A History of Biblical Israel

Worlds of the Ancient Near East and Mediterranean

Series editor: Diana Edelman, University of Oslo

Worlds of the Ancient Near East and Ancient Mediterranean brings alive the texts, archaeology and history of the cultures of the regions around the Mediterranean Sea and eastward to ancient Iran and Iraq, from the Neolithic through the Roman periods (ca 10,000 BCE-393 CE). Studies of one or more aspects of a single culture or of a subject across cultures in the regions outlined will form the foundation of this series, in which interdisciplinary approaches are encouraged. Studies can be based on texts, on material remains, or a combination of the two, where appropriate. In the case of a project that focuses on either the memory or the reception history of a place, person, myth, practice, or idea that arose or existed within the prescribed time, chapters that trace ongoing relevance to the present are welcome. The volumes are meant to be accessible to a wide audience interested in how the inhabitants of these parts of the world lived or how they understood their own pasts, presents, and futures, as well as how current scholars are understanding and recreating their pasts or their future aspirations.

Forthcoming titles:

Burial Practices in Ancient Israel and the Neighboring Cultures (c. 1500-330 BCE)
Jürg Hutzli

Ancient Cookware from the Levant
An Ethnoarchaeological Perspective
Gloria A. London

Recovering Women's Rituals in the Ancient Near East
Julye Bidmead

A History of Biblical Israel

The Fate of the Tribes and Kingdoms from
Merenptah to Bar Kochba

Ernst Axel Knauf and Philippe Guillaume

SHEFFIELD uk   BRISTOL ct

Published by Equinox Publishing Ltd.

UK: Office 415, The Workstation, 15 Paternoster Row, Sheffield, South Yorkshire S1 2BX
USA: ISD, 70 Enterprise Drive, Bristol, CT 06010
www.equinoxpub.com

First published 2016

© Ernst Axel Knauf and Philippe Guillaume 2016

All rights reserved. No part of this publication may be reproduced or transmitted in any form or by any means, electronic or mechanical, including photocopying, recording or any information storage or retrieval system, without prior permission in writing from the publishers.

British Library Cataloguing-in-Publication Data
A catalogue record for this book is available from the British Library.
ISBN 978 1 78179 141 7 (hardback)
978 1 78179 142 4 (paperback)

Library of Congress Cataloging-in-Publication Data
Knauf, Axel, author.
  A history of biblical Israel : the fate of the tribes and kingdoms from Merenptah to Bar Kochba / Axel Knauf and Philippe Guillaume.
     pages cm. -- (Worlds of the ancient near East and Mediterranean)
  Includes bibliographical references and index.
  ISBN 978-1-78179-141-7 (hb) -- ISBN 978-1-78179-142-4 (pb)
  1. Bible. Old Testament--History of Biblical events. 2. Bible. Old Testament--Antiquities. 3. Palestine--History--To 70 A.D.--Historiography. 4. Bible. Old Testament--Criticism, interpretation, etc. I. Guillaume, Philippe, author. II. Title.
  BS1197.K57 2015
  221.9'5--dc23
                                    2014047866

Typeset by ISB Typesetting, Sheffield, UK
Printed and bound by Lightning Source Inc. (La Vergne, TN), Lightning Source UK Ltd. (Milton Keynes), Lightning Source AU Pty. (Scoresby, Victoria)

TABLE OF CONTENTS

List of Illustrations ix
List of Tables x
Preface xi
Introduction 1

PART I
THE PRE-HISTORY OF BIBLICAL ISRAEL 27
1 From Merenptah to Rameses VI 29
   1.1 The Egyptian Province of Canaan 30
   1.2 Merenptah: How the Israelites Came to Egypt 32
   1.3 Sethnakht and an Exodus (1186 BCE) 36
   1.4 Rameses IV–VI and the End of the Egyptian Province of Canaan 37
2 From Ephraim to Mamre: The Tribes in the Early Iron Age 42
   2.1 The Emergence of the Tribes of Israel 42
   2.2 Tribal Life 48
   2.3 Tjekers, Philistines, and Phoenicians 52
   2.4 Religion and Literature in Iron Age I 53
   2.5 Festivals and Customs 57
3 From Saul to Jeroboam I: State Formation 62
   3.1 The Beginning of an Economic Recovery in the Second Half of the Eleventh Century BCE 64
   3.2 Saul 65
   3.3 Eshbaal 70
   3.4 David 71
   3.5 Solomon 76
   3.6 Shishak and the Egyptian Revival 80
   3.7 Jeroboam I 82
   3.8 Religion and Literature in the Tenth Century BCE 83
4 From Omri to Jeroboam II: The Consolidation of Levantine Kingdoms 85
   4.1 State Formation in Southern Syria-Palestine in the Ninth and Eighth Centuries BCE 85
   4.2 Aram and Israel 87
   4.3 The Dynasty of Omri 88

	4.4	Israel Under Aram-Damascus	95
	4.5	Religion and Literature in the Ninth Century BCE	96
	4.6	Jeroboam II	98
	4.7	In the Shadow of Ashur	101
	4.8	Religion and Literature in the Eighth Century BCE	101
5	From Tiglath-pileser to Ashurbanipal: The Integration of Levantine Kingdoms in the Neo-Assyrian Realm		103
	5.1	Tiglath-pileser III	105
	5.2	The Demise of Israel as Kingdom (727–720 BCE)	109
	5.3	The Integration of Judah in the Neo-Assyrian Empire (720–701 BCE)	112
	5.4	Judah's Neighbours: Ammon, Moab, Edom, the Arabs, and the Philistines	115
	5.5	King Manasseh	119
	5.6	The Demise of Ashur and Egypt's Return	124
	5.7	Josiah (640–609 BCE)	126
	5.8	Religion in the Seventh Century BCE	129
	5.9	Literature of Assyrian and Post-Assyrian Times	132
6	From Nabopolassar to Nebuchadnezzar		134
	6.1	The Neo-Babylonian Empire	134
	6.2	The First Deportation	135
	6.3	The Second Deportation	136
	6.4	King Gedaliah and the Third Deportation	137
	6.5	The End of the Kingdom of Yehud	139

PART II
THE FORMATION OF BIBLICAL ISRAEL IN YEHUD AND SAMARIA IN THE PERSIAN PERIOD — 143

7	From Nebuchadnezzar II to Xerxes I: Mizpah, Samaria, and Jerusalem's First "Second Temple"		145
	7.1	From the Neo-Babylonian to the Persian Empire	145
	7.2	Yehud from 582 to 525 BCE	150
	7.3	Yehudites in Babylonia	153
	7.4	Cambyses, Darius, and the First "Second Temple"	156
	7.5	Persians, Phoenicians, Arabs, and Greeks	160
8	From Artaxerxes I to Ptolemy I: The Second "Second Temple" and Torah		169
	8.1	Nehemiah and the Persian Fortress at Jerusalem	170
	8.2	Economic Crisis in Yehud?	173
	8.3	The Military Colony at Elephantine	177
	8.4	Arabia and Idumea	178
	8.5	Yehud and Samaria	180
	8.6	Ezra and Torah	182

	8.7	Torah and Identity	184
	8.8	Literary Developments after the Torah	186
	8.9	Bethel's Legacy	188
	8.10	Alexander and the Diadochi	190

PART III
THE DISINTEGRATION OF BIBLICAL ISRAEL   197

9	From Ptolemy II to Antiochus III: The Bible in Greek		199
	9.1	Alexandria	199
	9.2	Hellenistic Biblical Texts	200
10	From Antiochus III to Salome Alexandra		203
	10.1	Antiochus III and Hellenism	203
	10.2	The Breakup of the Seleucid Empire and the Rise of the Hasmoneans (187–130 BCE)	205
	10.3	From John Hyrkanus to Salome Alexandra	210
11	"Pax" Romana and Jewish Wars		215
	11.1	Pompeius (63 BCE)	217
	11.2	Herod the Great (40/37–4 BCE)	219
	11.3	Ethnachs and Procurators	220
	11.4	The Jewish Wars (66–73 and 132–136 CE)	223
	11.5	From Judea to Palestine	228

Appendix	230
Bibliography and Abbreviations	232
Index of Biblical and other Ancient References	254
Index of Modern Authors	260
Index of Subjects	264

List of Illustrations

1	Merenptah Israel stele (after ANEP #342)	2
2	250 mm isohyet (T. Guillaume)	15
3	Camel-rider (after Drijvers 1976, pl. LXV)	18
4	Canaanites (after Lepsius 1859, pl. 133)	20
5	Mediterranean shipwrecks (T. Guillaume)	24
6	First record of the name YHW' (after Jaroš 1974, 122)	29
7	Shasus (after Rothenberg 1972, fig. 38)	33
8	Moses' name (after CSAPI 3 Tell Fārʻa South #525)	35
9	Philistine ceramic (A. Knauf)	53
10	Egyptianized storm god (after IPIAO 2 #478)	54
11	Baal-Seth (after *GGG* 87b)	55
12	Suckling calf motif (after Meshel 2012, fig. 6.8)	55
13	Hathor (after IPIAO 2: #421)	56
14	Seal of Jaazanyahu (after Badè 1933).	60
15	Centre and periphery eleventh–tenth centuries BCE (T. Guillaume)	66
16	Shishak's campaigns in Canaan (T. Guillaume)	69
17	Centre and periphery ninth–eighth centuries BCE (T. Guillaume)	74
18	Baal-Seth-Sun (after Keel 2007, 126)	77
19	Detail of Shishak Karnak relief (after Wilson 2005, 108)	80
20	Shishak stele (after Lamon and Shipton 1939, 60 #70)	81
21	Jehu (after Layard 1849, pl. 53)	94
22	Storm god (after Keel 2007, 126)	100
23	Horus child from Samaria (after Crowford and Crowford 1938, #1,1)	100
24	Lord of the animals (after *GGG* #197b)	102
25	Centre and periphery in the seventh century BCE (T. Guillaume)	104
26	Lion of Megiddo (after *GGG* #205a)	105
27	Lachish (Judith Dekel in Ussishkin 1982, 86, 100)	114
28	Arabian trade routes (T. Guillaume)	117
29	Deportation of gods (after Layard 1849, pl. 65)	121
30	Seal of Gedaliah (after Keel 2007, #506)	125
31	Asherah (a–b after Keel 2007, #332, 333; c after *GGG* #323)	128

32	Seal of the city commander (after *GGG* #346)	129
33	Sin (a after *GGG* #295a; b after Keel 1977: #222; c after *CSAJ* #2)	130
34	Ishtar Arbela (after Uehlinger 1994, 101 #6)	131
35	Ishtar (a after *GGG* #331a; b: after Schroer 1987b, # 98)	131
36	Map of Persian Empire (T. Guillaume)	158
37	Galleys (a Meshorer 1985, #20; b Madden 1881, #116)	166
38	Hoplites (a after Leith 1997, 32; b after CSAPI 2 Dor #12)	167
39	Seal of Elnatan (after Avigad 1976, #5)	170
40	Centre and periphery, fifth century BCE to sixth century CE (T. Guillaume)	175
41	Athena owl (after Elayi and Elayi 2009, #1378)	176
42	Samaria coins (a–e after Meshorer and Qedar 1991, #23, 40, 88, 152, 179)	181
43	Coin of Hezekiah (after Meshorer 2001, #3,22)	194
44	Coin of Yohanan the priest (after Meshorer 2001, #3,20)	194
45	Coin of John Hyrkanus I (after Ostermann 2005, #1)	210
46	Coin of Alexander (both after Ostermann 2005, #10)	212
47	Coin of Aretas IV (after Meshorer 1985, #49)	213
48	Coin of Gabinius (after Hendin 2001, #874a)	218
49	Coins of Antigonus (after Ostermann 2005, #41-42)	219
50	Coin of Agrippa I (after Madden 1881, #136)	221
51	Coin of Herod Philip II (after Madden and Fairholt 1864, 101)	222
52	Coin Iudea capta (after Brin 1986, #93)	226
53	Coin of Bar Kochba (after Madden 1881, #202)	227

List of Tables

1	Traditional and low chronology	13
2	Main forms of Hebrew	64
3	Sizes of four Levantine cities	65
4	Dates of state formation and provincialization	147
5	Judean and Biblical Hebrew	154

Preface

Daily life can be managed with little awareness of the past, but the prospects for the future are bleak when lessons from the past are not learnt.

The issue is particularly acute when the past in question is loaded with religious values, as is the case with biblical Israel. It is crucial to place sacred texts in their historical context. The ancient world, like the modern world, is a field of interaction between economic, technological, and ideological centres and their various peripheries.

This book is based on courses we taught on the History of Israel for years in Heidelberg, Geneva, Beirut or Berne. The present manuscript reflects our present views on the subject, while we are well aware that the field is in constant change. Not only do archives and sites provide a constant flow of new data that needs to be integrated, but our own interests and perspectives on the past are constantly changing and thus require revisions.

We thank David Ussishkin for granting gracious permission for Figure 27, Georges Mills for polishing the English, Tania Guillaume for the maps, Diana Edelman for her guidance in the preparation of the manuscript in the *The Worlds of the Ancient Near East and Mediterranean* series and for the dedicated staff at Equinox with whom it is always a great pleasure to work.

E. A. Knauf and P. Guillaume
Spring 2015

Introduction

The terms *history* and *past* are often used as synonyms, although technically they are not. Since most of us presume there is only one world, we also assume there is only one past made up of a single succession of past states of this world. By contrast, history is a mental representation of narrow segments of the past. There surely is only one past; but there are many different histories, false ones and more correct ones, each reflecting different cultural contexts and different historians. History is a scientific enterprise whenever it processes representative data using rational and controllable methods to work out hypotheses and theories that are empirical, improvable through the application of recognized criteria of falsification.

Delimiting the Time-Span: from Merenptah to Bar Kochba

There are histories of Israel that begin with Abraham or David and continue until the "Exile" (586 BCE), Alexander the Great (333 BCE) or Bar Kochba (132–136 CE). Here, the limits are established by two documents.

Our starting point is provided by the stele erected in 1208 BCE by Pharaoh Merenptah, on which he recorded his victories in Canaan over the cities of Ashkelon, Gezer, and Yanoam and over a group named Israel (*CoS* 2.6; in *ANET* 376–378; Figure 1). Where in Canaan this Israel was to be found, what happened to it, and how much of it is reflected in biblical Israel is not easy to determine, but since the Merneptah stele is so far the earliest mention of the name Israel, it is a natural starting point for a history of Israel. Obviously, things happened before this beginning. Apart from the mythical beginning at Creation and the hypothetical beginning of the Big Bang, one may ask why a Pharaoh should have led military campaigns in Canaan. Answers can be found at various earlier points, but the most relevant one here is the presence between the Red Sea and the Dead Sea of a commodity coveted by Egypt and Assyria alike: copper.

Our closing point will be 136 CE, when four Roman legions crushed the revolt of Simeon Bar-Kosiba, later known as Bar Kochba, "Son of a Star." The document that establishes this date consists in the legends on the coins Bar Kosiba struck during the war with Rome: "Year one of the redemption of Israel," "Year two of the freedom of Israel," and "Simon Prince of Israel" (Mildenberg 1998, pl. 44). No coins bearing the name

Figure 1: The upper part of Merenptah's Israel stele depicts in mirror image the Pharaoh receiving the sacred scimitar (Hebrew כידן, Josh. 8:18; 1 Sam. 17:6; Job 39:23; Jer. 6:23) from the god Amon under the winged solar disk. The Pharaoh also receives the blessing of the goddess Mut (left) and of the moon god Khonsu (right). The name 'Israel' is found in the second last line (after *ANEP* #342).

Israel would be struck again until 1948 CE. Bar Kosiba is thus the last ruler of a political entity using the name Israel in antiquity, closing a history that began in 1208 BCE. The various groups that claimed to be the real Israel after 135 BCE—Samaritans, Jews, and Christians—are indeed repercussions of the previous Israels, but as non-political entities they fall outside the history delimited here between 1208 BCE and 136 CE.

The history of ancient Israel is commonly split into two: the history of the "First" Temple (until 586 BCE) and the history of the "Second" Temple (520 BCE–70 CE). The gap between 586 and 520 BCE is commonly described as a templeless period or the "Exile," which articulates the pre-exilic and post-exilic periods. These designations are problematic, so we prefer a tripartite division centred on the concept of biblical Israel: the pre-history of biblical Israel, including the history of the kingdoms of Israel and Judah, the formation of biblical Israel in the Persian period, and, finally, the fragmentation of biblical Israel in the Hellenistic and Roman periods. The first part corresponds to the times narrated in the bulk of the Hebrew Bible, except for Haggai, Zechariah, Psalms, Esther, Ezra, Nehemiah, and Daniel. The second part covers the period when the Hebrew Bible was finalized as a large narrative from Creation to the Persian era. Books that are only found in Greek and some Christian Bibles (Ben Sira and Maccabees, for instance) correspond to the last part.

Defining Terms

Israel
The term Israel covers different realities at different times, and it is the burden of historians to account for the differences, in contrast with the cultural memories of Judaism and Christianity, both of which stress continuity (Davies 1997). Israel was a Canaanite tribe in the late thirteenth century BCE, a tribal kingdom in the tenth century BCE, and a regional power in the ninth and eighth centuries BCE. After the disappearance of the kingdoms, the population of the provinces of Samaria and Yehud that recognized the Torah was the Israel of the Persian era, which generated several religious groups—Jews and Samaritans and, later, Christians—in the Hellenistic and Roman periods.[1] These groups spread across the empires that followed the Persians. Finally, a modern State of Israel was founded in 1948 CE, adding the western European notion of citizenship

---

1 In late antiquity, Islam became the form in which Jewish and Christian traditions were accepted on the Arabian Peninsula.

to the religious overtones conveyed by the term Israel. History must deal with each of the groups that claimed the title Israel for themselves.

History

History as an academic discipline deals critically with all available data in order to answer the fundamental questions of what happened, when, where, to whom and, equally important, why it happened (Knauf 2001a; Gaddis 2002; Swain 2006).

Besides the pattern of events, always somewhat hypothetical, historical inquiry seeks to determine *conjonctures* and structures in the ocean of the past. Events, *conjonctures* (a French word meaning circumstances used mainly in economics), and structures stand for the different velocity of change, from the most fickle aspect of events that can be overturned within the same day to structures that are most stable and evolve very slowly, such as climate. To retain the marine metaphor, structures are currents, while *conjonctures* are waves. Events are the foam that crowns the waves (Braudel 1972). A caricature of history would focus mostly upon events, listing the names of kings and the dates of the battles they won, dealing only with the foam and forgetting the mighty current and undertow against which the greatest individuals can do little to resist, even if they are kings. Winning a battle is no guarantee the war will be won. The challenge is to avoid taking an event for a *conjoncture*. Hence, the rise and fall of the Neo-Assyrian Empire is the *conjoncture* in which events such as King Jehu's coup and King Josiah's so-called reform occurred. It is against the backdrop of the slow transformations experienced by the Empire that the significance of local events in peripheral Israel and Judah can be assessed correctly. But *conjonctures* are themselves determined by the geographical structure, which, around the Mediterranean, establishes marked differences between plain and highland. The major climatic differences between plains and upland translate into marked differences in lifestyle, culture, and religion. In the Iron Age, the difference between lowland Canaan and Israel in the highland was structural. Three millennia later, the structure has hardly changed. The highland remains poorer and hardier than the coastal plain, but the *conjoncture* has changed. The lowland is now inhabited by people who call themselves Israel, while the highland, the cradle of Israel, is occupied mostly by Palestinian Arabs. Histories of Israel in antiquity have to take into account structures and *conjonctures* to interpret the events related in the Bible as much as modern historians have to take into account the geopolitical position of the Middle East (the structure) and the Cold War and its aftermaths (the *conjonctures*) to interpret the conflict between the modern State of Israel and its neighbours. Otherwise, one is blinded by daily events and mistakes a tree for a forest.

The Latin word *historia* gave two separate words to English: story and history. As narrative, history, with its ideological premises, remains a literary scheme. The difference between what historians and authors of fiction write lies in their subject matter rather than in the truthfulness of their writings. In fact, fiction, especially when it is infused with mythological themes, conveys more truth than histories, in the sense that it deals with universals that are relevant across the ages. In the realm of truthfulness, historians are at a disadvantage, since their burden is trying to piece together what may have happened from scraps. When it comes to explaining why something happened, the hypothetical nature of the historian's work becomes even more blatant. In fiction, the image is the original itself, or, at least, it is an adequate representation of the truth it conveys, while in history, the narrative can only be a partial representation that can never come as close to the original as would a photograph. What actually occurred is long gone and has often left precious few traces. The historian's ability to write the past is limited by the amount of available relics as well as by the historian's own political and religious outlook. Scientific history is also a critique of political and religious stories and myths social groups construct to build their own identities and hopes. But historians do not work in isolation from their own context. As actors in the production of the social memory of the group to which they belong, historians write narratives about the past that are loaded with their authors' own ideologies (Halbwachs 1992). This fact adds to the difficulty of deconstructing the ideological constructs produced by past societies. When historians leave the level of reconstructing social and economic processes and address collective memory, myths, and legends, they can no longer hide behind the mask of scientific objectivity. Their deconstructions of past ideologies are themselves ideological constructs.

As an empirical social science, history had to get out of the ghetto of narrativity. Each narrative, whether intended as fictional or factional, creates a "narrated world" which is usually related to the real world of the narrators, but in a rather large number of possible ways and degrees of facticity. In postmodernism, the specious identification of "history" with "historical narrative" has led to the proclamation of "the end of history," because all narratives, conflicting as they are, are deemed equal in relevance (or rather irrelevance) (Evans 1997; Sokal and Bricmont 1999; Knauf 2011). By contrast, science feeds on quantitative data, and history has no problem with the plausibility and usefulness of such quanititative studies of humanity and of the worlds it has produced (Popper 1963, 1979).

As with any other science, scientific history operates "as though there is no God" (*sicut Deus non daretur*). This premise is particularly important when dealing with a religiously sensitive subject like Israel. The postulate "as though there is no God" does not imply that the historian is an atheist. It is a methodological starting point that forbids using miracles as evidence or proof, although it does not necessarily imply that miracles never occur. Empirical science analyses what occurs in the world; in other words, in reality as we perceive it. As Ludwig Wittgenstein argued, "the world is everything that is the case" (Wittgenstein 1922, 29), and "God does not reveal himself *in* the world" (Wittengenstein 1922, 107). The historian can only speak of gods as human perceptions. Naturally, the Bible was written from an entirely different point of view, but the Bible is not a history in the modern sense. As a narrative in which God makes a lot of appearances, it is the defining myth of Israel and all who claim its heritage. By contrast, it is the duty of theology to remember and remind us that there is more to the world than what is "the case": "Ah, but a man's reach should exceed his grasp / Or what's a heaven for?" (Robert Browning).

History of Israel
History of Israel, being an academic branch of the scientific study of the Old Testament / Hebrew Scriptures, supplements the exegesis of individual biblical books or sections of books, to produce a general view informed by the wider context of the ancient Near East and organized along chronological and geographical lines.[2] We consider the History of Israel to be a productive tool for biblical exegesis and theology, given that the composers of the Holy Writ were children of their time. Because of the logic of its sequential arrangement, a History of Israel can serve to sum up or recapitulate the First Testament or Hebrew Bible, as can a "Theology of the Old Testament," except that it does not seek to distil a unified system. Because History of Israel is not the history of Israel only, it contributes to the overall contextualization of Israel and to a better understanding of the religions of Canaan as well as of the empires within which Judaism and Christianity arose.

As primary sources for the History of Israel, we have texts in the form of royal inscriptions, letters, records, and graffiti in Egyptian, Assyrian, Israelite, Judean, Moabite, Aramaic, Greek, and Latin, as well as images. Written documents provide data beyond events that were considered worth reporting; they can also be mined for information on onomastics, prices, vocabulary, linguistic histories, and communication patterns. A second set of data is provided by the archaeology of relevant sites. Although archaeology retrieves only minimal amounts of ancient material, and even then lacks much of the context that would help make sense of it, it is an irreplaceable tool for the reconstruction of daily life. It sup-

---

2   Seen from China, our European Near East is the Far West, but we take the Eurocentric designation as an inherent feature of the English language.

plies an ever-growing amount of quantitative data concerning the wealth of households, settlement patterns, food habits, the natural environment, trade networks, and imports. Meanwhile, iconographic depictions of the divine world provide our sole consistent database for the history of religion across the millennia (in the case of ancient Israel, see *IPIAO*).

Data is interpreted within the theoretical framework of cultural anthropology, including the geography of cultures and ethnology (Wagstaff 1985; Levy 1995). The living conditions and the organization of farming communities in late Ottoman Palestine are relatively well documented. They are useful guidelines for the structures that prevailed in biblical times, since the extent of climatic and geographic change over time is limited. The Nile still flows through Egypt, and the Central Palestinian Range has not moved. Ottoman- and Mandate-era studies are also a mine of information on *conjonctures*, once the modifications resulting from the introduction of modern techniques are taken into account. Even the present geopolitical position of Syria-Palestine is relevant to the History of Israel: besides Egypt, the other regional heavyweights, Iraq and Turkey, are heirs of the Assyrians, Babylonians, and Hittites of old. Analogies can also be drawn from ethnological studies of nomadism and of life in the desert fringes of the Middle East.

To organize the mass of relevant data, we use the basic principles derived from Cultural Materialism (Harris 2001) and World-systems Theory (Wallerstein 1984), which examine ways in which humans tend to act according to what they perceive as being in their best interest. We also make use of the distinction between centre and periphery.

Our interpretation of data is shaped by a distinction between primary and secondary sources, made according to the amount of interpretation incorporated into the data conveyed by any given source, rather than whether the data is factual or not. Information drawn from archaeology involves a lot of interpretation, although based on inherently silent vestiges such as walls, bones, and ceramic. Yet, compared with eloquent sources such as texts, a certain amount of background noise needs filtering before texts can be assessed correctly. Hence, the development of archaeology has altered the status of the Bible as a source for the reconstruction of Israel's past. For a long time, biblical narratives used to be the only source for many periods. Now, the Bible is one among several sources. Other texts have come to light, sometimes from Israel's enemies, transmitting a different point of view of the same events, which shows that all literary texts are secondary sources as far as events are concerned. History is not found as such in the texts. The ideology of the texts needs to be deconstructed before history can be constructed (Wellhausen 1885). At first sight, the evidence provided by the silent witnesses of the past that archaeology reveals appears more straightforward, requiring less decoding. They qualify as primary sources. Caution, however, is required, as biblical archaeology arose in reaction to Wellhausen's understanding of biblical history: the pioneers of biblical archaeology sought to recover concrete evidence that would prove that the Bible was right after all. The results went quite contrary to expectations, which, by itself, is a token of the scientific quality of the work accomplished. Many genuine discoveries were serendipitous. As the number of excavated biblical sites grew, so the database expanded. Pottery sequences could be established and progressively refined through ^{14}C analyses of organic material recovered from the same strata.

Martin Noth (1960) and Herbert Donner (1984-1986) primarily used archaeology to write their histories of Israel for early periods about which the Bible is silent. But with the biblical record of the reigns of David and Solomon, even critical historians believed they possessed sources that were contemporary to the events they recorded and were thus reliable primary sources. The excavations of Solomon's stable cities mentioned in 1 Kings 9 were accepted as providing final proof of the historicity of the biblical Books of Samuel and Kings.

Today, the stories in Samuel and Kings are considered to have been written centuries after the deaths of the kings they discuss, because they depict a world that differs greatly from the one that archaeology for the period has reconstructed. As archaeology revealed the similarities between the material culture of Israel and that of its immediate neighbours, historians changed their view of Israel's status in the ancient Near East. Martin Noth still claimed that the task of the historian of Israel was to reveal Israel's uniqueness from neighbouring cultures. Although Israel lived and behaved like the surrounding people, it was a stranger, separated from the world by its very being (Noth 1960, 2-3). The histories written during the following decades devoted increasing attention to the broader Near Eastern context, searching more for analogies rather than particularities.

The changing approach to the texts produced by Israel resulted from a new understanding of the difference between primary and secondary sources: primary sources tell too little, while secondary sources are too loquacious. Both require interpretation, but there is a difference between a piece of papyrus that records that no bricks were delivered on a day designated "Sabbath" (Tcherikover and Fuks 1957, 10) and a biblical text claiming that God commanded Israel to do no work on the Sabbath (Exod. 16:23). The papyrus in question is the earliest attestation of the ban on work, but it was written a millennium later than when the god of Israel is supposed to have dictated the Ten Commandments to Moses, and by someone whose primary concern was to keep exact records. The scribe's sole concern was to avoid trouble from his superiors, and he did not note whether the brickmakers he was in charge of were Jews, or what kind of Jews they might be—questions irrelevant to him but crucial to the historian. Nor was the delivery record destined for posterity. It is by mere chance that we can read it today. By contrast, the biblical text is the result of a long process of composition and canonization for transmission to posterity in order to sustain the identity of its re-readers and weld them into a religious community. The Jewish scribes who penned the Bible succeeded beyond their expectations in transmitting a text that became the basis of three major world religions. We can take the date supplied by the Egyptian scribe almost at face value, but we cannot do so with the biblical claim, because to assert that God spoke to Moses face-to-face breaches the limits imposed by the premise of *sicut Deus non daretur*. Contrary to the Egyptian records, that, for the most part, fail to provide information of interest to the historian of Israel, the biblical text says far too much. Its claims have to be downsized, while the historian can hardly avoid over-interpreting the meaning of the brick delivery. Eventually, however, both primary and secondary sources have to be integrated into a coherent picture to produce a history of Israel.

The various histories of Israel on the market today can be evaluated on how they differentiate between primary and secondary sources. The still-current history by Miller and Hayes (2006 [1977]) is less factual than the work of Grabbe (2007b), which has turned the primacy of the biblical text over archaeology on its head. Yet, biblical archaeology does not supply purely objective data. The study of the past cannot be disentangled from the present. Even when digging an Early Bronze layer, an archaeologist of the Near East can hardly ignore fighting occurring not too far away. Archaeologists are also citizens, and those who are citizens of democracies are called on to vote. They may belong to a progressive or a conservative university. Archaeologists also need funds provided by agencies that have their own agendas, which necessarily influences which personnel and sites are chosen. Hence, modern ideologies invite themselves into the debate; labels such as Zionist, Evangelical, or Materialist convey a certain amount of truth that cannot be ignored, although they are quite often used in a derogatory manner to disqualify opponents and rivals.[3]

Confidence in the ability of dating any biblical text with precision through literary and redaction criticism has declined dramatically among the recent generation of exegetes. Much of the production of the Hebrew Bible is today assigned to the Persian and early Hellenistic era, half

---

3 "Minimalist" and "maximalist" are polemical designations, more revealing about the person who uses them than about the person spoken about.

a millennium later than the reign of Solomon that was once viewed as the Golden Age of biblical production. This down-dating has definitively removed the biblical texts from the category of eyewitness accounts. A narrower timespan, comprised of between the sixth and the second centuries BCE, has eliminated much of the once fashionable speculations of verse-by-verse reconstructions of the composition of biblical texts and the search for the exact circumstances that led to the various additions. Certainly, some traditions like the Song of Deborah in Judges 5 go back to the ninth century BCE, if not earlier, and underwent several stages of redaction and expansion during the seventh and sixth centuries BCE, but the once common belief that each stage could be identified within the final text is now mostly rejected. The notion of "Scripture" or of the Pentateuch as "Law" did not arise before the Persian period. The collection designated as the Historical Books in the Greek and Latin Bibles is no earlier. It does not correspond to a history, despite the all-too-common habit of referring to it as the "Deuteronomistic History." The synchronized chronology of Israelite and Judean kings in 1 and 2 Kings began as a chronicle based on earlier material, while the other texts in Samuel and Kings are short stories and are mostly secondary insertions (Kratz 2005, 158–186; Grabbe 2007a). Historiography is more fitting a title for Ezra–Nehemiah and Chronicles, produced in the fourth and third centuries BCE, although their reliability as historical sources is limited. First Maccabees imitates Kings, while Esther, Judith, and Tobit are novellae which play with history rather than write history. Only 2 Maccabees follows the rules of Hellenistic historiography.

The annals of the Neo-Assyrian kings (Luckenbill 1924; Grayson 1991, 1996; Tadmor and Yamada 2011), the Babylonian Chronicles (Grayson 1975; Glassner 2004), and royal Persian inscriptions (Kent 1953) are the main extra-biblical literary sources for the Israels of the ninth to sixth centuries BCE, most of them now available in reliable publications. These texts must be interpreted in light of the "Tiglath-pileser principle" (Halpern 2001, 124–129): because they addressed their inscriptions to the gods, they could not lie, but they did not tell the whole truth. One must read between the lines to recover the facts. According to their annals, the great kings always won, but mapping the locale of the "victories" allows a fairly accurate assessment of their significance. A series of victories sited ever closer to home betrays a pattern of successive defeats.

A middle course will be followed here between two extreme positions. Radical sceptics, often called "Minimalists" by their opponents, consider all texts to be false unless proven otherwise, while those in turn described as "Maximalists" regard all ancient texts as telling the truth unless there is strong reason to suppose otherwise. Underlying these two extremes are different views on the nature of the Bible: a cultural product for the Minimalist position, and the careful record of honest authors for the Maximalist camp. Factuality lies in between, but where exactly is never certain. No statement is ever one hundred per cent correct, and there is rarely enough evidence to make an irrefutable case (Moore 2006).

Identifying a narrative's bias or how a writer has spun the evidence helps to construct a more balanced picture of historical reality. One example here is the biblical depiction of David as a great king, and of Saul as a failure.

Defining Notions

Time

Attributing dates to individuals and events is the first task when producing a history, although this is particularly challenging when it comes to the history of the ancient world. Besides the use of different calendars, kings with the same name are not easy to differentiate and the sources are always lacunary.

The first period ever calculated continuously from a fixed point was the Seleucid era. Its starting point was the return to Babylon of Seleucus I Nicator following his exile in Ptolemaic Egypt, which the Seleucids regarded as the foundation date of their empire. According to the Babylonian calendar, the Seleucid era began from a date during 311 BCE, although in the Macedonian calendar, which was observed in Asia Minor and Syria, the start corresponded with a date in 312 BCE. The biblical Books of Maccabees reckon dates according to the Seleucid era, as the Yemenite Jews do to this day. Before this, years were dated according to reigns. In Egypt, when pharoah B took over from pharoah A, scribes numbered the year as Year 1, but not always indicating to which pharoah it referred. Meanwhile, in Mesopotamia, Year 1 began on the New Year that followed the accession of a new king. The problem here is that we do not have the entire sequences of kings or pharaohs, or the duration of their reigns. Consequently, there are gaps and scholars have devised long, medium, short, and very short chronologies. For instance, Hammurapi of Babylon probably ruled either from 1792 to 1750 BCE (medium chronology) or, more likely, from 1728 to 1696 BCE (short chronology). But according the very short chronology, he ruled between 1696 and 1654 BCE, while the now defunct long chronology had him reign between 1848 and 1806 BCE (Gasche et al. 1998). However, records of eclipses and other astronomical phenomena mean that it is possible to create a more reliable absolute chronology for Mesopotamia than for Egypt. In this book we adopt the short chronology for Egypt (Hornung 1999).

In Israel and Judah, the situation is even more complicated. It is not clear whether the accession year was determined according to Egyptian or Mesopotamian usage (see above), whether Israel and Judah used the same system, or if the system was changed over time. Co-regencies are further complications. For instance, it is not certain whether the regnal years of Manasseh include the years he ruled with his father Hezekiah (2 Kings 20). Whether dates were reckoned from the spring New Year, around the vernal equinox, or from the New Year at the autumn equinox adds another six-month uncertainty. Hence, there is no absolute chronology for successive reigns. According to 1 Kings 12:32, it seems that, at times, the kingdoms of Judah and Israel used different systems, but little is known about which calendar they followed. It is not possible to be sure even whether the best attested calendar of the Bible, the sabbatical or 364-day calendar, was ever used. Intercalation is yet another problem, since all calendars, except for the Islamic, intercalate days in order to keep in step with the seasons, months, or years at strict or variable intervals. Hence, different scholars have produced different chronologies for the biblical kings (Miller and Hayes 1977, 678–683; Thiele 1983; Hayes and Hooker 1988; Galil 1996). Nebuchadnezzar stormed Jerusalem for the first time in 597 BCE, but he destroyed it in 587 or 586 (here we choose 586). There is a two-year uncertainty for the death year of King Manasseh, but the regnal dates of the last three kings of Judah are firm. We will mention both the highest and lowest dates, for instance for Omri 886/876–875/869 BCE (see Appendix). Rather than learning these dates by heart, the reader should learn to situate each king in the correct century.

Besides the political chronology, archaeology uses a succession of "ages" that have much broader delimitations. Dates obtained through ^{14}C analyses are expressed by a date within two brackets. Hence, 875 ± 15 means, with a probability of 68%, between 890 and 860 BCE. The duration of transitional phases between different ages varies from region to region, as cultural innovations do not spread evenly across space. It used to be common to organize the chronology of cultures along political lines. Beginning around 1200 BCE, the settlement of the highlands and the formation of Israel were defined as Iron Age I. Iron Age II began around 1000 BCE with the rise of King David and the consolidation of the kingdom of Israel.

Today, the cultural sequence is established by the pottery assemblage that characterizes each phase. Here, we take it as an established fact that the "low chronology" (Knauf 2000b; Münger 2005; Finkelstein et al. 2011) has been vindicated by a series of ^{14}C samples from different sites. However, as the traditional chronology remains current in many handbooks, Table 1 sets both chronologies side by side.

The new chronology entails transitional phases of some 25 years. The full impact of Hellenism was not felt before the second century BCE in Palestine, half a century after the conquests of Alexander the Great. The beginning of Roman rule over the Near East in 63 BCE had no immediate impact on the local Hellenistic culture.

Table 1. Traditional and low chronologies.

Era	Traditional chronology	Low Chronology
Late Bronze IA	1550–1450	1550–1450
Late Bronze IB	1450–1350	1450–1350
Late Bronze IIA	1350–1250	1350–1300/1275
Late Bronze IIB	1250–1200	1300/1275–1250/1225
Late Bronze III	unattested	1250/25–1125/1100
Iron IA	1200–1130	1125/1100–1050
Iron IB	1130–1000	1050–1025
Iron IC	unattested	1025–950/925
Early Iron IIA	1000–	950/925–875
Late Iron IIA	–925	875–800/775
Iron IIB	925–750	800/775–725/700
Iron IIC	750–586	725/700–575/550
Persian	539–333	575/550–300/250
Hellenistic	333–63	300/250 BCE–25/125 CE
Roman	63 BCE–323 CE	25/125 CE–

Space

Engaging the history of Israel requires a good understanding of the geography of the region. From west to east, at the latitude of Jerusalem, the plain along the Mediterranean coast was the domain of the Philistines in the south and of the Phoenicians in the north. Then comes the Shephelah, a region of low rolling hills rising steeply towards the central ridge on which Jerusalem sits at an altitude of over 800 m. Continuing eastward, the relief drops extremely sharply to the western coast of the Dead Sea (423 m below sea level), the lowest point on the Earth's surface. The Judean desert is the area between the central ridge and the Dead Sea. From the eastern coast of the Dead Sea, the altitude rises again sharply to the Moabite plateau. From north to south, the mighty Mount Hermon (over 2,800 m) closes the Jordan depression, which flows towards Lake Kinneret and the Dead Sea. West of the Jordan, the Lebanon range slopes down southwards into the Galilean hills as far as the narrow Jezreel Valley that runs from Beth-She'an to the Bay of Acco. South of the Jezreel Valley, on the west, is the Carmel range and then the Sharon plain. Inland the relief rises again to form the Central Palestinian Range—the Israelite and then Samarian cradle—that continues southwards into the Benjaminite plateau opening onto the high point of Jerusalem and then dropping gradually past Hebron as far as the lowlands of the Negev and the Beersheba Valley, a natural corridor between north Arabia and Gaza. Reflecting the topography, the hygrometry is extremely contrasted. The upper Jordan basin, the sandy coastal plain and the Jezreel Valley were swampy during periods of heavy deforestation. Lake Kinneret is the largest body of freshwater in the entire region. Halfway between the Kinneret and the Dead Sea, the Jordan receives the waters of the Jabbok (Arabic *nahr ez-zerqā* "Blue River") that come down from the Ammonite plateau. The Arnon (Arabic *wādī el-mūǧib*) flows from the Moabite plateau down into the Dead Sea. South of the Dead Sea, the *wādī el-ḥasā* separates Moab and Edom before contributing its meagre flow to the southern tip of the Dead Sea. Also south of the Dead Sea, the Arabah depression continues down to the Red Sea, as part of the Great Rift Valley that spans 6,000 km from the Taurus in modern Turkey south to Lake Malawi between Malawi, Mozambique, and Tanzania. At the level of the Jordan Valley and the Arabah, the Arabian and Mediterranean tectonic plates collide at a speed of 2 cm per year, with much seismic activity. The western side of the Central Range benefits from the humidity brought by the Mediterranean, but the Central Range acts as a barrier that leaves little rain for the Judean Desert. In the southern Jordan Valley, some oases like Jericho depend on springs. On the other side of the Jordan River, the Golan—with its extinct volcanoes, the Hauran (biblical Bashan), and its fertile basaltic soils —and the hills of Gilead are better watered. As a general rule, rain levels decrease from north to south and from west to east. In the south, the Negev marks the limit of dry cultivation (Hütteroth and Abdulfattah 1977; Karta 1985; Khalidi 1992; Krämer 2002).

The large range of altitudes and rain-levels within such a restricted territory (barely 100 × 250 km) produces dozens of ecological niches belonging to no less than four climatic zones: the Mediterranean in Galilee, Samaria, and Gilead; the Irano-Turanian in the Negev and Lower Jordan Valley; the Saharan in the Arabah; and the Sub-tropical, for instance in the Jericho oasis. Agricultural production is equally diverse. In the mountains olives, grapes, and almonds dominate. The valleys and plateaus are suitable for dry grain cultivation until precipitation falls below the 250 mm isohyet in southern Negev and east of the narrow Moabite and Edomite fringes (Figure 2: 250 mm isohyet). The sandy coast between Gaza and Acco offers but poor shelters for navigation. Acco, Dor, and Jaffa are the main harbours in the north, while Ashdod and Ashkelon were the natural outlets for the produce of the Judean hills.

The climatic diversity is reflected in the ethnography, which is as diverse as could be. The area is a matrix for cultural plurality that works against consolidation into a single political entity. The modern State of Israel is a patchwork of ghettos built from massive immigrations from Europe, North Africa, the Soviet Union, the USA, and the Middle East; the diasporas feel little affinity with each other. On the Palestinian side, the genesis of a common identity has not progressed much since the 1930s.

Figure 2: 250 mm isohyet (T. Guillaume).

Had it been sited in a place less coveted by mighty neighbours, Israel/Palestine could have become another Switzerland, a place where, after 550 years of civil war (1291–1847 CE), small groups eventually managed to cohabit peacefully, with each continuing to use its own dialect and religion to mark its difference from its immediate neighbours rather than building a common identity. Like Switzerland, Israel/Palestine is a periphery over which the zones of influence of several powerful neighbours overlap. From the fourth millennium BCE, Canaan, the Egyptian designation for Israel/Palestine, was where Egypt obtained wood, copper, olive oil, wine, and slaves. Commercial relations between Egypt and Canaan were like the relationship between a first- and a third-world country. In return for raw materials, Egypt, followed later by Assyria and the Phoenicians, supplied luxuries that strengthened the status of subservient local elites. Israel/Palestine was also a crucial land bridge, a passage between the great centres of the region, Egypt and Mesopotamia. Hence, it was a thoroughfare for goods exchanged between the Nile and the Euphrates as well as for imperial armies marching against one another. As was the case in the second millennium (Late Bronze Age), the Mediterranean world became a third actor in Israel/Palestine along with Egypt and Mesopotamia. The eighth century BCE saw the arrival of Arabia as a fourth actor, using Israel/Palestine for what became known as the incense road towards Gaza and Damascus. Ever since, Israel/Palestine has remained open on all sides.

Roads, therefore, are Israel/Palestine's greatest asset, resulting from the area's physical geography, which has hardly changed across the millennia. Even the opening of the Suez Canal in 1869 CE strengthened rather than weakened the strategic position of Israel/Palestine. The canal redirected the traffic between Asia and Europe through the Red and Mediterranean seas. The Via Maris "Road of the Sea" (Isa. 8:23; Mt. 4:15) connected Egypt to Syria by following the northern coast of the Sinai Peninsula and the Mediterranean coastal plain towards the Carmel. It took a shortcut through the Nahal "Iron Pass" guarded by Megiddo, into the Jezreel Valley, following its easy terrain down to the Kinneret, where it followed the upper Jordan Valley to cross the river halfway before Lake Huleh. Across the Jordan, the Via Maris climbed towards the Golan Heights before reaching Damascus. From the Via Maris, four connections branched off in an East–West direction. From the Jezreel Valley one could cross the Jordan south of Lake Kinneret at the level of Beth-She'an towards Pella and the Ammonite Plateau. Before the "Iron Pass," one could reach Shechem and travel down again through Wadi Far'a to the Jabbok, or more to the south through Jerusalem or Gibeon towards Jericho, crossing the Jordan above the Dead Sea to reach the Moabite plateau. These passages were active during the Bronze Age. During the Iron Age, the crossing south of the Dead Sea opened a southern connection between the Via Maris at Gaza and the "King's Way" (Num. 20:17, 21), as the Assyrians called it. The King's Way ran north–south parallel to the Via Maris across the Transjordanian Plateau, meeting the Via Maris at Damascus in the North and at Elat in the South. After the annexation of the Nabatean kingdom in 106 BCE, this road became the Via Traiana from Bostra to Aila and continued to Hegra.

As geography represents space as maps, the present volume includes a number of maps to guide readers through space, though mapping the physical geography of Israel/Palestine is a recent phenomenon. Geographical maps do not reflect the way ancient or modern populations experience space, nor the way they orient themselves to where they live. While most editions of the Bible include maps, the Bible itself transmits mental maps that represent another aspect of space. The mental maps of the Hebrew Bible use the Dead Sea and the Mediterranean as markers of the eastern and western sides of Canaan, but when it comes to the southern and northern sides, the transposition of "borders" runs into inextricable problems. Biblical passages disagree with each other and the vague points mentioned in the text hardly allow one to trace a coherent line on a map. It was the British Empire that introduced modern cartography in the Levant and improved the methods used by the Ottomans to describe and register land and territories (Mundy 1986, 78). Modern cartography established precise geodesic points that are irrelevant to mental maps. Hence, the maps found in most Bible editions are as misleading as they are useful. As a result, modern cartography has opened an unbridgeable gap between the inaccuracy of textual descriptions and the expectations of modern readers (Lissovsky and Na'aman 2003, 320). Even if cartographers avoided rendering frontier areas as lines, maps would nevertheless remain over-simplifications, since space in the ancient world was represented as lists of cities on royal inscriptions, rather than taking the form of maps (Smith 2003, 112–148). While the history of Israel requires the study of maps to remedy the lack of direct experience of the geography of Israel/Palestine as it was lived on foot and donkey-back, cartography cannot reproduce mental maps or, even less, tribal territories that reflect identity rather than administrative realities. Geography is only one way to describe space.

The difference between the administration of natural resources and the administration of identity corresponds to the difference between politics and economics, two related spheres that are not to be confused. Both place expectations and duties on their constituencies, but their spheres of influence rarely coincide. Today, Levantine villages are composed of more than one religion and clan because, as a rule, they are much larger than the corresponding settlement type in antiquity. Yet, not all combinations are possible. For instance, in Lebanon Sunni and Shi'a Muslims coexist only in cities and rarely in the same quarters. Muslims and Christians cohabit at village level, but not every denomination of Christians live in the same village. Orthodox Christians and Protestants have little or no place in Maronite villages. Orthodox churches are prominent in the lowland with Sunnis, while the mountains serve as a refuge for minorities: Alawites in the Gebel Ansarye in Syria. In Lebanon, the Qadisha Valley and the Metn are the traditional refuges for the Maronites, the Shouf for the Druzes, and the Gebel 'Amal for the Shi'a. Despite the demographic explosion of the last centuries and the profound population redistribution caused by the creation of the modern State of Israel, the Levant is not an American-style melting-pot. Pockets of ancient identity resist, such as Circassian villages and Sunni wadis in Galilee. The Jewish population is itself resettling into separate ghettos, with Orthodox in Jerusalem, Mizahis and Francophones along the northern coast, and Russians on the southern coast.

Peasants, Urbanites, and Nomads
The combination of space and time into a physical continuum illustrates how humans associate with each other and with the rest of their natural environment. They create a worldview that turns the chaos of crude representations of reality into an ordered and manageable whole.

The social reality of the ancient Near East, and in some measure of the modern Near East as well, can be illustrated through three different survival strategies represented by the categories of the farmer, the urbanite, and the nomad (Sussnitzki 1966; Rowton 1973, 1977; Herzog 1997). These three are not present at all times, but they keep reoccurring in various combinations for the rational division of labour under the prevalent *conjoncture*.

Parallel to the selection of wild grains for cultivation, the domestication of animals enabled human groups to survive major climatic changes and adapt to previously hostile ecological niches. Farmers raised goats and sheep, cattle, donkeys, and pigs; as a result, they became less dependent on protein obtained through hunting. The camel was kept for its milk from the third millennium BCE in some parts of Arabia and became a pack animal in the second millennium. From the ninth century BCE, camel-riders appeared as warriors in parallel with horse riders in the north (Figure 3) where, throughout the second millennium BCE, horses were used only to propel chariotry (Bulliet 1977; Betts 1992; Levy 1995).

Figure 3: Arab camel-rider with lance. Palmyra, second century CE. The riding position indicates that the rider is sitting on a šadād saddle. Attestations of this kind of saddle on Achaemenid and Roman coins are doubtful (after Drijvers 1976, pl. LXV).

After the farmer arose the nomad, or rather the first type of nomad (here called "type 1"). Once farmers occupied the most favourable locations, close to reliable fresh-water springs and arable land, the human population grew faster than farmers' ability to clear the more difficult land. Exploiting the huge tracks of wasteland, in which villages were but tiny islands, remained more profitable than building terraces around the villages. As long as the human population was small enough to leave the wasteland largely underexploited, the farming communities relegated the exploitation of the wasteland to type 1 nomads. These nomads specialized in tapping the wasteland beyond the immediate reach of the villages, rather than working their fields, although they never entirely abandoned a farming lifestyle since they were an extension of farming villages. This type was the only type of nomadism found during the third and second millennia BCE (Köhler-Rollefson 1987).

Before we turn to the other types of nomads, we must focus on the farmers and the structure of their villages. Huddled closely on a natural outcrop for mutual protection against winds, sun, and predators, their houses were surrounded by a belt of walled gardens, the domain of women (Song of Songs). The gardens combine vegetables, pulses, and trees, olives, figs, pistachios, and almonds, which represent long-term investments requiring stability in order to obtain a return. A second belt is formed around the village by the arable land (*'adamah*) used for dry cultivation of grain, mostly barley and wheat. The third circle is the grazing land, either the arable land left uncultivated (*sadeh*) or the *midbar*, a word usually rendered "desert" although it means "drove," the place where the herds and flocks of the village are driven by children or men, since the safety and honour of women cannot be guaranteed in the open field (Deut. 22:25). Genesis 2–4 depicts two of these circles, omitting the crowded and unsanitary village, selecting the garden as the locale for paradise, where the woman is most at ease. The other space is the place of punishment. Ploughing and harvesting make the fields the place of sweaty brows, and make the driving of animals over the *midbar* a relative pastime (Wagstaff 1985).

The bones of wild animals recovered in ancient villages show that the limits of the cultivation potential of Israel/Palestine was not reached even at the end of the nineteenth century CE, despite the dramatic population increases during the Roman and Late Ottoman periods, resulting in an overall population of one million inhabitants. It is only with the 10 million inhabitants of the present day that the water resources of the region have become over-exploited. Most of the inhabitants of any given village are interrelated, despite the prevalence of farmer mobility as a strategy to overcome various constraints. Strangers are soon integrated, since the well-being of villages continues to depend heavily on the size of their workforces. In the absence of machines, all activities were done by hand and apart from a few donkeys, cows, and camels to pull the plough and carry loads, every man, woman, and child was mobilized for the harvest. Villages were and are also related to others nearby in a network of blood ties resulting from exogamy and a hierarchy of settlements in which larger villages assumed administrative and commercial functions for their periphery. Under the constraints of the geographical structure, satellite villages were grouped around a primary centre situated downhill, towards which trickled surpluses and taxes (Sugerman 2009). A similar hierarchy operated until surpluses reached the closest harbour or marketplace on one of the great commercial highways. Returns made it uphill as luxury goods and credit supplied by traders who owned stores in urban centres (Figure 4).

Figure 4: Fresco from Beni Hassan showing Canaanites bringing copper ingots to Egypt (indicated with arrows), Middle Kingdom (after Lepsius 1859, pl. 133).

These urban centres, the size of the villages of today, were the places where surpluses were stored and dispatched to be transformed into commodities other than consumables used for immediate survival. As the locations of writing, used to record taxes and stock-keeping, cities were the cradle of statehood, in the form first of city-states and later as territorial states. Hence, the rise of the Kingdoms of Israel and Judah is concomitant with the spread of writing, beginning respectively in the ninth and eighth centuries. At every level, one family held a commanding position expressed through a larger house and other status symbols such as the donkeys ridden by the sons in Judges 10:4 and 12:14. Village communities were not inherently egalitarian, unless poverty is taken as shared equally. The slightly higher status granted to the local chief entailed a greater share of the communal burden to assume representational responsibilities towards the outside and regulatory functions within, arbitrating conflicts and taking the final decision in communal affairs. But for the rest, the daily routine of the family was run along private lines.

Major differences in altitude within short distances enabled farmers to tap different stages of vegetation, sending animals to graze in uplands in the summer and in the lowlands in the winter. This is the standard Mediterranean transhumance, when unmarried men were sent off with the animals that were not needed at the village. Animals were also grazed in fallow fields, about half the total arable surface, and in the other fields between harvest and ploughing times for manuring and weed control. When the village did not own enough animals, the fallows could be rented out to type 2 nomads.

What is commonly assumed by the term "nomad" is type 2 nomadism: non-sedentary tribes specialized in raising animals, who relied for their needs for non-animal products on the exchange of wool, hides, cheese, meat, and transport facilities, as well as on raiding and protection money. This type of nomadism corresponds to an ethnic division of labour (Sussnitzki 1966). Type 2 nomadism is not attested before the ninth century

BCE. It became possible with the advent of the great empires of the first millennium BCE. Hence, biblical Hebrew has no term for nomad and modern Ivrit had to borrow it from European languages, while Arabic uses the term ʻarab to designate Type 2 nomads.

Toponyms
Toponyms, the names given to places, are important markers of how humans construct the world in which they live. Place-names often transmit historically relevant information. In Semitic languages, most names are transparent (Zadok 1985; Halayqa 2008). For Arabic speakers, Muhammad is "the highly praised," while Petach Tiqwa is the "Gate of Hope" for Israelis. Most Arabic toponyms in Israel/Palestine have either a Canaanite or an Aramaic substrate that often transmits the ancient name of the site. Hence, Rabbat (Bene) Ammon is ʻAmmān, Heshbon is Ḥisbān, Rabbat Moab is er-Rabba, and Bozra is Buṣēra; these names are all of Canaanite origin. Krak Moʼabā, "Fort of Moab," became Kerak and Rāmtā, "Height," became Ramtha (biblical Ramot Gilead). These are Aramaic names, as the Irbid plateau was settled by Arameans from the eleventh century BCE. Aramaic words indicate that no previous Canaanite settlement existed, or that the place only became prominent in Persian times when the use of Aramaic was generalized. Canaanite names reveal settlement continuity, sometimes as far back as the third millennium BCE, particularly when they end in -ān/-ōn, like Gibeon (Isserlin 1956; Aḥituv 1984; Knauf 1988b). As expected, they are more frequent in the heart of the country than on the fringe areas that were settled later and often on a more intermittent basis. Names with baʻal elements are typical of new foundations of the Iron Age in the Central Range (Rosen 1988). Some names have been "translated" into Arabic. Hence, *Tell el-Qāḍī*, "Ruin of the Judge," has to be translated back to reveal the name Dan, "someone who is judging."

Despite a millennium of Hellenistic and Roman rule (333 BCE–694 CE), during which Greek and Latin names were given to the free cities (*poleis*) established next to Pre-Hellenistic settlements, the Pre-Hellenistic names reappeared. "Philadelphia" became Amman again, Antioch on Chrysorrhoas later reverted to Jerash, Scythopolis returned to Beisan (Beth-Sheʼan), while Hippos was turned into Khirbet Sūsīye, "Horse Ruin." Hellenism was restricted to the upper classes; the majority of the population spoke Semitic languages like Aramaic and Arabic throughout the period.

Latin names that persist include Capitolias, a Roman foundation which survived in arabized Aramaic translation as Bēt Rās, "Summit House," and two different places called La(ǧ)ǧūn, from [*castra*] *legion(is)*, "legion camp": one close to Megiddo, the other east of Kerak. Both were places where legions were stationed. Only Nāblus, Sebastīye, and Qēsarīye remain close to their Greek origins, respectively Neapolis "New City," founded by Vespasian in 72 CE to settle veterans; Sebastos, founded by Herod the Great on the ruins of Samaria in honour of Augustus; and Caesarea, another foundation of Herod the Great, also in honour of Augustus, this time on the basis of the name of his family.

Epochs and Conjonctures

The social appropriation of the past requires division into epochs. Hence, the Bible presents a succession: the time of the Patriarchs; the period in Egypt; the wandering in the wilderness; the periods of the Conquest, of the Judges, and of the Kings; followed by the Exile and the Return. This periodization presents two major obstacles.

First, these periods are a theological construct by the elites of Persian Jerusalem and Samaria for building a common identity (Edelman 2013). Using these periods to organize a history of Israel runs the risk of fostering the confusion between theology and history. Hence, the present history is articulated around the concept of biblical Israel. In this way, the epochs that structure the biblical narration of Israel's past correspond to the prehistory of biblical Israel. The chronological distance separating the events narrated in the Bible and the production of the biblical scenario is thus established. The formation of biblical Israel occurred when the stories it narrated belonged to the past and could thus serve as the basis of a common identity for people scattered to the four corners of the various empires that integrated the kingdoms of Israel and Judah. The formation of biblical Israel began in the Neo-Babylonian era and continued through the Persian period until the early Hellenistic era. Biblical Israel then disintegrated into rival religious groups: Jews, Samaritans, Christians, and Muslims.

Second, periodization both constrains and enables history writing. Although it is hard today not to think of Israel's past in terms of distinct periods, periodization identifies particular events as turning points and *caesura* that were not experienced as such at the time. For instance, 333 BCE, the arrival of Alexander the Great in the Levant, was not as significant as modern histories suggest. Cities in Egypt and Asia Minor simply struck coins of Alexander in Persian attire, as they considered Alexander as the successor to their local Persian satrap. Alexander the Great can be considered the last of the Achaemenids as much as the founder of a great empire. Yet, it is a requirement of periodization that forces historians to lump together some events while exaggerating their difference from other events, so that the past can be organized in a way that meets contemporary social needs (Zerubavel 2003). In many cases, periodization is a literary artifice that does not reflect socio-political phenomena, which are characterized by continuity rather than by clear-cut periods.

To avoid the idiosyncrasy of historical periodization into distinct epochs, history might be organized into *centuries*, understood as social categories that roughly correspond to 100-year periods. In recent European history, one refers to the "long" sixteenth century (1492–1618 CE), the "long" nineteenth century (1789–1914 CE) and the "short" twentieth century (1914–1989 CE) (Hobsbawm 1994). In the history of Israel, a "short" eighth century is encountered (796–734 BCE) and a "long" seventh century (734–609 BCE).

Given that Israel belongs to the fringes of the Mediterranean world, the micro-history of Israel can be synchronized with the macro-history of the Mediterranean systems through Braudel's economic *conjonctures*. The first half of the second millennium BCE saw the rise of the first Mediterranean economic system, limited to the eastern side of the Mediterranean with Egypt, Babylonia, Asia Minor, and Crete as the main actors. This network did not survive the Bronze Age. The second Mediterranean economic system began with the "Canaanite revival" of the eleventh century BCE and ended with the collapse of Mediterranean trade in the seventh century CE. In the **middle** of the eighth century BCE, Phoenician trade networks operated fom southern Spain to southern Arabia. In 671 BCE, Assyria subdued Egypt, making the eastern Mediterranean a monopolar world for the first time, realizing the old Egyptian and Mesopotamian concept of a world empire spanning the four corners of the world. The concept was taken over with much élan by the Neo-Babylonians, Persians, Macedonians, and Romans, gradually shifting the centre of gravity westwards. When Egypt and Arabia became Roman provinces (in 30 BCE and 106 CE, respectively), the **domination** of Rome over the entire Mediterranean expanse was completed. In the process, Rome was deeply orientalized, and the Republic gave way to the oriental notion of empire.

In the fourth century CE, when the Mediterranean economy contracted again, Rome found itself sidelined, the centre of the Empire having shifted back to the eastern side of the Mediterranean world at Constantinople. The resulting vacuum in the West fostered the development of the fringes that primed the Germanic invasions. These invasions were the consequence, rather than the cause, of the Roman Empire's collapse. The third Mediterranean economic system is beyond the purview of the present volume.

The pre-history of biblical Israel unfolds during the first half of the second Mediterranean system in the framework of the kingdoms of Israel and Judah (Coote and Whitelam 1987). The integration of the kingdoms into the empires spurred the rise of a new identity to overcome the physical distance between the Diaspora and the Israelite cradle. As charter of the cultic centres of Jerusalem and Mount Gerizim, the Torah founded a new identity that made loyalty to any particular king irrelevant. A social memory based on biblical Israel rooted the new identity in Creation, and this fostered peaceful cohabitation with other groups in the Diaspora as much as in Palestine. Declaring the Others legitimate offspring of the original couple and of the survivors of the Flood gave biblical Israelites a sense of common destiny, thanks to the Israelite patriarchs and matriarchs, as well as Moses, Aaron, and Miriam who brought them out of the house of slavery. The translation of the Torah into Greek in Egypt (the old house of slavery), along with the Hellenistic concept of history, prepared the way for the disintegration of biblical Israel. The constitution of a post-Torah history that narrated what happened after Israel's entry in Canaan until the days of Nehemiah caused a gradual rift with the Samaritans, who rejected the notion of history and insisted on the uniqueness of the Torah. The extension of the biblical canon by Jerusalem and its translation by Alexandria introduced Judaism into the thriving cultural scene of Hellenism and fostered the spread of Judaism far beyond its natural boundaries through the agency of Christianity and Islam (Pirenne 1939); after providing a sense of common identity, biblical Israel gave birth to three of the most successful monotheisms. Judaism eventually rejected Greek but split between Palestine and Mesopotamia, Christianity adopted Greek and tried to ignore the thriving Aramaic churches, while later Islam also splintered into central and peripheral groups. As children of the Torah, the Tanakh, the Mishnah, the New Testament, the Talmud, the writings of the Church Fathers, the Qur'an, the Sunna, and the writings of Jewish and Muslim authorities are the continuation of a thought process that began millennia earlier in Egypt, Mesopotamia, and the Levant as a whole.

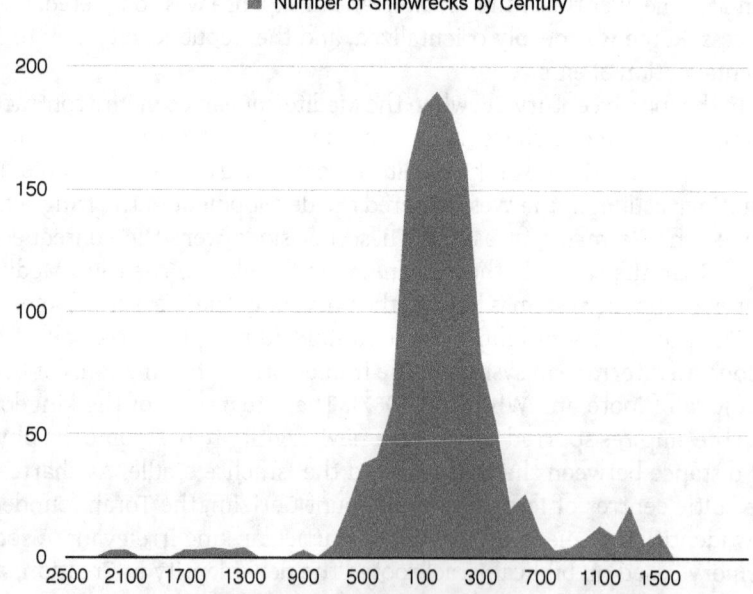

Figure 5: Mediterranean shipwrecks (T. Guillaume).

The rise and fall of the two older Mediterranean economic systems is reflected in the number of shipwrecks that litter the Mediterranean seabed (Parker 1992; Horden and Purcell 2000; Knauf 2008). As the climate and the nautical technologies experienced no major revolutions between 2000 BCE and 1500 CE, the loss ratio through shipwreck can be considered fairly constant for the period (Figure 5, shipwrecks). The Canaanite system of the Bronze Age (seventeenth to twelfth centuries BCE) is modest and limited to the eastern side of the Mediterranean. The number of wrecks for that period is too low to reconstruct an unequivocal "bell curve" as an indicator of the intensity of Mediterranean trade. The second system lasted three times as long (ninth century BCE to eighth century CE). The third system, only partially represented here, was stronger than the first one but much weaker than the second system. The Israel of the Bible appears on the scene after the collapse of the first system and at the beginning of the second system. Setting ancient Israel in its macro-historic context shows why there could be no kingdom in Israel and Judah before the ninth and eighth centuries BCE. The Neo-Babylonian interval, the so-called "exilic period," does not mark any change in the number of shipwrecks. From the seventh to the end of the fourth century BCE, Judah owed its existence to a favourable international *conjoncture*. The transition between the Persian and Macedonian powers is reflected in the recession of the fourth century BCE. It was followed by the booming third to first centuries BCE, bringing levels of prosperity that remained unmatched in Israel/Palestine until the nineteenth century CE. Rome arrived on the Levantine scene as the downturn set in.

Part I

The Pre-history of Biblical Israel

Chapter 1
From Merenptah to Rameses VI

The relations of Egypt with Canaan in the Late Bronze Age establish the framework for development in the Iron Age.

In this first part, we cover the time when there was no Bible, although most of the traditions the scribes of Jerusalem elaborated upon arose in this period. Like the authors of the present history, the scribes who produced what became the Torah and the Prophets sought to face the challenges of their own time. The Persian context in which the biblical scribes worked must be understood before setting out to deconstruct the biblical texts and reconstruct the history of ancient Israel. But since history is best served in a chronological sequence, we begin with an inquiry into the situation in Canaan at the end of the Bronze Age.

It is in Egyptian texts that a political entity named Israel and the divine name YHWH are first attested (Redford 1992; Figure 6). Some biblical

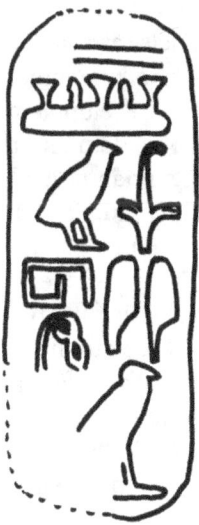

Figure 6: First record of the precursor of the name YHWH in the list of Shasu-lands of the temple of Soleb (Sudan): t3 š3-św y-h-w3 'Shasu-land: Yhw'. From top to bottom: ta /sha / (right to left) sw (w) / yhw3 (after Jaroš 1974, 122).

passages would appear to reflect this notion (Exod. 1:1-8; Ezek. 20:5-9; Hos. 11:1), with others claiming a different origin (Deut. 32:8-9 [LXX], 10-14; with Ezek. 16:3; Hos. 9:10). The historical background of the Exodus tradition is rooted in the Late Bronze Age (1550–1130 BCE), when Israel/Palestine was an Egyptian province called Canaan. The weakening of Egyptian influence over the region fostered the development of a number of local autonomous entities, Philistine and Canaanite city-states as well as the groups that later would coalesce into Israel and Judah (Na'aman 2011b).

1.1 The Egyptian Province of Canaan

The existence of Canaan as an Egyptian province lies beyond the reach of the Israelite collective memory transmitted in the biblical traditions, except for a few reminiscences such as such as the name מעין מי נפתוח *ma'yan mê neftoaḥ* "the waters of Neftoah," which is a corruption of "the source of Merenptah" in Joshua 15:9 and 18.15. The use of Canaan as the name of a son of Ham and brother of Egypt in Genesis 10:6 reflects the renewal of Egypt's influence over its old province during the seventh century BCE. Israel/Palestine had always served as a strategic northern buffer zone for Egypt: Egypt established commercial outposts in southern Palestine as early as the fourth millennium BCE (Arad), and further north on the Lebanese coast by 2600 BCE. By 2000 BCE, Egyptian influence spread east to the Golan and the Hauran (CoS 1.38). Deportees and migrants from Canaan inhabited northern Egypt and founded a Canaanite city-state in the eastern Nile Delta at Avaris (Bietak 1996; Oren 1997). Avaris was the centre of a Canaanite kingdom that subdued northern Egypt between 1680 and 1550 BCE, a development referred to as the "Hyksos period," between the Middle Kingdom and the New Empire; "Hyksos" is the Greek rendering of the Egyptian *ḥq3wt ḫ3śwt*, "Rulers of the foreign lands," and from the third millennium onwards this term had designated the kinglets of Canaan rather than a particular people. In the middle of the sixteenth century BCE, Egypt expelled the Canaanites and subdued the homeland of the invaders. In the fifteenth century BCE, Pharaoh Thutmosis III campaigned as far as the Euphrates. The large fourteenth-century BCE archive recovered from the Egyptian site of Tel Amarna contains the correspondence of Canaanite kinglets with their Egyptian overlord (Moran 1996; Goren *et al.* 2004). Yearly reports were sent to the pharaoh as clay tablets which transcribed in cuneiform the Canaanized Akkadian language (Rainey 1996).

The Canaanite city-states developed in the first half of the second millennium BCE as the southern extension of Syrian culture (Ilan 1995). By the middle of the millennium, even before the advent of the Egyptian New

Empire (1550–1050 BCE), the Canaanite city-states experienced a sharp decline (Marfoe 1998, 153–216). Only Hazor and Megiddo survived as sizable cities (Herzog 1997, 164–1655); the others were but shadows of what they had been (Bunimovitz 1995). The situation in the highlands was even worse. Robber barons controlled Shechem and Jerusalem, their respective northern and southern fortified residences on the central mountain range where no other settlement existed. The Amarna letters reveal how 20 "cities" squabbled and fought each other, each "king" assuring Pharaoh of his unwavering loyalty while accusing his neighbour of rebellion (Na'aman 1996). The pharaoh considered them for what they were —village mayors— and turned a deaf ear to their bickering as long as the interests of Egypt were not threatened.

The recovery of Egypt in the sixteenth century BCE resulted in massive deportations from Syria-Palestine to Egypt (CoS 2.276–277, in ANET: 280–281), adding to the prevalent insecurity. From a population of 140,000–180,000 in the seventeenth century BCE, Israel/Palestine experienced a severe phase of depopulation, with only 30,000–45,000 people in the cities during the fifteenth century BCE.

As a whole, the Late Bronze (sixteenth to twelfth centuries BCE) was an age of decline for Canaanite culture (Finkelstein 1994). The principalities of Lab'ayu at Shechem and 'Abdiḫepa at Jerusalem disappeared from the scene after the fourteenth century BCE, not reappearing until the tenth century BCE as the tribal kingdoms of Saul and David. If "f" indicates the social and economic level in Canaan in a given century n, then f (fourteenth century BCE) > f (thirteenth century) > f (twelfth century); f (twelfth century) < f (eleventh century), but f (fourteenth century) = f (tenth century), which means that the downward trend was reversed in the eleventh century with a rapid expansion in the tenth century that regained the level of the fourteenth century BCE.

Small mobile groups, designated as *shasu* (*š3św*) in Egyptian texts and as *sutû* in Akkadian texts, roamed the Central Palestinian Range and the east Jordan plateau. These type 1 nomads survived on the fringe with minimal interaction with the population on the other side of the Jordan and were considered dangerous strangers by Canaanites and Egyptians alike. These *shasu* were the remnants of the local population from the hill country of the Middle Bronze Age.

With the shrinkage of the influence of the Canaanite city-states over the highlands, bands of *'apiru* (= "dusty men?") appeared. Also spelled *habiru* or *hapiru* in modern books, they were outlaws *à la* Robin Hood, raiding villages for their own gain or serving as mercenaries for whoever hired them, until they became slaves, either voluntarily or after being caught in slave-hunts. Etymologically, the term Hebrew derives from *'apiru* (Loretz 1984; against, Rainey 2007).

Shasu and *'apiru* shared the same geographic zones and more or less the same survival strategy (Na'aman 1982). They were considered hostile to civilized society, although there would necessarily have been symbiotic aspects in their relationship with settlements. Minimally, they constituted a ready source of slaves, without which civilized society could not develop. At the end of the thirteenth century BCE, Pharaoh Sethos I encountered a group of *shasu* named Tayru near Beth-She'an (Figure 7).

These *shasu* had joined up with the *'apiru* from the mountain of Yarmuth against loyal Asiatics of Ruhma' (*CoS* 2.4D). The stele that narrates the encounter attests to the beginning of some kind of ethnogenesis by which a group of *shasu*, who up to then had never represented an ethnonym, began to display a supra-clan social organization that entailed collaboration with a group bearing an Aramaic name, Tayru.

The Egyptians also encountered some *shasu* further south in the Arabah, where they worked copper mines at Timna. From there, the Egyptians heard about a mountain or a group whose name they transcribed as *yhw3*, which corresponds exactly to the biblical name of Israel's God YHWH (*DDD* 1: 1712-1730; *DDD* 2: 910-919). The Hebrew Bible also claims a southern origin for YHWH, from Seir (Judg. 5:4-5) or further south, from Midian in the northwestern Arabian highlands (Exod. 2:15-16; Hab. 3:7).

The *shasu* were frequently hired or forced into working in the local mines as well as marched off as slaves to Egypt; but in times of drought, they would also seek refuge in Egypt. In any of these different ways, YHWH came into contact with Egypt.

1.2 Merenptah: How the Israelites Came to Egypt

The empires that arose during the third millennium BCE along the Nile and between the Euphrates and the Tigris came into contact in the fifteenth century BCE through war and diplomacy. These contacts challenged the notion of empire as covering "the entire world," as the notion of empire had been conceived up until then. How can two empires coexist if both claim to rule the whole world? The question had theological repercussions and led to the formulation of the idiosyncratic religion of Pharaoh Amenophis IV/Akhenaton (1353-1336 BCE), which elevated the sun god Aton above all other gods. Aton was the sole emperor in heaven if not on earth (Redford 1984). The crisis exacerbated by Akhenaton came to a resolution of sorts at the end of the second millennium, with what is now called "implicit monotheism" emanating from the three hundred chapters of the Hymn to Amon:

> All gods are three:
> Amun, Re, and Ptah, and anyone like them does not exist.
> He who conceals his name as Amun,
> he is Re in his face, and his body is Ptah.

1. From Merenptah to Rameses VI 33

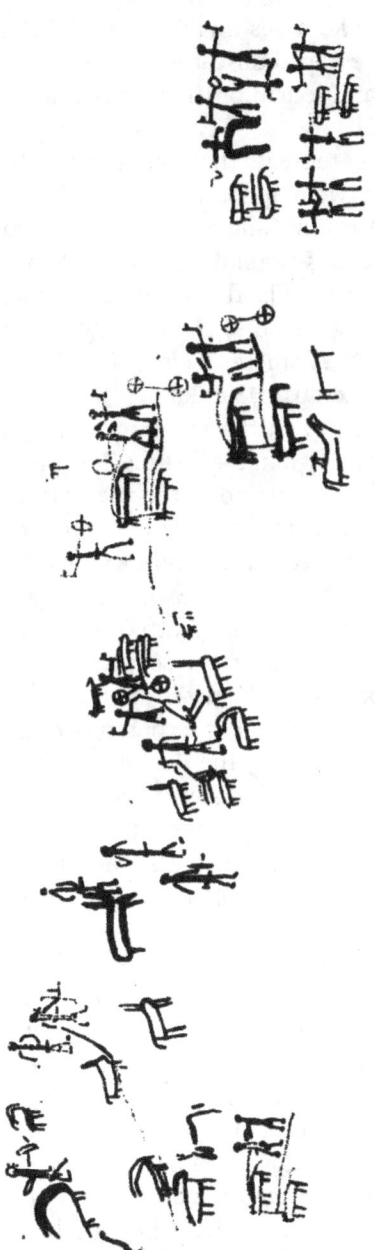

Figure 7: Rock drawing of the Egyptian army perceived by friendly Shasus (after Rothenberg 1972, fig. 38).

This type of monotheism claimed that a single divine essence was at work in every known god.

By the thirteenth century BCE, the Egyptian and Hittite empires entered into direct confrontation as they spread their influence over Syria and Lebanon. The showdown took place at Kadesh on the Orontes in 1275 BCE. Although Pharaoh Rameses II (1279-1213 BCE) claimed the victory because he personally escaped unscathed, the small print on his victory inscription reveals that a fourth of the Egyptian forces was annihilated (Lichtheim 1976, 57-72).

The international peace treaty that followed, the first of its kind, fixed the limits between the two empires slightly north of the present Israel-Lebanon border, thus turning Canaan into a frontier zone. This new configuration led the Egyptians to reinforce their rule over Canaan through the dedication of vast tracts of land to Egyptian temples, the replacement of kinglets by Egyptian governors, and the Egyptianization of the local elite (Higginbotham 2000). Rameses II also built a new city in the eastern Nile Delta known from Exodus 1:15 as Rameses.

In view of Exodus 1:15 and the mention of a tribe named Israel in Canaan during the days of Rameses' successor, Merenptah (1213-1203 BCE), older histories of Israel commonly took Rameses II as the "Pharaoh of the Exodus." Israel's 40 years in the wilderness fitted nicely within Rameses' 60-year reign. These speculations, however, fail to take into account that the Exodus Conquest Narrative in Exodus 2-Joshua 10 is not a factual report of what took place in the thirteenth century BCE but a theological construct by Judean scribes during the seventh century BCE, at the earliest. The Israelites labouring at Rameses are not a feature of a tradition from the second millennium BCE but a construct of the first millennium BCE. This is clearly established by the Hebrew forms of the names Moses and Rameses (משה *Moše*, רעמסס *Raʿmesses*), which render the same Egyptian sound /ś/ in different ways. Both names contain the Egyptian verb *mśy*, "to be born." Rameses means "the sun god (Ra) gave birth to him (Pharaoh)," while Moses reproduces only the "born" part, omitting the divine element (Figure 8 Rameses).

Around 1000 BCE, the sound /ś/ was rendered into Canaanite as /s/ (*samek*), so the current form of Ra-meses, rendered with two *sameks* (רעמסס), indicates its borrowing into Canaanite after 1000 BCE. By contrast, Moses became *Moshe* because the name entered Hebrew tradition before the sound shift in Canaanite which occurred around 1000 BCE (Knauf 1988a: 73-76). The different transliterations indicate that the link between Moses and Rameses II is secondary and that their combination in the story in Exodus cannot establish a date for the historical Moses. The memory of the city of Rameses survived through the writings of the Israelite and Judean scribes in the eighth and seventh centuries BCE.

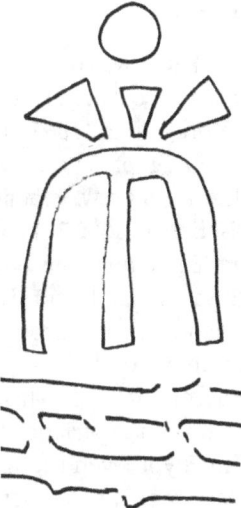

Figure 8: The name Rameses on a seal from Tell Farʻa South, with the hieroglyph Raʻ above and *msw* below from which the Hebrew name *Moshe* is derived. Pharaonic names were believed to be endowed with power because they were formed with divine names. They were often reproduced on amulets (after *CSAPI* 3, Tell Fārʻa South #525).

As long as the *shasu* were involved with declining city-states, they did not constitute tribes, i.e. political organizations beyond the extended family. The first tribal names appear at the point when they encountered a world power, such as Egypt. Between 1213 and 1208 BCE, Merenptah defeated three rebellious Canaanite cities (Ashkelon, Gezer, and Yanoam) and a tribe named Israel (*CoS* 2.6). At that time, Israelite prisoners of war entered Egypt. By 1211 BCE, archer contingents had secured the central ridge by patrolling the roads that connected watchtowers. One station along that road was called Springs of Neftoah, likely located northwest of Jerusalem, in the vicinity of the modern suburb of Lifta. The highlands of Canaan now came under Egyptian rule, too. The subjection of the first Israel probably occurred during the Egyptian occupation of the Central Range, the military pacification of which probably began during the reign of Rameses II (Kitchen 1964, 66).

Merenptah's Israel cannot be identified as the direct precursor of the tribes of biblical Israel. In the twelfth and eleventh centuries BCE, various tribes formed in the mountains of Galilee and Samaria, where Merenptah's Israel should be sought: Naphtali, Zebulon, and Ephraim. The god of Merenptah's Israel was probably El. The title *ʼel ʼelohe yisraʼel* (אלהי ישראל אל) in Genesis 33:20 seems to be a relic of the period when Israel's god was called El rather than YHWH.

1.3 Sethnakht and an Exodus (1186 BCE)

As the Nineteenth Dynasty in Egypt was dying, the Grand Vizier Bay/Beya, of Canaanite origin, tried to seize power. Beya was defeated by the founder of the Twentieth Dynasty, Sethnakht, in 1186 BCE. In the ensuing confusion, Canaanites were expelled from Egypt. These events could be the nucleus around which the Exodus tradition grew. Israelites who had been brought to Egypt as Merenptah's prisoners in 1208 BCE, or slightly earlier, had come into contact with *shasu* from Edom and thus encountered the god YHWH. Evicted after the failure of Beya's coup, the survivors settled in the northern Central Range, where Egyptian control was on the wane (1150–1130 BCE). There, they articulated the memory of their salvation as recorded in Exodus 18:1: YHWH had brought Israel out of Egypt. This slogan appealed equally to the local *shasu* and to *'apiru* who had experienced the loosening of the Egyptian grip as a liberation from Egypt, even though most of them had never seen the Nile. Others may have remembered how their ancestors had been forced to seek refuge in the highlands to escape Egyptian rule. Hence, the "Exodus" reflects the conflation of various memories of the encounter with Egyptian colonialism rather than the displacement of populations following the breakdown of the Canaanite city-states.

Other scenarios are possible, such as the flight of an Edomite *shasu* group from the mines of Timna, where they had been press-ganged. In any case, it is crucial to note that the Exodus tradition moved from Israel to Judah and not the other way round.[1] More cannot be said about the historicity of the Exodus, but it is clear that in the centuries that saw the formation of biblical Israel, various groups experienced liberation from the Egyptian yoke in more than one way and on more than one occasion. Rather than focusing on a particular event, the Exodus reflects the interaction of the populations of Israel/Palestine with Egypt from the sixteenth to the twelfth centuries BCE (Na'aman 2011b). In this sense, the Exodus tradition is the aggregation of these memories, which were updated when Israel and Judah interacted with the colonial powers of later times, Assyria and Babylon.

As indicated above, the name Moses is based on Egyptian *mśy*, which was used to form many names in Ramesside times. The Egyptian name of Beya/Bay was Ra'-mes-su-ğa'u-em-nečeru ("Ra is born in the midst of

---

1 The Exodus motive is linked to Israelite sanctuaries (1 Kgs 12:28) and prophets (Hos. 2:17 [MT 2:15]; 8:13; 9:3; 11:1; 12:9 [MT 12:10], 13[14]; 13:4); it is in Hosea that the word "Egypt" has the highest frequency of any biblical book (3.6‰ according to Accordance™). On the other hand, there is no allusion to the Exodus in Isaiah 1–39 or Micah 1–3, presumably predating the second half of the seventh century BCE (Schmid 2010, 158–159; Gillingham 1999).

the gods"). A chamberlain called Ra'messes-em-per-Re' ("Ra is born in the House of Ra") led a series of expeditions to the copper mines of Timna. His career can be followed over several decades (Schulman 1976). Both of these Egyptian officials of Canaanite origin were involved in the muster of groups from YHWH's homeland. Other Egyptian officials of Asiatic origin with a *mśy*-name may stand behind the figure of Moses, but these are the two who are attested in the documentation retrieved so far.

1.4 Rameses IV–VI and the End of the Egyptian Province of Canaan

In the wake of the break-up of the Late Bronze economic and city-state systems during the thirteenth century BCE, warring and plundering bands appear in the written records and are designated as the Sea People by the Egyptians (Breasted 1906, II §307; III § 574, 587; IV §44; *ANET* 262–263). Various groups are recorded under this label. Already at Kadesh (1275 BCE) Rameses II hired the Shardana (*š3-r'-d-ï-n3*). In Libya between 1213 and 1208 BCE, Merenptah fought the Aqawash (*3-q-3-w3-š3*), Tur(u)sha (*t-w-rw-š3*), Luku (*rw-k-w*), Sikil (*š-k-rw-š3*), and Shardana. In 1175 BCE, Rameses III confronted Peleshet (Philistines, *p-w-r'-š3-t'*), and Tjekkel (*č-3-k-k3-r'*), Danyuna (*d-3-yn-yw-n-3*), and Washash (*w3-š3-š3*). As far as can be seen, these groups originated from the periphery of the Hittite Empire. That empire came apart at the beginning of the twelfth century BCE, enabling the rise of the small Luwian kingdoms that survived until the eighth century BCE. The Sikil and Shardana may have spread west in the Mediterranean and founded colonies on the islands of Sicily and Sardinia. The names of the Aqawash, Danyuna, and Luku recall the Greek names of the Achaians, Danaeans, and Lykians.

The end of the Hittite Empire was precipitated by a major climatic change around 1200 BCE that dramatically reduced the amount of agricultural surpluses that fed the Mediterranean trade system. The sharp reduction of overseas trade rendered many cities irrelevant once the bulk of human activity had begun focusing exclusively on subsistence food production. After 1190 BCE Ugarit was deserted, soon followed by Hazor. Only the largest centres located in the most favourable surroundings of Phoenicia, the Nile Valley, and Mesopotamia survived the crisis.

As is the case with the barbarian invasions of late antiquity, the migration of the so-called Sea Peoples at the end of the Bronze Age is often understood as the arrival of new ethnic groups that overran the Hittite Empire. This view confuses the effect with the cause. It was the power vacuum following the collapse of the Empire that enabled the rise of new political entities. Hence, the *ahlamu* ("youngsters") founded "Aramean" kingdoms on the ruins of the Syro-Mesopotamian Bronze Age civilization from the eleventh century BCE onwards without large-scale migrations of exogenous groups. There were no Aramean people as such. They spoke various dialects that were later standardized into Imperial Aramaic by the resurrected Mesopotamian empires. Neither the Arameans nor the various Sea People groups formed into ethnic units before consolidating in the territories they had acquired.

Prior to 1190 BCE, the Sea Peoples are only attested as raiders by sea and as mercenaries. In 1175 BCE, however, Pharaoh Rameses III claims to have stopped a massive invasion by sea and land by migrating Sea Peoples. The assumption of much previous scholarship was that the Pharaoh fought them off at the Nile Delta, i.e., the innermost border of Egypt. He then settled the vanquished in military colonies at Ashdod, Ashkelon, Gaza, Ekron, and Gath, where they became the biblical Philistines.

If prisoners-of-war were indeed incorporated into the Egyptian forces, they were certainly not stationed on the frontier they had recently threatened. They would have been stationed on the other side of the realm, as an inscription of Rameses II in the Great Temple of Abu Simbel indicates:

> The Good God, slaying the Nine Bows [...] who carries off the land of Nubia to the Northland (or Delta), and the Asiatics to the land of Nubia; he has placed the Shasu in the Westland, and he has settled the Libyans (*Tjehenu*) on the ridges.
>
> (Kitchen 1996, 67)

The text continues with a mention of the *shasu*, who are said to have been settled in a land the name of which is unfortunately lost. Nevertheless, on the basis of the previous lines, it is clear that vanquished people were deported far away and that the Philistine coast would have been the last place to settle the defeated Sea Peoples. Hence, the arrival of the Philistines in southern Canaan should be explained differently. Rameses did stop an invasion of Sea Peoples, somewhere in Syria, Lebanon, or Palestine, but not in the Nile Delta as was long thought. North of the Egyptian sphere of influence, these people established the kingdom of Palastin in the area encompassing Tell Ta'yinat, between modern Antakya, Aleppo, and Hamath (Hama) (Sass 2010). An 11-line Hieroglyphic Luwian inscription (Aleppo 6) is incised and almost completely preserved on the statue of the king, placed opposite the statue of the storm god of Aleppo in the temple of this god recently excavated in the Aleppo citadel (Hawkins 2009, 169).

After 1135 BCE (the demise of Megiddo VIIA), a group that split out of Palastin penetrated into southern Canaan (Ussishkin 2008). The name Palastin survived in the Luwian Aramean kingdom of Pattina-Unqi. It stands to reason that Rameses III stopped a mass migration somewhere south of Hama and restricted the Sea Peoples for the time being to central and northern Syria. Confrontations on the Nile were the work of pirates.[2]

---

2 As Heather (2009) shows, mass migrations might be accompanied by raids or

It was the destruction of the Egyptian strongholds at Megiddo and Lachish around 1130 BCE and the end of Egyptian control over Canaan that allowed the rise of the Philistine Pentapolis (Ashkelon, Gaza, Ashdod, Ekron, and Gath). The Pentapolis, however, never formed a political entity. The kinglets were often at war with one another, but their dynasties ruled the area for the next five hundred years. The notion of a "Philistine land" is first attested around 800 BCE on a stele of the Assyrian king Adadnerari III. All inscriptions from Philistia between the tenth and the seventh centuries BCE are written in Canaanite, with only a few names such as אכיש *'Akish* (Anchyses) and עלית *'Olyat* Goli-ath, צקלג Ziklag, סרן *seren* (from the pre-Greek *tyrannos* employed exclusively in the Bible for Philistine rulers) and פלגש *pilegesh* "concubine" or "secondary wife" (Greek *pallax*, Latin *pellex*).

Rameses III explains how he checked an invasion of Sea Peoples in the Nile Delta:

> The foreign countries made a conspiracy in their islands. All at once the lands were removed and scattered in the fray. No land could stand before their arms [...] They were coming forward toward Egypt [...] Their confederation was the Philistines, Tjeker, Shekelesh, Denye(n), and Weshesh, lands united [...]. I organized my frontier in Djahi, prepared before them: princes, commanders of garrisons and *maryanu*. I have the river-mouths prepared like a strong wall, with warships, galleys and coasters, (fully) equipped, for they were manned completely from bow to stern with valiant warriors carrying their weapons. The troops consisted of every picked man of Egypt. They were like lions roaring upon the mountaintops. The chariotry consisted of runners, of picked men, of every good and capable chariot-warrior [...] I (Ramses III) was the valiant Montu [the War God], standing fast at their head [...]. Those who reached my frontier, their seed is not, their heart and their soul are finished forever and ever. Those who came forward together on the sea, the full flame was in front of them at the river-mouths, while a stockade of lances surrounded them on the shore. They were dragged in, enclosed, and prostrated on the beach, killed, and made into heaps from tail to head. Their ships and their goods were all fallen into the water. (Medinet Habu, ca. 1175 BCE, *ANET* 262)

There is no mention of any settlement of the surviving foes in "Philistia." To the contrary, in the summary of his northern wars, Rameses III mentions the settlement of some Sea Peoples (but not the Philistines) in Egypt itself:

---

piracy, 'jump' from one relatively consolidated state to the next, and re-arrange the ethnic composition of the migrating entity with every step. Instead of one or two 'waves' of Sea people at fairly precise dates, one better assumes stages: end of the thirteenth / beginning of the twelfth century, to Cilicia with raids against Cyprus and northern Syria (Ugarit); 1175 BCE, push of the Palastu to central Syria; after 1135 BCE, further push of some Philistines to southern Canaan.

I [Ramses III] slew the Denyen in their islands, while the Tjeker and the Philistines were made ashes. The Sherden and the Weshesh of the Sea were made nonexistent, captured altogether and brought in captivity to Egypt like the sands of the shore. I settled them in strongholds, bound in my name [...]. I assigned portions from them all with clothing and provisions from the treasuries and granaries every year. (Papyrus Harris I.76, 6–9 in *ANET* 262)

The Onomasticon of Amenope (ca. 1100 BCE) lists over 600 entities or classes of entities in the physical world. Besides the toponyms along the Nile, the cities of the Philistine coast hold a prominent position: the Land of Asqalon, the Land of Ashdod, the Land of Gaza, the Land of Asir, the Sarden people, the Land of the Teucri, and the Land of the Philistines (Gardiner 1947). "Asir" is probably western upper Galilee / southeastern Phoenicia (biblical Asher), with the "Teucri" (Cheker) occupying Dor, as mentioned in the tenth-century BCE travelogue *The Voyage of Unamūn* (Schipper 2005). The list then seems to turn south again, ending with Philistia. How the "land of the Philistines" at the end relates to the "lands" of Ashkalon, Ashdod, and Gaza at the beginning is hard to tell. Did the author distinguish between the Philistine cities and the Philistine hinterland, or is our assumption wrong that the sequence turns back from Asir, and that this "Philistia" is identical with Palastin?

Despite the weakening of Egyptian influence, southern Canaan remained in the Egyptian orbit throughout the reign of Rameses III (1184–1153 BCE). The temple of Amon in Gaza was renovated (*ANET* 260–261), and other Egyptian sanctuaries in the area received endowments. Rameses II (1279–1213 BCE) had initiated expeditions to the copper mines of Timna, and Rameses III maintained the Egyptian presence in the Arabah:

I sent forth my messengers to the country of 'Atika, to the great copper mines that are in this place. Their galleys carried them. Others, on the land journey, were upon their asses. Their mines were found abounding in copper. It was loaded by the ten-thousands in their galleys. It was sent forward to Egypt and arrived safely. (Papyrus Harris I 78, 1–5; Schulman 1976, 124)

Egyptian mining expeditions continued in the area until the reign of Rameses V (1146–1142 BCE). By contrast, during the Amarna period (*EA* 33–37, 40), Egypt and Syria-Palestine received copper from Cyprus (*Kypros*, Copper Island), where the production and transport of copper ingots was cheaper than those smelted in the Arabah and carried by donkeys and camels to Gaza. Therefore, the exploitation of the mines at Timna and Fenan (biblical פונון *Punon* or פינון *Pinon*) was only viable when the disruption of international trade rendered Cyprian copper inaccessible.

As for the *shasu*, some were brought to Egypt as booty in the wake of Egyptian slave-hunting expeditions in the Sinai Peninsula:

I destroyed the people of Seir, of the tribes of the Shasu; I plundered their tents of their people, their possessions, their cattle likewise, without number. They were pinioned and brought as captives, as tribute to Egypt. I gave them to the gods, as slaves into their house(s). (Papyrus Harris I 404; Breasted 1906, 4.201)

Other *shasu* came to Egypt of their own accord during times of famine. Around 1200 BCE, an officer posted to an Egyptian border fortress recorded the entry of *shasu* tribes:

> we have just let the Shasu tribes of Edom pass the Fortress of Merneptah-hetep-hermaat, LPH, of Tjeku, to the pool of Pithom of Merneptah-hetephermaat, of Tjeku, in order to revive themselves and revive their flocks from the great life force of Pharaoh, LHP, the perfect sun [...]. (Papyrus Anastasi VI 54–58; *CoS* 3.5, in *ANET* 259)

Egyptian relief operations are also mentioned in Genesis 12:10-20 and chapter 46, revealing a pattern in the relations between Egypt and Canaan in the second and first millennium. Yet, these migrants were not nomads, nor did they represent a specific group or political entity.

The last Pharaohs attested to in Canaan are Rameses IV (1153–1146 BCE), who controlled Lachish, and Rameses VI (1142–1135 BCE), who controlled Megiddo. After the destruction of Lachish Stratum VI around 1130 BCE, the site was abandoned until the establishment of a Judahite village in the ninth century (Lachish V). The ruins of Megiddo remained occupied by squatters until the mid-ninth century BCE (Megiddo VA), when Canaanite tradition revived.

Chapter 2
From Ephraim to Mamre: The Tribes in the Early Iron Age

The rise of proto-Israelite tribes in the Central Palestinian Range is placed in the context of Canaanite revival spurred by the exploitation of copper mines in the Arabah following the collapse of the first Mediterranean economic system.

What Israel may have been between the fall of the first Israel around 1208 BCE and the rise of the tribal kingdom of Israel under Saul ben Kish at the beginning of the tenth century BCE remains unknown. The pre-state Israel was neither a distinctive people nor a federation of tribes. On the basis of Judges 5:11 and 5:13, we can only state that the tribes that became Israel between the eleventh and the ninth centuries BCE understood themselves as the people of YHWH when they came together as a warring band that followed its god in the fight (Dever 1995a, 1995b, 2007).

2.1 The Emergence of the Tribes of Israel

The various groups that eventually formed the kingdoms of Israel and Judah in the tenth century had very different origins. The tribe of Ephraim derives its name from the mountains of Ephraim. It is from the vantage point of Ephraim that the name Benjamin was coined to designate the "Southern people," the *Bene Yamin*. The name "Judah" stems from the designation of the local landscape as "rugged mountains" (Arabic *wahda*). As these groups derive their name from the region they inhabited, it is clear that they did not all come from outside, as the Bible suggests. Some emerged from the local population, though this does not exclude the possibility of outsiders settling in the region and taking over the local territorial name. Besides those territorial tribes, biblical Israel was also composed of eponymous tribes, groups such as Simeon or Manasseh, which were named after an ancestor.

The process of tribal formation corresponds to the rise of rural settlements in the highlands, which were virtually devoid of permanent human presence in the Late Bronze Age (Finkelstein 1998; Bunimovitz 1994). At this point, one must differentiate between political and economic motives. The decision to organize gangs and clans into a tribal structure is a political move. When groups practising extensive farming decide to settle, they are motivated by economic considerations. Extensive farming requires no long-term investment. As long as plenty of unoccupied prime sites are freely available (good soil near permanent sources of water, game, and wild fruits), small groups find it easier to change location frequently than to settle down permanently. They would remain at one location while waiting for the little grain they sowed to ripen. Such extensive farming corresponds to the practices of type 1 nomads, not to be confused with Bedouin, and type 2 nomads. Due to climatic changes or demographic pressure, extensive farmers (type 1 nomads) may decide to invest in developing more permanent settlements, clearing more land, and building defensive walls to produce, store, and protect marketable grain surpluses when rising demographic levels and active inter-regional trade networks make it preferable to mobility. The shift from extensive to intensive modes of production is not a once-and-for-all move. Mobility remains an option at all times. Across the millennia, rural and urban populations adapted to economic and political changes by alternating between one mode and the other.

In the case of the kingdoms of Israel and Judah, the settlement process in the Iron Age only reached its climax in the eighth and seventh centuries BCE. In the Levant, the full supporting capacity of the land was never reached. The greatest challenge for local populations was under-population. In the absence of machinery, prosperity was strictly tied to demography. Even during the heyday of the kingdom of Israel, the Israelites shared the country with lions and bears (1 Samuel 17; 2 Kgs 2:24) as the areas of wasteland were extensive enough for large predators to breed. Hence, throughout the Iron Age, the notion of demographic pressure is only relevant to the gradual shift from extensive to more intensive modes of food production. Demographic pressure, however, never reached the point that would spur processes often mentioned in exegetical literature: latifundia, absentee landlordism, landless farmers, and the rise of a proletarian class (Guillaume 2012, 90–97).

Politics and economics should neither be conflated nor isolated from one other. They interact constantly and it is their interaction that leads human groups to choose between more or less intensive modes of production. The appearance of small villages throughout the Palestinian highlands should be placed in the context of the enforcement of the Pax Aegyptiaca in Canaan between 1225 and 1125 BCE. The needs of the small Egyptian military stations and mining expeditions were significant enough to create a demand for local products and services (grain, fodder, transport, meat, wine, beer, oil, figs, cooking, entertainment, etc.). The new market fostered the rise of enterprising locals who received protection in exchange for a reliable supply of the needs of the Egyptian garrisons. Another effect of the Pax Aegyptiaca was the pacification of the area, which in turn fostered long-term agricultural investment in the form of the construction of walled settlements and terraces, the planting of trees, and the clearing of more land to produce surpluses for which there now was a market. What is more difficult to explain is how these local trade networks survived the withdrawal of the Egyptians. If tribal societies often pay homage to the ideal of self-sufficiency, they rarely fully achieve it. When they do, it is at the cost of general pauperization, due to the rupture of trade networks.

The survival of the modest economy of early Israel after the withdrawal of the Egyptian troops is illustrated by the analogy of the urbanization of central Europe emanating from the native suburbs of the Roman military camps. The names of modern cities such as Utrecht (Traiectum), Nijmegen (Oppidum Batavorum—Noviomagus), Xanten (Castra vetera—Colonia Ulpia Traiana), Neuss (Novaesium), Cologne (Colonia Claudia ARA Agrippinensis), Koblenz (Ad Confluentem), Mainz (Castrum Moguntiacum), Basel (Basilea), and Zurich (Turicum) reveal how villages that had sprung up in the vicinity of Roman garrisons took over the role of the defunct Roman centres. Due to a favourable political and economic *conjoncture*, towns in medieval Europe and Israel/Palestine in the eleventh century BCE were in both cases founded on the sites of the disused garrisons. A later example of this kind of settlement process is Gadara/Umm Qēs on the Jordanian plateau during the nineteenth and twentieth centuries CE (Mershen and Knauf 1988).

In a multi-polar world, the consolidation of tribes occurs at the non-urban peripheries. By contrast, a monopolar world leads to fragmentation at the periphery. These contrasting trends are illustrated by the hundreds of Safaite tribes that arose in Arabia during the *floruit* of Roman dominion in the second century CE and by the tribal kingdoms of the Ghassanids and Lahmids that formed in the same area in the sixth century CE when Byzantium and Sassanid Persia vied with each other for the control of Greater Syria. In other words, the rise of the Israelite and Judean kingdoms presupposes the Canaanite revival that followed the withdrawal of the Egyptian overlord in the middle of the eleventh century BCE.

This Canaanite revival took place in a multi-polar world driven by the Philistine centres in the south, the Phoenician centres in the north, and the copper production and distribution zone in the Jordan Valley and Arabah. This third centre of activity was the main one until deliveries of Cypriote copper to the Levant resumed in the ninth century BCE. The traffic between the coast and Rift Valley through the Jezreel Valley, the pass of Shechem and the Benjamin Plateau sustained the economy of the tribes that controlled them. The New Canaan of the Iron Age differed from the Old Canaan of the Late Bronze Age by its greater demographic and political weight, thanks to the settlement of the highlands. Before the advent of machinery, agricultural prosperity was relative to demography and *vice versa.* Once there is more to share because there are more producers, it is no longer viable to help oneself by raiding the next settlement, because the shrinking distance between them increases the likelihood of devastating reprisals. Hence, it becomes worthwhile to sit down with one's neighbours and organize cohabitation along political and military lines.

Statehood never erases the tribes out of which it arises. The urbanite Paul knew that he was from the tribe of Benjamin (Rom. 11:1; Phil. 3:5), not from Judah. Tribes do not vanish the moment a chief declares himself king. Israelite and Judean dynasties represented thin layers of "statehood" on top of a largely tribal society. Tribes take over again at the first sign of the weakening of the state. Therefore, the social memory transmitted in the Hebrew Bible does not reach back earlier than the tenth century BCE, apart from the Exodus motif and Moses' name. The collections of tribal sayings (Genesis 49; Deuteronomy 33; Judges 5) were transmitted in the palace schools of Samaria and Jerusalem (Gen. 49:21; Deut. 33:22) and integrated much later into the Pentateuch (Gen. 49:5-7).

The debate over the relation between the Israelites and the *shasu* or *'apiru* presupposes the erroneous notion of a people as an entity displaying intangible characteristics. It is plausible that the Israelite tribes emerged from groups of *shasu* and *'apiru*, but Israel never became a people as such. The tribes and kingdoms that arose in Israel/Palestine gathered together a mosaic of groups with distinctive economic activities and folklore, epitomized in the names of Jacob's wives: Leah the "cow" (לאה) standing for agriculture, and Rachel the "ewe" (רחל) standing for type 1 nomads.

The question of the origins of Israel is of no more relevance than the knowledge of what exactly happened in the Exodus because the identity of Israel, as defined by the Torah and Prophets, is marked by the experience of a more recent past, considered from the perspective of the Persian period. There is no such thing as a fundamental Exodus experience that would have put an indelible mark on the character of Israel and Judaism. The meaning of the Exodus tradition was constantly updated and transformed. The collective total of actual memories transmitted in biblical texts declines steadily in the centuries before the sixth century BCE, when the production of biblical texts was getting under way (Knauf 2010a, 2010b).

The notion of the so-called conquest of Canaan by the Israelite tribes can now be laid to rest. The three models it revolved around (discussed below) are all incompatible with currently known records and theoretical models (McDermott 1998, 36-45). They are based on the dubious premise that historical change is induced by mass immigration or class struggle. However, as these models are still encountered in exegetical literature, it is necessary to mention them here.

At this point, it is useful to remember that the Hebrew Bible rarely mentions the land of Israel but very often the land of Canaan, the area that was granted by its God and not conquered by Israel on its own initiative. The *conquest model* developed by W.F. Albright has the tribes of Israel spring out of the desert and conquer the country, as portrayed in Joshua 1–12. It is now clear that the tribes originated from within the country and not from outside. Late Bronze destruction layers spread over a much larger period than the five years covered by Joshua 14:7-10, while they are missing at Jericho and Ai, the two cities whose destructions are related in detail in Joshua 6 and 8. A further problem is that most burnt layers, which Albright and his students used to prove the historicity of Joshua's conquest, could have resulted from accidental fires started by the negligence of smiths, potters, or cooks or when earthquakes crashed flammable roofing materials onto a hearth. To prove that a destruction layer results from a military attack, one needs to find underneath the debris the bodies of the slain, with arrowheads stuck into them. The case of Stratum VII at Dan is particularly striking in this respect, since the ash layer considered the destruction layer of the Canaanite city is consistent with a fire breaking out among shrubs that had overgrown a city that had been abandoned 50 to 100 years previously. The fire may have been lit by the new settlers of Stratum VI but certainly not by Joshua.

The second model, Albrecht Alt's *infiltration model*, is based on the correct observation that the tribes of the future Israel formed where there were no Canaanite towns, between 1500 and 1150 BCE. The problem is that Alt used the concept of transhumance to explain the arrival of Israel in the unsettled mountains of the West Bank, thus turning the concept upside-down, since transhumance would have been initiated by settled farmers on the western side of the Jordan sending their flocks eastwards to pasture.

While Alt ignored the *'apiru*, they are the basis of the third model for Israel's origins, the *social revolution model* developed by G. Mendenhall and N.K. Gottwald. According to these scholars, the ancestors of the Israelites, the *'apiru*, were Canaanite peasants who rebelled against their feudal lords and took to the hills, where they united as a group of anti-feudal covenanters in a spirit of brotherhood and egalitarianism. This is an anachronistic projection of modern ideals onto the Bible, presupposing the appearance of freedom rhetoric in reaction to the consolidation of the kingdom of Israel in the eighth century BCE. Compared with these out-dated models, current research favours small-scale and evolutionary approaches to the formation of Israel.

The representation of Israel as 12 tribes is a theological construct elaborated at the earliest in the days of Jeroboam II but more probably in the fifth century BCE (Levin 1995). The symbolic sum of 12 is reached by adding Judah to the 10 tribes of Israel listed in Judges 5 (1 Kgs 11:30-32), plus the priestly tribe of Levi. Ephraim and Manasseh (called Machir in Judges 5:14) may be counted as one tribe designated as the House of Joseph (Gen. 35:23-26; 49:2-27; Josh. 17:17; 18:5) or as two tribes, in which case Levi disappears (Gen. 48:5; Num. 1:4-16). Hence, there are more than 12 tribes in the biblical record, but they did not all exist at the same time. The complexity of the formation of Israel is illustrated by Judges 5:3 and 5:5, which state that it was as the people of YHWH that the warring bands came together. As such, Israel was the people of YHWH rather than the people of El. The process of tribal formation should be considered region by region.

In Galilee, the names Naphtali for Upper Galilee and Zebulun for Lower Galilee are territorial designations with an Aramaic base. The Aramaic root *ptl*, "to weave" could possibly be a reference to the dense scrubland in Naphtali. The root *zbl* with the affix *-on* is fitting for the "princely" or "rich country" of Zebulun (Knauf 2000a). Dan was never anything other than an Aramaic city that was integrated into the kingdom of Israel during the reign of Jeroboam II. Issachar, "wage labourer," includes the Canaanite population of the Jezreel Valley, which did not come into Israel's orbit before the tenth and ninth centuries BCE. Asher is a ghost tribe. In Joshua 19:24-31, it constitutes Tyre's hinterland and may have come under Israelite rule under Jeroboam II (Lipiński 1991). Genesis 49:13 assigns Asher's territory to Zebulun. The question of where the language border between Aramaic, Phoenician, and Hebrew ran can only be tentatively answered. The inscriptions found in Galilee dating from the tenth through to the eight centuries BCE are Phoenician in the west and Aramaic in the east. Hebrew seals only appear in the eighth century BCE onwards, in the days of Jeroboam II. Hence, the designation of Naphtali as אמרי שפר in Genesis 49:21 is likely Aramaic for "beautiful lambs," but was later taken for the Hebrew "beautiful(?) words."

On the east bank of the Jordan, Judges 5:14-17 mentions Gilead, a territorial designation, and Machir, "sold," a personal name possibly designating a warring band that later became known as the son and grandson of Manasseh (Num. 26:29; 27:1; 32:39-40; 36:1). While Ephraimites and Manassites may have settled in Gilead, Joshua 17:14-18 refers to Manasseh in Cisjordan. South of Gilead, on the northern Moabite zone, Reuben, Jacob's firstborn (Num. 32:37-38; Judg. 5:15-16), must be an old designation because it is no longer detectable after the tenth century BCE (Schorn 1997). Gad, between the Transjordanian plateau and the Arnon river (Num. 32:34-36), was Israelite only during the ninth century BCE, under King Omri. The division of Transjordan between Reuben, Gad, and Half-Manasseh in Joshua 13 is a geographical fiction of the Persian era.

Ephraim, in the central Palestinian Range, means "dust-land." Since Merenptah's Israel supposedly lived in the same area, the formation of

Ephraim implies the disappearance of the first Israel. A remnant of Merenptah's Israel is probably found in the clan of Asriel (אשריאל) mentioned in Joshua 17:2 (Lemaire 1977, 283–289). Manasseh, "forgotten," may have split off from Ephraim during the wars between Baasha and Omri (1 Kgs 16:21). South of Ephraim, Benjamin, "Son of the South," is named from an Ephraimite standpoint that ignores Judah because it did not exist at the time. Around 900 BCE, the Central Range was the home of Ephraim, Machir, and Benjamin. That Benjamin is named in reference to Ephraim makes it likely that the tradition of Jacob as the ancestor of the tribes of the Samaritan mountains had arisen already in the eleventh century BCE, at a time when Judah and the other tribes were still not considered Jacob's sons. The stories of the birth of the 12 sons of Jacob date to the Persian era. The sons of Rachel (Joseph and Benjamin) form the core of the tradition. The sons of Leah (Reuben, Simeon, Levi, Judah, Issachar, and Zebulun) cover the periphery of Mount Ephraim, while the concubines share out between them the rest of Galilee (Dan, Naphtali, Gad, and Asher). The Shibbolet incident (Judg. 12:6) reveals linguistic differences between Ephraim and Gilead according to which Gileadite, like old Aramaic until the end of the eighth century BCE, preserved the phoneme *t* (*tha*) east of the Jordan River. West of the Jordan River, this phoneme merged with *sin* in the course of the second millennium BCE and changed into *shin* after 1000 BCE. Hence, contrary to Judges 12:6, the tell-tale sign was not between *samek* and *shin* but between *tha* and *shin*. What the fleeing Ephraimites pronounced wrongly was not sibbolet but Thibbolet.

By 1000 BCE, there still was no tribe of Judah. Judah, "rugged mountain," takes its name from the steep and rocky scenary south of the Benjaminite plateau. The Calebites were remembered as being associated with Hebron. Hebron's other name, Qiryath-arba, "City of the Four" (Josh. 14:15; 15:13), could imply that Hebron was the central place of four clans in pre-and early Davidic times. Further south, different parts of the Negev bore the names of groups which had controlled them: the Othnielites, Jerahmeelites, and Kenites (1 Sam. 27:10). In the case of Judah, tribe formation and initial state building coincide. From the eighth century BCE onwards, the Arab groups of the Ishmaelite confederation settled on the southern fringe of Judah. The Bible designates these groups as the tribe of Simeon, whose name is based on the same root as Ishmael (Josh. 19:1-9). Levi, Asher, Dan, and Simeon are ghost tribes that never existed outside the Bible.

2.2 Tribal Life

The tribes of Israel were not an egalitarian society like Stone Age hunter-gatherer groups but a developed tribal society with an egalitarian ideology within the ruling class only (Dostal 1985). A tribe is a political organization of clans, usually a mutual defensive alliance. The tribal chief exercises his leadership together with the heads of families (the elders) on the basis of the voluntary consent of the tribal brothers. Recognized for his wisdom and his personal wealth, the chief was called upon to arbitrate internal and external disputes: a rich man is less easily corrupted than a poor one. He was not paid for his work but he could receive some compensation for the hospitality he was expected to offer to travellers and for the tribe's palaver. To secure some level of self-sufficiency, tribes united clans that managed different eco-zones (forest, savanna, steppe, and shore). They welcomed specialized craftsmen (blacksmiths, but also priests) among them, granting them the status of *gerim* (גרים), a term mistranslated as "strangers, foreigners, or aliens" (Achenbach *et al.* 2011). Since different biblical texts use the term in different ways, the discussion is vitiated by presuppositions regarding the relative date of the relevant biblical passages as well as by the impossibility of establishing a link between legal texts and practice. Nevertheless, the sense of "client" is generally preferable. Clients may originate from another village or a clan outside the tribe, and for this reason they have no say in the assembly, but they do not necessarily come from afar. As a client, the *ger* is an *obligée* rather than an invited guest, a person or a group in an inferior position that accepts subordination in exchange for protection.

The regular occurrence of *gerim* in the Hebrew Bible underlines the necessity of taking into account the interplay between kin and geography. Whether settled or mobile, tribal societies administer a more complex reality than smaller clans, under whose jurisdiction everyone may be considered related through blood ties even if this may require a little fiction. Hence, villages, unless they number only a few dozen souls, soon comprise members of more than one clan. In this case, the village assembly that manages the communal aspects of agricultural production (e.g. water rights, land-strip distribution, fallow cycles, pasturing, collective taxes, and beginning the harvest) does not constitute the same reality as the tribe. This point must be emphasized, because the influence of the biblical notion of tribal territories is pervasive in exegesis.

Tribal societies are divided into four layers (rather than classes): an aristocracy composed of the family heads, then tribal brothers, clients, and slaves (cf. Exod. 21:18-32). As voluntary and provisional aggregations of clans, tribes fluctuate greatly. They continually split and recompose. In the early stages of statehood, the king and his entourage formed an additional layer tolerated by the tribal leaders because the king served functions that the tribal leaders could not fulfil. The development of statehood was the answer to the challenges of a broadening horizon. At first, a charismatic leader would prove himself to be the man of the situation at a critical moment. Hence, Saul the Benjaminite was acclaimed king of Israel once his military prowess had been proven (1 Sam. 11:11-15), despite the fact that the previous chapters insist that it was YHWH and Samuel who first made him king, only to change their minds afterwards.

In an ideal situation, where all the residents of a village belong to the same clan, every adult male is the brother of every other adult male and each owns shares in the communal land of the village, besides owning whatever private property he inherited from his father or acquired by his own means (parts of a house, garden, tools, weapons, wives, animals, and slaves). In this ideal village, where kin and territory or blood and land demarcations are identical, the assembly decides matters of communal agricultural production as well as tribal matters. Each brother has a vote and the obligation to fight when the chief calls up the tribal militia, the ʿam (עם). The term ʿam can be rendered "people" as long as one remains in the ideal situation of ethnic purity imagined in Deuteronomy. In the fiction of the wilderness, before Israel enters "real life" in Canaan, Israel is indeed identical to the sum of adult males recorded on the musters of Numbers 1:46 and 26:51. Each clan belongs to a single tribe and everyone lives in close proximity, ready to answer Moses' summons to war. Women and children are excluded (Deut. 3:19; 29:11), not only because they are too precious to be put at risk in war, but also because they are the source of the complications against which the ideal schemes of the Torah flounder. Despite the prevalence of marriage between paternal cousins (Gen. 24:29-30) to this day in the Levant, Numbers 36 presents the daughters of Zelophehad as a case that anticipates a real-life challenge, where husbands die and leave behind widows for whom no one wants to assume care. The text glosses over the tricky matters that are dealt with in the Book of Ruth with some realism: Widows may have given birth to male children, to girls, or worse, they may have remained childless. Despite Moses' instructions in Numbers 36:8-9, not every woman marries within her father's tribe. The birth of cousins who do not belong to the same tribe soon interferes with the solidarity between tribal brothers, blurring clan divisions and introducing extra-tribal ties. Hence, in the narratives of the Books of Samuel and Kings, the reader encounters figures that do not fit tribal maps: Doeg the Edomite (1 Samuel 21–22), or the Rechabites, who appear to live in Israel and are better YHWH-worshippers than native Israelites, although they do not belong to Israel (Jeremiah 35). The so-called legal codes of the Torah, that before the Hellenistic era were not codes of laws enforced by judges, admit to the presence of residents (תושבים) who live in Canaan next to Israel without being subjected to the same rules as Israel (Lev. 25:45-49). The famous command to love in Leviticus 19:18 is particularly revealing, since it forbids hating one's tribal brother (בני עמך), while exhorting the love of one's fellow tribesman rʿh "neighbour" (רעה) as oneself. Tribal solidarity is a duty, not a choice, and it renders the emotional level of love irrelevant. Hate and love in the biblical world are modes of action rather than emotions. You hated someone when you did something detrimental to him or her. You loved somebody when you did something helpful to him or her. In Canaan, Israelites cohabited with people who did not belong to their tribe and these had to be treated with respect, even though they did not fit the tribal map.

The Levites, "followers of YHWH," are designated *gerim* (Num. 18:19-24; Deut. 10:9; 12:12; 14:27-29; 18:1) and a priestly tribe as well. Slaves (עבדים) are subject, like women and children, to the authority of the head of the family. Slaves were prisoners-of-war or disfranchised members of other tribes, as were the *'apiru*. Or, as temporary slaves, they were pawns sent by their own family to serve a creditor for a set time as security against loans (Exod. 21:2-6). Slaves had the same obligations as other family members (Deut. 5:14; 12:18). Like daughters, they inherited nothing though, unlike daughters, they were inherited. Male slaves were circumcized (Gen. 17:12-13) and as a result, were counted as Israelites. The title "Slave of the King" (עבד המלך) that designated a high royal officer shows that slaves could obtain high responsibilities. Since slaves were members of the household, the social ranking of a slave depended on that of his owner. Hence, the slave of a king was a high-ranking person.

Apart from the specialized skills offered by the *gerim*, the division of labour followed gender and generational lines rather than social ones. The oldest woman of the compound supervised in-house production of poultry, vegetables, foods, and utensils, plus the raising of children. This meant endless grinding, kneading, cooking, baking, washing, hauling fresh water, weaving, milking, curdling, churning, and sometimes pottery production. Men were in charge of fieldwork: ploughing, sowing, harvesting, hunting, cutting wood, making bricks, building walls. Young people of both sexes herded flocks beyond the ploughed fields except after the harvest, when flocks were driven over the fallow quarters to keep weeds down and spread manure. At harvest time, all available hands of both sexes and all ages would be busy scything stems, binding sheaves, and piling them on the threshing floor. Ploughed fields, grazing areas, water sources and canals, middens, threshing floors, paths, and any other installation or space of public interest were held communally and managed by the village council. Fields were not enclosed, because they were subdivided into narrow strips redistributed on a regular basis between all the male members of the village commune (Guillaume 2012, 28–53). By contrast, homes, gardens, women, slaves, animals, tools, and weapons were privately owned.

Although humans have no influence over the weather, the yield depended on the available labour force as well as the wisdom and luck of the farmer. Famine was chronic in the months before harvest, but roasting unripe grain could reduce the waiting time (Josh. 5:11). Harvest failure, which meant yields that did not cover the yearly food requirements plus seed needed for the following year, occurred at least once every decade. In the absence of grain merchants to offer credit, the group survived by starving its youngest and oldest members first. In the absence of chemical fertilizers, yields could only be increased by putting new or more land under the plough. The reserve of available land was virtually inexhaustible and it was freely available. The limiting factor was the labour force: human hands and draught animals. In the absence of taxation enforced by a strong authority, there was little incentive to produce surpluses beyond maintaining reserves for the regular occurrence of harvest failures. As is the case everywhere with agricultural work, but even more so in the Mediterranean climate, intense labour at ploughing and harvest times alternated with lengthy periods of near idleness for men, who thus had time to go to war.

2.3 Tjeker, Philistines, and Phoenicians

After the fall of Egyptian rule about 1140–1130 BCE, the Canaanite culture of the Bronze Age survived on the Lebanese coast due to the lack of competitors. In Ashkelon, Ashdod, Gaza, Ekron, and possibly Gath, the cities of Philistia survived the crisis that swept the East Mediterranean trade system, thanks to the 'Arabah copper that shifted economic predominance to southern Israel/Palestine when the supply of cheaper Cypriote copper became depleted. The copper trade fostered a Canaanite revival that spurred a significant population increase in the southern parts of Israel/Palestine. Philistine ceramics dominated the market for luxury goods in place of Aegean imports that were no longer available (Figure 9). The distribution of Philistine pottery distinguishes the Philistine centres with higher population concentrations from the Philistine periphery with lower concentrations.

A group of the so-called Sea Peoples is attested at the coastal city of Dor, possibly the Teukrians of Greek tradition (Egyptian *tjeker*) who later assimilated with the Phoenicians (Gilboa 2006). The distinctive material culture of the Phoenician cities, spanning Acco in the south to almost as far north as Ugarit, does not reflect any political unity (Lehmann 2001; Gitin *et al.* 1998). Homer knew of Sidonians but not of "Phoenicians." The Phoenicians identified themselves rather by their home town and sometimes by the moniker "Canaanites". The *Journey of Wen-Amon* (CoS 1.41; Lichtheim 1976, 224–230) is a travel account written during the reign of Shoshenq/Shishak, but apparently using sources from the first half of the eleventh century BCE, warning traders of the perils of travel in foreign countries. Wenamun visits Dor and its Tjeker king, Byblos, and then Cyprus, revealing Mediterranean trade networks controlled by the Sea Peoples (Schipper 2005).

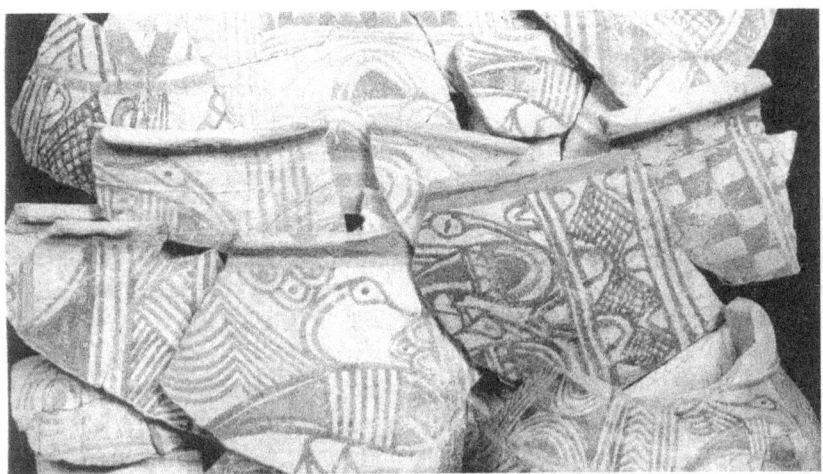

Figure 9: Sherds of Philistine ceramic.

2.4 Religion and Literature in Iron Age I

Sources for the religious history of Israel/Palestine before the Persian era are supplied mainly by iconography, supplemented by sporadic epigraphic finds (including personal names), a number of toponyms, and some archaeological data. The presentation of Israel's past in the biblical narrative from Genesis to 2 Kings is an ideological construct by intellectuals during the Second Temple period who, nevertheless, transmitted some memories dating from the tenth to the sixth centuries BCE. The problem is that the older material, when it is at all distinguishable from the rest, has been processed under the perspective of an Israel deemed monotheistic from its very origin, which it was not.

Egyptian influence on the iconography of Israel/Palestine is pervasive throughout the early Iron Age. The Egyptians rarely depicted Amon, the hidden and highest-ranking of the gods; they preferred to identify him by means of his symbol, the lion, which is also a hieroglyphic element of his name. For propagandistic purposes, seals of Amon continued to be disseminated in Palestine even after 1130 BCE. They were probably received there as symbols of El, the highest god of Canaan. These were often aniconic (*GGG* 130 b), and they may be at the root of the later biblical ban on images. The fact that Amon/El was accepted as the highest-ranking god does not imply, however, that he was the only god. There were other divine entities besides him (*GGG* 180B).

Iron Age I was not a peaceful era. War gods were popular, especially Baal-Seth (*GGG* 138a) and Resheph (*GGG* 137a, 138a), who were most often represented with a raised arm holding a mace ready to strike the vanquished. The goddess Anat was also a fierce fighter, but she never lost her attributes of love and fertility (*GGG* 163a). Toponyms with the divine epithet *ba'al*, like Ba'al-Gad and Ba'al-Hazor, are innovations from Iron Age I; they first occur when the designation *ba'al*, "lord," rose to prominence in connection with various deities (Rosen 1988).

The title "ba'al" is attributed to various gods. It never designates a specific god Ba'al. Yet, because the influence of the Ugaritic myths of Ba'al and 'Anat and of the narrative of 1 Kings 16–2 Kgs 10 that polemically designates the god of Samaria as *ba'al* and presents him as the competitor of YHWH, previous scholarship reconstructed a god named Ba'al. Yet, *ba'al* means "lord," as do Adonai and Adonis. These terms apply to men as much as to gods, as is common in English. Ba'al is always "Lord of something or somewhere"; "something" is dropped when there is no ambiguity for the ancient audience as to the location of the particular *ba'al* being referred to. The *ba'al* of Harran is the moon god Sin. Ba'alshamim ("Lord of Heavens") became the Hebrew name of Zeus Olympios in the first half of the second century BCE. The proper name of the *ba'al* referred to in the Ugaritic texts was Haddu, who later became the Syrian Hadad. Thus, when King Saul named one of his sons Jonathan, "YHWH gave," and another son Ishba'al, "man of ba'al," it cannot be inferred that he converted to Ba'alism between the birth of Jonathan and the birth of Ishba'al. YHWH was viewed as the storm god, a crucial attribute for the fertility of the fields since in the Levant, rain often falls during storms (Figure 10). As storm god, YHWH was the same type of god as Ba'al-Hadad, and the name Ishba'al honors YHWH as much as does the name Jonathan (Figure 11). The violent Mediterranean storms also fittingly evoke the war god (Judg. 5:5).

Figure 10: Egyptianized storm god on a seal from Ashkelon. The Pharaonic crown is typically Egyptian, while the twig in the left hand is a Levantine attribute of fertility (see Figure 31b) (after *IPIAO* 2 #478).

Figure 11: A complex combination of the storm god Ba'al and the warring Seth defeating the chaos-snake Apophis under the supervision of Shamash the sun god, on a seal from Tell Far'a South (ca. 1100 BCE). In Job 38–41, all these motifs are combined in YHWH (after *GGG* 87b).

Unlike the polemical designation of the Samarian god as *ba'al* by the editors of the Book of Kings, older texts tend to refer to gods other than YHWH as the *ba'alim*, a plural form (Zevit 2003). In the absence of epithets or names, iconography can only classify gods as El, Ba'al, or Asherah divine types. The goddesses 'Anat and 'Astarte began to merge into a single deity in the Late Bronze Age, later to become 'Atargatis. The goddess is represented by different symbols: a suckling mother (human or animal, Figure 12), dove, lion, or tree (Figure 13).

Figure 12: The suckling cow fertility motif drawn on a jar at Kuntillet Ajrud (after Meshel 2012, fig. 6.8).

Figure 13: Two worshippers flanking a stylized Egyptian goddess Hathor influenced by representations of the Levantine fertility tree (after *IPIAO* 2 #421).

In the Hebrew Bible, Asherah is used polemically to designate the fertility aspect of the *baʿal* of Samaria associated with the tree of life (Franklin 2011). In the eleventh and early tenth centuries BCE, ʿAnat is attested in the personal names *ʿabdlabiʾat ben ʿAnat*, "Servant of the Lioness, son of Anat," inscribed on arrowheads from el-Khader near Bethlehem, and by the sons of ʿAnat in Judges 3:31 and 5:6. These sons of ʿAnat may designate some sort of warrior caste. In light of the Ugaritic fragments of the myth of ʿAnat, "Lioness" is a fitting epithet for ʿAnat. Despite the efforts of later editors to disguise it, the place name Baʿalat Judah, "Lady of Judah," is still recognizable behind a number of faultily transmitted names in Joshua 19:44, 2 Samuel 6:2, 1 Kings 9:18, and 2 Chronicles 8:6. These names support the assumption that ʿAnat was the tribal deity of ancient Judah.

Some seals of the eleventh to ninth centuries BCE from the Central Range depict the Lord of the Ostriches, a title evoking the desert (*GGG* 162a-d). At the time, the religion of YHWH was not widely practised at the level of family devotion, or his aspect as a desert god was less emphasized than his links with war and rain. The subtype Lord of the Animals is applied to YHWH when he is identified with El-Shadday (*DDD* 2: 749–753), the protector against the many dangers encountered in the wilderness (Gen. 17:1).

Apart from the slogan "YHWH has led us out of Egypt," Moses' name, a few poetic snippets in Exodus 15:21 and the Book of the Wars of YHWH (Num. 21:14-15), there is nothing in the Bible that can be dated before the tenth century BCE with any reasonable degree of plausibility. As extra-biblical sources, we have a few personal names on arrow-heads, jar handles, seals, and an abecedary (Finkelstein *et al.* 2008). The Egyptian texts of the second millennium BCE that found their way into the Hebrew Bible (Psalm 104, Proverbs 22-23) likely arrived in the course of the ninth to fifth centuries through Phoenician mediation. The Covenant Code (Exodus 21-23) is no older than the eighth century BCE, but it has been used for the reconstruction of the early Iron Age tribal class society on the assumption that the similitudes reflect a common tradition of Amorite (early West Semitic) customary law. In fact, "codes" like Exodus 12-23 and Hammurapi's stele were compilations to train scribes and were never meant to guide judges. Customary law has no need of codes, treatises, and constitutions.

2.5 Festivals and Customs

The most important feasts of the Hebrew Bible (Passover/Matzot, Shavuoth/Succoth) are commonly said to be rooted in the rural society of the eleventh to sixth centuries BCE. Passover has been related to the departure of young villagers and shepherds when the summer heat resumes and it becomes necessary to pasture the flocks further away from the settlements. For farmers in the highlands, however, the departure probably occurred earlier than the biblical date of Passover, which is set around the spring equinox. This seems rather late for the beginning of transhumance in the Levant, if the flocks were to benefit from the fresh grass that started growing after the first rains in the lowlands, in the Shephelah, and in the Jordan Valley in early winter. Except for the highest parts of the Lebanon and Anti-Lebanon, where the cold and the snow prevent growth after the first rains, at the time of Passover, grasses are closer to the end of their annual cycle than its beginning. As the nutritive quality of grass is inversely proportional to its maturation, the best grazing season would begin in the lowlands soon after the first rains, in December, with a delay of several months for the highest pastures, which enabled herders to move up and tap into the fresh reserves of young grass. By keeping the rams away from the ewes, herders could restrict lambing to the few months prior to the period when the best supply of fresh forage would be expected, which occurs earlier than the spring equinox (Dalman 1939, 183).[1]

The early lambs are the best. When the ewes are inseminated in June, the lambs are born in November. They suckle for a month and a half. At the time of weaning, they benefit from the best grass in January–February. Thanks to the availability of fresh grass, the ewes continue their lactation and their owners milk them to make cheese. Postulating the use of a cal-

---

1 Ewes' milk production peaks three to four weeks after lambing, which occurs about 140–150 days after insemination.

endar beginning with the autumnal New Year[2] would set Passover in early October, which is too early for the beginning of the lambing season or the departure of the flocks. Hence, rather than marking the departure of the flocks, Passover celebrates the slaughter and consumption of the first early male lambs, as Exodus 14 indicates. These lambs are the first to be culled before the summer. Other views on the origins of the paschal lamb sacrifice are found in Steinberg (2009) and Prosic (2004).

Matzot, the biblical feast of unleavened bread, is celebrated in the week that follows Passover (days 15–21 of month 1). Matzot comes too early for the beginning of the grain harvest, but it could anticipate it with unleavened bread, remembering that the sour dough made with last year's harvest is all gone. Equating festivals with actual farming activities can only be approximate. As different calendars were used at different times, the meaning of festivals changed over time. Hence, the linking of Passover and Matzot is not earlier than the Persian period.

Shavuoth, the festival held during the seventh week after Matzot, would have celebrated the completion of the grain harvest, while Succot, the other autumn festival, would have celebrated the wine and olive harvest, a time when family members took turn day and night in huts set up in the vineyards and in the olive groves to guard the ripening fruits from their many predators. In their effort to dissociate Yahwism from ba'alism, the biblical redactors minimized the association of feasts with the fertility rites that celebrated the important moments of the agricultural cycle, especially since these rites were practised in the open, away from the temple's jurisdiction. Therefore, there is little hope of recovering the pre-biblical significance of the festivals. In the Bible, festivals have been keyed into the Exodus story and fitted onto the sacred, seven-fold structure of the sabbatical calendar, which is rooted in Creation (Gen. 2:1-3).

Scholarly reconstructions of the evolution of the biblical festivals suffer from artificial oppositions between Israelite/Canaanite, nomadic/settled, pre- and post-exilic categories, the relative date of legal codes and sources of the Pentateuch, and unconfirmed historical events like a cultic centralization during King Josiah's reign. The discovery of seven-day and seven-year calendar units at Emar in eastern Syria in the fourteenth and

---

2 The Mediterranean climate makes the autumnal equinox the natural time for the celebration of the New Year, since it corresponds roughly to the arrival of the first rains. After a six-month summer during which hardly a cloud is seen in the sky (1 Kgs 18:43-45), new life returns with the onset of autumnal rains (Gen. 18:10). In the river oases of Mesopotamia and Egypt, on the other hand, the year begins with the snow melt in the mountains, which feeds the Nile, Euphrates, and Tigris in the spring.

thirteenth centuries BCE has overturned the schemes that were current in twentieth century CE scholarship (Fleming 1999). The sequential development of biblical festivals from Canaanite to Jehovist, Deuteronomistic, and Priestly redefinitions are over-simplifications based on the notion that prescriptive biblical texts reflect actual practices at given points of Israel's and Judah's past.

The origin of the pork taboo is often deduced from the higher proportion of pig bones recovered by the excavations of Ekron and Ashkelon, compared to highland Palestinian, Aramean, and Transjordanian sites. The difference varies between 20% and 0% (Sapir-Hen *et al.* 2013, 4–7). Although no archaeozoological data exist for Ashdod (hardly any bones were saved during the excavations there) and for Gaza (unexcavated), the common wisdom is that proto-Israelites and Judahites established an ethnic boundary between themselves and the pork-loving Philistines by banning pork from their diet (Sapir-Hen *et al.* 2013, 13). Yet, Iron Age I rural sites close to Philistine cities display very low pig-bone ratios while lowland Israelite sites of Iron Age II have fairly high pig-bone ratios (Sapir-Hen *et al.* 2013, 9–10), which further undermines the notion of a Philistine trait based on pork consumption. Since Edomite settlements display the same rarity of pork consumption as Israelite settlements, an argument that uses this to infer ethnic differentiation is not valid. Despite better retrieval methods and greater attention to bones than was the case on older archaeological digs, this particular criterion, in which pork consumption is inferred precariously from the pig-bone ratios, remains based on "small sample sizes and only scant consideration of possible alternatives which may explain the perceived phenomenon" (Lev-Tov 2012, 597).

Instead of being an identity marker by which the highlanders marked their difference from the lowland Philistines, the pork taboo has been understood as a practical adaptation to the living conditions on the edge of subsistence. Pigs and humans are omnivores and occupy the same position on the food chain. The calories or proteins eaten by pigs could be more profitably by eaten by humans. The problem with this explanation is that pigs are excellent foragers in woods and thickets and that, until the generalization of industrial in-door piggeries, pigs were driven out of villages in the morning, returning at night, satiated with berries, mushrooms, worms, insects, and acorns. Free-range pig husbandry afforded plenty of opportunity for hybridization with wild pigs, which renders biometrical differences used by archaeozoologists to distinguish between wild and domestic pigs (for instance Sapir-Hen *et al.* 2013, 3) irrelevant (Albarella *et al.* 2007, 305).

Whether domestic, semi-wild, or wild, pigs did not constitute a threat to the diet of humans. On the contrary, in marginal zones occupied by Edomites and Israelites, there was no need to raise pigs. Wild pigs were numerous in the wasteland between settlements as they are today south of the Dead Sea, thanks to the limited amount of hunting (Mendelssohn and Yom-Tov 1999).[3] Besides providing excellent meat, hunting wild pigs was necessary to keep them away from the ploughed fields. The rarity of pig bones in the archaeological record almost certainly reflects the weight of the carcasses of wild boars. Rather than carrying them back home, Israelites and Edomites probably roasted most wild boars in the open, wherever they killed them. As archaeologists only excavate settlements, pig bones remain archaeologically invisible.

Another factor in the rise of the pork taboo was the loss of the economic appeal of domestic pigs when olive oil offered an alternative source of fat for human food, lighting, and the production of leather and soap. Since no other animal can compete with pigs for the production of grease, it makes sense that the pork taboo arose in the home of the olive tree. In the Levant, the chicken gradually supplanted the domestic pig as a food source. The cock depicted on the Jaazaniah seal from Mizpah (Figure 14) reflects the increasing popularity of chickens in the Central Palestinian Range in Iron Age II.

Figure 14: Seal of Y'ZNYHW servant of the king, found at Mizpah, the earliest representation of the domestic chicken (*Gallus gallus*) in the Levant. The aggressive posture of the cock and the rarity of chicken bones retrieved from Iron Age sites suggest that chickens were first raised for cock-fighting and that their consumption developed to compensate for the effects of the pork taboo (after Badè 1933).

---

3 The presence of pigs in the Negev is attested at Aroer with pig bones at 3% of the total (Motro 2011).

Although biblical translations render the word תרים in Leviticus 1:14 as turtledoves, it probably refers to chickens (Staubli 2008): from the Persian era, the bones of domestic chickens become far more common at Jerusalem than the bones of doves (Horwitz and Tchernov 1989). In the the sanctuary area at Khirbet et-Tannur, chickens are the only identifiable species of birds (Whitcher Kansa 2013). The domestic chicken gradually supplanted the pig in the human diet, and the dove as a sacrificial victim.

The biblical ban on pork consumption arose when the temple sought to tighten its grip on the economy to satisfy the demands of Persian and Hellenistic overlords who used the temples as tax authorities. Declaring pork impure discouraged hunting and fostered the production of olive oil, since it is easier to collect a portion of the product as taxes directly from the press than to tax movable assets like animals, which tended to vanish before the tax collectors reached settlements. Hence, the pork taboo is the final stage in a long evolution that has little to do with the taxonomy that was supposed to explain why only animals that fit squarely in their class defined by their mode of locomotion could be edible (Douglas 1966).

The tradition of the sacred grove of Mamre, the core of the Abraham tradition, is probably rooted in Iron Age I. As a sanctuary dedicated to a tree goddess, Mamre would have been visited by women and couples longing for a child (Schroer 1987a). The laughter around which Genesis 18 is built could have been part of the Mamre ritual, a laughter that may well be euphemistic (see Gen. 26:8). Despite living in a tent at Mamre, Abraham is clearly depicted as a farmer: he sacrifices a calf (Gen. 18:7). Mamre lies at the junction of two clan territories (Lehmann 2004) and in tribal terms, it would have been situated between Judah and Caleb.

Chapter 3
From Saul to Jeroboam I: State Formation

The rise of territorial kingdoms in Palestine is placed in relation to Egyptian revival and Shishak's campaigns.

According to the biblical account, Saul united the tribes of Israel into a kingdom, and David united the clans of Judah into a separate kingdom before creating the kingdom of Judah-Israel his son Solomon would inherit. In reality, state formation took longer. Solomon's kingdom in 1 Kings 1–11 is a retrojection, composed between the seventh and fifth centuries BCE. In Israel, there were three attempts at state formation: under Saul, under Jeroboam I, and then under Omri. Only the last attempt somewhat succeeded. In Judah, the early tribal state of David was transformed into a more durable structure by the Omride princess Athaliah, who married the Judahite king Jehoram and became the mother of King Ahaziah (2 Kgs 8:6; 11:1-20). Although the author of the Book of Kings has tried to disguise the fact that the kingdom of Judah developed largely under the influence of Israel, Athaliah's status as an Omride princess strongly points in this direction. The kingdom of Judah was a complex of tribal structures in response to the challenges of a broadening political and economic horizon. As the realm expanded, face-to-face interactions had to be supplemented by specialists like scribes and military and religious personnel, who became the arm of the State. Tribes agreed to relinquish some of their sovereignty and revenues as long as they felt the state apparatus delivered greater security and prosperity than they would have obtained on their own. At first, this state apparatus would have been limited to the royal family and its entourage, and early tribal states therefore appear in the record as the house of the founding king of the dynasty, Beth-Saul and Beth-David (2 Sam. 3:1, 6).

State formation in Israel and Judah should be placed in the context of a comprehensive view of state formation across the Syro-Palestinian and Syro-Mesopotamian regions. Usually, the processs began in an existing city where the family of the local chieftain assumed crucial functions beyond the confines of the tribe and the catchment area of the city. Since the chief could not raise taxes from his own tribe, he covered his expenses by drawing on outside resources: raids on neighbouring tribes, the proceeds from mercenary service, road tolls, returns from food-loans granted to his own people, and the sale of grain to regional partners, given that the primary function of any city was the storage of agricultural surpluses from the surrounding area. In the Assyrian and Babylonian empires, war booty and tribute were an integral part of government revenues, although their actual significance is inflated on royal inscriptions, because the portrayal of the king as a great warrior had greater appeal than his portrayal as a wise accountant or shrewd negotiator. Empires as much as tribal structures relied on the surpluses they managed to collect and transform into non-foodstuffs such as prestige items made of non-perishable, and hence precious, material. Tribal states or early stages of statehood are unstable, as the narratives of the rise and fall of Abimelech and Saul show (Judges 9; 1 Samuel 10–31). In Israel, most dynasties ruled for two generations only, the exceptions being the Omrides, with three generations and four kings, and the Nimshides, with five generations. Judah enjoyed greater stability because it was on the sidelines of world politics.

Any use of the term "nation" and its derivatives is better avoided in biblical studies, because the concept of nation is too modern to render ancient realities adequately. Even modern concepts of nation vary. In the Anglo-American and French traditions, the nation is equated with its citizens, forcing marginal groups to assimilate, while Germanic and Balkanic traditions limit the nation to the state-supporting ethnic group, marginalizing other ethnic groups. The nation-state as such did not arise before the nineteenth century CE. There was no nation-state in the ancient Near East. Assyria was the kingdom of the God Ashur; the Assyrian king was Ashur's deputy on earth, and he felt called to subject the entire known world to the god Ashur.

The biblical tradition transmits a number of accurate memories from the tenth and ninth centuries BCE, but they are filtered by the experiences and mentality of the seventh to fifth centuries BCE. In the time of Saul and David, the Philistines played a greater role in the formation of the kingdoms of Israel and Judah than the Bible allows. However, the kingdoms interacted mainly with the cities of Ekron and Gath rather than with the Philistines as a whole, despite the fact that the role of Ekron was forgotten in the Davidic tradition. As a general rule, the traditional elements that have the greatest historical plausibility are those contradicted by the tradition's overall emphasis. Hence, Saul was a successful king rather than the failure he is presented as in the Bible: he extended his tribal kingdom from Benjamin to the northern end of the Central Range and transmitted the realm to his son, who extended it even further. David was an opportunist who failed to bring most of Saul's dominion under his rule. Solomon was king of Judah and Benjamin only.

In one important respect, the ancient biblical traditions are supported by archaeological and epigraphic findings: in the tenth century BCE there was no state of Israel, but two proto-states, Israel and Judah. The older layers of the Book of Jeremiah (sixth century BCE) differentiate between *beth yehuda* and *beht yisra'el*. The language of the Bible that we call Hebrew is a late form of the official language of the kingdom of Judah. From the kingdom of Israel, we know of three different written languages, none of which matches Judean. The clearest difference between the written Israelite and Judean languages is found in the way the theophoric element YHWH is transcribed in personal names. *Natanyahu* 'YHWH has given' is so transcribed in Table 2. In this book, the names of the kings of Israel and Judah follow the orthography of the NRSV, but the appropriate Judean and Israelite form is added at the first occurrence in brackets.

Table 2.   Significant differences between Israelite, Judaean and Late Biblical Hebrew.

	Israelite	Judean	Late Biblical Hebrew
Subject-object	נתניו Natanyô	נתניהו Natanyáhu	נתניה Netanya
Object-subject	יונתן Yônatan	יהונתן Yehonatan	יונתן Yonatan

3.1 The Beginning of an Economic Recovery in the Second Half of the Eleventh Century BCE

The main driver of state formation in Israel/Palestine was the void left after the collapse of the first Mediterranean economic system. The second Mediterranean economic system emanated from Phoenician cities in the late eleventh century BCE. At first, maritime trade was not as significant as it had been during the Bronze Age, but inland trade compensated for this weakness with renewed mining activities at Timna and Fenan in Wadi 'Arabah as long as the supply of copper from Cyprus fell below local demand (Artzy 2003; Tebes 2007). Copper production and trade was in the hands of specialists from Edom and Midian, and new settlements appeared along the copper trade routes, like Tel Masos in the Negev, Tel Rehov south of Beth-She'an, and Kinneret on the northwestern shore of Lake Kinneret. Evidence of iron or copper processing has been found at each of these places.

In the absence of interference from Egypt and Mesopotamia, the Canaanite renaissance of the eleventh and early tenth centuries BCE involved the old city-states of Phoenicia and Philistia and the new centres on the copper route. This network constituted potential power bases for the tribes in northern and central Palestine. An echo of the fight over control of this new economic system is to be found in the narrative of the battle of Gibeon (Joshua 10). The victory song embedded in the Joshua narrative reflects a conflict that originally opposed the cities of Gibeon and Jerusalem around 1025–925 BCE. Like Jerusalem, Gibeon was a strategic stage on one route between the Jordan Valley and the Mediterranean coast. For Joshua 10:12-13, the writer indicates that he quoted from a Book of Jashar:

> The sun god remained still at Gibeon, and the moon god in the valley of Aijalon!
>
> And the sun god remained still, and the moon god did nothing, until the nation [*goy*][1] took vengeance on their enemies. (author's translation)

The economic and political dynamics of the Philistine centres are reflected by the size of the settled area in Ekron, Gath, and Ashdod, listed in hectares in Table 3 (Finkelstein and Singer-Avitz 2004; Maeir and Uziel 2007). The data for Gaza and Ashkelon are currently lacking.

Table 3.   The Sizes of Four Cities

Centuries BCE	Ashdod	Ekron	Gath	Jerusalem
12	7	20	4	3
11	7	24	2	4
10	1	24	4	5
9	7	4	30	8
8	30	4	1	12
7	15	24	1	50
6	15	0	1	0

Ekron's supremacy lasted from the twelfth to tenth century BCE. Dominance then passed to Gath in the ninth century, until Gath was taken over by Ashdod in the eighth century, and then returned to Ekron in the following century. The displacement of Ekron by Gath in the ninth century provides an interpretive framework for the wars between the Philistines, Saul, and David in the Bible, where David becomes a mercenary leader of the king of Gath (1 Samuel 21; 27). The table also shows that the short-lived rise of Jerusalem as the most important centre in Israel/Palestine occurred in the seventh century BCE (see Figure 15).

3.2 Saul

In the Bible's black-and-white representation of the rise of David to prominence (1 Samuel), Saul is the dark backdrop against which David shines forth (Edelman 1996; Knauf 2001b; Grabbe 2007a: 111–115). Historians have to work against the grain to reconstruct more balanced portraits of the two leaders, except in the case of the representation of Saul as the first

---

[1]   On the basis of the Amorite term *gāwum* attested at Mari, the *goy* here is a tribe, probably Benjamin according to the geographical context.

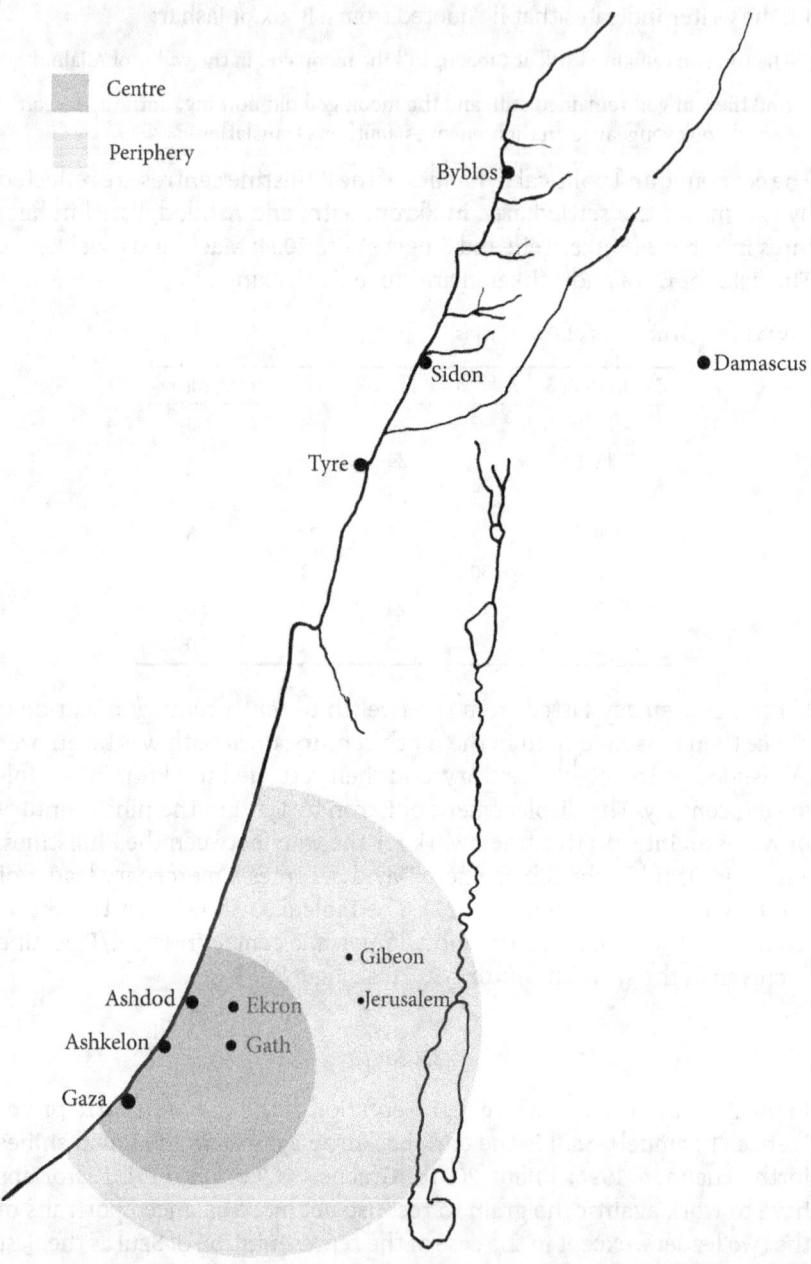

Figure 15: Centre and periphery eleventh–tenth centuries BCE (T. Guillaume).

king of Israel, which sits too uncomfortably within the overall ideology of the story to be the creation of pro-Davidic writers. In Saul's days, however, Israel was not the Israel of the Persian era, which encompassed the whole of the Central Range. The core of Saul's Israel was the tribe of Benjamin. Judah entered Israel's periphery as the dowry of the Omride princess Athaliah in the middle of the ninth century. The centrality of the Benjaminite factor in the formation of the kingdoms of Israel and Judah is no accident.

The 40 years ascribed to the reigns of David and Solomon correspond to a scribal convention by which the composers of the narrative indicated that they had no precise data to hand. By contrast, they had the exact duration of Saul's reign, but the first part of the number was "lost" and the Hebrew text transmits only the last digit, two (1 Sam. 13:1). Number two and 12 being grammatically impossible, Saul would have reigned for 22, 32 or 42 years. After Solomon, a fairly reliable chronology is transmitted from King Rehoboam and Jeroboam I onwards. Hence, from the accession of Jeroboam I in 932/922 BCE, Saul's reign can be dated roughly to the first quarter of the tenth century BCE, followed by David and then Solomon. Saul's reign was neither felicitous nor a failure. Even Davidic propaganda concedes that Saul's military prowess was proverbial. David, nevertheless, had to be credited with the killing of 10,000, because women used to sing of Saul's thousands (1 Sam. 18:7-8; 21:12; 29:5).

The biblical explanations for the origin of the monarchy (1 Samuel 8, 12) reflect the theological perspective of the Persian period, when the kingdoms of Israel and Judah were viewed as unfortunate experiences never to be repeated. The biblical notion that the kingdom of Saul was a response to the "Philistine threat" is neither wrong nor entirely correct. It is indisputable that Saul founded his Benjaminite tribal kingdom on the periphery of Ekron (Figure 15).

The 3,000 warriors Saul musters in 1 Samuel 13:2 represent a significant force in a country that numbered a total population of 100,000–120,000 by 1000 BCE, and as such justified putting a crown on his head. Saul's economic base was the trade between the Jordan Valley and Philistia, from which he collected protection money from caravans or robbed them. Bellicose reactions from Ekron had the same character as the preventive actions of the Egyptians in the thirteenth and twelfth centuries BCE: tight control over the mountainous areas is rarely worth the trouble, and even less so for Ekron with a population that totalled 12,000 at most, including women, old men, and children.

The kingship of Saul was a complex chieftaincy rather than the headship of a state. It was too small to need officials beyond Saul's family (Abner) and household (Doeg). The primary power base was the tribal levy of Benjamin (1 Samuel 11) sent by the clans loyal to Saul. Whereas Abimelech's attempt to found a tribal state at Shechem failed (Judges 9), Saul's succeeded, thanks to the presence of Gibeon in Benjamin. Situated closer to the mining centres of the 'Arabah, Gibeon provided a more favourable base than Shechem in the economic network that spurred the Canaanite revival. Gibeon collaborated with Saul, hiring his tribal forces to defend itself against other threats such as David, who is depicted several times under the walls of Gibeon (2 Samuel 2; 20). The regional significance of Gibeon is revealed in the fact that it was the only highland centre Shishak I destroyed in the second half of the tenth century BCE (Figure 16).

The evolution from Abimelech at Shechem to Saul at Gibeon is a fairly correct reflection of the process at work in the Central Range from the eleventh century BCE onwards. Four chiefdoms—Dothan, Tirzah, Shechem, and Shiloh—arose within Lab'ayu's fourteenth-century BCE realm (Finkelstein 2006). Shechem was laid waste from 1025 BCE to 925 BCE. In the same period, Shiloh, a regional pilgrimage shrine, was the victim of a destruction that became proverbial (Jer. 7:12-14; 26:6-9; Ps. 78:60). Israelite state formation did not emanate from Ephraim but from Benjamin, which was closer to the Philistine economic centres. As is the case with Helsinki, London, and Washington, eccentricly located capitals are good indicators of which country these towns depended upon when they were founded. Finland belonged to Russia, London to Normandy, the former American colonies to Great Britain, and Gibeon to Philistia. Saul's primary power base was the tribe of Benjamin, but there were also loyal components in Ephraim (according to Judges 5 Manasseh did not yet exist), and the city of Jabesh-Gilead on the other side of the Jordan (1 Sam. 11:1-13). The area in which Saul searches for his father's asses (1 Samuel 9-10) probably covers his primary power base. Saul's activities did not reach beyond the central hill country, and he fought his last battle at its northeastern tip (1 Samuel 30). Saul lost that battle and his life, but his son Eshbaal won the war and ruled over a wide territory that included the Jezreel Valley and possibly some parts of southern Galilee (1 Sam. 2:8).

Ever since their formation, the tribes of Benjamin, Ephraim, and Gilead had stood in close relationship with one another. It is possible that before Saul came on the scene, they expressed their relationship through a common forefather named Jacob. If he were to retain the loyalty of Ephraim and Gilead, the title "king of Benjamin" would have been out of the question for Saul's new role, though "king of Jacob" might have been an option. Like Israel, it was also a personal name in origin, not a geographical term. If, however, the mention of the "people of Israel" in Judges 5:3 and 5:5 reflects the situation before Saul, it was as "king of Israel" that Saul led the warring tribes.

Were one to deem Saul a failure, the same verdict would have to be applied to Sargon II and to Cyrus, both of whom also died on the battlefield while extending their realms. Despite the pro-Davidic bias of the

3. From Saul to Jeroboam I   69

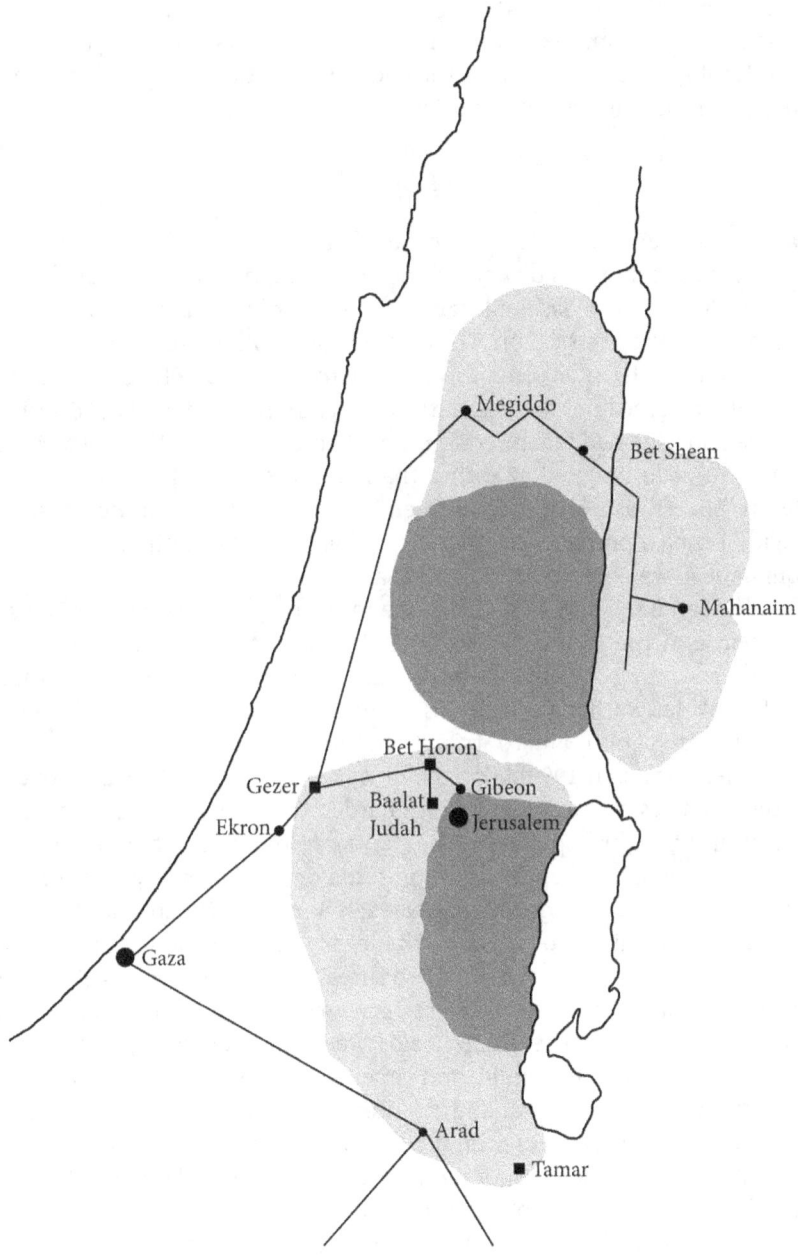

Figure 16: Shishak's campaigns in Canaan (T. Guillaume).

Books of Samuel, Saul's legacy lived on and prospered under his son and successor, Eshbaal. The next kings, however, seem to have lost much territory, and Israel shrank again to the Benjaminite plateau until Jeroboam ben Nebat gave it a new start at the end of the tenth century BCE, but in a very different political constellation.

3.3 Eshbaal

Saul was succeeded by his son Eshbaal, "man of the Lord" (1 Chron. 8:33; 9:39), whose name was disfigured into Ishbosheth, "man of shame" in 2 Samuel 2–4 due to a *"ba'al*-allergy" on the part of the Hasmonean editors of the Torah-Prophets canon. The tradition about him is so sparse that the second king of Israel is often forgotten, wrongly so. One hardly needs to read between the lines to see that the death of Saul was not a total disaster for the tribes he had federated. If Eshbaal became king at the age of 40 (2 Sam. 2:10), Saul reigned 32 rather than 22 years, but since 2 Samuel 3:1 claims "there was a long war between the house of Saul and the house of David," Eshbaal probably reigned more than two years and David's reign commenced well before the death of Saul.

Although Benjamin was a war zone in the conflict between the House of David and the House of Saul, that Eshbaal resided at Mahanaim in Gilead (2 Sam. 2:12) must not be misunderstood as an attempt to evade the Philistines. Rather, Eshbaal was moving his residence beyond the Benjaminite core of his realm to strengthen the tribal state he inherited from his father (Na'aman 1990). Mahanaim was closer to the 'Arabah copper-trading centres than Gibeon and it guarded the entrance to the sources of iron in the Ajlun upstream. The move can be interpreted either as a stronger grip on the copper and iron trade or as the consequence of the loss of Gibeon. According to 2 Samuel 2:9, Abner made Eshbaal king *over* Ephraim, Benjamin, and all Israel (the legacy of Saul) and king *to* Gilead, *to* the Asshurim, and *to* Jezreel. These three "to" (אל) elements get lost in the NRSV translation. Had the verse been written in Late Biblical Hebrew, one could argue that the difference between the proposition "over" (על) in front of Ephraim, Benjamin, and Israel is negligible because Late Biblical Hebrew tends to use אל and על interchangeably. Second Samuel 2:9, however, is archaic, because the spelling of "all Israel" (ישראל כלה) is written with the old suffix pronoun *heh* instead of the standard *waw*. Hence, "to make [Eshbaal] king to" instead of "to make [him] king over" is a telescoped version of the statement, "Abner brought him to [*place name*] and made him king there." The enigmatic Ashurites (האשורי) probably reproduce the Phoenician and Canaanite designation for Galilee. Therefore, an Ashurite is indirectly related to the tribe of Asher (Knauf 2009b). Under Eshbaal, Israel took control of the rich landscapes of Gilead, the Jezreel

Valley, and Lower Galilee, well beyond Saul's original realm, and now included most of the 10 tribes of the Song of Deborah in Judges 5 (Guillaume 2000; Knauf 2005a).

For this reason, the earliest date for the Song of Deborah is the time of Eshbaal, although the reigns of Jeroboam ben Nebat or Baasha are not impossible either. Later, the song was put into writing at the court of the Omride dynasty. It celebrates the victory of the Galilean tribes of Zebulun and Naphtali (Judg. 5:18) in association with Ephraim, Benjamin, Machir, and Issachar, while Reuben and Gilead are blamed for their inactivity. Dan and Asher are probably later additions from the time of Jeroboam II. The tribes did not disappear with the rise of the monarchy: the Song of Deborah calls up followers of YHWH, the God of Israel, given that early states have to be theocracies because they lack the legitimacy that mature states acquire through routine interaction with their subjects. The early state is built on hope and its cohesion needs to be corseted by a transcendent concept. The king comes second only to God. The name "Sisera" is most likely Philistine or Teukrian, but the kings of Canaan (Judg. 5:19) show how well the Philistines were acculturated in the tenth century BCE.

According to 2 Samuel 3, the defection of Abner put an end to the war between the House of Saul and the House of David (2 Sam. 3:1). The murder of Eshbaal by two officers, one bearing the Canaanite-Phoenician name Ben 'Anat, is part of an elaborate narrative from which it is impossible to retrieve what precisely took place because it is entirely driven by the glorification of David. Yet, the presentation of the crown of Israel to David by a delegation of tribal representatives is plausible (2 Sam. 5:3). In a similar situation, King Abdullah of Transjordan, whose troops occupied the West Bank in 1949 CE, summoned an assembly of notables that proclaimed him king on both sides of the Jordan River. As became the rule in ancient Israel, the dynasty of Saul did not survive beyond the second generation, and Israel became the stomping ground for various pretenders until Jeroboam ben Nebat and Omri reunited Israel under their able leadership.

3.4 David

To a large extent, the Davidic traditions originate from the royal family and its immediate entourage, the families of notables at Jerusalem. A dynasty needed legitimizing traditions that accounted for the fate of its various family members, winners as well as losers. Three layers of tradition can be identified, each represented by a queen: Bathsheba for Jerusalem, Maacah for Hebron, and Athaliah for Saul (Knauf 2002b). Storytellers and court scribes embellished the tradition with a wealth of details that give the false impression that the Davidic narratives were produced by eyewitnesses. The enormity of the claims wins the sympathy of the audience for the unscrupulous but initially successful politician who failed miserably in the end: the Jerusalemite tradition shows an exhausted King David as the pawn of the parties at the court. The biographical connection between Saul and David is mostly fictitious, but it became important under Queen Athaliah, who represented the Omrides as legitimate successors to both Saul and David.

The stories about David were updated as late as the fourth century BCE as part of the continuing conflict between Judeans and Benjaminites. David was remodelled into a singer at the court of Saul, a person who could not help being successful, and who eventually marries the king's daughter despite the king's devious machinations (Halpern 2001). This portrayal turned David into an icon of piety in Judaism, Christianity, and Islam.

Despite literary embellishments, the inscription of Hazael found at Tel Dan has confirmed that David was the founding father of the tribal state of Judah, which was also known as the House of David (2 Sam. 3:1). David's kingdom was a complex chieftaincy: under particular conditions, such a political unit may cover a considerable area. As founder of the state and tribe of Judah, who also managed to integrate Jerusalem, David became the stepfather of the three monotheistic world religions (Moses is the father) and the cause of the sanctity of Jerusalem and the political dilemmas that are currently associated with this concept. The portrayal of upstart David as a Mafioso racketeer extorting southern business owners with his band at the beginning of his career (1 Samuel 25) is consistent with what we know of *'apiru* chiefs like Idrimi of Alalakh (*ANET* 557). The transition from an *'apiru* regime to statehood was facilitated by the king of Gath, who hired David and provided him with at fief at Ziklag (1 Samuel 27, 30).

From Ziklag, David was expected to keep the Wild East of Gath in check. Despite suggestions to the contrary in 1 Samuel 27:8-12, David fully accomplished his mission. Without the blessing of the king of Gath, David would not have managed to federate the Judeans, Jerahmeelites, and the Kenites (1 Sam. 27:10), conquer the Calebites, and set up a tribal state at Hebron (2 Sam. 2:1-4). It was politically advantageous to tell the Judean audience, and later the audience of the Bible, that David tricked the Philistines with YHWH's blessing. While 2 Samuel 2:4 gives the erroneous impression that David was crowned when Saul died, it also suggests that the war between the House of David and the House of Saul had begun already when David was a vassal of Gath. To gain a free hand for his expansionist policy in the north, Saul may have associated himself with Ekron. Hence, David's struggles against the Philistines is plausible, as long as these are understood to have been Philistines from Ekron (2 Sam. 5:18-25).

According to biblical tradition, David was attempting systematically to destabilize the rule of Saul in Israel (2 Sam. 2:4-7; 3:12–21:36). Upon Eshbaal's death, David claimed the Israelite heritage for himself and was proclaimed king of Israel. As was the case initially in Judah (2 Sam. 2:4), David's rule over this complex chieftaincy was an elective monarchy based on the consent of the tribes (2 Sam. 5:1-3). Naturally, 2 Samuel 4:3 describes the agreement as a *berit*, a term rendered "covenant'" when in fact it would have been an agreement of submission. The riots that marked the end of David's reign show that the consent of the tribes could be reversed, and it is only in 1 Kings 12 that the allegiance of Judah to the House of David is deemed final. David's united kingdom was a personal union, as was the case between Britain and Hanover from 1714 to 1837 CE. The kingdoms of Israel and Judah were formed independently from one another and remained separate. In the tenth century BCE, Judeans were not Israelites.

The uprisings led by Absalom (2 Samuel 15-18) and Sheba (2 Samuel 20) reveal how fragile David's rule over Israel was. Apparently, David had no military bases in Israel, since the nucleus of his army was in and around Jerusalem; he is said to have set up garrisons in Edom (2 Sam. 8:14), but never in Israel. On the broader scene, alliances were struck with at least one Aramean kingdom through a diplomatic marriage with Aram-Geshur (2 Sam. 3:3).

Sheba was a Benjaminite, and his rebellion was triggered by a local Judeo-Benjaminite dispute. The "city and mother in Israel" that handed over Sheba's head (2 Sam. 20:19) was probably Gibeon, a city that had no interest in getting involved in tribal squabbles. Beth-maacah, where the present narrative locates the showdown with Sheba, was far beyond David's grasp or that of any king of Israel prior to Jeroboam II (Finkelstein 2011). By the end of David's reign, Jerusalem's hold over Israel/Benjamin had virtually collapsed. The northernmost place mentioned in the old Davidic tales is Baal-Hazor, between Bethel and Shiloh. The list of David's commanders in 2 Samuel 23:8-39 reveals a sphere of influence extending towards the Philistine periphery in central and southern Palestine, from where he recruited his followers (Figure 17).

After securing the crown of Judah and Israel, David became king of Jerusalem. However, the biblical text here (2 Sam. 5:6-10) is largely incomprehensible. In all probability, a capitulation agreement must have been reached, for Jerusalem remained for the most part culturally and politically distinct, as shown by the story of Solomon and by Ezekiel 16:3. Between southern Judah, controlled by David with the backing of Gath, and Benjamin controlled by Saul, Jerusalem had every reason to be on good terms with David and Saul. The decisive factor for David's choice of Jerusalem could have been a wish outdo nearby Gibeon; the city seems to have served as Saul's residence for a while, as the execution of Saul's sons by the Gibeonites suggests (2 Samuel 21). After Solomon had become king of Jerusalem/Judah by *coup d'état* (2 Kings 2), he claimed the Saulide inheritance, Israel, by ritual act at Gibeon.

74   A History of Biblical Israel

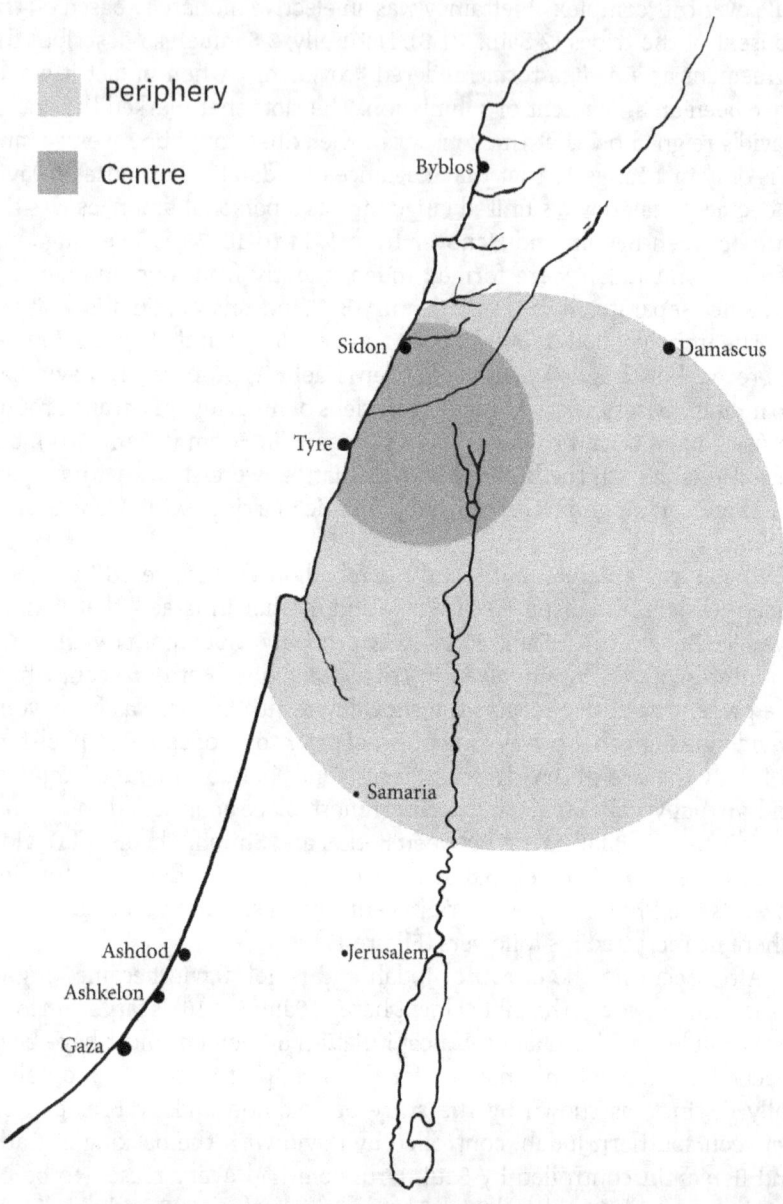

Figure 17:   Centre and periphery ninth–eighth centuries BCE (T. Guillaume).

Gibeon's appearance in the narrative of Solomon's coronation (1 Kings 3) suggests that Gibeon had meanwhile been subjugated by Jerusalem. Jerusalem was the residence of David but not the capital of a "united kingdom." Judah remained focused on Hebron (2 Sam. 15:7-12), while the metropolis of Israel remained Gibeon, probably extraterritorially so. In fact, the notion of a single capital is quite modern. Instead of a capital, the Omrides and Nimshides had residences in the different regions they controlled.

In this turbulent era of small competing power centres, David may have crossed swords with Aram, as 2 Samuel 8 suggests. Damascus, however, only became a significant kingdom in the time of Solomon (1 Kgs 11:23-25), and Aram-Zobah is probably a retrojection from Omride times. Battles against Ammonites, Moabites, and Edomites would have led to more crowns on David's head, but claims to sovereignty do not mean effective rule. The sparse population of the Moabite and Edomite regions would have made them logical targets for raids, as would the Ammonites and the caravans on the 'Arabah trade route, but there were no Ammonite, Moabite, or Edomite states in the tenth century BCE. In the eleventh and early tenth centuries BCE, there were some smaller polities, probably chiefdoms, in western Ammon / northern Moab (Tell el-'Umērī) and in southern Moab (Tell Mudēyineh), all linked to the 'Arabah copper trade (see Finkelstein 2013). On the other hand, the scuffle around Rabbath-Ammon in 2 Samuel 10–12 could be authentic, since it betrays no knowledge of the effective siege techniques introduced into the region in the second half of the ninth century by Hazael of Damascus and subsequently perfected by Tiglath-pileser III at the end of the eighth century BCE.

David's kingship over Judah and Israel did not necessarily mean a break with the Philistines of Gath. At best, David controlled a stretch of Ekron's hinterland from Gibeon to Gezer (2 Sam. 5:25) with the help of Cherethites, Pelethites, and other contingents from Gath (2 Sam. 15:18). David was fighting for rather than against the Philistines of Gath. Hence, the Metheg-ammah (מתג האמה), an obscure expression which the NRSV leaves untranslated, would signify the iron fist of Philistine rule over the highland. Although the text indicates that David subdued the Philistines before being able to remove the Metheg-ammah from their hands, David did not liberate the highlanders. More likely, David ruled the tribes of the Central Range on Ekron's behalf (Figure 17). As such, David's kingdom matched the territory controlled by 'Abdiḫepa of Jerusalem during the Amarna period, just as Saul was a Lab'ayu *redivivus*. Only in the imagination of later generations did David rule a great empire.

At the end of his reign, David's designated successors were dead or would soon be dead. North of Benjamin, Israel was lost, as was David's old power base in the Negev of Judah. Memories of David's "empire" were produced during Josiah's reign at the earliest, and more likely by the

Hasmoneans and Herodians who took the biblical David as a model and proceeded to "restore" what they believed was his empire. Of these epigones, Herod the Great was the most successful, thanks to the backing of Rome. The rise and fall of Daher ibn Omar, who governed Palestine from 1750 to 1775 CE, presents interesting parallels with David's career (Volney 1787). Other parallels to the careers of Saul and David can be found in the rise and fall of the Shammar of Hā'il and Saudi state formation in the nineteenth and twentieth centuries CE in Arabia (Musil 1928, 236–255; Flanagan 1988, 304–311, 325–341).

3.5 Solomon

The story of Solomon (1 Kings 1–11) is the overture to the history of the kingdoms of Israel and Judah, projecting all the glory of the Assyrian Empire onto a fabulous past to show how such an empire can only lead to ruin. The prosperity of Israel in the time of the Omrides in the ninth century BCE was transferred to Solomon, including the boats sent to Ophir, the mighty palace, and the list of 12 districts (1 Kings 4). The portrayal of David the warrior and Solomon the builder corresponds, with some exaggeration, to Omri the founder of the dynasty and to Ahab his son (Niemann 1997). The biblical Solomon inherited from Jeroboam II the building of Hazor, Megiddo, and Gezer and the horse trade from Egypt to Assyria. The judgment of Solomon (1 Kgs 3:16-28), his wisdom (1 Kgs 5:9-14), and the visit by the Queen of Sheba (1 Kgs 10:1-10, 13) are legends of the seventh to fifth centuries BCE, when Arabian queens are known from Assyrian records.

Solomon's reign was not peaceful, despite a folk etymology that derives his name from the word *shalom*, "peace." The campaigns of Pharaoh Shishak in Israel/Palestine began in Solomon's day. Solomon was probably named after the Jerusalem god Shalem, a companion of the sun-god (Figure 18); Jerusalem means 'Foundation of Shalem.'

The explanation of Solomon's name as a replacement or compensation for Bathsheba's firstborn son (2 Sam. 12:24) is a fitting pseudo-etymology because the Hebrew root *šlm* expresses the notion of compensation. The notion of peace is but a consequence of compensation. Between David and the immediate predecessors of Omri, the biblical account of the first kings is far from peaceful:

–There was a long war between the house of Saul and the house of David (2 Sam. 3:1).

–There was war between Rehoboam and Jeroboam continually (1 Kgs 14:30).

–The war begun between Rehoboam and Jeroboam continued all the days of his life (1 Kgs 15:6).

Figure 18: Baal-Seth combined with two astral symbols (compare Figures 11–12) (after Keel 2007, 126).

–There was war between Abijam and Jeroboam (1 Kgs 15:7).

–There was war between Asa and King Baasha of Israel all their days (1 Kgs 15:16, 32).

For a more peaceful period, one must await Ahab.

As the son of a Jerusalemite mother, Solomon succeeded David, who was probably not his biological father (Veijola 1979). The succession was orchestrated by the leading members of the Jerusalemite party at David's court: the courtier Nathan, Zadok the priest, and Benaiah, the commander of the guard. The coup eliminated the Judahite elite, the crown prince, Adoniah (the military commander), Joab, and Abiathar the priest (1 Kings 1). David is depicted as senile and impotent. He rubber-stamps the actions of his supposed son, who subdues the tribe of Judah and places the area around Jerusalem under the control of the city-state. The lists of David's officers (2 Sam. 8:16-18; 20:23-26) mention one "recorder" (ספר), Ahilud, who, in the list of Solomon's officers (1 Kgs 4:2-6), is flanked by Elihoreph and Ahijah, sons of Shisha. Hence, after the takeover of David's entourage, Jerusalem could boast of having three persons who could write. The story of 2 Samuel 10–11 and 1 Kings 1 was enough to legitimate Solomon's dynasty in the eyes of Jerusalem. Judah had no say in that matter, but regarding Israel, Solomon's legitimacy was affirmed through the episode of incubation at the shrine of Gibeon, Saul's old residence (1 Kgs 3:4-15).

The area over which Solomon ruled effectively is covered by the list of construction projects in 1 Kings 9:17-18 and matches the map of the campaigns of Shishak (Figure 16). Solomon controlled the western part of Israel (Gezer, Beth-Horon) and central Judah (Baalat Judah), with a southern outpost on the southern edge of the Dead Sea (Tamar = *'ain al-'arūs*). At the end of the reign of Solomon, Jeroboam I became king of Israel at the newly founded capital of Shechem. The core of the list of Solomon's officials in 1 Kings 4:8-12, 14 betrays an attempt to regain the Samarian mountains, the Jezreel Valley, and Gilead for the House of David but it was probably composed later than Solomon's days, as the reference to Gath cannot predate the rule of Omri. In this list of 12 "districts," the first seven form a logical sequence; starting with Ephraim, the territories surrounding it follow clockwise from Gezer via the Jezreel Valley to Gilead. "Districts" 8-10 (Naphthali, Asher, Issachar) and 11-12 (Benjamin and Northern Moab) are additions.[2] Shishak had to subdue the Negev tribes with whom David had built his power base (1 Samuel 27-30), but from then on, the territory of the kingdom of Judah remained constant until 597 BCE, the greatest amount of fluctuation occurring on the Benjamin Plateau. From Solomon on, Jerusalem lost control over northern Israel, but territorial claims can survive setbacks on the ground for centuries. Although Britain lost Calais in 1558 CE, the last remnant of its possessions in France, it was only in 1801 that the British crown renounced the title "king of France".

The temple of Jerusalem where David prayed (2 Sam. 12:20) was sited where the Dome of the Rock stands today. It is built over a cave which is partially artificial and resembles a typical burial cave of the Intermediate Bronze Age (2300-2000 BCE). Despite the antiquity of this sanctuary, the Bible transmits no legend relative to its foundation as a Yahwist cultic place, in contrast to Bethel (Gen. 28:11-19). The building report in 1 Kings 6 deals with the decoration of an existing temple, which indicates that Solomon introduced the Judean and Israelite tribal deity YHWH next to one of the Jerusalemite gods, El or Amon (1 Kgs 8:12-13 LXX), into the pre-existing temple. The subordination of YHWH to El reflects Bath-sheba's coup (1 Kings 1) in the divine sphere. The elite of the old Jerusalemite

---

2 Following Finkelstein (2011), Phase I ("districts" 1-7) represents pre-Omride Israel (which might have been coveted by Solomon), Phase II (8-12) Omride expansion. See also Knauf (2001d). Niemann (2000) attributes also Phase I to the Omrides.

city-state subordinated the tribe of Judah and domesticated its once-free tribal god:

> [El] set the sun in the heavens: but YHWH prefers to dwell in thick darkness. So I have built you an exalted house, a place for you to dwell in forever. (1 Kgs 8:12-13 LXX)

> When Elyon apportioned the nations, when he divided humankind, he fixed the boundaries of the peoples according to the number of the sons of El; YHWH's own portion was his people, Jacob his allotted share. (Deut. 32:8-9 LXX)

The notion that at Jerusalem YHWH was placed next to El in a temple that was not built from the start for him alone did not fit the canonical view. Although the Hebrew text turned the "sons of El" of Deuteronomy 32:9 into "sons of Israel" and erased the sun god from 1 Kings 8:12, the polytheistic traits of these old texts are preserved in the Dead Sea Scrolls and in the Septuagint, textual traditions that were less troubled by the idea that the YHWH of the wilderness had entered the local Canaanite pantheon.

The three adversaries of Solomon in 1 Kings 11 weave threads of various periods into an elaborate theological overture for the synchronic narrative of the kings of Israel and Judah that follows (Edelman 1995). The adversaries have to be sent by YHWH in punishment for Solomon's sins in order to explain the severe shrinkage of Solomon's virtual domination from the Euphrates to the border river of Egypt (1 Kgs 5:11; 2 Kgs 24:7) to the narrow confines of the Central Palestinian Range, where the power and the riches of Solomon left no traces. Although 1 Kings 11 is completely unhistorical, it bears tenth-century BCE traits of verisimilitude. That an Edomite tribal leader escaped a Judean raid by fleeing to Egypt (1 Kgs 11:14-22) would be consistent with the 'Arabah trade system and the renewal of Egyptian–Edomite cooperation in copper mining at Timna during the reign of Shishak (Knauf 1991). That this Edomite prince fled from Judean occupation of his land, however, is an ingredient of the seventh to fifth centuries BCE. Permanent occupation of Edom would have far exceeded the capacity of David's 200-man army. Rezon son of Eliada was, like David, an Idrimi-like *'apiru* leader. The kingdom he founded at Damascus (1 Kgs 11:23-25) must have suffered the same fate as David's and Idrimi's, since the next attested king of Damascus (1 Kings 15) traces his pedigree to a different ancestor.

The conclusion of the chapter (1 Kgs 11:29-40) is a similar patchwork. Following the same pattern as the story of David's service at Saul's court (1 Samuel 16–18), it sets Jeroboam's rebellion in the days of Solomon to introduce the story of the division of Solomon's empire at the great assembly of Shechem (1 Kgs 12:1-20). In fact, the synchronism that makes Jeroboam and Rehoboam's reign begin in the same year presupposes that the father who disciplined Israel "with whips" was Solomon and that the son who promised to do so "with scorpions" was Rehoboam (1 Kgs 12:11).

3.6 Shishak and the Egyptian Revival

In a new cycle of the standard sequence of political and economic powers, the Canaanite revival was followed by a revival of Egyptian Canaan. In Egypt, the Libyan Twenty-Second Dynasty rose to power. Its first pharaoh, Shishak (1 Kgs 11:40; 14:25), never abandoned Egypt's claim over Canaan, which the Egyptians considered as an eternal possession (Figure 19).

Figure 19: Mahanaim and Gibeon on Shishak's triumph relief. Following previous models, Shishak's triumphal relief inscribes toponyms inside crenalated ovals on the sides of small kneeling Asiatic captives (after Wilson 2005, 108).

The Libyan chieftain took control of a weakened Egyptian power and tried to have his tribal government establish control over the realm his pharaonic predecessors had ruled (Ritner 2009). Yet, Shishak's mentality was closer to that of Solomon and Jeroboam than it was to that of the pharaohs of earlier dynasties. Hence, the Libyan did what previous pharaohs would never have done: he married his female relatives to foreigners in order to secure tribal alliances. The Egyptian marriages attributed to Solomon and Jeroboam I are plausible in the historical context of Shishak's reign.

The Hebrew Bible records a single Canaanite campaign, presented as a mere plundering raid, which brought Shishak to Rehoboam's Jerusalem (1 Kgs 14:25-26). However, an inscription belonging to a member of Shishak's court states that he accompanied the pharaoh on his campaigns (plural) in Syria-Palestine (Wilson 2005, 70). Thus, the damaged inscription listing his conquests might reflect multiple, conflated campaigns. One campaign appears to have targeted Philistia and Benjamin, and a second one the Negev. In a possible third and final campaign, Shishak might have led his troops through Philistia, the Jezreel Valley, and the Jordan Valley, with a foray into the valley of the Jabbok east of the Jordan (Figure 16). Jerusalem could have been the intended destination of the first campaign, but the portion of the inscription where Jerusalem would have been mentioned is perfectly legible, so it is clear that Rehoboam never paid tribute to Shishak I. Moreover, Shishak erected a monumental victory stele at Megiddo, which reveals a greater involvement in Canaan than a few raids (Figure 20).

Figure 20: Fragment of a stele Shishak erected at Megiddo (after Lamon and Shipton 1939, 60 #70).

The map of Shishak's conquests (Figure 16) indicates that he sought to support rather than destroy the kingdoms of his sons-in-law, Solomon's Jerusalem and Jeroboam's Shechem, by knocking out their immediate rivals. He conquered Gibeon, Gezer, and Beth-Horon. He apparently gave Gezer and Beth-Horon to Solomon for rebuilding (1 Kgs 9:16-17) but left Gibeon, Jerusalem's immediate rival, in ruins. Shishak's activities east of the Jordan enabled Jeroboam to build a centre at Penuel (1 Kgs 12:25), below Eshbaal's former place of coronation, which gave Jeroboam control over the access to the Ajlun iron deposits. All these works are explicable only as the sequel to the preceding Egyptian destructions. Southern Judah, long lost by Jerusalem because it had been David's personal power base, was conquered again by Shishak and placed once more in the orbit of Jerusalem. The impact of Shishak's campaign on the development of the kingdom of Judah is downplayed in the Bible, but its remembrance on the ground is indicated by the frequent reproduction of Shishak's cartouche on Judahite seals of the tenth to eighth centuries BCE (Staubli 2007, 65, #48).

In Galilee, Megiddo Stratum VB seems to have become the new administrative centre of the Egyptian Canaanite province (Ussishkin 1990; Knauf 2001c). It played this role again under Necho (2 Kgs 23:29). There are no differences in material culture between Megiddo V and the adjoining hill country, which indicates that Israel was now integrated into the Egyptian structure of Megiddo and the Jezreel Valley, or *vice versa*, depending from whose vantage-point one considers Shishak's achievements in Israel/Palestine.

In contrast to previous research, it now appears that Shishak's activities in Canaan had a significant impact in the Levant. The restoration of Egyptian sovereignty over Canaan lasted until about 850 BCE in the form of a loose supervision of vassals. The pharaohs of the Twenty-Second Dynasty secured the loyalty of their vassals occupying the Syrian coast by sending wives and statues. Israelite and Judean seals of the ninth and even eighth century BCE use the title Shishak/Shoshenq (š3šnq or š3šq) as a kind of protecting power. The influence of the Twenty-Second Dynasty over Canaan was pervasive. The Omride architects used the Egyptian cubit rather than the Syrian cubit their predecessors had used and that their successors resumed using in Israel/Palestine (Franklin 2004, 2008). The presence of 500 Egyptian soldiers is recorded at the battle of Qarqar 853 BCE. It is possible that Rehoboam paid tribute to the Egyptians in his fifth year (1 Kgs 14:25-27), but not to Shishak I. In the biblical narrative, this note explains the disappearance of Solomon's virtual wealth from further Judaean history

3.7 Jeroboam I

In light of the revival of Egyptian Canaan, the success of Jeroboam ben Nebat in founding a new Israelite state with the northern tribes can be explained by the support he received from Egypt (Galpaz 1991). According to 1 Kings 12:20, the decision was taken by the tribes. Jeroboam set himself up at Shechem, which had lain desolate for the previous 50-100 years. In a second step, he fortified Penuel at the lower Jabbok, which had probably been granted to him by Shishak (1 Kgs 12:25). Hence, Jeroboam I reproduced the growth pattern of Eshbaal's Israel—a pattern directed by geographical *structure*. From Shechem, Jeroboam I controlled the northern Jordan Rift Valley and the passages to and from the coast, while Peniel gave him a stake in the 'Arabah trade route (Olivier 1983). The choice of the name Jeroboam by the subsequent Nimshide dynasty (2 Kgs 13:13), under whose reign the kingdom of Israel reached its greatest territorial extent, indicates that in the eighth century BCE, Jeroboam ben Nebat was remembered locally as the founder of Israel as vividly as Saul is in the Bible and Omri is by the Assyrians.

The sin of Jeroboam (1 Kgs 12:26-33) was establishing bull statues or stelae in Bethel and Dan. It does not hark back to Jeroboam I (Berlejung 2009). It may have been a ritual action by Jeroboam II transferred to Jeroboam I by the editors of the Book of Kings to de-legitimize the entire kingdom of Israel by portraying its blatant idolatry right from its beginnings. If Benjaminite Bethel was a contested zone between Israel and Judah at least until about 900 BCE (1 Kgs 15:16-22), Dan was probably uninhabited in 925 BCE and only became Israelite during the reign of Jeroboam II (Arie 2008).

Until the demise of the kingdom of Israel in 722–720 BCE, Judah stood in the shadow of its northern neighbour. Bethel, Gezer (Josh. 16:10; Judg. 1:29), and Beth-horon (1 Chron. 7:24) reverted to Israel before Omri's reign. From around 900 BCE, the dividing line between the spheres of direct control of Judah and Israel was set north of Ramah (1 Kgs 14:30; 15:6, 16-22, 32). The revival of Israel in the last quarter of the tenth century is a consequence and an indication of the recovery of the Phoenician economy and its effects in its southern periphery. As long as Philistine dominance in central Palestine was unrivalled, Benjamin and Judah blossomed at the expense of Israel. Yet, the Phoenician and Israelite recovery remained dependent on the 'Arabah trade system, as the location of the residences of the kings of Israel at Shechem, Penuel, and Tirzah (1 Kgs 15:21, 33; 16:6, 8-9, 23) indicate. It was Omri who moved his residence to Samaria, following the shift of the economic centres from the 'Arabah to the Lebanese coast, a position more favourable within the second Mediterranean trade system (Figure 17).

Little more can be said about Rehoboam, Solomon's son and successor, than that he reigned for 17 years and that his mother was an Ammonite princess (1 Kgs 14:21). Since the queen mother of his son and successor Abijah was Maacah, daughter of Ab(i)shalom (1 Kgs 15:2), Rehoboam's wife was probably a granddaughter of David (Halpern 2001). That Abijah ascended the Jerusalemite throne in Jeroboam's eighteenth regnal year (1 Kgs 15:1) indicates that Jeroboam began to reign one or two years before Rehoboam. After three years of Abijah's reign, Asa reigned for 41 years (1 Kgs 15:9-10).

3.8 Religion and Literature in the Tenth Century BCE

The religion of the tenth century BCE still belongs to the Iron I period. The most important changes were David's placement of his dynasty under the protection of the Israelite war god YHWH and Solomon's introduction of YHWH to the cult and theology of Jerusalem. These steps were the first in a long process that would eventually make Jerusalem the holy city of three worldwide, monotheistic religions.

The Israelite traditions of the tenth century BCE that were put in writing in the next century and eventually found their way into the Bible are polytheistic poems (Josh. 10:12-13; Judges 5; 1 Kgs 8:12-13). Because of the biographical parallels between Moses and Jeroboam I in the biblical texts, it can be surmised that the Exodus tradition was alive at the court of Shechem and was cherished along with the tradition of Jacob, whose oldest layer connects the two residences of Jeroboam: Shechem and Penuel (Genesis 31-33). Under David and Solomon, there was probably no court literature: epigraphic evidence from the tenth century is limited to the area of the Shephelah and consists of writing exercises, such as the Gezer Calendar and the Qeyyāfa ostracon, that have but distant links with biblical Hebrew. The royal house of Judah started elaborating the traditions of the House of David in writing at a later date. The earliest are the Bathsheba-layer in 2 Samuel 11-12 and 1 Kings 1, and the Maacah layer in 2 Samuel 13-20 and 1 Kings 12 (Knauf 2002c).

CHAPTER 4
FROM OMRI TO JEROBOAM II:
THE CONSOLIDATION OF LEVANTINE KINGDOMS

The consolidation of Levantine kingdoms and the rise of secondary states are set in the context of the second Mediterranean trade system.

4.1 State Formation in Southern Syria-Palestine in the Ninth and Eighth Centuries BCE

From the fragmented economic centres they were in the eleventh century BCE, the coastal cities of the Lebanese coast became the hub of a pan-Mediterranean economic system whose leadership remained unchallenged until the fifth century BCE. Tyre founded Carthage in modern Tunisia, and by the end of the eighth century Phoenician trade reached southern Spain (Sagona 2004). In the meantime, Philistia stagnated. The cities of the Canaanite revival in the Jezreel and Jordan valleys were integrated into the states of Israel and Aram-Damascus. While the kingdoms of Saul and David were ephemeral formations at the edge of the Philistine centres (Figure 15), the Mediterranean revival fostered a steady process of secondary state formation from the ninth century BCE onwards in the hinterland of Phoenicia, supported by a favourable *conjoncture* that had not existed in the previous centuries (Figure 17). Statehood in Aram-Damascus and Israel (900–850 BCE) spread to Ammon (875–850 BCE), Moab (850–825 BCE), Judah (850–700 BCE), and finally, to some extent, to Edom (725–600 BCE) (Knauf 1992). Compared with earlier tribal states, these states were dominated by the figure of the king as the most visible element of an administrative apparatus composed of a standing army, a bureaucracy, and a monumental architecture of palaces, temples, and fortresses. The population of the coastal cities increased steadily. Tyre's 50,000 inhabitants, compared with Jerusalem's 15,000–20,000 at its peak of prosperity in the seventh century BCE, could not feed themselves from surrounding gardens and fields. Statehood means a greater amount of specialization, implying the ability to extract foodstuffs from producers to feed the state apparatus. Yet, most people, even in the cities, continued to produce some of the food they ate, and in Hellenistic times soldiers were "paid" with land on which they were expected to grow their own food. The revenues of the state derived from its ability to tax its own subjects, something tribes were unable to do because they relied on a militia of volunteers drawn from their own ranks. A standing army of the State, however small it may be, is accepted as enforcing tax collection when taxpayers experience the benefits of taxation in the form of enhanced security and stability, the *sine qua non* conditions for long-term investments in trade and agriculture. Before the seventh century BCE, however, taxes were primarily imposed in the form of corvée, mandatory free labour, for public building projects.

Jeroboam's son Nadab succeeded his father for about a year. The "two years" of 1 Kings 15:25 means that the New Year occurred during his regnal year, after which the Issacharite (Jezreelite) Baasha ben Ahijah murdered him and made himself king (1 Kgs 15:25-29, 32). Baasha (בעשא) is a diminutive form for Baalshama, "Baal hears," or Baal Shaphat, "Baal reigns." The usurper killed his predecessor's entire house (1 Kgs 15:29), including the slaves, which corresponds to the entire state apparatus.

The fortification of Geba and Mizpah (1 Kgs 15:16-22, confirmed by Jer. 41:9) shows that King Asa of Jerusalem stabilized the northern margin of Judah with the help of King Bar-Hadad bar Tabrimmon bar Hezion, who reigned in Damascus and was clearly not a descendant of Rezon. To relieve the pressure on Judah, Bar-Hadad devastated Galilee (1 Kgs 15:20). At the time, Dan belonged neither to Israel nor to Aram-Damascus, but to Beth-Rehob, Beth-Maacah, or Geshur (Finkelstein 2011).

Elah ben Baasha reigned for about a year, before Zimri, an officer of the chariot corps, assassinated him (1 Kgs 16:8-11). This is the first credible mention of war chariots in Israel. Zimri reigned seven days, until Omri, another commander, attacked the usurper and replaced him on the throne, thanks to the support of the militia (1 Kgs 16:15-18). Zimri and Omri are both designations of places of origin rather than personal names. Pre-Arabic place names suggest that Zimri came from *Zimrin* or *Zamarayn*, villages in the vicinity of modern Tartus in Syria, while Omri's family would have been from *'Ammurin* near Hama, also in modern Syria. Hence, it is likely Zimri and Omri were Arameans serving in the army of the Israelite kingdom, which had emancipated itself from its tribal structure with a more or less private army of mercenaries (Rosenfeld 1965). As happened with the Mamelukes in Egypt in 1250 CE, the servants became the lords of the kingdom. In the wake of the revival of Mediterranean trade, Jehoshaphat of Judah made peace with Israel (1 Kgs 22:45), ending a century of constant skirmishing and making Judah a vassal of Israel. Judah sent auxiliary troops as support in Israel's wars (2 Kgs 8:28, 9-10). Judah was drawn into the Phoenician trade network through the marriage of Jehoram ben Jehoshaphat with Athaliah, a daughter of Omri (2 Kgs 8:26).

As was the case with the pharaohs of the Libyan dynasty, the stronger party in the diplomatic marriage was the wife-giver (Niemann 2006).

4.2 Aram and Israel

The kingdom of Aram-Damascus, like Israel, did not belong to the first wave of Aramean state formation; 2 Samuel 8:5-6 forms a parenthesis in the report of the story of David's dealings with Hadad-Ezer of Beth Rehob in the Lebanese Beqaʿ. This was inserted either under the Omrides or, more likely, by the Nimshides since, as 1 Kings 11:23-25 shows, Damascus became a kingdom later than Beth-Rehob, which, with its more western situation, was thereby closer to the Phoenician coastal cities. It was not before 900 BCE that Damascus gained dominance over the Aramean dynasties of Arpad, Hamath, and other cities of Inner Syria.

The rise of Aram-Damascus was slower than how it is presented in the Bible. At first, Hazael subdued only the small Aramean states on the border of Israel (Beth-Rehob, Aram Beth Maacah, and Geshur); 1 Kings 20:1 and 20:24 wrongly attribute to Hazael the imperial policy of Tiglath-pileser III. It was only after Hazael's kingdom had brought Israel and Damascus into direct contact that the two kingdoms fought one another (the Ben-Hadad mentioned in 1 Kings 15:18-20 is not necessarily Ben-Hadad I, since the Bible designates every king of Aram-Damascus who was not called Hazael to be "Reson" or "Rezin 'Ben-Hadad'"). Ben-Hadad II, the enemy of Ahab (1 Kings 20, 22) and Hazael's predecessor (2 Kgs 8:7-15), is entirely fictitious and based on the backward projection of Israel's wars against Ben-Hadad III, the son of Hazael.

King Baasha of Israel moved the royal residence from Shechem to Tirzah (1 Kgs 15:21, 33; 16:6) after a coup during the siege of Philistine Gibbethon, which belonged to the declining kingdom of Ekron (1 Kgs 15:27-30). As discussed above, Baasha's son Elah fell victim to a coup by the chariot-general Zimri, who reigned seven days and was ousted by the army, which then proclaimed Omri king (1 Kgs 16:9-20). Omri thus did not come to power through the will of the tribal aristocracy but, as with Solomon, by a military coup. The military, however small, was the political arm of the incipient state. For the first half of his reign, Omri struggled against a rival king, Tibni (1 Kgs 16:21-22)—a rivalry that marked the split of Mount Ephraim between Ephraim and Manasseh, later deemed sons of Joseph. Tibni is the first Israelite ruler named only according to his place of origin, either in Lebanon or in Gilead, where one finds some places named Tibna, Tibnin, and Tibne. That Zimri was counted in the list of kings despite his very short reign betrays the aim of the composers of the Book of Kings, who recorded 18 Israelite kings between 927 and 724 BCE and the same number for Judah between 926 and 586 BCE.

4.3 The Dynasty of Omri

To the Assyrians, Omri was the founder of the kingdom of Israel, which in the ninth century BCE they regarded as a tribal government and referred to disparagingly as the "House of Omri" (Assyrian: Bit Umrī). In the same period, Aram-Damascus and Moab mentioned "Israel," but Judah continued to be described as the "House of David." In his first report on the Battle of Qarqar, however, Shalmaneser III mentions "Israel," which shows an awareness of the changes that had occurred in Israel. Omri and Ahab built fortresses, palaces, and a new residence at Samaria (1 Kgs 16:23-24). Despite the story of the purchase of the hill of Samaria from a man named Shemer, the name *Shomron* is a Canaanite toponym, as the ending *-on* indicates. From Samaria's commanding position, it was indeed easy to guard (שמר) the surrounding area.

The alliance of the Omrides with Phoenicia was sealed by the marriage of Omri's son Ahab with the Sidonian Princess Jezebel (1 Kgs 16:31). Summarizing Omri's reign with the word "his bravery" (גבורתו) in 1 Kings 16:27, the writer indicated that Omri was a successful warrior who, after pacifying Israel, subdued the surrounding cities of the Canaanite revival and skimmed the wealth they had accumulated in the previous century to the point that Ahab, his son, was able to maintain 2,000 chariots. The Bible devotes a mere eight verses to Omri (1 Kgs 16:21-28). On the achievements of his successors, the Hebrew Bible is mute apart from charging them with the "sin of Jeroboam." The Elijah-Elisha traditions in 1 Kings 17 to 2 Kings 8 contain no report from the ninth century BCE. The good relations of the Omrides with Phoenicia and their impressive achievements were all transferred to Solomon.

Compared with the other Israelite dynasties that lasted no more than two generations, Omri's dynasty lasted between 46 and 49 years, with four rulers in three generations: Omri for 12 years, Ahab for 20 years, Ahaziah for two years, and Joram for 13 years (1 Kgs 16:29-34; 22:51; 2 Kgs 1:17). Around 843 BCE, the chariotry officer Jehu staged a military coup—the third in the kingdom's troubled history as it is recorded in the Bible (2 Kings 9–10).

Thanks to Egyptian and Phoenician backing, the Omrides expanded the territory of Israel in all directions (Knauf 2007). They advanced north to the detriment of the small Aramean kingdoms in Upper Galilee and established a garrison at Hazor for a chariot regiment and two small forts on the Phoenician fringe, at Har Adir and Tel Harasim. Another chariot base was set up at Jezreel. In Transjordan, the Omrides extended Gilead to the Yarmuk River, where they founded a fortress at Ramoth-Gilead. From the designation of a landscape, Gilead became the name of a province that included the Land of Argob (Deut. 3:4), and probably most of the territory of the Aramean kingdom of Tob (Judg. 11:3, 5).

In 853 BCE, the southward advance of the Assyrian King Shalmaneser III was halted at Qarqar, a battle the Great King claimed to have won although it brought him no strategic advantage. On the contrary, the same coalition faced the Assyrians in 849, 848, and 845 BCE, each time north of Qarqar. The detailed report for the Battle of Qarqar in 853 BCE attributes the leadership of the coalition to Israel, Damascus, and Hamath. Ahab's 10 infantry regiments are only the second largest, but he also supplied the largest chariot corps (two regiments). The figures can be questioned, but they present an overview of the tactical units at the beginning of the battle as Assyrian intelligence estimated the military strength of the individual states:

> 1,200 chariots, 1,200 cavalry, (and) 20,000 troops of Hadad-ezer (*Adad-idri*) of Damascus; 700 chariots, 700 cavalry, (and) 10,000 troops of Irḫulēni, the Hamathite; 2,000 chariots, (and) 10,000 troops of Ahab the Israelite (*Sir'alāia*); 500 troops of Byblos; 1,000 troops of Egypt; 10 chariots (and) 10,000 troops of the land of Irqanatu (Irqata); 200 troops of Matinu-ba'al of the city of Arvad; 200 troops of Usnatu (Usnu); 30 chariots (and) [ ],000 troops of Adon-ba'al of the land of Šianu (Siyannu); 1,000 camels of Gindibu' of Arabia; [ ] hundred troops of Ba'asa, (the man) of Bīt-Ruḫubi, the Ammonite... (Shalmaneser III in *CoS* 2.113)

Five Phoenician cities provided 40 chariots, while the the 1,000 Egyptians represent the Egyptian garrison sent by Sidon and Tyre. Egypt supplied the prestige, Phoenicia the money, Aram and Israel the men and the horses. Forces from Judah are not listed, either because they were too insignificant or because they were incorporated into the Israelite contingents. Aram-Beth-Rehob is not yet a vassal of Damascus, and for the first time an Arab tribal confederation occurs as a military-political entity. The Battle of Qarqar may have left a literary sequel in the Karkor of Judges 8:10, the place of Gideon's battle against Midian. As with most battles in military history, no one won at Qarqar, and the balance of power remained unchanged after the carnage.

Na'aman (1997) suggests that Ahab died the same year that the Battle of Qarqar took place, possibly from a wound received there (1 Kgs 22:34-37). If that had been the case, however, Shalmaneser III probably would have taken credit for the fatal shot, as Hazael did in the case of the deaths of Joram and Ahaziah on the Dan inscription. In fact, Ahab's death imitates the death of Joram in 2 Kings 8:29. According to 1 Kings 22:40, Ahab "slept with his ancestors," which means at the very least that he was buried in his family tomb. Of course, he could have been wounded on the battlefield and managed to get home before dying, but the notion of a peaceful end for a king deemed as evil as Ahab by the editors of the Book of Kings was probably unbearable. As the king of Israel is only named as Ahab once in the entire episode (1 Kgs 22:20), the otherwise anonymous king who died of an arrow shot in 1 Kings 22:35 only became Ahab after some creative scribal rewriting.

Shalmaneser's reports of the battles of 849, 848, and 845 BCE no longer use the descriptive *Bit-* (House of x). As these reports are summaries, it cannot be concluded that Israel had dropped from the coalition. Indeed, Joram had to deal with the defection of Mesha, who set himself as king over Moab, but this would not have diverted Israel's entire military force.

Israelite troops were probably organized into nominal regiments of 1,000 men, like Assyrian troops, and companies of 50 men (1 Sam. 8:12; 2 Kings 1). In this way, a small standing army could be maintained on the basis of tribal militias mustered for short spells. The companies of each regiment manned the forts one at a time. The 10 infantry regiments correspond to the 10 tribes of Omride Israel (Judges 5; 1 Kgs 4:7-19; 11:30). The charioteers were stationed at Jezreel and Hazor, where fodder for the horses was assured. Given the requirements of ancient agriculture, one man out of 20 was all families could relinquish to the state besides workdays spent on royal projects in the non-busy period between harvest and sowing. Since the crown could not extract more taxes (in the form of manpower) from its own population, the largest share of the state's revenues consisted of the proceeds from crown estates, trade, and to some extent the spoils of war. Assyria waged war to finance its army. Rather than recording the payment of taxes-in-kind, the Samaria ostraca (eighth century BCE) are receipts for food supplies sent to Samaria from the home villages of Manassites serving at the royal residence (Niemann 2008):

Year 10. From Geba to Adoniam: 1 jar of old wine. (Samaria ostrachon #8)

Year 9. From Hatzerot for Gaddyau: [1] skin of refined oil. (Samaria ostrachon #18)

The list of Manassite possessions within the territory of Issachar and Asher could reflect Omride royal estates in the vicinity of Beth-She'an, Ibleam, Dor, En-dor, Taanach, and Megiddo (Josh. 17:11). Samaria lay in Manasseh and ran estates in the countryside of these Canaanite cities to feed the state apparatus without encroaching on the economic structure of the cities themselves; the amount of available fertile land was endless compared with the size of the population.

With the rise of a royal entourage less dependent on the tribal elite came the ability to mobilize the tribal workforce for more constructive activities than inter-tribal feuds. Although secondarily attributed to Solomon, the officers who were in charge of forced labour (1 Kgs 4:6; 5:13-14; 9:15-21) belonged to the supra-tribal caste that arose in the immediate entourage of the Omride royal household. These officers drew their own revenues from agricultural surpluses produced on empty Canaanite land beyond the tribal area from which they originated. Moreover, the cost of transporting surpluses produced near Beth-She'an, Ibleam, Dor, En-dor, Taanach, and Megiddo to the Phoenician export centres was lower than it would have been for surpluses produced in the Samarian highlands. The transport would have been provided outside the war season by the horses trained to pull the Israelite war chariots recorded at the Battle of Qarqar. As long as there was a Mediterranean market for Canaanite produce, anyone who could force farming families to clear arable land during non-demanding periods of the agricultural cycle would consolidate his economic and political dominance.

In pre-industrial worlds, political leverage results from wealth. Wealth in turn results from agriculture, the yields from which can be increased only by tapping under-employed manpower to enlarge the amount of land put to the plough. Since no one willingly clears stones and bushes from someone else's fields, wealth is relative to the ability to force farmers to work outside their own villages. Hence, the amount of forced labour is relative to the size of the army, and *vice versa*. Besides the occasional plundering of areas beyond the realm, the proceeds of which are offset by retaliatory raids on the territory of the original plunderer, the primary activity of a standing army is the organization of work-gangs on royal estates. Since a soldier will protect rather than put pressure on his cousins, the Omrides' success was based on the ability to put Manassites in charge of the forced labour in areas Joshua 17:5 describes as the territory of Issachar and Asher. Despite the framework of Greater Israel from Dan to Beersheba, Joshua 17:11-13 and Judges 1:27-28 transmit an accurate picture of economic processes by distinguishing between the countryside and the cities and by admitting that the Manassites could not take possession of the cities, so that Canaanites continued to live in them. The only required corrective is to recognize the anachronism. The time "when the Israelites grew strong and put the Canaanites to forced labour" was in the days of the Omrides.

It was only under Omri and Ahab that Gad became part of Israel. The list of Solomon's administrative officers (1 Kgs 4:7-19) reflects the basic elements of the rudimentary administrative districts of Omride Israel. Of the 12 districts, only the first seven follow a meaningful geographical order (Niemann 2000, fig. 1). Starting from the centre of Ephraim and proceeding clockwise, the text lists the northern Shephelah, the Sharon plain, the Phoenician city of Dor, the Canaanite cities in the Jezreel Valley and Beth-She'an, and Ramoth-Gilead (Mount Gilead). From there, it makes a big leap to Naphtali (Hazor) and to Lower Galilee with Issachar, and then from there to Benjamin and Gad in two further leaps. The third Gilead at this point in the Hebrew Bible is one too many. Nevertheless, three distinct waves of expansion are identified and remembered: to the coast, the Jezreel Valley, and northern Transjordan, then to Upper Galilee, and finally, to Benjamin and southern Transjordan.

The fortification of Jericho, after a long occupational gap at this oasis in the marshy and malaria-infected area of the lower Jordan Valley (1 Kgs

16:34), served as the basis for the control of northern Moab (the northern half of the tribe of Gad). It presupposes the control of Benjamin at the expense of Judah. The rest of Moab was made a tributary as far as the regions controlled by the fortresses at Ataroth and Jahaz. The city of Nebo guarded the route to Jericho. In the days of Joram, the Gadite Mesha from Dibon rebelled and captured the north of Moab and some Israelite territory around Nebo (2 Kgs 3:4-5). Since the Bible refers to Mesha's capital as 'Dibon-gad' (Num. 33:45-46), it is clear that Mesha established his kingdom by securing control over a fortress Omri had built in Gad. On the stele he erected in Dibon, Mesha justifies his conquest of the Israelite city of Nebo by stating that it was ordered by his god Kemosh (line 14).

The Mesha inscription (CoS 2.23; Dearman 1989) describes the foundation of a state. This is the result of the somewhat clumsy editing of annals, except for the standard 40 years of the Omride oppression, which is incompatible with the chronology of the Omrides but indicates the absence of written records in Moab before Mesha. The script and the language of Mesha's stele are Israelite, even the plural ending *-in* (Knauf 2005a). The text represents a review of Mesha's deeds distributed over several decades (Na'aman 2007a). That "Israel has perished" (line 7) is correct in relation to the downfall of Omride Israel prior to the Nimshide restoration. What Mesha fails to mention, however, is that he exchanged his vassalage to Israel for vassalage to Damascus. The off-centre capital at Dibon reflects the power structures of the ninth century BCE. The Mesha stele is the first epigraphic evidence of the divine name YHWH and the third epigraphic attestation of the name Israel. The second is the Dan inscription, Merenptah's stele being the first.

The transition from a tribal state to a dynastic chiefdom or kingdom through the rise of a military and administrative apparatus required the quenching of ensuing conflicts and social upheavals. In Judah, Jerusalem's grip over the tribes began in the second half of the tenth century but remained incomplete until the seventh century BCE. In the ninth and eighth centuries BCE, integration into the Mediterranean economy only concerned the extended royal family. The collection of taxes-in-kind began in Judah in the seventh century BCE. The annexation of the Canaanite and Aramean cities in the plains that surrounded the hill country of Samaria enabled the Omrides to wage war and build forts. The cities supplied capital and know-how, the mountains the manpower. The officers and officials in the entourage of the king formed a group of upstarts that outclassed the old tribal and urban nobility. Hence, the conflict in the ninth century was not between the upper and lower classes but between ascending and descending elements within the elite. Religious conflicts played no role in the ninth century BCE, and the Elijah stories are a back-projection.

The end of the dynasty of Omri came about suddenly and unexpectedly. In 842 BCE, Hazael took the throne of Damascus. For reasons that are obscure, his accession to the throne corresponds with the end of the successful anti-Assyrian coalition, resulting in the war between Aram and Israel at Ramoth-Gilead. Judah was enlisted on Israel's side (2 Kgs 8:28). On his Tel Dan inscription, Hazael claims to have killed Joram of Israel and Ahaziah of Judah. In the biblical tradition, both succumbed to wounds they may have received in the fight against Aram. Both kings apparently died too young to secure the throne for a son. In Israel, the queen mother Jezebel tried, apparently unsuccessfully, to take over the regency. A coup was staged from the fortified camp of Jezreel by Jehu ben Nimshi (2 Kgs 9:30-33). Jezebel's sister-in-law Athaliah survived in Jerusalem a little longer. Shalmaneser III exploited the disintegration of the coalition to advance as far as Damascus in 841 BCE (CoS 2.113E, in ANET 280). He ravaged the countryside but could not take the city. Together with Tyre and Sidon, Jehu submitted to Shalmaneser (not mentioned in the Old Testament but depicted on the Black Obelisk, the only known drawing of a biblical king: Figure 21), which marked the end of Egyptian influence in Canaan and sealed the enmity between Jehu and Hazael. The tribute of Jehu (CoS 2.113F, in ANET 281a) includes an amount of gold and tin, two metals Israel could have only obtained from Phoenicia.

Jehu ben Nimshi was from a wealthy family of the Beth-She'an region, as attested by three ostraca of the late tenth and early ninth centuries BCE (Mazar 2003). The Nimshides wrote their clan name in Phoenician orthography (נמש). While the Omrides were possibly of Aramean origin, the Nimshides were Canaanites. The biblical account in 2 Kings 9–10 makes Jehu a hero fighting for the true faith. The story includes revisions from the Persian period, but its features may go back to a basic component in the founding legend of the dynasty elaborated under Jehoash or Jehu ben Nimshi. While the legendary Jehu is a fearless ruler whom his successors set up as their model, Jehu was, in fact, a weak and ineffectual ruler. It was necessary to hush up the role Hazael played in Jehu's career, and the glorification of violence in the Jehu narrative betrays the influence of later Assyrian propaganda. The notion of Yahwism as the state religion seems to be an innovation of Jeroboam II, who appears to have been the first to build sanctuaries to 'the gods who led Israel out of Egypt (1 Kgs 12:28).

For Israel, Jehu's coup and submission to Shalmaneser was a disaster (Figure 21). Israel lost its international position, and control of Galilee and the Jezreel Valley passed to Damascus. From his little kingdom in Moab, Mesha could see that Israel's power base was entirely gone.

Three fragments of an inscription from Tel Dan were found on the pavement before the gate of Dan Stratum II. The inscription, a stele or an orthostat, was erected by Hazael in Dan Stratum III and shattered when

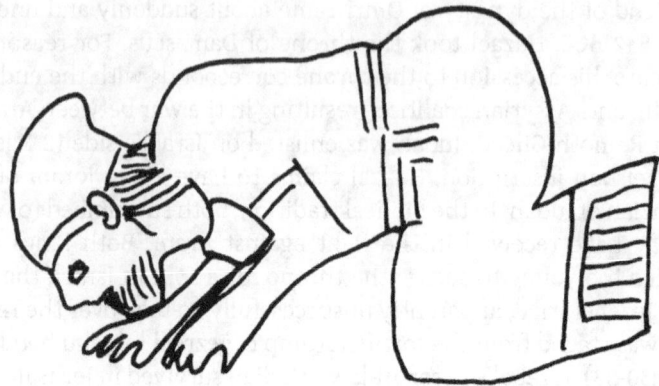

Figure 21: "Jehu son of Omri" kneeling and paying homage to Shalmanassar III on the black obelisk erected in 827 BCE in the palace of Nimrud (after Layard 1849, pl. 53).

Israel conquered Dan in the days of Jeroboam II. The correlation of Fragments II and III (B1 and B2) is undisputed, but the commonly suggested relationship between Fragment I (or A) and II + III (or B) is wrong. A shift of one line up or down in the relation between Fragments II–III and Fragment I is plausible, but the line length cannot be determined:

Fragment I (or A)

1.
2.] my father went up [
3.] My father lay down; he went to [his ancestors
4. the king of Is]rael had gone into my father's land [
5.] I/Me. And Hadad went in front of me [
6.] my becoming king, and I killed [two] kin[gs
7. two thousands cha]riots and two thousands horsemen[
8. I killed] the king of Israel, and [I] killed [
9. and overth]rew the House of David. I set [
10.]?? their land into [
11.] other(s) and ??[
12. k]ing over Is[rael
13.] siege upon [

Fragment II (or B)

1.] and he cut [a treaty
2.] he united with him at A[feq/bel
3.]? the king marched against ??[
4.] Hadad made king [
5.] I departed from the com[pany] of [
6. power]ful harnessed thou[sands of

7. [Jo]ram son of [Ahab
8. Ahaz]yahu son of [Jehoram

(Ghantous 2013, 50)

The horses and riders must have been Syrians or Assyrians, since Israel and Judah at that time had no cavalry. The common translation "fight" in B 2 is erroneous, since in Aramaic, the root לחם means "to join together."

4.4 Israel under Aram-Damascus

It is only recently that scholarship has begun to assess the importance of Hazael. As is also said of Solomon (1 Kgs 5:1), Hazael and his son and successor Bar-Hadad (Hebrew Ben-Hadad) reigned for 40 years "over all the kings of the boundary river of Egypt to the Euphrates." Shalmaneser III designated Hazael a "son of a nobody" (CoS 2.113G, in ANET 280b), to show he considered him illegitimate. On the other hand, the Tel Dan inscription leaves no doubt that Hazael was of royal descent but had inherited the throne of Damascus in an indirect way, by the will of the God Hadad (Na'aman 2000; Athas 2003; Hasegawa 2010; Ghantous 2013). Hazael was probably the legitimate heir to the throne of Beth-Rehob, and in the face of the Assyrian threat, he assumed the throne of Damascus as well, presumably because no suitable heir apparent was available. The biblical writers, who probably knew of the irregular succession of Hazael, had Hazael designated king by YHWH and made him the murderer of his predecessor, who had nothing to do with the real Hadadezer (1 Kgs 19:15-17; 2 Kgs 8:7-15). Shalmaneser presents Hazael as the aggressor, but the first battle took place on Mount Hermon, between the territories of Beth-Rehob and Damascus in 841 BCE when Shalmaneser subjected Israel, Tyre, and Sidon and was faced by Hazael alone. Yet, instead of caving in, Hazael withstood the pressure, and Shalmaneser returned in 838 BCE and again in 837 BCE, when he could only capture some relatively insignificant towns in the Hauran. In fact, Shalmaneser's forces were seriously overstretched and the battle in 837 BCE was probably a crushing defeat for Shalmaneser, who never came back. Hazael had turned the tables. He had eroded Assyrian influence and extended his own control to the Euphrates, something that can be seen in the later editions of the annals of Shalmaneser. The wording describing the wars against the Syrian coalition changes from "Hadadezer and twelve kings of the sea" to "Hadadezer and twelve [or even fifteen] kings of the sea coast *and along the Euphrates.*"

Since Jehu had sided with the Assyrians against Hazael, Israel suffered greatly once Hazael was relieved of Assyrian pressure (1 Kgs 19:15-17; 2 Kgs 8:12; 10:32; 13:3). Israel lost Galilee; Hazor was destroyed and rebuilt as an Aramean stronghold (Hazor Stratum VIII). On Tel Kinrot, Hazael had a watchtower built. Hazael founded Dan III, which includes the restored city wall and the monumental gate through which modern visitors enter the city. The Jezreel Valley was systematically plundered. Megiddo, Jezreel, and Taanach were destroyed. Tel Rehov and Tel Amal in the vicinity of Beth-She'an suffered. Israel lost its most productive lands, its economic basis, and became a vassal of Damascus, which controlled Israel's trade (1 Kgs 20:34). Under Jehoahaz, Jehu's successor, Israel reached a low point. Its levy amounted to 50 riders (something new in Israel), 10 chariots, and 10,000 men (2 Kgs 13:7). In 738 BCE it rose again to 50,000–60,000 men.

In the south, Hazael destroyed Philistine Gath (2 Kgs 12:18), which was the leading centre of the area at the time. Gezer Stratum VIII seems to have been destroyed as well. Second Kings 12:19 associates the payment of a tribute by Judah with the conquest of Gath, but Judah had probably come under Damascene vassalage earlier. After the death of Ahaziah, Queen Athaliah assured the regency for her son Jehoash. However, after seven years, she was murdered in a coup, an indication that an external force, in all likelihood Hazael, was involved in Judah's affairs. The narrative of 2 Kings 11 is marked by the language and ideology of the Second Temple to such a point that it lacks credibility. Had Athaliah removed her grandson, she would have lost all legitimacy.

In 796 BCE, an Assyrian intervention led by Adadnerari III rescued Zakkur, the king of Hamath, from a coalition led by Bar-Hadad of Damascus, thus marking the end of Hazael's empire. Whether it led to a siege of Damascus (CoS 2.114F) is doubtful, but the situation was hopeless enough for Bar-Hadad to capitulate immediately. Besides the 2,000 talents (6 tons) of silver, 1,000 talents (3 tons) of copper, and 2,000 talents of iron that Bar-Hadad delivered, Tyre, Sidon, and Jehoash paid tribute as well. In a later version of the same text (CoS 2.114G), the Damascene tribute is even larger: the tribute of the most distant vassals of Aram-Damascus, Edom, and Philistia has been added. Joash now became an Assyrian vassal instead of a Damascene one. Israel appears here for the first time as Samaria, reflecting how Hazael had shrunk it to no more than the Samarian mountains. Assyria kept up the pressure on Damascus and in 772 BCE, Shalmaneser IV appeared before the city, ruled at the time by a king called Ḥadyān or Ḥaḏyān. Another unspecified tribute of gold, silver, and copper was paid, as well as the royal bed, and a princess (CoS 2.116).

4.5 Religion and Literature in the Ninth Century BCE

From the ninth century BCE we have royal inscriptions from Aram-Damascus, Ammon, and Moab. That these monuments were preserved at the periphery suggests that they also existed in Israel, just as the best-preserved Roman cities are found on the edges of the Roman Empire, in North Africa, Syria, and Jordan. In these inscriptions, the gods address the kings: Damascene, Ammonite and Moabite inscriptions quote divine messages given to the kings, and prophets are mentioned explicitly at Hamath. Prophecy was a common phenomenon throughout the ancient Near East, even if the evidence is sporadic: from the seventeenth century BCE kingdom of Mari on the Euphrates and from the ninth to seventh century BCE in Israel, Assyria, Syria, and its outlying areas. Prophecy is based on the assumption that the gods determine the fortunes of the world and that their intentions can be divined by trained experts. Technical divination in the Hebrew Bible was accomplished through use of the Urim and Thummin (Exod. 28:30; 1 Sam. 14:41; 28:6) and the *goral* "lots," pebbles, dice, astragali (sheep and goat knuckle bones), or sticks thrown during ritual, military, or many other occasions (Lev. 16:8; Num. 34:13; Josh. 13:2; Judg. 20:9-10; 1 Sam. 14:41; Jon. 1:7). Given the number of astragali found in Israelite and Judean occupational levels (Sasson 2007), these were very popular and enabled anyone to obtain simple yes/no answers to queries relative to everyday life. Prophets might have dreams and visions that would be interpreted as messages sent by the gods. Words pronounced by epileptics during seizures were also considered ominous (Grabbe 2000).

The idea that in Israel, contrary to other places, there were prophets who wrote the books that bear their names is anachronistic. In the ancient Near East and Israel, writing was exclusively a matter for professionals who were trained by their fathers or senior colleagues and who, as one of their tasks, played the role of ideologues for their respective employers (Nissinen 2002; Knauf 2004; Edelman and Ben Zvi 2009). As Assyrian prophecy of the seventh century BCE shows, it was a long process before the words uttered by a prophet or a prophetess became part of a literary canon. First, the words were interpreted and reported to the central administration, where they were archived. Then, when the king sought religious legitimation, scribes searched the archives for relevant oracles that were then copied onto a separate tablet or scroll. In the case of biblical prophecy, the thematic collections of oracles were updated from time to time until they were given a coherent literary form, complete with a title and a date, and canonized as such. Hence, the biblical prophet is a literary figure that usually arose at the end of the process. The prophet did not write his book: the figure of the prophet was created by the book.

The Book of Isaiah was written about Isaiah, not by Isaiah. The more biography of its prophet a book contains, the more fiction it transmits. The core of the Book of Isaiah is a collection of oracles from several prophets. The core of the Book of Hosea is a collection of prophetic oracles from the reign of Hosea, the last king of Israel. The Book of Nahum is not a prophecy but a gloat over the fall of the hated Nineveh (Berlejung 2006), except for the Psalm in Nahum 1 that may provide guidelines for an elaborate method to draw oracles from prophetic books to answer specific queries

(Guillaume 2009b). Divination was an important motivation for the canonization of prophetic books (Davies 2007); it is in their canonical form that the prophetic scrolls speak out the divine word.

The iconographic evidence for Iron Age IIA shows no break from the Iron I period. Military gods continue to dominate until the clear break that occurred in the eighth century BCE. What is new in the ninth century BCE is the rise of court literature. In a process similar to that which occurred in thirteenth-century CE Europe, the fast growth of commerce and credit spurred the development of writing; people could no longer rely solely on their memory (Fishman 2011, 91–120). In turn, the growing number of available scribes fostered a new kind of intellectual who, besides recording transactions and keeping ledgers, recorded oral traditions and copied existing texts, and thus produced literature. The Iron Age Mediterranean revival led to textualization at the royal court, where literati had enough spare time to emulate each other in copying each other's literary production. The Song of Deborah (Judges 5) displays some Omride-period features, like the absence of articles and the masculine plural in -īn (Knauf 2005a). The *Sefer ha-yashar* or Book of the Righteous, which is quoted in Joshua 10:13 and 2 Samuel 1:18, also dates to this period. Psalm 45, a wedding song for an Israelite prince marrying a Phoenician princess, and 1 Kings 6–7 also both reflect Omride templates (Finkelstein 2000). The *Sefer Balaam* of Succoth (Tell Deir 'Alla) is an original Omride text (*CoS* 2.27). It reflects the Israelite language under the Omrides rather than a Gilead dialect, because in the ninth century BCE writing was done by court scribes who wrote the language they learned—that is, the language of the royal court.

4.6 Jeroboam II

Renewed Assyrian pressure on Damascus enabled Israel to free itself from its vassalage to Damascus. After the low point reached during the reign of Jehoahaz (2 Kgs 13:4-5, 7), the turning point occurred in the reign of his son Joash (2 Kgs 13:22-25). After 796 BCE, Joash appears in the tribute list of the Assyrian king Adadnerari as king of Samaria. Yet, Joash recovered northern Galilee and part of Transjordan. Adadnerari was the saviour mentioned in 2 Kings 13:3-5, who enabled Joash to obtain a favourable peace treaty with Bar-Hadad, alias Ben-Hadad III (1 Kgs 20:34). The three victories of 2 Kings 13:25 correspond to the three victories in the Elisha cycle (2 Kgs 13:14-19), Ahab's three Aramean campaigns (1 Kings 20 and 22), and the three wars of Elisha (2 Kgs 3:6-27; 6:8-7:20). According to 1 Kings 20:34, Israel recovered its status of being equal partner with Damascus. Under Joash or Jeroboam II, Israel even seems to have gained the upper hand (2 Kgs 14:27-28). The choice of the name Jeroboam reflects a programme of recovery for the Israel of the tenth century BCE. According to 2 Kings 14:25, Jeroboam II expanded

Israel's sovereignty from the entrance of Hamath to the Dead Sea. Second Kings 14:28 even claims that Jeroboam recovered Hamath itself and Damascus "for Judah in Israel" (ליהודה בישׂראל). This awkward expression shows that the territory over which Jeroboam ruled is the model that was used to describe the extent of the kingdom of Judah in the days of David and Solomon. Jeroboam II was the first ever king of Israel to control Dan (Stratum II). Therefore, the description of Israel as extending "from Dan to Beersheba" (Judg. 20:1; 1 Sam. 3:20; 2 Sam. 3:10; 17:1; 24:2, 15; 1 Kgs 4:25) can be dated to the eighth century BCE at the earliest.

From the Bible all we learn about Jeroboam is that he reigned 41 years, that he was a great warrior, and that in his days there was a prophet named Jonah ben Amittai (2 Kgs 14:23-28). The date given in Amos 1:1 could be authentic, since it admits the vassalage of Judah, but Amos' prophecy against Jeroboam is legendary (Amos 7:10-17). How much text in the Book of Amos goes back to the eighth century BCE is hard to say. Jeroboam built up Dan (Stratum II), smashed the stela Hazael had set up at the gate of the city, and established fortresses at Kinneret (II), Hazor (VI), Megiddo (IV), and probably at Gezer and Jokneam. Jeroboam II was the only Israelite king who ruled over Hazor, Megiddo, and Gezer, a feat 1 Kings 9:15 attributes to Solomon along with Jeroboam's trade in horses between Egypt and Assyria (1 Kgs 10:28-29). The large "stables" of Megiddo with the arsenal, barracks, and warehouses beside them might have been part of the horse export infrastructure (Cantrell 2011). After the experience of 841–837 BCE at Damascus, when the fortress was inaccessible to the Assyrian army that flooded the countryside, Jeroboam II stopped relying on a mobile field army. Instead, every town was fortified to withstand sieges. Whatever archival material is transmitted in the tribal lists of Galilee in Joshua 19 originates from the administration of Jeroboam II. He participated in Phoenician trading expeditions in the Negev. Inscriptions recovered from Kuntillet 'Ajrud, a caravan station in the Sinai, shed light on Phoenician, Israelite, and Judahite religion (Hadley 2000).

As Jeroboam I could not have built the royal temples of Bethel and Dan, it must be Jeroboam II who set up the golden "calves" there (1 Kgs 12:26-30). These bull images were either small statues representing the pedestal of the invisible YHWH or symbols of his power and strength (Figure 22).

Every Israel but the first was defined by the worship of YHWH as its god. The control of religion by the state at the temples of Bethel and Dan, in addition to the elusive temple in Samaria, was meant to serve the peripheral areas of the kingdom. Although 1 Kings 12:26 presents Jeroboam's action as an anti-Jerusalem measure, 1 Kings 12:28 is an accurate description of Jeroboam's religious programme: "These are your gods, O Israel, which brought you out of Egypt." The religion of Israel in the eighth century BCE was both iconic and polytheistic (Figure 23).

100   A History of Biblical Israel

Figure 22: The bull pedestal of the storm god on a stele from Tell Ahmar (Syria) is reflected in the story of the Golden Bull in Exodus 32 (after Keel 2007, 126).

Figure 23: One of 600 ivory fragments from Nimshide Samaria: the Horus child in a lotus blossom, a typical Egyptian motif, originally inlaid with gold, glass, and lapis-lazuli (after Crowford and Crowford 1938, #1,1).

Beside YHWH stood the wife he had inherited from El (Dever 2005). When the Assyrians conquered Samaria, they deported several divine images from the temple.

4.7 In the Shadow of Ashur

After a six-month reign, Jeroboam's son Zechariah was assassinated by Shallum, who succumbed to the hand of Menahem a month later. According to 2 Kings 15:12, the death of Zechariah marked the end of Jehu's dynasty and the fulfilment of the promise that his sons would sit on the throne of Israel to the fourth generation. Menahem, who seems to have been the governor of Tirzah (2 Kgs 15:14), managed to rule for 10 years (2 Kgs 15:8-16; see also Hos. 8:4). The difference in Israel's fortunes between Jeroboam II and Menahem may be due to the erasure of some Israelite kings in between to obtain the same number of kings as is recorded for Judah. In 738 BCE, Tiglath-pileser III conquered Hamath and received from Menahem a tribute of 1,000 talents of silver (3 tonnes) in exchange for being confirmed over Israel (2 Kgs 15:19). Second Kings 15:20 explains that Menahem's tribute was raised from each member of the elite, 50 shekels a head. In exchange, Pul (Tiglath-pileser) did not set foot on Israelite territory. Depending on whether one sets the talent at 3,000 or 3,600 shekels, the tribute payers numbered 50,000 to 60,000 men, from whom the total population can be estimated at 350,000 people, a number so large that it would include Judah. This is the first evidence of the collection of tax in Israel. It is also an indicator of general prosperity. Fifty shekels were roughly the equivalent of two slaves. These figures refute the notion of a widespread impoverishment of the peasantry during the eighth century BCE popularized by "social scientific" theologians (Gottwald 1979; Chaney 1993) from texts such as Amos 2:6-8; 3:10; 4:1-2, and 5:7, 10-12.

4.8 Religion and Literature in the Eighth Century BCE

State formation became noticeable in the iconography as representations of imperial symbolism. Instead of being the Lord of the Crocodiles, the Lord of the Ostrich, and the Mistress of Animals (Figure 24), three symbols of fertility, Baal-Hadad was given attributes celebrating cosmic order and stability.

The sun god (popular as the supreme god of imperial states such as Egypt) previously played no major role in Palestine except perhaps in the local cult in Jerusalem (Niehr 1997; Uehlinger 1997; Na'aman, 1999). By now, the supreme god had become the state god (Baalshamim, YHWH-El), the guarantor of cosmic order enforced on earth by the state. In Israel, the high quality of Egyptian-Phoenician representations reflects the

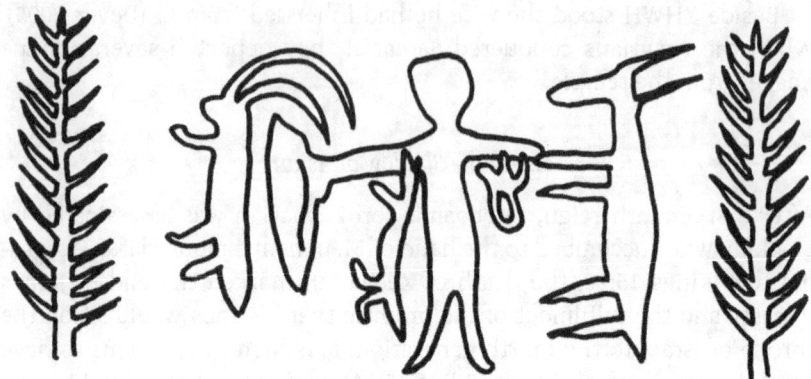

Figure 24: Crude "Lord of the Animals" on a cylinder seal from Ta'anach. The Lord of the Animals motif was common on mass-produced seals produced in Egypt and widely distributed as amulets in the Levant (after *GGG* #197b).

economic prosperity of the kingdom (*GGG* 246, 250b), while Judah remained very provincial (*GGG* 265a, 267a). Only towards the end of the eighth century BCE did Judah display proper seal cutting (*GGG* 274d).

According to the inscriptions of Kuntillet 'Ajrud and Khirbet el-Qom (near Hebron), YHWH had a wife named Asherah and thus took the role of the god El (*GGG* 268abc; 210). Seals, of course, only provide limited information about the religion of the layer of society that owned seals. Below the level of state religion, there was local (or regional) and family religion. Well-known local gods were worshiped in Beersheba and Dan (Amos 8:14). The seal of a priest of Dor was found in the port city of Dor. It does not state which god this priest served. In the Samaria ostraca, some names are formed with the Baal element instead of the YHWH element, but that does not mean that the Manassites worshipped two different gods.

The stories relative to the House of David transmitted at the court of Jerusalem were given a broader outlook by integrating the ideology of the Nimshides, possibly in order to cope with the earthquake that had caused much damage in Jerusalem around 760 BCE. This earthquake is well attested in the archaeological record (Megiddo IV). It is also mentioned in Amos 1:1 and 9:1 and possibly in Isaiah 6. With the oldest layers of the David stories, these references indicate the beginning of the Isaiah and Amos formation now contained in books of later dates. In Israel, the Exodus tradition was militarized (Exodus 14). Other Israelite collections that found their way into the Bible (Judges 3–12, 4–11; the Elisha cycle in 2 Kings; Hosea) emerged after the downfall of the kingdom (724–720 BCE).

CHAPTER 5
FROM TIGLATH-PILESER TO ASHURBANIPAL:
THE INTEGRATION OF LEVANTINE KINGDOMS
IN THE NEO-ASSYRIAN REALM

The integration of Israel and its neighbours into the Neo-Assyrian orbit marks Manasseh's reign as the climax of the kingdom of Judah and the ideological context of the Deuteronomistic literature.

The Assyrian supremacy over Syria deeply affected relations between Israel and Judah. Israel became the Assyrian province of Samaria; Judah remained a vassal state, formally independent. Most importantly, the Israelite economy regressed to pre-Omride levels and the centre of power shifted southwards. Not having a navy, the Assyrians could never fully control the Phoenician cities, and rebellious Phoenician vassals repeatedly escaped by sea. Since Assyria could never trust the Phoenicians, the Assyrians isolated the Phoenician cities and hindered the overland movement of goods to and from Tyre and Sidon. Instead, the Assyrians favoured Ekron and Gaza, which benefited from their position further south along the East-West trade route between Arabia and the Mediterranean. Philistia again became a hub for long-distance trade, with consequences similar to those seen in the tenth century BCE. In the Phoenician periphery, Israel declined, while Judah flourished in the periphery of a booming Philistia (Figure 25). For the first time, in 727 BCE, an Assyrian inscription mentioned Judah (Cogan 2008, 51–60). Whereas in the ninth century Hazael and Mesha only knew the House of David, a tribal government, under Uzziah Judah had become a bureaucratic state, about a hundred years after Israel.

From the three to five hectares it covered at the time of David and Solomon, the city of Jerusalem grew from between six and eight hectares in 750 BCE to 20 hectares in 700, and up to 50 or 60 hectares in the seventh century BCE. Lachish III was converted into a military and administrative centre comparable to Megiddo IV under Jeroboam II (Herzog 1997, 236–249) (Figure 26).

104 A History of Biblical Israel

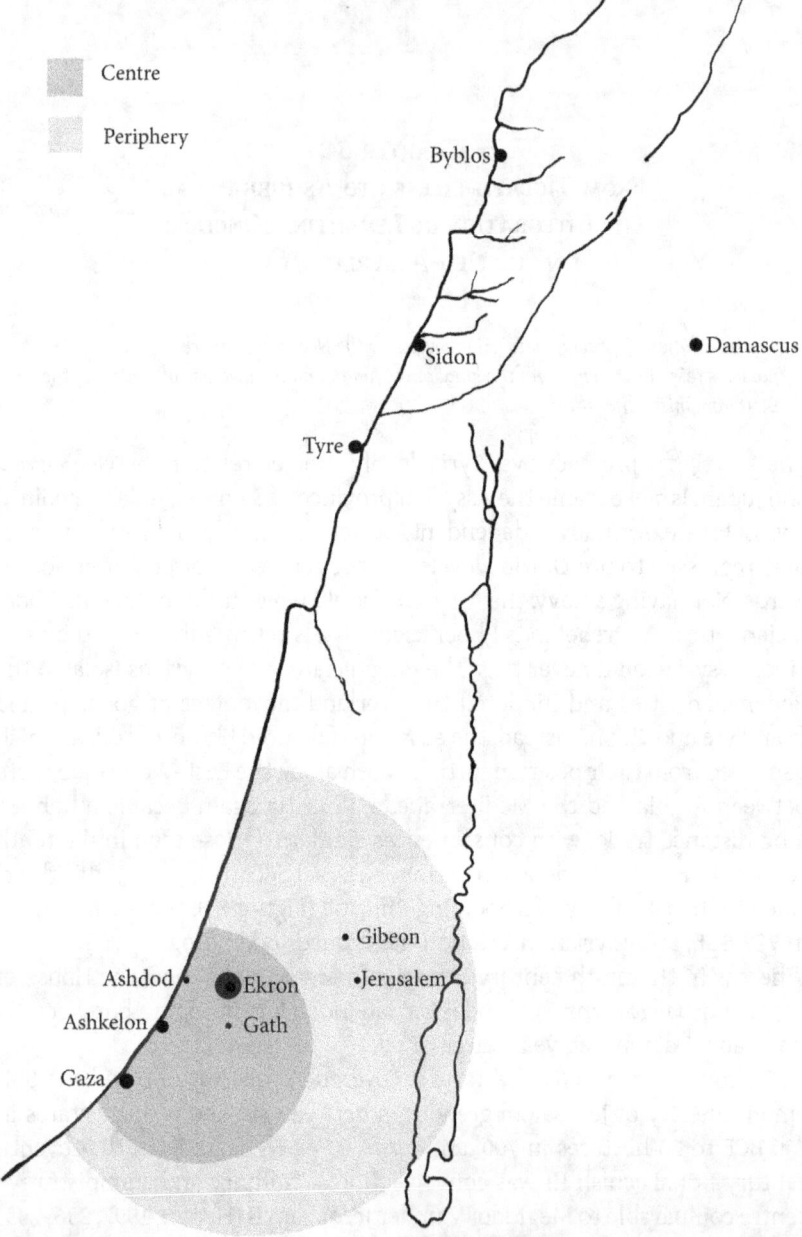

Figure 25:   Centre and periphery in the seventh century BCE (T. Guillaume).

5. From Tiglath-Pileser to Ashurbanipal

Figure 26: Golden seal of Shema, minister of Jeroboam II (לשמע עבד ירבעם) found at Megiddo, now stolen. The lion was and remains a symbol of royalty (after *GGG* #205a).

5.1 Tiglath-pileser III

The birth of the Neo-Assyrian Empire can be set in 734–732 BCE, when Tiglath-pileser III managed to put an end to the constant struggle between Samaria and Damascus, the two regional powers of equal force that had fought each other throughout the ninth and eighth centuries BCE but were able to block any Assyrian western expansion whenever they got together to fight a common enemy. Until then, Assyria had only played the role of third party in the Israel-Damascus-Assyria triangle, first with Shalmaneser III, then Adadnerari III in the days of Hazael. After the last foray of Shalmaneser IV towards Damascus (773 BCE), Assyria fell into a deep slumber until the reign of Tiglath-pileser III. At first, the Syrian kingdoms thought they could use the Assyrians as an ally against their immediate neighbours and continue playing the power game of the last two hundred years. Inherited from Egyptian imperialism of the second millennium, this brand of power politics was satisfied by occasional forays into Canaan to collect tribute, which was then displayed back home for the glorification of the pharaoh. Such a model of limited dominance was no longer adequate in the Iron Age, when long-distance trade required open borders. Hence, a new kind of empire that was far more effective arose with the Neo-Assyrians. An empire can be defined as an

> expansive and incorporative kind of state, involving relationships in which one state exercises control over other socio-political entities (e.g. states, chiefdoms, non-stratified societies), and [...] imperialism as the process of creating and maintaining empires. The diverse polities and communities that constitute an empire

typically retain some degree of autonomy—in self- and centrally-defined cultural identity, and in some dimensions of political and economic decision making.

(Sinopoli 1994, 160)

Due to the larger geographical size or the larger population they control, empires have to make a greater display of military force to suppress rebellions and express greater manifestations of ideology to sustain loyalty than is the case with more limited territorial entities such as tribes and states.

With Tiglath-pileser III (745–728 BCE), symbol politics gave way to *realpolitik*. Whenever a vassal state rebelled, it was lucky if it lost only the best part of its territory, as happened to Israel in 733 BCE. On a second instance, the rest of the kingdom would be turned into an Assyrian province, as happened to Damascus in 732 BCE. If the local king remained on his throne, he was flanked by an Assyrian governor and an Assyrian administration that made his rule nominal. Deportations were the motor of the Empire. Occasional deportations had occurred back in the second millennium under Adad-Nerari I (1295–1263 BCE); they now became systematic. Contrary to the idea conveyed by the Book of Kings, only the state apparatus and the military officials were deported, not the entire population. Being deported was not necessarily a hardship for the deportees. They were simply displaced to the opposite end of the Empire, where they continued to exercise their previous occupations.

Deportation severed their ties of loyalty to their own people, and instead introduced loyalty to the Empire. When the deportees found themselves serving the Empire as a small minority in the midst of a foreign people, they had to secure their position through loyalty to Assyria. In return, they retained their elite status. Being part of the imperial administration offered more opportunities for ambitious individuals than if they had remained at home. The growing Empire needed a unified official and administrative language: this was the Imperial Aramaic, which was used for everyday administrative matters in addition to one's own ancestral languages or dialects. Only the highest echelon of the Assyrian administration employed scribes versed in cuneiform Akkadian, which was used for the annals and for inscriptions that were viewed by only a very few people. The Aramaic version of the annals has not survived, but we know that it existed. Assyrian reliefs show the Great King on the battlefield dictating to two scribes: one, who holds a clay tablet and a stylus, is writing in Akkadian, while the other has a piece of leather or papyrus and a pen for writing in Aramaic.

Before Tiglath-pileser, the Assyrian army was superior to that of its opponents only in numbers, so there were setbacks. However, from Tiglath-pileser III to Ashurbanipal (668–627 BCE), the Assyrian military history reads like one long ongoing victory, not only because Assyrian propaganda disguised defeats but because of new techniques. Before the Neo-Assyrians, armies consisted mostly of chariot troops and foot soldiers with a spear and shield and maybe a dagger or short sword (Judg. 5:6). Contrary to popular perceptions and iconographic representations, chariots did not crush everything in front of them. The Persians tried using chariots in this way, with no success. A chariot was nothing other than a mobile platform for archers (Spalinger 2005). Placing elite archers on a chariot was costly. It required a driver and at least two horses besides the chariot but it offered no strategic advantage when faced with archers equipped with composite bows. Made of several materials, such a bow could propel six arrows per minute at a distance of 400 m. At 50 m, the arrows penetrated any armour. Half of the Neo-Assyrian infantry was equipped with composite bows, the other half were spearmen with large shields to protect the archers. Against such an army, any Syro-Palestinian levy stood no chance. Although Assyria kept some chariot corps, the development of the cavalry in the ninth century BCE made it superfluous. The Assyrian records of the battle of Qarqar list as many riders as chariots, meaning that the riders were on the reserve horses that went with each chariot. At first, the horse was no more than a higher platform for archers, but they were also far more economical since each rider needed only one horse, compared with two or four for a chariot. Nevertheless, chariots retained prestige for several hundred years.

Assyria was irresistible for two reasons, geographic and temporal. First, it was able to project its power further and displace the theatre of war far from the Assyrian heartland. Being able to raid far-away areas rather than just the adjacent neighbour reduced the likelihood of retaliatory raids, which would instead be endured by vassal states or provinces that served as a buffer zone. Second, the logistics of Assyria's standing army were such that the army could organize campaigns outside the traditional warring season of mid-October to mid-December (Andersson 2011). Setting off in the spring before the heat of the summer, and while the targets of the campaign were busy with the harvest, enabled the army to feed itself on the ripening corn and to disrupt the harvest to such a extent that either famine would strike the area in the following spring, or the lack of agricultural surpluses would at least weaken its economy while the Assyrians financed their wars on the back of their conquests.

Nothing illustrates the brutality of the imperial thrust better than the statistics for the Luwian inscriptions produced by the kingdoms of northern Syria (Hawkins 2000). The number of inscriptions rises between the twelfth and the first half of the eighth century BCE, reflecting the burgeoning economy of the time. With Tiglath-pileser III and his immediate successors, this thriving literary culture ends abruptly.

In 738 BCE, Tiglath-pileser subjected Hamath, making Assyria the immediate neighbour of Damascus and of the Israel of Jeroboam II. Together with Byblos and Tyre, Damascus and Israel submitted (Cogan 2008, 51-60).

Between 737 and 735 BCE, the Assyrians had their hands full in the north and east of their empire, leaving the Syro-Palestinian kings under the impression that the tribute they paid in 738 was a one-off occurrence. King Razyān of Damascus may have tried to revive the anti-Assyrian coalition of 853–845 BCE (Na'aman 1995). This could explain Pekah's coup (736/735 BCE) against Menahem's successor Pekahiah, who was murdered after reigning for two years (2 Kgs 15:25). It is likely that the Assyrians were pulling the strings, since in the same year Tiglath-pileser pushed on as far as Gaza to cut off any Egyptian support for the coalition and to avoid a repetition of the events of 853 BCE.

Northern Israel was probably devastated in 733 BCE (Cogan 2008, 76–79; 2 Kgs 15:29). Although the Eponym Chronicle states that the campaigns of 733 and 732 BCE were directed solely against Damascus, Tiglath-pileser mentions in passing previous campaigns on the occasion of the change of ruler in Israel in 732 BCE (Cogan 2008, 72). In this year, Damascus was an Assyrian province. In Israel Pekah was murdered by Hoshea ben Elah, whom Tiglath-pileser confirmed as vassal (Cogan 2008, 61) over the Samarian mountains and possibly also over Gilead, which was not an Assyrian province (Cogan 2008, 60). Galilee and the Jezreel Valley were assigned to the new province of Megiddo, while the Sharon plain became the Province of Dor. Israel was thus cut off from its best agricultural land and from direct access to maritime trade.

In 734 BCE, the Judaean king Ahaz seems to have refused to give the military support his Israelite suzerain requested against Assyria. To resist intimidation from Samaria and Damascus, Ahaz asked for Assyria's support. Contrary to what happened to Jehu in 841 BCE, Ahaz's calculation proved right. After the conquest of Gaza, Tiglath-pileser mentions tribute paid by Arabs, but no Judaean tribute. Ahaz's name appears again in the Assyrian records in 732 and 727 BCE. Judah's subjection to Israel, which Jehoshaphat had inaugurated, thus came to an end.

What is commonly referred to as the "Syrian-Ephraimite war" was unimportant in itself, but it gained much significance as the event that triggered the formation of a collection of oracles spoken by prophetesses and prophets. As the nucleus of the biblical Book of Isaiah, this collection was created to support the legitimacy of the pro-Assyrian diplomacy of Ahaz, and later of Manasseh. Despite the anti-Assyrian and anti-monarchical revisions, a collection of sayings from 734 BCE can be identified in Isaiah 7:4–8:4:

> [7:4] Do not let your heart be faint because of these two smouldering stumps of firebrands, because of the fierce anger of Rezin and Aram and the son of Remaliah. [7:5] Because Aram with Ephraim has plotted evil against you, saying, [7:6] Let us go up against Judah and 6d make the son of Tabeel king in it; [7:7] therefore thus says the Lord GOD: It shall not stand, and it shall not come to pass. [...]

[7:14] Look, the young woman is with child and shall bear a son, and shall name him Immanuel. [7:15] He shall eat curds and honey by the time he knows how to refuse the evil and choose the good [= things will be fine for us]. [7:16] For before the child knows how to refuse the evil and choose the good [= the next three years], the land before whose two kings you are in dread will be deserted. [...] [8:4] for before the child knows how to call "My father" or "My mother," the wealth of Damascus and the spoil of Samaria will be carried away by the king of Assyria.

Naturally, the Bible represents the events as if Judah had hired the Assyrians against its two enemies (2 Kgs 16:5-9). Assyria complied for reasons of its own. For Judah, the transition from Israelite to Assyrian dependency was quite a climb. Neutrality was not an option.

The fall of Damascus marked the end of the last Aramaean state, the kingdom Hazael had built out of the tribal-state of the tenth and ninth centuries BCE and which had enabled him to compete with Assyria for supremacy over Syria. Isaiah 10:9 summarizes the situation nicely:

> Is not Calno like Carchemish? Is not Hamath like Arpad? Is not Samaria like Damascus?

The largest part of the kingdom of Jeroboam II was now an Assyrian province; the kingdom of Israel was reduced to the size of Saul's Israel, the mountains of Ephraim. Judah, Ammon, Moab, and Edom became Assyrian vassals without a fight. Assyria ruled from the Euphrates to the Brook of Egypt, the extent of the land promised to Abram in Genesis 15:18.

5.2 The Demise of Israel as Kingdom (727-720 BCE)

At the end of the eighth century BCE, Samaria and Jerusalem expected Assyria to disappear from the horizon, as had happened between 836 and 797 BCE. Israel and Judah underestimated Assyria as much as they overestimated Egypt. After the loss of its supremacy in southern Syria in the middle of the ninth century, Egypt split into a series of small kingdoms, but its reputation in Canaan remained intact and Egyptian help was sought in the hope of resisting Assyria. The Egyptians lent a weak hand since the Assyrian conquest of Gaza in 734 BCE threatened the Nile Delta.

In 727 BCE, Hosea, the last king of Israel, judged that the death of Tiglath-pileser III was the right moment to break Assyria's yoke. This blunder reveals the political immaturity of the Samarian court. Hosea imagined that his subjugation to Tiglath-pileser was terminated by the death of Tiglath-pileser; for the Assyrians, however, the rule over the city of the god Ashur had no end. Shalmaneser V imprisoned Hosea (2 Kgs 17:1-6) and Samaria was besieged for three years. The Assyrian texts mention three sieges of Samaria: by Shalmaneser V, and then by Sargon II in 722 BCE and again in connection with the submission of Hamath in 720 BCE

(CoS 2.110–111, 118A, 118D–E). The various data can be harmonized so that 727 BCE corresponds to the change of rulers from Tiglath-pileser III to Shalmaneser V when, encouraged by the Egyptians (2 Kgs 17:4; Hos. 7:11), Hosea stopped paying the tribute. In 724 BCE, Shalmaneser V captured Hosea and had it recorded as the conquest of Samaria, although the city was not breached. The campaign was interrupted by the change of ruler from Shalmaneser V to Sargon II in 722 BCE. Finally, Sargon captured the city in 720 BCE.

The elite, that is, most of the population of Samaria, was deported to Assyria, which remained underpopulated in 700 BCE (Fales and Postgate 1995, 121–145). Some Israelites emigrated to Egypt and were settled in military colonies (Hos. 8:13; 9:3-6; 11:5, 11), but most of them remained in the country. Most revered YHWH, whose cult at Bethel was not yet aniconic (2 Kgs 17:27-28). The notion of a mass exodus of the Israelites into Judah at this time is baseless (Na'aman 2007b, 2014; Guillaume 2008). Farmer mobility was always a reality, but people did not emigrate *en masse*. The rapid growth of Jerusalem before or after 700 BCE is the result of the consolidation of statehood within Judah, and the reception of Israelite traditions in Judah at the end of the seventh century BCE reflects the influence of the sanctuary of Bethel, which is much closer geographically to Jerusalem than to Samaria. The alleged north-Israelite influences in the Siloam inscriptions are statistically insufficient to support the notion of a massive arrival of refugees fleeing the Assyrians (against Rendsburg and Schniedewind 2010).

The city of Samaria itself was not depopulated. Sargon claims that he rebuilt the city after 716 BCE and made it bigger and better (Becking 1992). We have no reason to doubt his word on the matter. The Israelite elite were simply replaced by the Assyrian governor and his entourage, most of them deportees from other parts of the empire (Na'aman and Zadok 2000). Hence, the excavations of Samaria did not identify Assyrian levels because the transition from Israel's capital to the seat of an Assyrian province did not translate into any visible changes in architecture and material culture. At the provincial capital of Megiddo, the changes were more drastic. The fortress of Jeroboam II (Megiddo IV) was destroyed. The city was rebuilt on a completely different plan after 716 BCE (Megiddo III). The residences for the provincial government covered about 20% of the city (compared with 75% of Megiddo IV occupied by administrative buildings). The remaining 80% were private houses in streets aligned on an impressive checkerboard pattern, the so-called Hippodamian grid, which obviously was not a Greek invention. Megiddo III was once again a city, which Megiddo IV had not been. The reconstructions at Samaria and Megiddo correspond to the time of the first deportation of Arabs to Israel/Palestine (CoS 2.118; Becking 1992, 111–112). Tellingly, no name in the list of 2 Kings 17 has a clear Arabian origin. The story is a polemic against Samaria, claiming that the cult rendered to YHWH north of Israel is heterodox. The story also presupposes the myth of the empty Judean land, which emerged around 400 BCE. Yet, the plague of lions evoked for the return of an Israelite priest to Bethel (2 Kgs 17:26-28) is a faithful reflection of the consequences of the southward shift of the economic hub of the Levant at the time. The Ephraimite highland around Samaria lost out to Bethel and to the Benjamin region, which were closer to the booming Assyrian centre at Ekron. If an Israelite migration did indeed occur, it was an internal migration that saw a decrease in the population in the region of Samaria, which in turn fostered reforestation and the multiplication of large predators such as lions. The maintenance of the existing capital was economically meaningless, but it made political sense to assert Assyrian domination as the legitimate successor of the Israelite kingdom; hence, Sargon's boast to have beautified Samaria.

Assyrian officials also resided at Hazor (IV-III) and Kinneret (I). Assyrian economic and administrative texts were retrieved from Gezer, Tel Hadid, and Samaria (Becking 1992, 112–118; Na'aman and Zadok 2000). The personal names are mostly Babylonian or Assyrian. A minority are Aramaic, but Judean names are found in Gezer and Israelite names at Tel Hadid. Difficulties in the collection of the grain tax in Samaria are attested (Becking 1992, 107–108), confirming that collecting grain from the threshing-floor never was an easy task. The amount collected was proportional to the force mobilized to supervise the harvest; farmers had an array of methods at their disposal to evade tax (Judg. 6:11), all the more so in depressed areas like the Ephraimite mountains where the Assyrian administration could not control what was going on in scattered farmsteads. The Pax Assyriaca rendered the safety of walled settlements redundant and enabled the Israelites to live in isolated villages of one hundred to five hundred inhabitants (Amos 5:3), as well as hamlets and isolated rural estates in the more exposed lowlands. The agricultural conquest of the plains led to a reforestation of the mountains that was accelerated by the ethnic division of labour of the imperial state, which assigned the livestock industry to the Arabs, who exploited the resources of the desert fringe rather than in the highlands.

The Samarians, the Samaritans of the Hellenistic period and after, are the descendants of the ancient Israelites. The search for the "10 lost tribes of Israel" is absurd, because these tribes were never lost. The Samaritans claim to be the true Israelites, and the claim is correct insofar as the Israelite-Samaritan language sides with Phoenician vis-à-vis Judean and Aramaic. While the lateral /s2/ sound evolved into *sin* in Judean and Aramaic, in Phoenician and Israelite it became *shin*. As attested by Egyptian and Assyrian transcriptions of the name "Israel," the Israelites pronounced it

"Yishrael" instead of "Israel" and this remained the pronunciation of the Samaritans.

The demise of the kingdom of Israel did not mark the end of the existence of Israel. On the contrary, the story of biblical Israel is just beginning now, and 734 BCE is perhaps the most important date in this story. The traditions of Israel and Judah became what they are today when they were used to address Assyrian, Babylonian, and Persian imperialism and its religious expressions. Judah soon claimed the legacy of Israel for itself when the fall of the kingdom of Israel left Judah as the only surviving state that named its main divinity YHWH. Hence, instead of wiping out Israel, the demise of Israel in 720 BCE resulted in two Israels.

5.3 The Integration of Judah into the Neo-Assyrian Empire (720-701 BCE)

In 716 BCE, Sargon II also received tribute from Egypt (*ANET* 286-287). From now on, Assyria was the only superpower. Nevertheless, Ashdod, along with the rest of Philistia, Judah, Edom, and Moab, rebelled in 712 BCE. Only Ashdod was crushed in 711 BCE (*CoS* 2.118E-F in *ANET* 286; cf. Isa. 20:1). Misinterpreting the absence of significant retaliation, Ashdod's allies rebelled again in 705 BCE upon hearing about Sargon's death on the battlefield, taking the Assyrians' inability to recover Sargon's body and give it a proper burial as a sign of divine wrath against Assyria (Cogan 2008, 103-105; see also Isa. 14:4-20). It took several years for Sennacherib, Sargon's son and successor, to impose his authority over Babylonia, which, since Tiglath-pileser III, had been ruled in a personal union. During that time, Sidon, Ashkelon, and Judah took an anti-Assyrian stance, and the pro-Assyrian King Padi of Ekron was imprisoned in Jerusalem (*CoS* 2.119B). The Twenty-Fifth Kushite Dynasty that took over in Egypt (712-664 BCE) supported these efforts, hoping to shift the Assyrian threat away from Gaza and the approaches of the Nile Delta.

In anticipation of possible Assyrian retaliation, Hezekiah expanded the city walls of Jerusalem to protect the southeast hill (Ophel and Temple Mount) and the southwestern hill (later named "Zion" by Christian clerics, and still known as such today), in order to accommodate 12,000-15,000 people. This far exceeded the population of Jerusalem, despite the boost the Arabian-Philistine trade gave to the Judean economy, meaning that the extended fortification was meant to offer temporary shelter to most Judeans when the Assyrian troops came to devastate the countryside. The distribution of the older royal stamps on storage jars suggests that supplies from the royal demesne were stockpiled in the city. The so-called "Hezekiah tunnel" at Siloam has nothing to do with Hezekiah. The water Hezekiah brought into the city (2 Kgs 20:20; Isa. 7:3; 36:2 // 2 Kgs 18:17) came from the north. The subterranean chamber source of Siloam was already accessible through a tunnel (Reich 2011). It is only in Sirach 48:17, dating to the Hellenistic period, that the impression is given that Hezekiah is associated with the tunnel and pool of Siloam.

Sennacherib's campaign of 701 BCE is one of the best documented moments of Judah's past, thanks to Sennacherib's reports (*CoS* 2.119B–D) and to 2 Kings 18:13-16, which is embellished in Isaiah 36–39. Isaiah 37:9 and 2 Kings 19:9 mention King Tirhakah of Egypt, who ruled from 690 to 664 BCE and was remembered because he lost his land to Esarhaddon. Isaiah 30:1-3 and 31:1-3 appear as "prophecy from the event" (*vaticinia ex eventu*) because they presuppose the neutral stance that characterizes the theology of the Book of Isaiah.[1] Elements of pro-Assyrian or pro-Babylonian propaganda may be reflected in Isaiah 30–31, but they do not have to come from the years 705–701 BCE. Sennacherib's records of the 701 BCE campaign are arranged geographically to give the impression of an unbroken victorious sweep across the Levant, but judging by the results of the campaign, this was not so. The return of King Padi to the throne of Ekron does not imply the defeat of Hezekiah.

Sennacherib's first victim was King Luli of Sidon, who escaped by sea and ceded the throne to the pro-Assyrian Ittobaal. We learn on this occasion that the territory of Sidon reached as far south as Acco. Tyre is not listed among the other coastal cities that paid tribute in 701 BCE. Ashdod learned its lesson in 711 BCE and was the only Philistine city to pay homage while Sennacherib was still in Sidon. Ammon, Moab, and Edom probably waited until after the showdown to pay their tribute to the victor. The war against Ashkelon took place around Jaffa. The people of the city were soon convinced they should free their pro-Assyrian king with his followers and his family. After Elteqeh and Timnah, Sennacherib turned against Hezekiah. The 46 fortresses Sennacherib claims to have conquered (2 Kgs 18:13) lay in the Shephelah and perhaps in the western Negev. The Judean mountains and Benjamin lay beyond Sennacherib's destructions. Sennacherib's main focus was Lachish, which was depicted in a series of reliefs in his palace (Uehlinger 2002; Figure 27).

After the capitulation of Lachish, Hezekiah freed Padi (2 Kgs 18:14). Hezekiah and Sennacherib had every interest in avoiding a lengthy confrontation, meaning that Jerusalem was not besieged. Meanwhile, an Egyptian force was approaching. Sennacherib's battle-weary troops wavered and Sennacherib himself had to join the fray, barely saving the day (Knauf 2003). In the short version of the report (*ANET* 288), Sennacherib speaks only of Sidon and Judah.

---

[1] Such "I told you so" prophecies are common in the Hebrew Bible.

Figure 27: Detail of the conquest of Lachish depicted on reliefs found in Sennacherib's palace at Nineveh, today in the British Museum. (a) Deportees leaving with entire families and animals. The skinning of two rebels in the lower register underlines the desirability of the status of the deportees. (b) An Assyrian siege machine ramming the city wall while a soldier pours water to quench the fire lit by torches thrown down by the city defenders (Judith Dekel in Ussishkin 1982, 86, 100).

Sources differ regarding the size of the tribute imposed on Hezekiah. According to 2 Kings 18:14, it amounted to 300 talents of silver and 30 talents of gold, an astronomical sum. The 30 talents of gold, 800 talents of silver and soldiers and princesses in CoS 2.119B correspond to a normal annual tribute. The conquered area was devastated. The Judean Shephelah was given to Ashdod, Ekron, and Gaza, which apparently had remained neutral.

The loss of the lowlands was a severe blow to Judah because it was the economic centre of the kingdom. Hezekiah's successors had to compensate for the loss as a means to continue to pay the tribute. Yet, in 701 BCE, Jerusalem was not the "watchman's hut in a cucumber field" (Isa. 1:5-8) that it became in the third century BCE. Also, the 200,150 people Sennacherib claims to have deported could not have all come from Judah, because the total population of the kingdom came to only half that number. The total, however, could include the casualties and prisoners of the whole campaign (including the Assyrians) or the total number of prisoners, including horses, mules, donkeys, camels, cattle, sheep, and goats. But the essential fact is undisputed: that Hezekiah led his kingdom to disaster. The annalists expressed their disapproval through an account of a disease that almost killed Hezekiah (2 Kgs 20:1). Nevertheless, Hezekiah was later glorified as a zealot for YHWH and was remembered as having initiated a cultic reform (2 Kgs 18:3-8).

5.4 Judah's Neighbours: Ammon, Moab, Edom, the Arabs, and the Philistines

According to the biblical scenario, 720 BCE closed the unfortunate parenthesis opened by Jeroboam I. The "fall" of Israel only marks the end of the kingdom, but from the point of view of the biblical writers, it allowed them to ignore further events north of Benjamin and to turn their full attention to Jerusalem and, to a lesser extent, on the Edomites and Arabs. Ammon and Moab entered the scene in the ninth century BCE in secondary roles. Ammon's incipient statehood is mentioned on a fragmentary inscription recovered from the citadel of 'Amman (Aḥituv 2005, 329 with additions by Knauf):

1. Milcom said to me: "Build yourself accesses all around
2. Whoever besieges they shall surely die
3. I shall thoroughly annihilate them but all who surrender
4. and in all chambers the righteous shall stay overnight."

The text records a command by the patron deity of the Ammonite kingdom, Milcom (1 Kgs 11:5, 33; 2 Kgs 23:13). The god orders the king to build a temple fortress and implies the presence of prophets serving as mouthpieces of the main deity in Ammon to as great an extent as there were prophets in Israel.

Thanks to their position on the Kings' Road (Num. 20:17; 21:22), which connects northern Arabia with Damascus, both Ammon and Moab drew benefits from the long-distance trade networks as suppliers to the caravans and the Assyrian garrisons that protected the routes from raiders. This favourable economic *conjoncture* promoted a significant demographic increase, with a population whose size would only be outdone in Roman times (second to sixth centuries CE) and in the twentieth century CE. They were no longer tributary to Israel and Damascus, though too backward for the Assyrians to turn them into provinces. First, statehood had to be consolidated in Ammon and Moab, and this process is visible in the Amman citadel inscription and in personal letters. According to the tribute list, Ammon paid twice as much tribute as Moab, whose territory was larger, and Moab paid twice as much as Judah (*ANET* 301).

While the rise of statehood in Ammon and Moab can be explained by their ability to produce agricultural supplies locally to service the trade routes, in Edom, which lies mostly outside the 250-mm isohyet where dry farming is no longer possible, the growth of incipient stages of statehood was due to the presence of iron and copper ore around Fainan. Copper was exploited there during the ninth century BCE by the Omrides and Hazael and again by the Assyrians in the seventh century BCE. There were Edomite chiefs prior to the seventh century BCE as there had been in Ammon and Moab before the ninth century BCE. But these chiefs who called themselves kings were merely kings *in* Edom or Moab (Gen. 36:32) rather than kings *of* Edom. Prior to the seventh century BCE, no significant trace of sedentary population is visible on the Edomite plateau. Edom was an appendage of Damascus and does not appear in the earlier Assyrian tribute lists. Once the Assyrians started investing resources and infrastructure in the Levant, they built a city at Bozrah to be the capital of the Edomites. Bozrah organized the distribution of the agricultural surpluses produced in the surrounding villages to the miners and the Assyrian troops. Nevertheless, Edom retained its tribal structure, as does modern Jordan, because most of the population had to remain mobile to survive, combining transhumance, irrigated agriculture, work in the mines, and transport services.

The Mediterranean revival also fostered demographic increases further south in Arabia. In the late eighth century BCE, Arabs appear regularly in Assyrian records, which tend to downplay their numbers. In 738 BCE, Zabibe, Queen the Arabs, paid tribute along with Israel and Damascus (Tadmor 1994, 105–108). Her successor, Samsi, submitted to Tiglath-pileser in the context of the conquest of Damascus (Tadmor 1994, 80, 228–229).

The Assyrian conquest of Gaza in 734 BCE forced Massa and Tema in the north (Gen. 25:13-15) and Sheba in the south to pay tribute; these cities were using Gaza as their Mediterranean outlet (Figure 28).

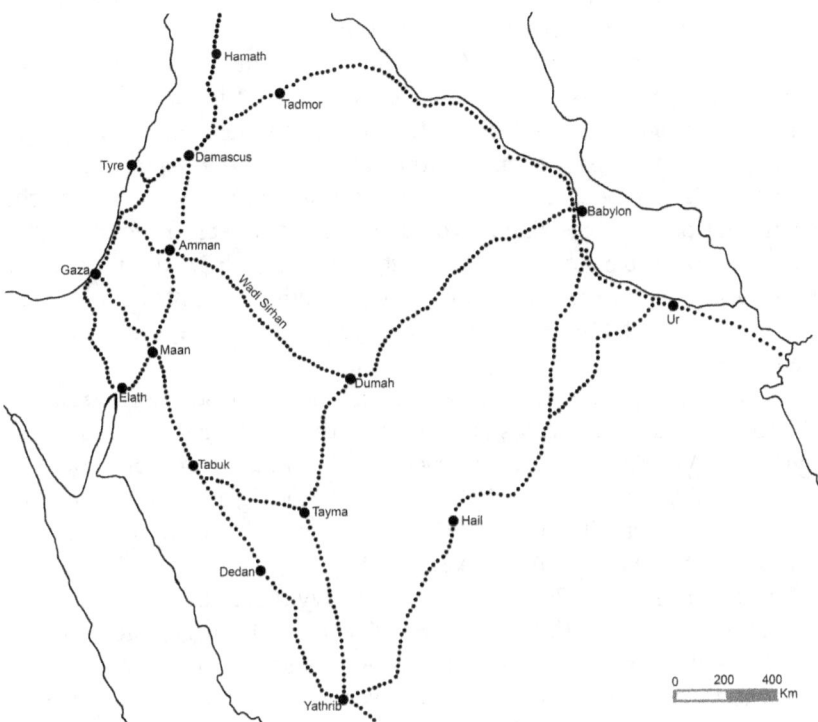

Figure 28: Arabian trade routes (T. Guillaume).

The cooperation between Sheba and Tema on the incense road had begun some 20 years earlier. They supplied frankincense, a resin tapped from bushes growing only in southern Arabia and Eritrea; as a dry good with a high per-weight value, frankincense was ideal for long-distance overland trade in the extreme conditions of Arabia and the Negev. The word for frankincense throughout the Mediterranean was *levona* ΛΙΒΑΝΟΣ (לבונה), a word that goes back to Sabean *lubān, rather than deriving from the geographical term, "Lebanon".

The tribe of Adbeel (Gen. 25:13) protected Assyria's frontier with Egypt. Roaming the Sinai with their large herds to secure the incense road, these tribes are the prototype of the Bedouin herding tribes that became a standard feature of Near Eastern fringes. The ethnonym "Arab" as *arubu* (Assyrian, Babylonian), *'rb* (Hebrew, Aramaic), and ΑΡΑΨ (Greek) is based on the Arabic designation for a nomad.

Hence, until the fourth century CE, in Arabic, "Arab" designated a nomad or a Bedouin. Today, Arabic speakers in the Levant do not consider themselves to be Arabs. For them, "Arab" remains a derogatory designation for the camel-herders of Arabia. The Assyrians considered the Arabian tribes to be serious political actors and treated them like other satellite peoples. Of the biblical sons of Ishmael (Gen. 25:12-15), Duma, Nebaioth, Naphish, Kedar, Tema', and Massa' appear in the Assyrian inscriptions of the eighth and seventh centuries BCE. The biblical Simeon derives from the same root as Ishmael and shares the same southern location in the Negev (Joshua 19; Judges 1). Sargon settled Arabs in Israel and Hezekiah settled some on the southern frontier of the kingdom of Judah, between Hebron and the Negev. Two Old-Arabic loanwords that are no longer current in Modern Arabic are preserved in biblical Hebrew: בכרת, "young camel" and צירה, "fold, pen" (Mic. 2:12; Isa. 1:8; Hab. 3:17), with its Imperial Aramaic equivalent טירה in Gen. 25:16.

By now, the Mediterranean revival spanned from southern Arabia to the south of Spain (Tartessos). Bringing southern Arabia into contact with Syria and Assyria, it spurred a process of secondary state formations in the tribal structure at Saba. Whereas in 734 BCE Tiglath-pileser recorded the Sabeans as a tribe, in 716 BCE Sargon designated the Sabean chief It'amra as the "man of Saba" (*ANET* 286a).

In Old Sabean inscriptions, Yitaʿamar Bayyin Sumuhū ali is *mukkarib*, probably a religious office held by the tribal chief. Then, Sennacherib designated Karib'il as the "king of Saba." At the same time, Karib'il Watar was the first *mukarrib* of Saba who took the title of king and subjected Saba's neighbours in Assyrian fashion. Since the second millennium BCE, Sabeans had formed agricultural tribes on the eastern and northern slopes of the Arabian Ridge, which benefited from rainfall. They also colonized the coast of Eritrea, where a descendant of the south Arabian script survives to this day. The strong aroma of incense was sought after to cover the stench of everyday life and gave rise to the legend of Arabia Felix, *felix* being a Latin mistranslation of Arabic *yaman* "right"; hence "south," the name of today's Yemen. The Queen of Sheba (1 Kings 11) was part and parcel of the legend.

The kingdoms of Hamath, Damascus, Ammon, Moab, and Edom left behind no political legacy, while the Philistines survive in the name "Palestine." The names on an inscription from Ekron preserve some typical Philistine elements (Gitin *et al.* 1997). 'Ikayuš, Assyrian *I-ka-ú-su*, and Hebrew אכיש, Achish in English, is a Philistine name borne by a king of Gath in the tenth century BCE (1 Samuel 27-29). The other names on the inscription are Canaanite (Paday, Yasud, 'Ada', Ya'ir). The letters are Phoenician, but the morphology is South Canaanite.

Ekron reached its heyday in the seventh century BCE. Over one hundred olive presses were found in the excavation of the city, revealing a specialization in oil production.

5.5 King Manasseh

At 55 years, the reign of Manasseh, the son and successor of Hezekiah, was the longest in Israel and Judah. Under his rule, the kingdom of Judah reached its economic peak, thanks to its integration into the trade networks and to the Pax Assyriaca (Ben Zvi 1996; Na'aman 2001; Knauf 2005b). Having learned from his father's mistakes, Manasseh was strictly loyal towards Assyria. The absence of external threats enabled Judah to compensate for the loss of the Shephelah by developing agriculture in the Negev. Although tribute is commonly seen as a burden with negative consequences on the local economy, the pressure of Assyrian tribute stimulated production and contributed to a sharp rise in the cultural level of the entire population. Ordinary households now had tableware of a quality that had been rare in the tenth century BCE. The poor were richer than three centuries previously, but they felt greatly poorer when they compared themselves with the elite of the seventh century. The population of Jerusalem filled the space fortified by Hezekiah and settled beyond the walls. Manasseh moved the wall from the east of the Ophel slope to the bottom of the Kidron Valley (2 Chron. 33:14). Manasseh's Jerusalem is celebrated in Psalm 48. The adjective *rab* rather than *gadol*, which qualifies the king in Psalm 48:3 (מלך רב), imitates the Assyrian *šarru rabbu*.

On the basis of the temporal distribution of jars marked with the royal stamp, Lipschits *et al.* (2011) question the notion that it was during Manasseh's reign that Judah reached its highest point. They claim that, compared with Hezekiah's time, the productivity of the crown estates regressed under Manasseh, and they suggest that Judah's high point was reached during the reign of Josiah, which was marked by renewed hostilities and the fragmentation of the Empire that started at the latest in 627 BCE. In fact, tax receipts from Lachish (Avigad and Sass 1997, #422), from either Manasseh's or Josiah's reign, show that the state began to collect taxes from its own people at about that time, which renders the productivity of royal domains less relevant to the actual finances of the state apparatus.

Historians cannot be satisfied with the evaluation of the kings of Judah by the writer of the Book of Kings. The section on Manasseh (2 Kgs 21:1-18) is a blanket condemnation according to which Manasseh transgressed all the religious prescriptions of the Torah, even though the Torah did not exist in the seventh century BCE. The aim of the writers was to explain the destruction of the state of Judah in 586 and 582 BCE as having been triggered by divine wrath, just as Mesha had explained Israel's occupation of Moab as a result of the wrath of Kemosh it had incurred (Halpern 1998). Contrary to Mesha, the writers wanted a specific scapegoat, and there were not many choices; the last kings after Josiah were insignificant figures compared with Manasseh. Moreover, 2 Kings frames Manasseh's reign with those of Hezekiah and Josiah, the two rulers who receive the most positive evaluations. Both walked in all the ways of their father David (2 Kgs 18:1; 22:2). Hezekiah's loyalty to his Assyrian overlord was the only way in which he surpassed Hezekiah and Josiah in emulation of David. The latter two are presented as having resisted the Assyrians and the Egyptians (2 Kgs 18:7; 23:29). This is counted to them as righteousness, although from a political point of view these acts of defiance were terrible blunders. Instead of admitting this, the writers "blackballed" Manasseh (Stavrakopoulou 2005) and, in a somewhat tragic way, they insisted that Manasseh's sins were so great that all of Josiah's virtues could not appease YHWH's wrath (2 Kgs 23:25-26).

That Manasseh rebuilt the high places Hezekiah supposedly destroyed is not proven. The text itself shows that the notion of altars for Ba'al was borrowed from 1 Kings 16:28, revealing the writers had no other sources apart from the annals of the kings of Israel and Judah. The altars for the host of heaven (2 Kgs 21:3-5) are more likely historical, since the worship of astral deities was in vogue at the time, and Josiah had probably removed their symbols from the temple. The passing of Manasseh's son through the fire (2 Kgs 21:6) may reflect a Phoenician burial custom involving the cremation of deceased infants.[2] Manasseh acted like any other king of his time when he practised soothsaying, augury, and ancestor worship (2 Kgs 21:6). Setting up a new cult image of Asherah (2 Kgs 21:7) makes sense from a literary point of view, since the writers found in the annals that the previous image had been donated by the Queen Mother, Maacah (1 Kgs 15:13).

Finally, the innocent blood that Manasseh "shed until he had filled Jerusalem from one end to another" (2 Kgs 21:16) may reflect the suppression of an opposition group that held the kind of anti-Assyrian ideas that inspired the anti-Babylonian politics of the last kings of Judah; ideas that the writers clearly supported. However, as the Book of Chronicles recognizes, a king who reigned for 55 years had to have been good at some point. Second Chronicles 33:10-13 invents a story of deportation to and conversion in Babylon. A less theological reason for Manasseh's success is that he effectively silenced all opposition to his pro-Assyrian policies, with murder when necessary. The story of Manasseh's repentance allowed the Chronicler to trans-

---

2 The debate is not yet settled whether the expression "to make one's child go through the fire" and the various tophets of Phoenician and Punic cities (cemeteries with infant urn burials) refer to a funeral custom reserved for children, the position adopted here, or to child sacrifice; compare Stavrakopoulou (2004) and Benichou-Safar (2004).

mit Manasseh's other achievements recorded in the annals: the construction of the outer wall of Jerusalem, the installation of specialists to train the militia in the cities of Judah, and certain cultic reforms (2 Chron. 33:14-17). Had the last kings of Judah followed Manasseh's policy, there would have been no "exile," but no Bible either.

The astralization of the pantheon – the worship of the heavenly army – is typical of the Assyrian and Aramean religions of the seventh century BCE. The Assyrians were too astute to force their vassals to worship the Assyrian gods. Instead, they manipulated local cults by claiming that they were sent to punish their enemies by the very gods of the people they had vanquished. This is the substance of the discourse of the Rabshakeh before Jerusalem (2 Kgs 18:25). Assyrian reliefs depict soldiers carrying off the images of the gods of the cities they have conquered (Figure 29).

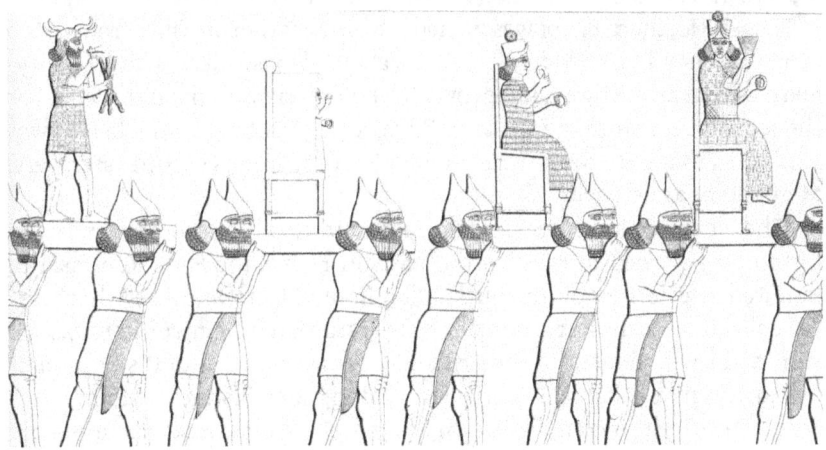

Figure 29: Deportation of the gods of a submitted city on a relief in the palace of Sargon II at Dur Sharrukin (Khorsabad), after Layard 1849, pl. 65).

The exile of the gods signified the wrath of the local gods against their own country. Their exile, however, was temporary. After a stay in the temple of Ashur, where they were "born again" as sons and daughters of the supreme god of the Assyrians (see Deut. 32:8-9), they returned embellished to their home sanctuary to mark the reconciliation of the gods with their people and inaugurate a new era of peace and prosperity under the aegis of Assyria (Pongratz-Leisten 1997). Describing YHWH as the supreme god would have been treason, but otherwise, the Assyrians encouraged rather than forbade the worship of YHWH in Jerusalem. Besides Ashur, the Assyrians recognized Sin of Harran as "Lord of the West," who appears increasingly on the seals of the elite in Judah, Ammon, and Moab (2 Kgs 16:10-12).

Manasseh served three Assyrian kings: Sennacherib (705–681 BCE), Esarhaddon (681–669 BCE), and Ashurbanipal (668–627 BCE). Contrary to the impression gained from reading 2 Kings 19:37//Isaiah 37:38, Sennacherib was not murdered immediately on his return home from his 701 BCE campaign, but 20 years later, after a civil war that brought his son Esarhaddon to the throne, even though he was not the crown prince Sennacherib had chosen. Under Esarhaddon, Judean workers were involved in the transport of timber from Lebanon to Nineveh, to be used for the construction of palaces and temples (*ANET* 291). When they returned home, they told of fabulous cities, 10 times larger than Jerusalem. Other Judeans visited Egypt as part of the Judean contingents that took part in the Assyrian conquest of Egypt under Esarhaddon and Ashurbanipal (Isa. 19:2-15). To celebrate the conquest of Thebes (No-Amon in Jer. 46:25; Ezek. 30:14-16; Nah. 3:8), Manasseh named his son Amon (Nelson 1983, 181). Following the conquest of Thebes, Northern Egypt was turned into an Assyrian province from 664 to 656 BCE, when Esarhaddon established a new dynasty at Sais, the Twenty-Sixth Dynasty, which remained loyal to the Assyrians to the bitter end. For the second time since the treaty of Kadesh (1270 BCE), the Middle East was made one, thanks to the mutual recognition of two of its two major players, Mesopotamia and Egypt.

The globalization of the Middle East spurred a literary reaction in the form of a renewed interest in the past. In Egypt, the Saite Renaissance imitated inscriptions of the third millennium BCE. In Nineveh, Ashurbanipal collected the available cuneiform literature in his famous library, now stored in the basement of the British Museum and most of it still unpublished. It is likely that in Samaria and among the Philistines, a similar process of transcription and collation of local traditions occurred. In Judah, scribes put the story of the House of David in writing at that time. The synchronization of the annals of the Judean and Israelite kings was probably produced in this context, along with the compilation of prophetic sayings that later became biblical prophetic books.

King Esarhaddon was the first Deuteronomist. Deuteronomists are often encountered in Old Testament studies, where scholars depict them in their own image: members of a school. If there ever were such a school, it had only one known pupil, the scribe Shaphan, King Josiah's secretary (2 Kgs 22; 25:22). At "school," Shaphan and his few schoolmates read Esarhaddon's annals, and from there they wrote in an easily recognizable style. Apart from this distinctive style, however, "Deuteronomism" does not designate any particular social reality. Deuteronomistic texts include quite realistic depictions of a "left-wing" internationalist Jeremiah as well as of ultra "right-wing" nationalists in Kings. Besides the fundamental idea that all misfortunes are the result of God's anger, Deuteronomism focuses upon the vassal treaties that the legitimate king established with dependents in the name of the gods. This type of treaty, the biblical *berit* or "covenant," forms the core of Deuteronomy 5–28. Israel is obliged to keep the Torah and in exchange YHWH endows it with land. In a rigid framework of retribution, both happiness and misfortune are meted out as reward and punishment, respectively, for the way in which the inferior partner observes the stipulations of the treaty:

> I call heaven and earth to witness against you today that I have set before you life and death, blessings and curses. Choose life so that you and your descendants may live, loving the YHWH your God, obeying him, and holding fast to him; for that means life to you and length of days, so that you may live in the land that the YHWH swore to give to your ancestors, to Abraham, to Isaac, and to Jacob.
>
> (Deut. 30:19-20)

Manasseh did more than Hezekiah to reform the cult. Yet, reform does not imply iconoclasm. The small sanctuary in the fortress of Arad is often invoked as proof of the historicity of Josiah's "reform." Yet, the sanctuary was not vandalized as one would have expected, had Josiah treated it as he supposedly did the cultic places from Geba to Beersheba (2 Kgs 23:8). The two standing stones at Arad were carefully buried with their incense burners. Whereas the stories of the patriarchs, the Judges, and Samuel give the impression that every tribal chief or king in Israel was free to build a temple or altar where it suited him (1 Kgs 8:12-13), Assyrian gods dwelt only in the statues that were erected in temples, built in places they had chosen and had made known to the king through one of the many divination techniques available. Whereas Exodus 20:24 states that earthen altars can be raised "in every place where I cause my name to be remembered," Deuteronomy 12:11 replies that all sacrifices and offerings must be taken to the place chosen by YHWH. Although this formulation does not exclude a plurality of legitimate places of worship, it nevertheless allows identifying illegitimate cult places.

Imitating Assyrian hydraulic technology, Manasseh and his successor built a royal garden at the southeast end of the Ophel, where he was buried with his son (2 Kgs 21:18, 26; 25:4; Jer. 52:7). This complex includes the Siloam canal, with its inscription, and a pool (*CoS* 2.28). The incipit of the inscription is missing: although the rock had been prepared to receive the incipit that would have mentioned the king who commissioned the work, the inscription and the garden remained unfinished (Ussishkin 1995) because of regime change in 640 BCE when King Amon was murdered. The layout of the royal residence of Ramat Rahel just south of Jerusalem could also be attributed to Manasseh, who either built it for himself or for the Assyrian Commissioner at the Jerusalem court. They would have preferred spending the summer outside the now densely populated and malodorous Jerusalem. A similar Trianon was established by the Ammonite King Amminadab at the place now occupied by the Mosque of the

University of Jordan in Amman, and from where a bronze bottle has been retrieved (Azize 2003).

5.6 The Demise of Ashur and Egypt's Return

With the conquest of Egypt in 664 BCE, the Assyrian Empire reached its climax. It stretched from Lydia in the west to Elam (western Iran) in the east (see Gen. 10:22). Three decades later, when Ashurbanipal died (between 630 and 627 BCE), the Empire vacillated. In 614 BCE the city of Ashur fell, followed by Nineveh in 612. By 605 BCE, there was nothing left, except the notion of empire (Machinist 1997; Stronach 1997). After Assyria, Israel/Palestine witnessed an almost unbroken sequence of empires: Babylon, Persia, Ptolemaic Alexandria, Seleucid Antioch, Rome, Byzantium, Umayyad Damascus, Fatimid Cairo, Crusader Jerusalem, Ayyubid and Mamluk Egypt, the Ottoman Empire, and the British Empire.

Having overstretched its resources, Assyria succumbed to setbacks from the periphery. It is also possible that the army experienced epidemics in Egypt and brought their diseases back to the motherland. Pestilence was proverbial (Exod. 15:26; Deut. 7:15; 28:60), and sword, famine, and pestilence form a deadly triad in the Book of Jeremiah. The smallpox epidemic that killed Pericles in Athens (Thucydides 2.47–55) may have been an offshoot of this seventh-century pandemic. The permanent state of fear evident in the letters of Esarhaddon and Ashurbanipal was perhaps not neurotic. In a similar fashion, after 542 CE, the plague of Justinian wiped out half of the population of the Byzantine and Sassanid empires, and both then fell to numerically inferior Arab invaders.

Another problem the Assyrians never managed to resolve was Babylon. After the death of Esarhaddon, who had ruled Assyria and Babylonia in personal union, rule was shared between Ashurbanipal in Assyria and his brother Šamaššumukin in Babylonia. Babylon, the cradle of the Akkadian language and literature, regarded Assyrians as barbarian upstarts in the same way as the Greeks considered the Macedonians to be. Babylon never accepted Assyrian rule. In 652 BCE, Šamaššumukin revolted against Ashurbanipal. When it fought outside the Empire, the Assyrian army was irresistible, but in Babylonia, it took four years of civil war to crush the rebellion. In 649 BCE, the lists of high officials after which years were named (the eponym-list) were terminated. After 648 BCE, the Assyrian-Babylonian heartland was devastated. Ashurbanipal came back victorious again from Elam in 644 BCE, but after that the annals are discontinued. The reality was so bad that the Assyrians had no words for it.

The chaos in Mesopotamia had consequences in Israel/Palestine. Amon, Manasseh's successor, was murdered in a palace revolution after a two-year reign in 640 BCE. Unlike Solomon's coup, the conspiracy against

Amon was no longer a purely Jerusalemite matter to settle the question of who would sit on the throne of David. This time, the "people of the land" (עם הארץ), the aristocracy of the Judean countryside, intervened and placed the eight-year-old prince Josiah on the throne (2 Kgs 21:19–22:1). The murderers of Amon were executed to eliminate the organizers of the coup (2 Kgs 21:24; 2 Chron. 33:25). Placing a child on the throne gave them a decade to consolidate their position, which they retained until the demise of the kingdom and beyond. The putsch was probably led by the secretary of state, Shaphan ben Azaliah ben Meshullam (2 Kgs 22:3), and different members of the Shaphan family are found in key positions until 580 BCE (Figure 30).

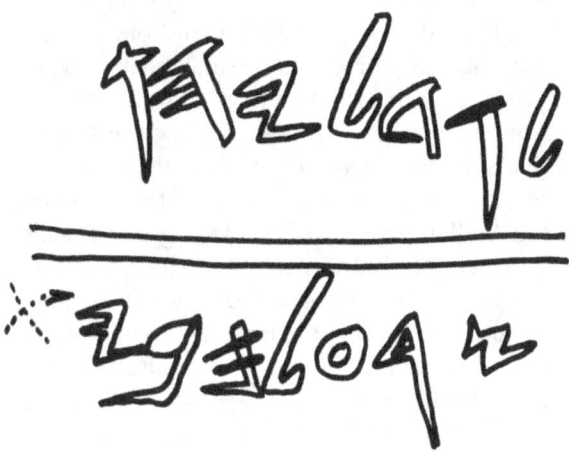

Figure 30: Seal of Gedaliah, overseer of the palace ([לגדליהו שר על הבית]) from Lachish (after Keel 2007, #506).

Shaphan ben Azaliah probably edited the annals and thus determined their presentation to posterity. Gemariah ben Shaphan was the secretary of state under Jehoiakim (Jer. 36:10, 12). With his brother Ahikam, they stood behind Jeremiah the Benjaminite "prophet" (Jer. 26:24; 36:25), which suggests that they all belonged to a Benjaminite lobby that left little leeway to the last kings of Judah. Elasah ben Shaphan was Zedekiah's ambassador in Babylon (Jer. 29:3), and Gedaliah ben Ahikam ben Shaphan was appointed the last king of Judah (2 Kgs 25:22; Figure 30).

During the revolt of Šamaššumukin (652–648 BCE), or shortly afterwards, most of the Assyrian army was deployed in Babylonia. The Levant was left in the care of the Egyptian Saite dynasty. In 609 BCE, Pharaoh Neco II came to the rescue of the Assyrians west of the Euphrates and thus completed the Egyptian takeover of Syria-Palestine "from the Euphrates to the brook of Egypt" (2 Kgs 24:7).

5.7 Josiah (640–609 BCE)

In the period of the transfer of power from Assyrian to Egyptian domination (622–609 BCE), Josiah seems to have tried to build an empire of YHWH's to replace Assyrian rule in the area:

> Pharaoh Necoh king of Egypt went up to the king of Assyria to the river Euphrates. King Josiah went to meet him; but when Pharaoh Necho met him at Megiddo, he killed him. (2 Kgs 23:29)

No reason is given for Josiah's execution, so the Chronicler felt obliged to supply one. Josiah would have tried to halt the progression of Necho's troops and was killed in battle (2 Chron. 35:20-24, compare with 1 Kgs 22:30-38). The annalistic material relative to Josiah is found in 2 Kings 21:19, 21:23-29, 22:1, and 23:8-12, 28-30. The rest of 2 Kings 22–23 consists of anachronistic fantasies. Josiah's successor, Jehoahaz, was not the crown prince but a prince chosen by the gentry (2 Kgs 23:30). On his way back from the disaster at Harran, where Necho saved the Assyrian Empire for another five years, Necho deposed Jehoahaz, deported him to Egypt to serve as hostage, and replaced him with his brother Eliakim.

Shaphan ben Azaliah must have been largely responsible for the policies applied by Josiah. The enthronement of the child-king is celebrated in Isaiah 9:1-7, a passage belonging to the anti-Ashur edition of the Book of Isaiah. Jerusalem believed that the time had come to replace the crumbling Assyrian Empire with a Davidic Empire after the Assyrian model. YHWH simply took Ashur's place as the highest God (Psalm 82). The oath of loyalty was sworn to YHWH, who made a treaty of vassalship with Judah-Israel (Deuteronomy 12–28). Just as Ashur did, YHWH required the extermination of his enemies (Deuteronomy 7 and 20; Joshua 6–12); Assyria had left the political sphere but remained on the theological scene, and its influence is significant in today's Middle Eastern politics. However, the problem with the above presentation is that the leadership of the Shaphan family in the post-Assyrian politics of Jerusalem sits uncomfortably with the consistent portrayal of Jeremiah as a vocal opponent of those who pushed the king to resist Babylon and of the nomination of Gedaliah ben Shaphan by the Babylonians after the destruction of Jerusalem. If Shaphan ben Azaliah was largely responsible for the Josianic programme, the Shaphans must have quickly converted to a pro-Babylon stance when they saw that the end of Assyria did not mean the end of Empire.

The extent and nature of Josiah's reform presented in 2 Kings 22–23 are controversial. For Wellhausen, 622 BCE was the chronological anchor for the dating of Proto-Deuteronomy, from which he worked out a relative chronological sequence for the sources of the Pentateuch: the Yahwist, Elohist, Deuteronomist, and Priestly sources. It is obvious that 2 Kings 22–23 wants to give the impression that Josiah enforced the centralization of the cult of Deuteronomy 12 in 622 BCE, when the book of the law was "discovered" in the temple of Jerusalem. Intent, however, is not equivalent to reality; the story is concerned with continuity between the First and the Second Temples. The replacement of the king by the Torah, the centralization of the cult, and aniconic monotheism were realities in Judah of the "Second" Temple era. Even 2 Kings 23:15 admits that the temple of Bethel was not destroyed in 622 BCE (Knauf 2006). Neither the temple nor the city were destroyed before the first half of the fifth century BCE. What may have happened in 622 BCE was the rise of YHWH in the temple of Jerusalem to the position of supreme god. Under Assyrian rule, this would have been an act of treason. As supreme god YHWH was now identified with the creator god, El. Psalm 47 suggests that the Babylonian New Year festival was performed in Jerusalem at the time (see Psalms 15, 24, and 68). Identified as the highest god (like Marduk in Babylon, Ashur in Assyria), YHWH arrived from the desert and entered his temple in solemn procession to signify the renewal of the world order.

From Joshua 15:21-62 and 18:21-28 it appears that the kingdom of Judah once more controlled Benjamin and the Shephelah at the end of the seventh century BCE. In addition to Bethel, Judah ruled over Gibeon (Jer. 28:1) and Jericho (2 Kgs 25:5), with Lachish (II) as the main stronghold of the kingdom. The material culture of the area forms a unit, with most households owning at least one pillar figurine representing either the goddess Asherah herself or a woman invoking the goddess's help, something rarely found outside Judah (Kletter 1999; Figure 31).

It stands to reason that these extensions were gained at the expense of the former Assyrian provinces between 622 and 609 BCE. In 609, Necho executed Josiah in retaliation for his anti-Assyrian promotion of YHWH as the supreme god, which Egypt had not considered problematic until Necho could not afford to leave a vassal of questionable loyalty when he travelled north to support Assyria in its fight with Babylon.

The Shephelah could even have been returned to the kingdom of Judah before the reign of Josiah. Manasseh could have received it as reward for his involvement in Esarhaddon's Egyptian campaigns in 664 or 648 BCE. In this case, however, the reason for the execution of Josiah at Megiddo is totally unknown. Whatever the reason, the northern limit of Judah at Josiah's death was probably the same as the boundary of the province of Yehud in the Persian period. Some likely reflections of Josiah's territorial gains are found in Joshua's conquests that cover Benjamin with Jericho, Ai, and Gibeon (Josh. 6:1-10, 14) as well as the Shephelah (Josh. 10:28-39). The dream of the reconstruction of the Davidic Empire was the first time that leaders became blinded to the contingencies of *realpolitik*. The illusion that small countries like Israel and Judah could play an independent role in the concert of the great powers, especially when they attributed this capacity to

Figure 31: (a) Terracotta pillar figurines are often found in Judean houses, probably imitating the statue designated "the image of jealousy" in or near the temple of Jerusalem (Ezek. 8:5); (b) a seal from Lachish shows Asherah under the winged sun. On her right, a monkey, symbol of adoration, and a sprig, symbol of the goddess' involvement in the fertility of the land. On the left, a worshipper (both after Keel 2007, #332, 333; *GGG* #321, 323).

their worship of the true god, should have been buried with Josiah. The base layer of the Book of Jeremiah and the Priestly Document in the Hexateuch drew this conclusion, but other biblical writers did not.

5.8 Religion in the Seventh Century BCE

Evidence for monotheism in Israel and Judah before 400 BCE is still lacking. The integration of the Levant into the Assyrian Empire between 738 and 701 BCE came as a shock for the petty kings of Syria-Palestine, who had taken the withdrawal of Egypt from Canaan as the occasion to behave as little pharaohs. Faced with Assyrian imperialism, one had the choice between collaboration and resistance. Resistance characterized the biblical Israelite religion. The existence of Judean seals in the seventh century BCE shows that aniconism began then, but iconic seals continued to be produced for the elite who collaborated with Assyria (Niehr 1997; Uehlinger 1997; Figure 32).

Figure 32: The officer in charge of the city (שׂר העיר) of Dor receives the bow and arrows with the blessing of the king (after *GGG* #346).

Stability was guaranteed by warring gods, and the king is represented carrying the bow of the supreme god as a symbol of domination (*GGG* 281, 284b, 285a). After the disasters of the sixth century BCE, the Persian-era YHWH would hang the war bow in the clouds (Gen. 9:13) to express that, henceforth, there would be peace. The astral symbol of the Assyrian-Aramean supreme god was not the sun but the moon (Figure 33). A goddess stood at his side as the Queen of Heaven, with the Venus-star (Dever 2005). She was the Assyrian Ishtar (Figure 34) and the Canaanite Asherah and Anath (Figure 35).

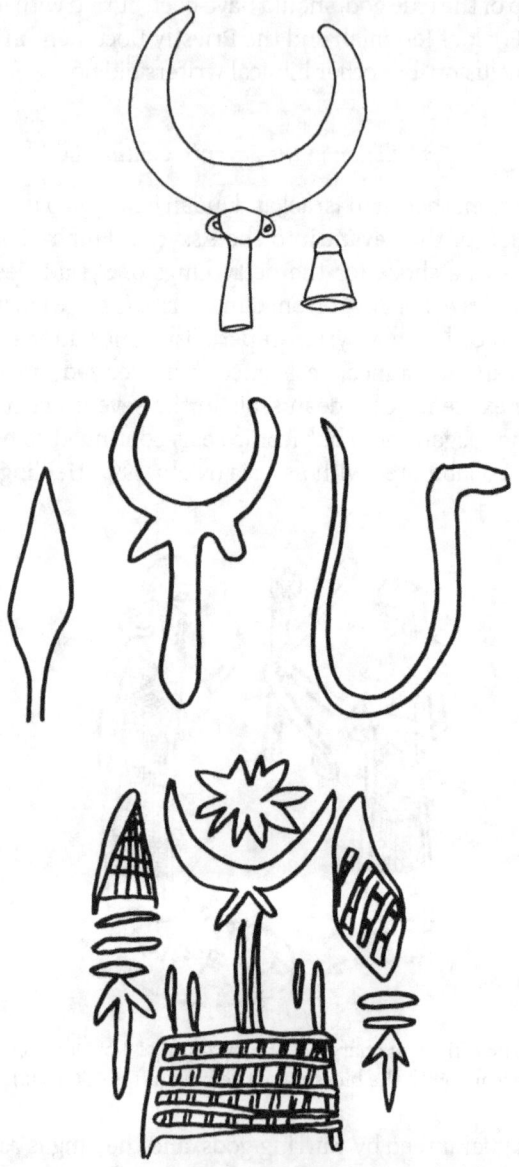

Figure 33: (a) Standard in the shape of the crescent of the moon god Sin found in the Assyrian camp at Tell Ser'a. After the Assyrian conquest of Egypt; (b) a cylinder seal from Tell Jemme combines Sin with the Uraeus; (c) an Edomite seal from Tawilan flanks Sin with two trees. The vision of Zechariah (Zechariah 4) replaces Sin with the seven-branch menorah (see Figure 49a) (a after *GGG* #295a; b after Keel 1977, #222; c after *CSAJ* #2).

5. From Tiglath-Pileser to Ashurbanipal   131

Figure 34: Ishtar of Arbela crudely engraved on an electron earring from Ekron. The goddess stands on her lion pedestal, blessing a worshipper. The prominence of the moon-crescent below the sun god and the Sibitti reflects a strong Assyrian influence (after Uehlinger 1994, 101 #6).

Figure 35: (a) Seal depicting a winged Ishtar holding two stars, an example of astralization under Assyrian influence. More common is (b), the simple representation of Ishtar within a starry circle, as on this seal from Ashdod (a after *GGG* #331a; b after Schroer 1987b, # 98).

The notion of a supreme god had not yet evolved into exclusive monotheism. Although the Assyrians could entertain the notion that all gods are one, represented by Ashur (Parpola 1993), the Assyrians still saw the moon god of Harran as the Lord of the West. As territoriality remained influential in the way gods were defined (1 Kgs 20:23), on the western side of the Euphrates, loyalty to Assyria was expressed through the worship of Sin rather than of Ashur. Against this background, the Harran-layer of the Jacob narrative (Genesis 26–35) expresses resistance through collaboration. Nabonidus (556–539 BCE), the last Neo-Babylonian ruler, went a step further and elevated Sin to the rank of the highest god. As a result, Nabonidus is ignored by the Bible (unlike in the Qumran texts), and Horeb is introduced as an alternative to Sinai to designate the mountain where YHWH met Moses, because the name Sinai evoked the name of the God Sin (Perlitt 1977, 311–313).

The Queen of Heaven (Jer. 7:18, 44) appears both as Anat (*GGG* 331a) and Asherah (*GGG* 317a, 331b). The goddesses can be represented either by their symbols or anthropomorphically. YHWH and his Asherah are displayed simultaneously as Cherub and Holy Tree and as God and Queen of Heaven (*GGG* 331b). Josiah removed neither the goddess that flanked YHWH nor the image of YHWH from the Jerusalem temple (Uehlinger 1997). The elimination of astral symbols (2 Kgs 23:5, 11–12) makes sense as an expression of anti-Assyrian politics. Given the quasi-divine status of Moses in the Hebrew Bible, the most fascinating episode in the long list of Josiah's destructions is the crushing of Nehushtan, the bronze serpent Moses had made in the wilderness (2 Kgs 18:4). Whenever this passage was written, it reflects a time in Jerusalem when the figure of Moses did not have the authority he has in later texts (Garbini 2003, 57).

5.9 Literature of Assyrian and Post-Assyrian Times

The destruction of Israel and the Assyrian pressure on Judah spurred the development of biblical literature. Hosea 4–11 was compiled at Bethel as an explanation of the disaster of 720–722 BCE and as the basis for a new beginning with YHWH but without kings (Hos. 10:3). In the Book of Saviours (Judges 3–9), another likely composition from Bethel, kings have a bad press too. The words of Hosea (Hos. 1:1) were not the words of a prophet named Hosea, but rather oracles collected during the reign of the last king of Israel of that name. The Harran layer of Jacob's cycle is probably the result of the adaptation of the cycle that suppresses the royal element and focuses on Jacob's mischievous collaboration with his Assyrian relatives at Padan-Aram to show that Israel could thrive without a king in Samaria. The anti-Assyrian Hosea tradition responded to Jacob's tricks with a particularly unfavourable comparison of the patriarch with Moses:

Jacob fled to the land of Aram, there Israel served for a wife, and for a wife he guarded sheep. By a prophet the YHWH brought Israel up from Egypt, and by a prophet he was guarded (Hos. 12:12-13).

Two concepts of Israel are at loggerheads here: a tribal Israel whose survival depends on the ability to accumulate herds and wives and a Deuteronomistic Israel whose survival depends on the strict observance of the terms stipulated by YHWH in the Assyrian-like vassal treaty. Like Jesus' question about what it takes to make sons of Abraham (Mt 3:9), Hosea 12:12-13 opposes genealogy with faithfulness. Eventually, the Torah juxtaposed the two conflicting positions.

In Judah, the destruction of Israel provoked the expansion of the oracles of Amos into a Book of Amos as a theodicy. It is not YHWH who failed, but his people (also Mic. 1:3-7). Isaiah, the pro-Assyrian court prophet of 734 BCE, was the hero of a tradition that assumed increasingly anti-Assyrian traits. In Isaiah 6-8, probably a piece of opposition literature from the time of Manasseh, YHWH is already enthroned as the supreme god (Isaiah 6:1). In the roughly contemporary story of Jacob (Gen. 28:12-13), YHWH stands at the top of the "ladder," the entrance to the heavenly throne room at whose end El is enthroned, showing that YHWH is *not* the supreme god. The collection of Proverbs 25-29 may date back to the days of Hezekiah, while the basic components of the geographical lists of Genesis 10, 25:12-15, and 36 could reflect the world of the seventh century BCE.

The production of Deuteronomistic literature began under Josiah and continued in the Persian period, when anti-Assyrian traditions were resisted by Persian-compliant groups (Knauf 2002b, 2004). In the Hellenistic period, the antithesis took the form of a conflict between the Hellenizers and those who were Torah-observant. In the days of Josiah or slightly after, Joshua 6 and 9-10 were combined to conclude a Moses-Exodus narrative. This narrative combined Bethel's Exodus tradition with the kingdom of Josiah described in Joshua 10:40-42 as the goal of the Exodus. In this context, the Book of the Acts of Solomon (1 Kgs 11:41), which covers 1 Kings 1-11, presents Solomon as a world ruler along the Assyrian model, ruling from the Euphrates to the Brook of Egypt.

Chapter 6
From Nabopolassar to Nebuchadnezzar:
Judah between the Great Powers

The deportations in the last decades of the kingdom of Judah produced among groups of tradents rival traditions whose debates were later recorded mostly in prophetic literature.

6.1 The Neo-Babylonian Empire

After the death of Ashurbanipal around 627 BCE, a rebellion broke out, led by Nabopolassar, an Aramean chief from southern Babylonia (Chaldea). At the time, Nabopolassar was the Assyrian viceroy in southern Babylonia (Kahn 2008). In 626 BCE, he ascended the throne of Babylon and took over the Empire chunk by chunk. Then, in 614 BCE, the tribal federation of the Medes led by Cyaxares invaded the Assyrian heartland and captured the city of Ashur. Despite Herodotus and Daniel (Dan. 2:39; 6:1; 9:1), the Medes did not constitute an empire (Sancisi-Weerdenburg 1988). Nabopolassar made an alliance with the Medes, and together they destroyed Nineveh in 612 BCE (Grayson 1975, 90–96). The biblical Book of Nahum gloats over the event in retrospect. Pharaoh Necho managed to hold the Euphrates border for four years, but in 605 BCE the Babylonians, under the leadership of the Crown Prince Nebuchadnezzar, inflicted a crushing defeat on the Egyptians at Carchemish. Nabopolassar died at the end of the year, and Nebuchadnezzar (or "Nebuchadrezzar" in Jer. 52:12) ascended the throne in 604 BCE. He campaigned in southern Syria-Palestine and accepted the submission of the Levantine vassals he inherited from Egypt (2 Kgs 24:1), including Jehoiakim of Judah. Only Ashkelon remained faithful to Egypt and offered resistance. It was destroyed in Nebuchadnezzar's first regnal year (Grayson 1975, 99–102). The plea of the king of Ekron, Adon, to pharaoh (Porten 1981) shows that in the next years Nebuchadnezzar kept his eye on the Levant, while the Egyptians continued to manipulate their previous vassals to destabilize the Babylonian control over this crucial area for Egypt's security. The Syrian campaign of Year 3 (602 BCE) (Grayson 1975, 99–102) was a demonstration of force and a rehearsal for the onslaught against Egypt in 601 BCE that would have made Nebuchadnezzar equal to Ashurbanipal. More realistic than the Assyrian annals, the Babylonian

Chronicles (Grayson 1975, 99–102) hint that the Babylonian king did not win the battle: instead of stating that he slaughtered his enemy, it records that both sides slaughtered each other.

In a replay of the geopolitical configuration of 732–701 BCE, Judah found itself once more in a region contested by two competing superpowers. The Jerusalemite court replaced Josiah with Jehoahaz. Three months later, however, Necho kept Jehoahaz as hostage in his camp at Riblah in Lebanon and replaced him with another son of Josiah, Eliakim, who took the throne name Jehoiakim (2 Kgs 23:31-35). The overdue tribute was raised through a levy (2 Kgs 23:35). The tax burden for Judah was the same under Egyptian and Neo-Babylonian rule. Both sides employed Greek mercenaries, the Kittim, mentioned in the Arad ostraca (Aharoni 1981) and stationed at key fortresses and checkpoints (Fantalkin 2001). These troops were fed with supplies delivered by the vassals, who also had to send workers for building and harvesting.

6.2 The First Deportation

Seeing the Babylonians beaten in 601 BCE, Jehoiakim decided to renounce his allegiance to Babylon (2 Kgs 24:1-2; Psalm 60). In 600/599 BCE, however, Nebuchadnezzar raised a new army and tried it out against the Arabs in the Syrian Desert (Grayson 1975, 99–102; Jer. 49:28-33). In November/December 598 BCE, he turned against Judah, where Jehoiakim was involved in a small-scale war against Arameans, or rather Edomites and Moabites that had remained loyal to Babylon. According to 2 Kings 24:2 and Psalm 60, Judah was attacked by these countries. Shortly before or during Nebuchadnezzar's approach, Jehoiakim died. Unless it was pure coincidence, he was possibly murdered by members of his entourage, who hoped in this way to save the city. Jehoiakim was succeeded by his son Jehoiachin, and it took three months of siege to negotiate the surrender of Jerusalem (2 Kgs 24:8-12). It occurred in Nebuchadnezzar's second year, on the seventh day of the month of Adar (March 16, 597) (Grayson 1975, 99–102).

Jehoiachin was taken captive to Babylon (2 Kgs 24:15-16). Sons and grandsons of Josiah found themselves hostage in Egypt (Jehoahaz) and Babylon. Being a hostage was not necessarily distressing. A tablet found at Babylon lists rations for Jehoiachin, which shows that he was surrounded by his family and retained his royal title and rank (*ANET* 308). The story of his pardon at the end of the Book of Kings (2 Kgs 25:27-30) conceals the devastation the Babylonians left behind in Judah and Jerusalem. Ten thousand members of the elite were deported together with the king (2 Kgs 24:14), but the suggestion that only the poor were left behind reflects more the social background of the authors of the text than the social reality. This high society comprised the royal family, the court officials (including the priest and "prophet" Ezekiel), the rural elite, 7,000 troops and 1,000 artisans (2 Kgs 24:15-16). According to Jeremiah 52:28, the total number of exiles in 597 BCE only amounted to 3,023, a more credible figure.

The temple and palace were plundered (2 Kgs 24:13). One may wonder whether the inventory of the furniture in Solomon's temple (1 Kings 6) is based on the inventory of the loss of 597 BCE. To replace the exiles of the first deportation, Jehoiachin's uncle Mattaniah took the name Zedekiah (2 Kgs 24:17-18) and was nominated as *nasi'* (נשיא), some kind of governor (Ezek. 21:25), though in the Book of Kings he is still called king. The south of Judah may have been placed under the supervision of the small kingdom of Edom.

It is common to mention an Edomite threat in the last decades of the kingdom of Judah, based on the reading of two lines of Arad ostraca #24 and #40 (Na'aman 2003, 2011a). In fact, these readings were heavily influenced by the circumstances of the archaeologist who excavated and published the Arad ostraca. The linchpin of the argument for a hostile Edomite pressure on Judean territory is to be found in the last four words of Arad Letter #24:20: "Lest Edom should come there" (Aharoni 1981, 46–49). It is not at all clear that what was requested from Arad was the dispatch of soldiers as reinforcement against an Edomite attack. The corroborating evidence found in the last line of Arad ostracon #40:15, read as "the evil that Edom has done" (Aharoni 1981, 71), is based on dubious reconstructions. Other possible readings of these crucial lines suggest that they discussed shepherding matters (Guillaume 2013). Moreover, renewed excavations in the Negev show that the conditions there at the end of the Iron Age were peaceful enough to allow the development of extra-mural settlements around forts (Thareani-Sussely 2008). If southern Judah had been taken over by Edom, it was the work of the Babylonians rather than the result of an Edomite conquest. As Sennacherib had granted the Judean Shephelah to Ashdod, Ekron, and Gaza, Nebuchadnezzar rewarded Edom for its help in the campaign against Jerusalem, as also suggested by the biblical Booklet of Obadiah. The biblical aversion to Edom is due to the Edomite occupation of the Judean centre of Hebron, granted to them by Nebuchadnezzar, rather than to specific aggressive acts on the part of Edom.

6.3 The Second Deportation

In Jerusalem, the struggle of the great powers for control of the Levant turned into a bitter struggle between two parties. One was pro-Egyptian and legitimized its stance as faithfulness to YHWH, who commanded Josiah to reconstruct David's empire. The other was the Shaphanides, who accepted with Jeremiah the new balance of power and defended a pro-

Babylonian stance, possibly taking King Manasseh as their model to ensure safety and prosperity for the kingdom. Despite the deportation of its main proponents in 597 BCE, Josiah's dream of a greater Judah survived, thanks to Pharaoh Psammetichus II (595–589 BCE), who came to Israel/Palestine in 591 BCE. The tour was a ceremonial display rather than a proper military operation (Kahn 2008). The Babylonian Chronicle for that year has not survived, so Nebuchadnezzar's reaction is unknown. But Egyptian interference in the area continued. In 589 BCE, Zedekiah rebelled with assurances of Egyptian support from Pharaoh Apries (589–570 BCE) (Ostracon #3 in ANET 322). Nebuchadnezzar reacted and arrived before the walls of Jerusalem on January 15, 588 BCE (2 Kgs 25:1; Ezek. 24:1-2). The Egyptians attempted to relieve Zedekiah, which forced the Babylonians to lift the siege and tackle the approaching Egyptians, who retreated to Egypt (Jer. 37:4-5, 11). Lachish was taken (Jer. 34.1-7; Ostracon #4 in ANET 322) and on July 18, 587/586 BCE (the exact year cannot be established) Jerusalem fell.

The temple, the palace, and the homes of leading politicians were destroyed. The temple was plundered again and a number of senior officials and priests were executed (2 Kgs 25:8-21). The Book of Kings (a single book in the Hebrew Bible) gives the impression that the rest of the population was deported, leaving only the poorest to till the land. Once Gedaliah was murdered, they supposedly all fled to Egypt. The end of 2 Kings leaves implicit what 2 Chronicles 36:20 states explicitly: during the exile, the country was empty. Behind the notion of the empty land is the ideology that only the descendants of those relocated in the deportations of 598 and 587/586 BCE, the first and second Golah, represented the true Israel (Barstad 1996). Members of the second Golah must have been involved in the compilation and editing of the Book of Kings, since 2 Kings 25 presents Zedekiah as king, which he was not in the eyes of the first Golah. The parallel tradition in Jeremiah 39–41 and 52 counters the notion of an empty Judah after 586 BCE. The rounded numbers in 2 Kings for the first and second deportations and the utter silence over the third deportation show that its author had no access to Judean archives, while the tradents of the tradition of Jeremiah in Mizpah and Bethel did. According to Jeremiah 52:29, only 832 persons were deported from Jerusalem in 586 BCE.

6.4 King Gedaliah and the Third Deportation

The Bible presents Gedaliah as a Babylonian officer who was active during one summer only (2 Kgs 25:22-26). The texts state that Nebuchadnezzar appointed Gedaliah in Mizpah (2 Kgs 25:22; Jer. 40:5), without indicating to which office he was appointed. Translators often fill the gap with the words "as governor," although there are good reasons to think that Gedaliah was appointed as king even though he was not a descendant of David but the grandson of Shaphan (2 Kgs 25:22; Jer. 39:14). This supplies a credible motivation for his assassination by a descendant of David with the backing of Ammon (Jer. 40:14). Had Gedaliah only been a governor, it is less likely that a son of David would have murdered him. Moreover, a seal was found in Mizpah, the residence of Gedaliah (with the inscription "Belonging to Ya'azaniah, minister of the king", ליאזניהו עבד המלך (Avigad and Sass 1997, 52). Jaazaniah is mentioned as a follower of Gedaliah in 2 Kings 25:23 and Jeremiah 40:8. The speculation that he could have been an official of Zedekiah (Mittmann 2000, 28–43) is unlikely, since in this case he would have been executed like Zedekiah or deported. Another element that supports Gedaliah's holding a royal title is the mention of princesses in Jeremiah 41:3. These princesses can hardly be daughters of Zedekiah. Nebuchadnezzar executed the sons of Zedekiah (2 Kgs 25:7) and would have enslaved the daughters or at least taken them hostage. He would not have left them behind in Judah to produce more descendants of David. So the princesses were probably the daughters of Gedaliah. Finally, at line 13 of Arad ostracon #40 Aharoni read *yd'. mlk. yhwd[h* 'The king of Judah should know' (Aharoni 1981, 71). Aharoni's own drawing supports reading *yr'. mlk. Yhwd*, "the king of Yehud will graze/befriend." Aharoni added a *heh* to *mlk. yhwd[h* to obtain a King of Judah rather than a king of Yehud because he wanted to find King Hezekiah in the letter (Aharoni 1981, 74). There is no trace of this *heh*, however. The physical evidence points to a king of Yehud, who would be Gedaliah. The conclusion is that Gedaliah (586–582 BCE) was the last king of Judah or the only king of Yehud and ruled from Mizpah over the cities of Judah (Jer. 40:5), which were all in Benjamin. The return of Judean refugees from Ammon, Moab, and Judah (Jer. 40:11-12) speaks in favour of a reign of more than two months. That neither Ezekiel nor the first Golah recognized Zedekiah as king, while the second Golah did not recognize Gedaliah as king, are not reasons to deny that they were.

The great abundance of wine and summer fruits gathered by the Judeans who had returned to the land of Judah after the departure of Nebuchadnezzar (Jer. 40:12) belongs to the topos of the redemptive rule of a new king (*CoS* 2.30). Thanks to the Babylonians who liberated Benjamin from the yoke of the House of David, Jacob now had a ruler of their own (Jer. 30:18-22).

The day after Gedaliah's assassination, 80 pilgrims from Shechem, Shiloh, and Samaria stopped at Mizpah, unaware of the murder. Had they wanted to go to Jerusalem, the murderers of Gedaliah would not have enticed them to come into Mizpah, the new capital of the land of Judah (Jer. 41:1-10). Mizpah is sited in Benjamin, which was spared the destructions wrought by the Babylonians in the region of Jerusalem. Thanks to the faithfulness of Jeremiah, who came from Anathoth in Benjamin (Jer. 1:1), and of the Shaphanides who opposed the pro-Egyptian party, the Babylonians had no interest in destroying Benjamin. The scribe Baruch ben Neriah was not Jeremiah's private secretary but his superior in the Shaffanid hierarchy. Baruch seems to have become Gedaliah's chief ideologue, in charge of archives and prophetic personnel. In this role, Baruch had access to the annals, which explains the precise figures for the deportees in Jeremiah 52 and the note about the cistern of Asa (Jer. 41:9) that he inserted when he edited an early version of the Book of Jeremiah.

6.5 The End of the Kingdom of Yehud

It is common in exegetical literature to distinguish a pre-exilic period until 586 BCE, a post-exilic period from 520 BCE to 70 CE, and to label the period in between as "exilic." The terminology is problematic because it is a theological construct that looks back on the exile from the perspective of the return. No one could foresee in 582 BCE that there would ever be a return and restoration. It was not desired in Benjamin and, if it were hoped for in Babylonia, the hope was probably akin to the nostalgia felt by people who have left their homeland even when their new circumstances are more favourable than the lands they have left behind. Despite representations such as 2 Chronicles 36:20-21, only a minority was deported. In contrast to 2 Chronicles 36:23 and Ezra–Nehemiah, only a few children and grandchildren of the deportees ever returned. In 582 BCE, there were at least four categories of Judeans. Three of them comprised the population of the Babylonian province of Yehud (mostly Benjaminites), the deportees in Babylonia, and the communities of migrant workers in Egypt (Jeremiah 42–44), in Transjordan (Jer. 40:11; 41:15), and in Arabia (Psalm 120). A fourth category was made up of Judeans who lived in the southern parts of the kingdom—the region of Hebron and the Negev—and found themselves under Edomite domination. Their names can be detected in large numbers in the ostraca from fourth and third century BCE Idumea. The "exiles" in Babylonia were thus just one segment of the Jewish Diaspora.

Taking into account the information in Jeremiah, around 600 BCE the total population of the kingdom of Judah amounted to about 120,000–150,000 people, and his figures can be compared to details in 2 Kings:

597 BCE: 10,000 (2 Kgs 24:14) versus 3,023 Judean exiles (Jer. 52:28);

586 BCE: "the rest" (2 Kgs 25:11) versus 832 Jerusalemite exiles (Jer. 52:29);

597 BCE: flight to Egypt (2 Kgs 25:26) versus 545 Judean migrants (Jer. 52:30).

It is unclear whether the 4,600 deportees Jeremiah mentions for the three deportations include every deportee or if they are only the heads of households. If the latter, then dependants have to be added. Assuming an average household of four persons, the number of deportees can be extrapolated to 18,400, probably about 10% of the population, mostly from the elite. The weight of the Golah remained important because the deportees generally did well in Babylonia, and they increased accordingly, while the population of Yehud fell from 50,000 in 582 BCE to 15,000 in 500 BCE. The southern Levant as a whole entered into a deep economic depression caused by the shift of economic centres to the northern Syrian coast, leaving the Central Range isolated.

The three deportations of 597–582 BCE produced four rival groups of tradents of the traditions of Israel and Judah: the first Golah of 597 BCE, the second Golah of 586 BCE, the third Golah of 582 BCE, and the Benjaminites who remained in Yehud. The four groups held in common the tradition of Jacob, the Moses-Joshua cycle, and the story of the House of David (approximately 1 Samuel 9 to 2 Kings 10).

The first Golah, represented by the tradition of Ezekiel in Babylon, was ultra-conservative. Its members considered themselves the only true Israel. For them, there was no legitimate king in Jerusalem after they left the city. In the eyes of the first Golah, those who replaced them in Jerusalem and who later became the second Golah were mere squatters (Ezek. 11:1-21). The divine presence had left the temple of Jerusalem; hence, the Book of Ezekiel has nothing to say after that. In its utopian vision of the restoration of Jerusalem and Israel in Ezekiel 40–48, the Ezekiel group rejected the restorations of 520–398 BCE as well as the traditions of the Benjaminites who stayed in the land (Ezek. 33:23-29). The patriarch Abraham was rejected as an innovation, although the figure and traditions relating to Jacob are viewed less negatively than they are in Hosea 12 and were integrated within the Exodus paradigm (Ezek. 20:5; 28:25; 37:25). The Ezekiel group agreed with the Jeremiah group over their rejection of the Deuteronomistic theodicy that explained the exile as punishment for the sins of the kings (Jer. 31:29-30; Ezek. 18:2). Ezekiel's prophecy that Nebuchadnezzar would conquer Tyre was not fulfilled (Ezekiel 28); it took several revisions and two centuries to make the book fit the requirements of Deuteronomy 18:21-22 regarding prophecy spoken in the name of YHWH. While the so-called Priestly Document is linguistically close to Ezekiel, it is theologically very different (Guillaume 2009a: 33–50).

The tradents of Samuel-Kings are associated with the second deportation (586 BCE). They combined the story of the House of David with a list of the kings of Israel reconstructed from memory. For them, the legitimacy of any future government was tied to the House of David. They recognized Zedekiah as the last legitimate representative of the House of David but expressed the hope of a restoration of the dynasty through the story of Jehoiachin's pardon in Babylon (2 Kgs 25:27-30) and the genealogy of 1 Chronicles 3:17-24.

The views of the members of the third Golah (582 BCE) are expressed in what is commonly designated as Second Isaiah (Isaiah 40–55, but especially 40–48), a corpus produced by a group trained in the poetico-prophetic tradition that recognized the legitimacy of Persian rule. The third Golah, the group that was the last to leave Jerusalem, was the first to return. They accepted Cyrus as YHWH's representative on earth (Isa. 44:24–45:13), which brought them close to the Jeremiah group that had recognized Nebuchadnezzar as such (Jer. 27:6-8). The main difference they had with the Jeremiah group, however, was their keen interest in the restoration of Jerusalem. Otherwise, they were more open to the traditions of those who had stayed in the land than was so for the Ezekiel group. Hence, the Isaiah group integrated Abraham and Jacob (Isa. 41:8, see also 29:22; 51:1-2; 63:16). Like the Priestly Document, Second Isaiah represents a royal anthropology of the people of Israel.

The Jeremiah group stayed in Yehud because it had recognized Nebuchadnezzar as YHWH's representative on earth (Jer. 27:6) and the legitimate ruler over Israel. Hence, it preserved the traditions relative to Gedaliah (Jeremiah 40–42) and accepted the dual existence of Israel in the land and in the Diaspora (Jer. 29:1-9, 45). Jeremiah 29:8-9 can be read as a polemic against Ezekiel. Jeremiah 40:7-10 is a polemic against 2 Kings 25:12, which views those who remained in the land as insignificant peasants. The Jeremiah group's reply was that the Golah should remain where they were and not interfere with the affairs of Yehud (Jer. 29:1-9). Jeremiah 7 and 26 are anti-Davidic. Subsequent editors brought Jeremiah (and Ezekiel) in line with the consensus of the prophetic canon, a consensus according to which the entire population of Judah was exiled and then returned, and the only legitimate king had to be a descendant of David.

In Mizpah or Bethel, the Jacob cycle was expanded with the Abraham tradition (Genesis 12–13; 16; 18–19; 21). Originally from southern Judah, the Abraham traditions were received in Jerusalem in 597 BCE, when they became part of the social memory of the elite. The episode of Sodom and Gomorrah (Genesis 18–19) takes the fall of Jerusalem into account and downsizes the land promised to Abraham to the territory of Yehud, the Babylonian and later Persian province centred on Benjamin without southern Judah (Gen. 13:14-17). This legitimizes Benjamin's claim to represent the whole of Judah. Besides the work on Jeremiah and Jacob in Benjamin, the oracles first collected in the days of King Hosea were gradually expanded into two prophetic works (Hosea and Amos). Thanks to a lengthy editorial process, the exact stages of which are beyond recovery, three books (Hosea, Amos, and Micah) grew into a six-prophet collection (Hosea, Amos, Micah, Zephaniah, Nahum, and Habakkuk) before the collection reached the canonical number of 12 Minor Prophets.

These different proto-biblical works reflect the controversy over the correct policy under Babylonian rule regarding the concrete political demands of the Judean elite towards their Babylonian overlords. Wealth was the only way to access power in the aftermath of the destruction of Jerusalem, and although Benjaminite Mizpah and Bethel held that power, the exiles in Babylonia were in a better position to accumulate wealth and power to feed the debate over the legacy of the kingdom of Judah.

Part II

The Formation of Biblical Israel in Yehud and Samaria in the Persian Period

CHAPTER 7
FROM NEBUCHADNEZZAR II TO XERXES I:
MIZPAH, SAMARIA, AND JERUSALEM'S FIRST "SECOND TEMPLE"

The integration of the last Levantine kingdoms and the transition from Neo-Babylonian to Persian rule foster the rise of new identities based on ancestry rather than on loyalty to a local ruler. In this framework, the various attempts to set up Jerusalem's first "Second Temple" appear as rearguard actions of little significance.

7.1 From the Neo-Babylonian to the Persian Empire

Once Tiglath-pileser III (745–728 BCE) had turned the notion of empire into a reality, the empires that succeeded one another in the Levant made sure to secure their control over the land bridge on which Israel/Palestine sits. To this day, the idea of the sovereignty of small states in the area is an illusion based on temporary neglect by imperial powers. The structure of the geographical position of Israel/Palestine makes the two sides of the River Jordan a strategic zone. Apart from one century of Umayyad rule (660–750 CE), when Jerusalem was one of the centres of an empire that extended from Spain to Afghanistan, Israel/Palestine has always been at the periphery of empire. A second effect of the geographical structure on the fortunes of Israel/Palestine stems from its inhabitants' different attitudes towards the imperial power, these being contingent on the country's three natural zones: the highlands, the plains, and the steppe. In short, the lowlands tend to be collaborative, while the highlands foster resistance and the steppe alternates between the two. Different types of empire must also be taken into account, since there are variations in the way imperial rule is administered.

The Neo-Babylonian Empire continued Assyrian practices like deportation, but under Nebuchadnezzar II the first steps towards the Persian model of a "federal" monarchy were taken. Local autonomy for the provinces was unthinkable in the universalistic framework of the Assyrians, who felt that their mission was to subject the entire world to the god of the city of Ashur and turn everyone into an Assyrian. The Neo-Babylonians managed to take over the Assyrian Empire with the help of the unruly Medes, but they could conquer neither Egypt nor the island of Tyre despite a 13-year blockade and the oracles in Ezekiel 26–28. Babylon had no navy, and the sign of Tanit found in Babylon implies the deportation of Tyrians from the suburbs of Tyre on the mainland rather than the conquest of the island itself (against Schaudig 2008). What Nebuchadnezzar II accomplished was a broadening of the notion of empire from a particular city, Ashur or Babylon, to heaven itself. Babylon always viewed itself as the navel of the earth, the earthly residence of the supreme god, Marduk. The blue hue on the bricks of the Ishtar Gate, now reconstructed in the Pergamon Museum in Berlin, represents heaven, while the mythical creatures embody the heavenly guard of the popular etymology of Babylon: *bab-ili* "Gate of the gods." The story of Bel and the Dragon in Daniel 14 preserves a memory of this worldview, against which the Assyrians could never compete. Their inferiority complex towards Babylon encapsulates Assyria's "Babylonian issue," that caused the collapse of the Assyrian Empire. The Babylonians had the same problem in reverse: like the Egyptians with their hypnotic attachment to the Nile, they were too focused on Babylon's uniqueness to produce a lasting empire.

The influence of the Bible on our collective memory tends to make the Assyrians and the Babylonians appear larger and more powerful than they actually were. The Neo-Assyrian Empire flourished for a century. Inaugurated in 738, it was comatose by 639 BCE, after which it came to a speedy end. That century saw two usurpers on the throne, Tiglath-pileser and Esarhaddon, and two civil wars related to the accession of Esarhaddon and Assurbanipal. Hence, the Assyrian Empire was hardly more stable than the kingdom of Israel. This applies even more to the Neo-Babylonian Empire; its floruit lasted less than a century (626–539 BCE). It was essentially a two-person affair. Nabopolassar founded it and Nebuchadnezzar II completed it. His son Amel-Marduk (Evil-Merodach in 2 Kgs 25:27; Jer. 52:31) reigned for two years and was murdered by his brother-in-law Neriglissar (560–556 BCE), a general of Nebuchadnezzar II (Jer. 39:3, 13). Neriglissar's son was displaced after three months by Nabonidus, a high court official of Nebuchadnezzar and Neriglissar.

Nabonidus (556–539 BCE), the last Neo-Babylonian king, was born in Harran, northwest of Babylon, in the Assyrian heartland. Nabonidus sought to make the moon god Sin of Harran the supreme god of the Empire, a heresy in regard to Marduk's one thousand-year supremacy over the Babylonian pantheon. Echoes of the outcry from the threatened priesthood of Marduk were recorded in the Persian Verse Account of Nabonidus, a text produced after the conquest of Babylon by Cyrus:

> [I.19–25] [...] he made the no-sanctuary. [...] made a wind arise. [...], and no one in the land saw him. [...] he set up upon a base. [...] he called its name "Sin." [...] of lapis lazuli, wearing his crown. [...] the form of Sin was the eclipse. (Smith 1924, 87)

The second column is better preserved. It states that the king who made a temple for Sin wilfully decided that

> [II.10-11] Until I complete this, and finish the mourning, I shall omit the festival, I shall cause the New Year feast to cease. (Smith 1924, 88)

The text goes on to explain that the king entrusted the kingship to his eldest son and left for Tema, where he slaughtered the population. Finally, Cyrus, the worthy successor of Nebuchadnezzar, brought back order to Babylon.

The violence of the polemic is surprising in the context of Mesopotamian polytheism. Although Sin of Harran was a time-honoured god, the Verse Account portrays Sin as a newly invented monster. The main issue is Nabonidus' long stay in Arabia (Gruntfest and Heltzer 2001; Beaulieu 1989). For several years in succession, the absence of the king prevented the celebration of the Babylonian New Year festival, which was considered essential to the renewal of creation and the stability of the world for the coming year. A substitute could probably have been acceptable, but Nabonidus' absence may have been deliberate. As the polemical tone of the Verse Account suggests, Nabonidus' absence was part of his struggle with the all-powerful Marduk clergy. In his last regnal year, Nabonidus was back home and the New Year festival was celebrated in Babylon again, but by that time, Cyrus already stood at the gates of the city (*ANET* 305–307, Year 17). A last-minute compromise was found, according to which Marduk was paraded as usual during the New Year festival, while recognizing Sin's temple in Harran (*CoS* 123A-B).

In 553 BCE, Nabonidus conquered Edom, the last tribal state of the Levant (Grayson 1975, 104–111). Having flourished under Assyrian rule as a relay on the incense road between Arabia and the Mediterranean, Edom was ripe to become a province. Statehood thus developed from the centre to the periphery of the greater Syrian region, as shown in Table 4.

Table 4.   From state to province

	State formation	Provincialization
Aram-Damascus	900–850 BCE	732 BCE
Israel	900–850 BCE	733/724/720 BCE
Judah	850–800 BCE	597/586/582 BCE
Ammon	850–800 BCE	582 BCE
Moab	850–800 BCE	582 BCE
Edom	750–700 BCE	553 BCE

For the next three hundred years Edom became the home range of Bedouin who serviced the trade routes (Jer. 49:7-22; Obadiah; Ezek. 25:12-

14). From Edom, Nabonidus moved further south and conquered Tema, Dedan, Padakku (Fadak), Hibra (Haybar), Yadihu (Yadi), and Yatribu (now Medina), the north Arabian caravan cities. Nabonidus resided 10 years in Tema and fought with the Bedouin (Gadd 1958, 56–59; Livingstone 2005, 30–34). He justified his absence from Babylon by stating that the Babylonians had insulted Sin, who had struck them with hunger and disease, whereupon the king had gone into exile. It should be noted, however, that an army that does not fight on a regular basis loses practice. Ancient armies were financed by the proceeds of their campaigns, but when the army had reached the physical limits of its ability to project its power, as happened to Ashurbanipal after 639 BCE, annual campaigns were discontinued becasue an overextended force had no more hope for substantial bounty. Nabonidus probably understood this and sought to station Babylon's army in the last available fringe of his empire. In the eastern, northern, and western frontiers, Cyrus had already established the foundation of his future empire, while Egypt, which Nebuchadnezzar II had failed to conquer, was out of bounds. Logically, Nabonidus targeted Arabia, the only area in which he could expand without challenging a mighty neighbour. Hence, besides his purported Sin-monotheism, Nabonidus' long sojourn at Tema saved the costs of yearly redeployment from Babylon and preserved the economy of the provinces in between. Their reserves were not depleted to feed the passing army. The incense trade involved very few people, who were comparatively very rich and thus constituted easy prey. Nabonidus' Arabian campaigns are reflected in Isaiah 21:11-15, Ezekiel 25:13, and Jeremiah 49:8. Since all the caravan towns Nabonidus conquered still had a large Jewish population a millennium later at the advent of Islam, the origin of these communities could go back to Judean soldiers enrolled by Nabonidus.

The Bible includes more texts from the time of Nabonidus. Job 1 alludes to the relations with Arabia in 553–543 BCE. In Daniel 5, Belshazzar is Nabonidus' crown prince, the last king of Babylon. The Aramaic narrative of "Nabonidus in Arabia" found at Qumran (4QOrNab) calls him Naboni (נבוני). This text served as a template for Daniel 4, where the king is named Nebuchadnezzar. The concealment of Nabonidus reveals the importance of his actual role in the formation of biblical Israel; a role similar to that of Cambyses, another king whose name never appears in the Bible.

Some Jewish theologians had no trouble with the notion of Marduk as the highest god who makes a veiled appearance in Genesis 1:1-8. The primordial chaos, the *Tehom*, recalls Tiamat, the monster Marduk filleted in Enuma Elish as the basis for the heavens and the earth. During the Babylonian New Year festival, Marduk was thought to write the tablets of fate that determined the structure of the coming year. In a similar way, in post-biblical Judaism, YHWH writes the names in the Book of Life on Yom Kippur, the Day of Atonement 10 days after the New Year.

After the conquest of Nineveh (612 BCE) and of Harran (610–608 BCE), the Medes struck a deal with the pre-Achaemenid Persians. Some Medes took over Elam, which the Assyrians had devastated in 639 BCE. An Elamite-Persian kingdom was established and Elamite, a language unrelated to other known languages, became the first written language of the Persians, using Babylonian cuneiform on clay tablets and stone. While Nabonidus was in Tema, the Persian King Cyrus overthrew the Mede Astyages (550/549 BCE) and took his capital Ecbatana (next to Elamite Susa) to establish a Medio-Persian kingdom that became the basis of the Achaemenid Empire (Dan. 5:28; 6:8, 12, 15). In 546 BCE, Cyrus conquered Lydia in western Asia Minor and thus surrounded the Neo-Babylonian Empire from the east, north, and west. In 539 BCE Cyrus marched into Babylon, apparently welcomed by the clergy of Marduk. Isaiah 45:1 shows how well integrated the Isaianic group had become in Babylon. Nabonidus retired and Cyrus acquired the Babylonian possessions in the west, but he had no time to organize them. He fell in battle against the Scythians in 530 BCE, and his son Cambyses (530–522 BCE)) succeeded him. For the Medes, Cyrus was a Mede appointed by Ahuramazda. For the Babylonians, he was a Babylonian called by Marduk (CoS 2.124 in ANET 315–316). For Isaiah 44–45, Cyrus was anointed by YHWH. The notion that the supreme god had different names in different regions was acceptable to all.

According to the canonical scenario of exile and return, the arrival of Cyrus in Babylon marked the end of the exile. According to the Hebrew version of the Edict of Cyrus (Ezra 1:2-4), he was called by YHWH to rebuild the temple in Jerusalem and to invite all the exiles to return. A general permission to return was meaningless to second- or third-generation Judeans born in Babylonia; many of them held land grants for which they paid rent and taxes. None of them would want to give up their position if the general permission to return did not stipulate a concrete counterpart in the "homeland." No such provisions are mentioned in the Aramaic version of the edict (Ezra 6:3-5), which deals only with the rebuilding of the temple, specifying its dimensions and the return of the temple equipment Nebuchadnezzar had confiscated. In 539/538 BCE, the rebuilding of the temple of Jerusalem would not have been an issue. Jerusalem and its vicinity were severely depopulated. Taking Cyrus' edict at face value implies a temple was to be built in a ghost city. Insisting that the return to Zion had no demographic impact on Yehud, Lipschits (2005, 372) nevertheless claims that several thousand of the priestly caste returned to Jerusalem to serve in the temple worship with or without any Persian support (Lipschits 2006, 38–39). According to this view, the temple was significant enough to foster a slow and gradual recovery of the social, religious, and economic power of Yehud. The scenario of the restoration of the temple within a deserted, war-damaged former capital is in line with biblical passages (Haggai–Zechariah 8; Ezra 1–6) that insist on a divine mandate to rebuild the temple and ignore whoever disagreed (Edelman 2005, 81–146). Such a miraculous scenario, however, does not correspond with the harsh realities prevalent in the province at the time. The economic role of temples is well attested (Tuplin 1987), but despite the promises of Haggai 2:15-20 and Zechariah 8:20-23, it is the generation of economic surpluses that enables the construction of temples, rather than the construction of temples that miraculously generates surpluses. Promises of great harvests are part and parcel of temple foundation narratives, but the return of waves of Jewish immigrants to Zion immediately after Cyrus' edict is as mythical as the empty land after the destruction of Jerusalem. The erection of a new temple in Jerusalem had to happen as part of a broader imperial strategy of regeneration of the province, something that occurred later than Cyrus. The attribution of the plan to Cyrus reveals some knowledge of an Aramaic version of wording written on the Cyrus Cylinder, which was buried as a foundation deposit and where Cyrus claims that upon his accession he returned to their sanctuaries the statues of gods that Nabonidus had assembled in Babylon (CoS 2.124 in ANET 315–316). The Cylinder presents the evacuation of the divine statues as proof of Nabonidus' malice towards traditional religion (which it was not), so that Cyrus appears as the restorer of the traditional order. Since Yehud was politically part of Babylonia, the writers of Ezra simply expand the application of the act of restitution from Babylon to Jerusalem. In fact, Nabonidus had either gathered the divine images to Babylon for the celebrations of the New Year or to protect them from the advancing Persian army.

7.2 Yehud from 582 to 525 BCE

It is common to assert that in the wake of the destruction of Jerusalem in 586 BCE, the southern part of the kingdom of Judah was amputated and Hebron and the Negev were turned over to Edom or to Kedar (Stern 2001, 369). This idea is based on the assumption that since Geshem the Arab is mentioned as one of the enemies of Nehemiah (Nehemiah 2, 6), he must have been governing the region adjoining Yehud to the south. It is not certain, however, that Geshem can be compared with Sinuballit and Tobiah and that he was the governor of the region that eventually became Idumea (Eph'al 1982, 212; Edelman 2006). All we know is that until 445 BCE, the centre of the province was Mizpah (2 Kgs 25:23-25; Neh. 3:7; Jer. 40:6–41:16). The main temple of Yahweh remained at Bethel until then. In contrast to the region of Jerusalem and to the lowlands, Benjamin was not devastated. Ezekiel 33:23-29, which reflects the polemics of the first Golah (597 BCE) against those who were not deported, criticizes the iconic cult at Bethel and describes the Benjaminite population as living in ruins, in the open field (tents), and in caves. Besides the polemic, living in caves, tents, and ruins was nothing new. It characterized the way of life of shepherds and mobile farmers. Their numbers rose after the devastation of 588–586 BCE, when many towns and villages were razed. Hence, Abraham the tent dweller reflects life in the Jerusalemite region after the Babylonian destructions rather than a memory of the Bronze Age. Ruins and caves were also good places to hide from the raids of the proto-Bedouin of Kedar, described as Midian in Judges 6:2-5.

The 4,600 Judean exiles (Jer. 52:28-30) amounted to about 5% of the total population of the kingdom. Yet, the population shrank from about 100,000 people around 600 BCE to 15,000 in 500 BCE (Lipschits 1999; Carter 1999), less because of war and deportations and more as a consequence of the marginalization of the southern Levant in the sixth century BCE that led to the exodus of the most productive segment of the population. Around 400 BCE, some 3,000 Judeans lived at Elephantine (Aswan), and at least 15,000 dwelt throughout Egypt.[1] At the time, the population in Judea reached 30,000, having doubled every 100 years since 500 BCE (Lipschits 2003). Hence, with a realistic factor of 2.3 children reaching adulthood per couple and five generations per century, the population decline of the sixth century BCE could be reversed without having to postulate a significant return of exiles.

Economic stagnation in the southernmost area of the Neo-Babylonian Empire was the result of Nebuchadnezzar's decision to shift the commercial hub away from Philistia and Phoenicia, both of which were turned into a depleted buffer-zone as a consequence of the cold war between Babylonia and Egypt. Nabonidus' campaign in Arabia aimed at diverting the Arabia–Mediterranean trade to northern Syria. Without copper exports and Arabian trade, Edom shrank to a few bases (Bozrah, Eilat), and the rest was left to the Bedouin. Nabonidus mentioned Gaza as the furthest point of his realm (CoS 2.123A). Unlike the Assyrians, the Neo-Babylonians did not invest in infrastructure and safety measures in southern Syria-Palestine; as a result, many residents of the area sought a livelihood elsewhere. Some of the Jewish mercenaries at Elephantine migrated to Egypt between 582 and 525 BCE. Other Judeans followed Nabonidus to

---

1   On the demography of Elephantine, see Knauf (2002a). According to Isa. 19:18, five cities spoke the "language of Canaan," i.e. Hebrew and/or Phoenician, in the Persian period when this "prophecy" was put in the mouth of Isaiah. The minimal number of Judeans at Elephantine, 3,000, is taken as the average of the five places.

Arabia and settled there. Israel/Palestine in the sixth century BCE became an economic backwater and its population declined. However, Persian rule reversed the trend and turned the entire coast, Philistia as much as Phoenicia, into a thriving zone. This favourable *conjoncture* persisted until the early Islamic period (Figure 5, shipwrecks), which in turn explains the steady demographic growth from the fifth century BCE to the first centuries of the Common Era.

The fact that Benjamin suffered little in 588–586 BCE fostered the rise of a new elite in the sixth century BCE: the Ḥorim (חרים), a distinctive category that appears for instance in Nehemiah 5:7. Neglecting southern Syria, the Neo-Babylonians let the local population organize itself in the absence of a royal institution. Local councils provided the basis of the local autonomy granted later by the Persians. The community's autonomous self-regulation was consistent with the Neo-Babylonian legal system, as illustrated by a trial and execution that took place in the reign of Nebuchadnezzar II (594/593 BCE):

> [Obv. 1–20] Baba-ahu-iddina, the son of Nabu-ahhe-bulliṭ, son of Sha-reshum-mani, instigated sin and crime and turned his mind to wickedness. He did not keep the sworn agreement of the king, his lord, and conspired (to do) evil. At that time Nebuchadnezzar, king of Babylonia... thoroughly examined the evil deeds of Baba-ahu-iddina and caught his conspiracy. Before the assembly of the people he proved against him the sin he committed, glared at him angrily, ordered that he will not live, and they cut his throat. (Na'aman 2008, 203)

The king had to argue his case in front of his peers, demonstrating the guilt before the assembly executed the conspirator.

Until the Ottoman era, legal practice was not based on law codes. In theory, the king was the incarnation of righteousness (Psalm 72) and its symbolic guarantor in everyday life. In practice, justice was rendered by local elders called upon to arbitrate disputes on the basis of customary law. Hence, the biblical collection of "laws," like the Covenant "Code" (Exodus 21–23), is a motley assemblage of extreme cases designed for the education of scribes rather than of judges. Actual legal practice cannot be inferred from the extant legal collections.

The Exodus-Joshua story (Schmid 2010) was expanded by inserting the Covenant Code as a constitutional treaty between Yahweh and Israel. The first step towards transforming the Exodus story into Torah was thus taken. Yet, the Judeans who lived in Yehud claimed privileges for themselves not with this story but with the promise of land granted to Abraham, their father (Ezek. 33:23-29).

The marginalization of the Exodus tradition in sixth-century Yehud is also reflected in the elaboration of a new foundation legend at Bethel. The gods of the Exodus were replaced by Jacob's heavenly vision in which he was promised offspring and return to the land of Canaan. Abraham thus became Jacob's (grand-) father (Gen. 28:11-22). In this vision, YHWH stands at the entrance of the heavenly throne room (Gen. 28:13), showing he is not yet the supreme god who sits on the throne. YHWH is presented in a subservient position and not as a rival of Marduk. Hence, Bethel recognized the suzerainty of Babylon.

Willing cooperation with the colonial power was always the hallmark of the Jacob tradition. Having served as the central sanctuary of the Judeans in lieu of Jerusalem, Bethel prepared the ground for the concept of biblical Israel in the Persian period. Although Judah had claimed Israel's heritage after the demise of the kingdom of Samaria, it is Bethel that produced the theological synthesis expressed in the creed of Judaism: "Hear, O Israel: The LORD is our God, the LORD is one" (Deut. 6:4). Rather than a monotheist confession, the *Shema' yisrael* is a confession of "monoyahwism." There is only one YHWH, whether he is worshipped at Samaria, Bethel, or Tema.

In the seventh century BCE, Ashurbanipal and his vassals in Transjordan fought against Arabs, mainly from the tribe of Kedar. Nabonidus annexed the north Arabian oases and eliminated the Transjordanian states (Moab and Edom), which benefitted the Arab tribes, especially Kedar. In the fifth century BCE, Kedar controlled the open country from Idumea to Egypt's eastern Delta and northwest Arabia (Isa. 21:13-17). The Edomite heartland in Mount Seir became the centre of a Kedarite clan, out of which the Nabateans later emerged. The traditions of Edom shifted west of the Arabah depression to the Negev, which became the province of Idumea in the fourth century BCE. Continuing a trend initiated by the settlement of Arab deportees in the province of Samaria by Sargon, the Edomites were increasingly Arabized; the geographer Strabo considered the Edomites to be immigrant Nabateans. The relations between Judeans and Kedar were sometimes hostile (Gen. 16:12) but not always so, because both groups shared the same interest in Arabian trade. Hence, Ishmael was deemed the son of Abraham and the beneficiary of the same covenant (Genesis 17), despite the reference to Isaac as Abraham's only son (Gen. 22:2). Proximity generates tensions that do not hinder cohabitation. So Isaac and Ishmael together are said to have buried their father at Machpelah (Gen. 25:9).

7.3 Yehudites in Babylonia

In Babylon, Jehoiachin and his sons (*ANET* 308) were housed in the royal palace. The other deportees lived in closed communities as colonists and vassals of the Crown. A "City of Judah" (Al Yahudu) is attested to by a group of tablets that currently are being published. The location of this "new Jerusalem" is unknown because the tablets come from illegal excavations (Pearce 2006). Yet, they illustrate the difference between Babylonian and

Assyrian deportation policy. The Assyrians had integrated deportees into Assyrian society while the Babylonians scattered them across the Empire. As a result, however, deportees were able to preserve their cultural heritage under the Neo-Babylonians.

Even so, Judean deportees did not form an ideologically homogeneous group. The deportees of 597, 586, and 582 BCE were probably settled separately. Besides the old elite of 597 BCE (the Ezekiel group), there were the upstarts of 586 BCE with the Samuel/Kings traditions, and the Zionists of 582 BCE (Isaiah 40–48). Yet, despite their ideological differences, they all followed the advice of Jeremiah 29:4-7. They settled down, made a career, intermarried and raised families, and generally sought the welfare of the city where they lived. They probably built a temple or shrines to worship YHWH, as did the Judeans in Elephantine (Egypt) and Idumea. Legal contracts from Elephantine archives mention a temple of Yaho in that community (Porten 1996, 139–147), and an ostracon from Idumea lists temples to YWHW, al-'Uzza, and Nabu somewhere near Makkedah (Porten and Yardeni 2007). Whether it did occur or not, the pardon of King Jehoiachin on the accession of Amel-Marduk (2 Kgs 25:27-30 // Jer. 52:31-34) presupposes that Judeans caused no trouble in exile and thus deserved the favour of the new king on the occasion of his celebration of his first New Year festival.

The Judean language written at the court of Jerusalem in the eighth to sixth centuries BCE evolved, as all languages do. It gave rise to the Hebrew of the consonantal text of the Hebrew Bible. The main differences between Judean and biblical Hebrew are orthographic, as shown in Table 5.

Table 5. Judean and Biblical Hebrew

		Judean	Biblical Hebrew
his tent	'oholo	אהלה	אהלו
her tent	'oholah	אהלה	אהלה
his tents	'ohalaw	אהלו	אהליו
her tents	'ohaléha	אהלה	אהליה

In the sixth century BCE, Judean was replaced by Aramaic as the language of officialdom. In Yehud, Judean religious texts were transmitted according to the Judean orthography.[2] The spoken language of Yehud,

---

2 The expension of an older Jacob story into a Abraham-Jacob story probably took place in the sixth century BCE: see Ezekiel 33:24 (Schmid 2010).

with its predominantly Benjaminite population, was a northern dialect out of which emerged Mishnaic Hebrew. In the Golah, where Judeans lived among non-Judean speakers, they became bilingual, preserving their Judean at home and communicating in Aramaic with the Babylonians. When members of the Babylonian Golah became the new elite of Jerusalem, they distinguished themselves from the "people of the land" by their spoken Judean. They appropriated the old literary heritage both from Babylon and Yehud and disinherited its Benjaminite keepers by changing the orthography from Judean to Biblical Hebrew, also referred to as Standard Biblical Hebrew. Archaic spellings such as אהלה, "his tent" in Genesis 13:3 are preserved in Standard Biblical Hebrew, which indicates the faithful transmission of older sources, including their archaic orthography.

In the ancient world, literature was produced in and for schools. Hence, there is no need to postulate the rise of private libraries in the Golah, preserving scrolls that the exiles took in their baggage. Jeremiah 52 (Yehud tradition) gives exact numbers for the deportees of 597, 586 and 582 BCE while 2 Kings 25 (586 BCE Golah tradition) transmits round and exaggerated numbers for the first two deportations and ignores the third one. Scrolls which survived 586 BCE in Yehud were evidently taken over by Mizpah and/or Bethel. The frequent reference to "the rest of the deeds of king NN'" in 2 Kings (for instance 2 Kgs 14:18; 15:11, 15, 21, 26...) might indicate that the scribes and priests of the Golah reconstructed books which they had partially learnt by heart in their own school days, without having access to the actual scrolls.

Cyrus' takeover in Babylon changed nothing for the Golah, except perhaps the addition of yet another name for the highest God besides YHWH in Jerusalem and Marduk in Babylon. In Susa and Ecbatana, the supreme god was Ahuramazda. This in itself would have corroborated the opinion that eventually spread: Marduk and Ahuramazda were other names for YHWH.

The most recent debate about the origin of biblical monotheism, which began in the 1980s, is now entering its fourth decade without any sign of a consensus in sight. The agreed points are that the religion of the First Temple was polytheistic, while the religion of the Second Temple was monotheistic from the beginning. Something occurred in between. What is meant by "monotheism" is, of course, crucial. Exclusive monotheism implies that all gods but one's own are false gods. Inclusive monotheism postulates a single god worshipped under different names. Inclusive monotheism was already known to the Egyptians at the end of the second millennium and to the Assyrians in the seventh century BCE. In its final form, the Bible contains both exclusive (Exodus 34; Deuteronomy 7, 20) and inclusive monotheism (Genesis 9; 17; Exodus 6).

The question whether some Judeans returned to Yehud before 500 BCE remains open. At first glance, the answer is negative. People were unlikely to give up favourable circumstances in Babylonia for the love of the home country. Yet, some degree of movement between Yehud and Babylon existed. Some members of the Judean Golah travelled on private business or were commissioned by the government.

7.4 Cambyses, Darius, and the First "Second Temple"

Cyrus' son and successor Cambyses (530–523/522 BCE) extended the Persian Empire into Egypt (525 BCE). Egypt remained more or less in Persian hands for over a hundred years, despite a series of challenges to the Persian hegemony. In Egypt, the Persian kings ruled as pharaohs and are counted as the Twenty-Seventh Dynasty, replacing the previous Saite Dynasty installed by the Assyrians. *De jure*, the Achaemenids now ruled Persia, Media, Babylon, and Egypt in personal union. *De facto*, Egypt became a province.

According to Herodotus (3.27–29), Cambyses supposedly killed the Apis bull, a living embodiment of the god Ptah, at Memphis, and the Egyptians never forgave him. It is hard to imagine that having just conquered Egypt, Cambyses would commit such a terrible blunder while presenting himself as the new pharaoh. While Cambyses was indeed influenced by Zoroastrianism, indicated by his giving his daughter Atossa a Zoroastrian name, would he have let his repulsion for the worship of a living animal override diplomatic considerations at such a delicate juncture of his career? Herodotus' report on the murder of the Apis bull is very problematic (Kahn 2007).

Cambyses seems to have died on his way back to Persia in 523 or 522 BCE under obscure circumstances. He may have fallen victim to a coup perpetrated by Darius, his successor. The Bible never mentions Cambyses. After Cambyses' nearly three-year absence from Babylon, his distant cousin Bardiya replaced him as either his legitimate successor or, if one is to believe the account of Darius, as a usurper.

After a civil war (522–517 BCE), Darius I killed all his competitors and recounted his victory on a rockface at Bisutun (or Behistun) in three languages: Elamite, Babylonian, and Old Persian, a cuneiform syllabary system invented for the occasion. An Aramaic version of the text was discovered in the archives of the Jewish military colony at Elephantine more than 2,000 km from Behistun on the overland route. The victory Ahuramazda granted to Darius was read as mass propaganda by every scribe across the Empire. Herodotus' report (3.70–86) largely coincides with the representation of Darius because he received his information from Persian officials who likely had learned to read and write with this text. Darius claimed genealogical ties to Cyrus and Cambyses, whom he presented as the successors of the Persian King Achaemenes. They were not, but the genealogical fiction founded the Achaemenid dynasty that ruled for about 200 years. The relative stability of the Persian Empire was largely the result of the shift of instability to Egypt, which now became the contested zone. Egypt had been a major logistical hurdle for the Mesopotamian empires, and even more so for the Persian Empire, its heartland being even further east. To overcome the fundamental problem of overextension, Darius I completed the canal linking the Nile to the Red Sea. The canal may be interpreted as an attempt to establish a direct maritime link between the Persian heartland and Egypt as an alternative to the land routes. How significant this naval link became is unknown, since the bulk of our sources on the Persian Empire are written in Greek and focus on the Mediterranean. The difficulties of Red Sea navigation seem to have limited the economic value of the canal (Redmount 1995; Burstein 2008, 135–148). Another solution to overextension was the desert road that linked Babylon directly to Arabia through Wadi Sirhan. Nabonidus' prolonged presence in Tema was probably related to this new route, even if he did not use it himself (Dalley and Goguel 1997, 174). This direct route to the southern periphery of the Empire was operating during Persian times (Byrne 2003, 12). It could not replace the Tadmor–Damascus route, but it reduced the importance of the Arabah that connected northern Arabia with the Mediterranean. As a result, the ability to move some supplies and troops between Persia and Egypt by ship around the Arabian Peninsula and overland through the route around the hostile Nafud Desert (the route on which Cambyses may has met his fate during his hurried return from Egypt) reduced the strategic importance of the Palestinian land routes (Arabia–Gaza, Egypt–Syria) and kept the Palestinian highlands in the margins (Figure 36).

The strategic insignificance of the Palestinian highlands is one argument against the idea that Cyrus and his troops, who probably never crossed the Euphrates, would have shown a particular interest in Jerusalem (Briant 2000, 238). To get around the problem, it is necessary to postulate an early restoration of the temple by Zionist enthusiasts from the Babylonian Golah. It has been claimed that they rebuilt the temple of Jerusalem independently, even against the will of the Persian administration (Lipschits 2006, 38–39). It seems unlikely, however, that residents in Babylonia would have been able to move to Jerusalem and build a temple there behind the Persians' backs. Another possibility has been suggested, that the temple was rebuilt by the local population (Bedford 2001). Would the Persians have allowed the restoration of the temple before it suited their strategic interests in the region? This point is likely to be one of the most debated issues in research in the years ahead.

If the Jerusalemite temple was not restored by returnees from Babylon, the next option is an early restoration of a fort in the ruins of Jerusalem in 520–515 BCE by the Persian administration to protect the flanks of the Via Maris. The citadel found in the vicinity of the temple during the Hel-

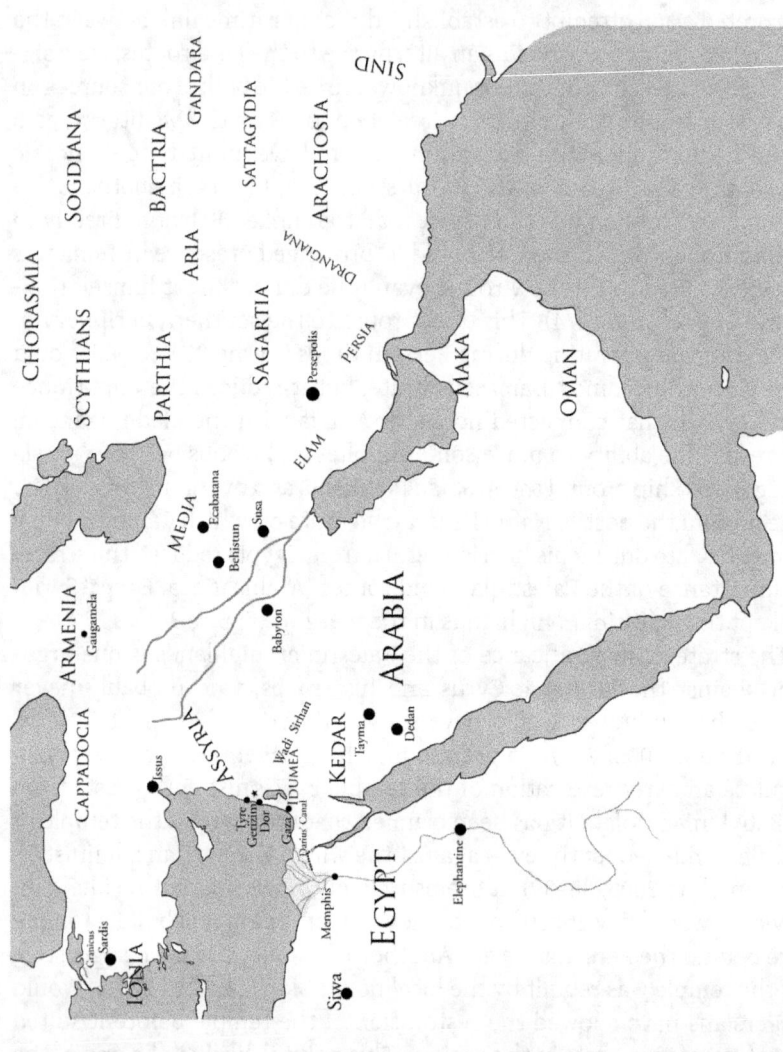

Figure 36: Map of Persian Empire (T. Guillaume).

lenistic period, the "Antonia" during Herod's reign, would have been the successor to this early fort. As was the case at Elephantine on the southern border of Egypt, the fort was an imperial fortress, a *birah* (Neh. 2:8; 7:2; 1 Chron. 29:1, 19). A shrine like the one built at Arad would have been erected inside the Jerusalemite fort. This small chapel (10 m sq at most) would not have been intended to compete with the provincial sanctuary at Bethel, the primacy of which was recognized (Zech. 7:1-2).

The manpower to serve the garrison of this fortress would have been recruited among the Judean deportees in Babylonia who came with Zerubbabel and a few other families in 525-520 BCE (Zech. 6:9-15). Other Judeans followed: Sheshbazzar with the temple vessels in 518-515 BCE (Ezra 1:5-11), 22 priests, and six Levites (Neh. 12:1-8), the governor Nehemiah and his household in 445 BCE (Neh. 5:16), and Ezra with a staff and retinue of 1,496 men and 220 Levites in 398 BCE (Ezra 7:11-28; 8:1-35). This latter group escorted a huge donation from the Babylonian Diaspora.

Just as the Elephantine fort guarded the southern border of Egypt, so the Jerusalemite fort would have guarded the southern border of Benjamin and the southern branch of the east-west route between the Transjordanian plateau and the Mediterranean coast from raiding bands, as depicted in Judges 6:1-4. A Jerusalemite fort was thus necessary, even if the Benjaminite and Kedarite elite entertained friendly relations. As military colonies were preferably not manned by locals, the Jerusalemite fort was not manned by Benjaminites but by descendants of the old Jerusalem elite who avowed their loyalty to Persia and represented no risk of collusion with the local Benjaminites.

A possible early restoration of a chapel within the fort does not challenge the notion that the "Second Temple" of Jerusalem was built in relation to Persian affairs in Egypt. When the Persians decided to regain control of the Nile Delta, something more than a fort and a chapel inside it was necessary. Jerusalem found a new place in the wider Persian strategy. Hence, Edelman (2005, 334) situates the rebuilding of the temple around 450 BCE in the context of the imperial policy of Artaxerxes I (464-424 BCE). Artaxerxes spent the early part of his reign regaining control over Egypt, which Persia had lost for the third time. At that time, the restoration of the city and its temple rose high on the Persian agenda. The 70 years of exile in Jeremiah 29:10 and 2 Chronicles 36:21 are stretched to a good 120 years, which is not a problem in itself, since "70" is clearly a symbolic number with little significance for the actual date of the restoration of the temple.

The problem with Edelman's hypothesis is that it turns all the texts claiming an early restoration into fiction (Ezra 6; Haggai 1-2; Zechariah 1-8). To save some degree of historicity for these texts, it is possible to claim that Cambyses or one of his generals had noticed the strategic importance of Jerusalem in the wake of the first Achaemenid campaign in Egypt (525 BCE). The campaign was successful and it shifted the frontier a thousand kilometers south to the middle of the Nile Valley (Figure 36). Cambyses would have had to have been particularly lucid to foresee the involvement of the Greeks to support Egypt following the disastrous campaigns of his successors in the Aegean world. The first Egyptian rebellion took place 40 years after Cambyses' conquest of Egypt, at the end of the reign of Darius I ca. 486 BCE. It was only then that continuous trouble in Egypt increased the strategic significance of the Palestinian land bridge.

The Aegean world had not challenged the Assyrian hegemony over Egypt, and the Neo-Assyrians had time to develop Palestine before expanding southward beyond the Nile Delta. Faced with Aegean enemies, Artaxerxes had to regenerate the Palestinian economy before troops could be concentrated on the frontier to regain Egypt. This marked the end of a century-and-a-half of Neo-Babylonian neglect (586–450 BCE) and the onset of a Persian era of active involvement in the highlands. Instead of ending with Cyrus' accession to the Persian throne, the so-called "exilic" period lasted until 450 BCE (Edelman 2005, 334–343).

Strictly speaking, the Persian era in Palestine runs from Artaxerxes I to the integration of Palestine into the Ptolemaic kingdom during the First Syrian War (276–272 BCE). At that point, Ptolemy II secured a hold over Palestine for almost a century and removed the area from the Mesopotamian orbit of which it had been a part since the seventh century BCE. Refusing to consider 333 BCE a major turning-point is justified, since Alexander's meteoric career did not translate into lasting changes in Palestine. On the broader scale of the ancient Levant, Alexander appears as the last Achaemenid ruler rather than as the founder of a new political entity (Briant et al. 2008, 109–146).

7.5 Persians, Phoenicians, Arabs, and Greeks

Cyrus and Cambyses conquered what would become the Persian Empire; Darius I (522–486 BCE) organized it. He made Old Persian a language of the Empire in addition to Elamite, Babylonian, and Aramaic. He restored the roads and postal service organized by the Assyrians and Neo-Babylonians and set up an intelligence service, the "eyes and ears of the king" (Job 1:6-12; 2:1-7; Zech. 3:1-2; 6:1-9). Next to the capital cities of Susa (in Elam), Babylon, and Ecbatana (modern Hamadan), he founded the palace city of the Persians, Persepolis (Figure 36). Inspired by the invention of coinage in Lydia (Asia Minor), he struck the Daric (1 Chron. 29:7; Ezra 2:69; 8:27; Neh. 7:70-72), coins of very high gold quality bearing the image of a kneeling archer ready to shoot. Contrary to a commonly held notion, the primary function of ancient coinage was not to finance trade, which was based mostly on credit and on weighted silver. Ancient coins were principally a convenient way to pay mercenaries and to give soldiers in exchange for booty (Vargyas 2000; Nimchuk 2002).

To counter-balance the physical size of the Empire, which rendered effective administration extremely difficult, the Persians granted the provinces greater levels of autonomy than had been the case with the Assyrians, who wanted to turn the entire world into Assyrians. Eschewing Empire-wide uniformity, the provinces developed their own characteristics, which laid the basis for what would become known as ethnicity in the Hellenistic period. The Table of Nations in Genesis 10 expresses Achaemenid imperial ideology (Uehlinger 1990, 578–583). "Nations" is a misnomer; tribes or peoples is preferable, because it was their tribal heritage that enabled the Persians to recognize other population groups as co-tribes. To be a Persian was to be different from others, and it was a matter of great pride. Cultural differences were cultivated, and this proto-ethnic consciousness spread to other peoples of the Empire. To be Judean gradually turned into possessing the condition of Jewishness, which meant also that one could be a Jew, i.e., eat, dress, and live like a Jew, without living in Yehud.

This aspect of Persianism is fundamental to the formation of the first part of the Hebrew Bible, the Torah. Before it became the "Law" under the influence of Hellenism, it was the "Teaching," a repository of traditions that provided the basis of a distinct identity within a wide empire in which the deportations of the previous centuries had mixed peoples of various origins, forcing them to live together. On an inscription from Persepolis, Darius I prays:

> [DPd §3] May Ahuramazda bear me aid, with the gods of the royal house; and may Ahuramazda protect this country from a (hostile) army, from famine, from the Lie! (Kent 1953, 136)

The word *dahyu*, translated "country," refers to a "tribe." Often combined with toponyms, it designates an ethnically defined population as reflected in the so-called Table of Nations in Genesis 10. The Lie refers to the rule of an illegitimate king. In another inscription from Persepolis, Darius states:

> [DPe §1] I am Darius the Great King, King of Kings, King of many tribes [*dahyu*], son of Hystaspes, an Achemenian. [§1] Saith Darius the King: By the favour of Ahuramazda there are the tribes that I got into my possession along with this Persian folk, which felt fear of me (and) bore me tribute: Elam, Media, Babylonia, Arabia, Assyria, Egypt, Armenia, Cappadocia, Sardis (Lydia), Ionians who are of the mainland and (those) who are by the sea, and tribes that are across the sea; Sagartia (Kurdistan?), Parthia, Drangiana (Helmand), Aria (Afghanistan), Bactria, Sogdiana, Chorasmia, Sattagydia, Arachosia, Sind (Pakistan), Gandara (Cashmere), Scythians, Maka (Oman). (adapted from in Kent 1953, 136, paratheses added)

Both inscriptions illustrate how the Persians conceived of their relationship with their subjects. The description does not correspond to the administrative division into satrapies. A satrap was a governor, be it of a large province or a small town. In the second inscription, Assyria refers to Syria, i.e. the entire territory west of the Euphrates as far south as the Wadi of Egypt, south of Gaza. Arabia does not yet correspond to the entire peninsula but only to the northern and eastern parts Nabonidus had conquered.

If the restoration of Jerusalem and its temple only became meaningful after the Achaemenids first lost control of Egypt (Edelman 2005), the biblical passages used to support the construction of the "second" temple already in the days of Darius I must be reconsidered. According to Haggai 1:1-6, the reproach for not rebuilding the temple was addressed to the governor of Judah on August 29, 520 BCE. At the time, the governor's seat was not at Jerusalem. It was transferred there in the days of Nehemiah. Hence, nothing indicates that the house of YHWH that lay in ruin at the time was the temple of Jerusalem.

The second oracle, in Haggai 2:1-9 (dated October 17, 520 BCE), addressed the governor Zerubbabel along with the high priest. Again, this is not evidence for the restoration of a temple and the priesthood at Jerusalem. The disturbances caused by the civil war before the accession of Darius I could have suggested that the current world order was about to collapse. Zerubbabel could have felt it was time to restore the Davidic dynasty (Hag. 2:20-23, December 18, 520 BCE). It was the eventual placement of the Book of Haggai between Zephaniah and Zechariah within the collection of the 12 Minor Prophets that made these oracles relevant to Jerusalem.

By contrast with Haggai, the Book of Zechariah is entirely focused on Jerusalem. In the first vision (Zech. 1:7-17, February 519 BCE), YHWH declares that he now wants to return to Jerusalem because the world is at peace. The building is to be measured out; therefore, construction had not yet begun. Then, the undated oracle of Zechariah 4:5-10 urges Zerubbabel to complete the temple he has begun.

Ezra 6:15 indicates an actual date for the completion of the temple (March 12, 515 BCE). Otherwise, the texts mention endless hurdles that render the successive royal edicts surprisingly ineffectual. At best, the construction of the Second Temple was initiated by two prophets during the political turmoil of 522–520 BCE. Much uncertainty surrounds the central figure of Zerubbabel, who was a son of Shealtiel son of Jehoiachin according to Ezra 5:2, or a son of Pedaiah according to 1 Chronicles 3:16-19. Whatever happened at Jerusalem in 522–515 BCE, it does look like something significant, in retrospect.

In light of the above, the description of the construction of the Second Temple in Ezra 1-6 appears as a propagandistic, post-332 BCE elaboration dotted with anachronisms. As in Daniel 11:2, the 12 Persian kings are reduced to four: Cyrus, Darius, Xerxes, and Artaxerxes. Cambyses, the

Persian ruler who physically passed closest to Jerusalem, is unknown to the writers for whom the Persian era was long past and for which they had little or no sources, depending on how reliable one considers the different edicts and dates. Given the lack of precise identification of the Persian rulers, the construction of the temple can be equally dated in the reign of Darius I (522 BCE), Darius II (424 BCE), or Darius III (336 BCE) (Ezra 4:5). Allegations against the project (Ezra 4:24) are submitted under Xerxes (486 BCE) and again (Ezra 4:7) under Artaxerxes I (465-425 BCE), Artaxerxes II (404-359 BCE), or Artaxerxes III (358-338 BCE). The work started again under one Darius (Ezra 4:24) and was completed under the same or another Darius (Ezra 6:15). Ezra 6:17-22 is full of anachronisms and errors concerning Persian history.

In the royal inscriptions from Darius I to Darius II (424-404 BCE), Ahuramazda is the only god, but the Persians were not monotheists any more than Jews were at the time. The Persian rulers were influenced by Zoroastrianism, a religion of obscure origins. Zoroaster is the Hellenistic name of Zarathustra, an Iranian prophet whose fictitious biography developed like those of the biblical prophets in the seventh and sixth centuries BCE. Zarathustra had lived in a remote valley of eastern Iran and left religious poems that hallow Ahuramazda as the creator of all, the supreme God (or supreme spirit) and the origin of both evil and good, involving individuals in a constant struggle between the two. The form and contents of Zoroastrianism in the fifth and fourth centuries BCE are at present undecided. Much of our knowledge is based on later sources. Herodotus (1.131) does not mention Zoroaster. For him, the Persians revered Zeus, the sky, the sun, moon, earth, fire, water, and air. Fire evokes the fire cult of modern Zoroastrianism, but it was not necessarily so in Achaemenid times.

The only sources for the religion of the Achaemenids are their inscriptions. Ahuramazda is the greatest of the gods, the god who grants the king his land (AsH §2 in Kent 1953, 116). Ahuramazda created the earth, the sky, humanity, and happiness (Dann §1 in Kent 1953, 137-138). Ahuramazda also created the king (DSF §3 in Kent 1953, 142-143) and his means of existence, namely the earth, people, happiness, good horses, and good chariots (DSs in Kent 1953, 146). The best thing for humans is to follow his instructions (DSs §6 and DNb in Kent 1953, 139-140; XPH §4d in Kent 1953, 151-152). Besides Ahuramazda, other gods or the gods of the royal family are sometimes mentioned (DSe §6 in Kent 1953, 142; XPC §3 in Kent 1953, 149; D2Sa in Kent 1953, 154). Xerxes (486-465 BCE) mentions *arta* as a hypostasis of righteousness besides Ahuramazda (XPH §4b, 4d in Kent 1953, 151-152). Beginning with Artaxerxes II (404-359 BCE), the goddess Anahita and the sun god Mithra are mentioned next to Ahuramazda (A2Sa in Kent 1953, 154). Mithra even replaces Ahuramazda in a request for protection (A2Hb in Kent 1953, 155). Compared with the exclusive monotheism of biblical Deuteronomism, the Achaemenid sources give the impression of a tolerant theological system.

There were, however, limits to religious tolerance. One of Xerxes' inscriptions mentions the destruction of the sanctuaries of "demons" (Kent 1953, 151). In 484 BCE Xerxes (486–465 BCE) destroyed the image of Marduk in Babylon, preventing the celebration of the New Year festival and marking the end of Babylon's special status as a kingdom ruled in personal union with the rest of the Empire.

With Cyrus' conquest of Sardis (546 BCE), the capital of the Lydian kingdom of Croesus in Asia Minor, the Persian Empire came into direct contact with the Aegean world and was irresistibly drawn into conflicts that eventually proved fatal to the Achaemenids. In 490 BCE, Darius landed an army at Athens to punish the Greeks for their support of a revolt of the Ionian cities (on the coast of Asia Minor). The Persian force was defeated at Marathon. In retaliation, Xerxes led an army and a fleet to Greece in 480 BCE. The fleet was sunk at Salamis; 50,000 sailors died in a few hours. As the Phoenicians had been the primary providers of the fleet, it is possible that the Sidonian king Eshmun'azor was granted the Sharon plain between Dor and Jaffa (CoS 2.57 in ANET 662) to compensate for the losses at Salamis.

Under Persian rule, the Phoenicians prospered as suppliers of warships and as intermediaries between the Mediterranean world and the Persian Empire. Phoenician merchants moved freely within the Empire (Neh. 13:16), but in the Mediterranean they increasingly encountered Greek competitors. The Aegean world even supplied models imitated by the Phoenicians. For instance, the early coinage of Phoenician cities was first based on the Athenian standard, which might suggest that Greek oarsmen were being used. If the defeats at Marathon and Salamis were little more than misfortunes encountered by the Persian Empire in the course of punitive expeditions, for the Greeks, these victories were the prelude to a new heroic period, a second Trojan War remembered as the victory of freedom over oriental despotism. In fact, Persian encroachments on the Aegean world marked the end of Greek "democracy." The independent cities gave way to an Athenian naval empire. While the Greeks won a few battles, the Persians won the war, as the Peace of Antalkias (386 BCE) demonstrates. Yet, half a century later, the Macedonians took over the entire Achaemenid realm.

As indicated above, coinage was invented to facilitate the conversion of war booty and the payment of mercenaries. The prosperity derived from trade between the Mediterranean and the Mesopotamian world and beyond enabled the enrolment of increasing numbers of soldiers. Besides the army, the Achaemenid era witnessed the rise of a navy and the invention of the trireme (Wallinga 1984, 1987). This ship was developed in two stages. First, the three-banked oarage was developed at Carthage around 535 BCE. Then, Saite Egypt fitted the three-banked oarage on its much larger ships. The first Egyptian triremes were used by Amasis (571–526 BCE) from his bases in Cyprus.

Cambyses' attack on Egypt can be interpreted as a reaction to the Egyptian use of this redoubtable new weapon. In 525 BCE, Cambyses' navy was entirely manned by Phoenicians (Herodotus 3.19.3). Before this date, there had been no need for Phoenician coinage. The 50- to 60-strong crew consisted mostly of oarsmen who, unlike soldiers, did not belong to the category of men of independent means who were liable for military service. Hence, the rowers had to be paid for their service, and the great demand for rowers led to the first production of Phoenician coins (Weiser 1989, 273). At first, the rowers were professional sailors whose involvement on the triremes disrupted the activity of the merchant ships they normally manned in peacetime.

Once the Persians joined the armament race, people soon became acquainted with the notion of coins representing the equivalent of rowing time on a trireme. Although a modest navy of 300 triremes employed between 18,000 and 51,000 rowers and thus required a large dispersion of coins, the circulation of coinage remained limited, because coins were often melted back into bullion. The majority of royal Achaemenid issues, specifically the gold and silver coins struck with the image of the royal archer, were found west of the Empire close to the Mediterranean coast, which confirms the link between coinage and naval operations (Nimchuk 2002, 55).

As noted above, the function of coinage in trade is secondary. The use of non-coined silver greatly outweighed that of coins, even in provinces that displayed an advanced economy (Vargyas 2000, 247–268). Coinage supplemented rather than supplanted the usual means of earning one's subsistence. While rowing required training, it was not beyond the abilities of farmers, to whom it offered new opportunities to earn extra revenues between June and November, the slack period between harvesting and ploughing (Figure 37).

Coinage is intimately related to Persian campaigns in the Aegean world, where an abrupt break in production of several series of coins occurred with the termination of Persian domination (Picard 2000, 250). In turn, the need for silver coinage benefited Athens, because the city controlled the Laurion silver mines. Classical Athens was financed primarily through its exports of silver and mercenaries to the Persian Empire.

Greek mercenaries started serving in the Egyptian and Babylonian armies at the end of the seventh century BCE, where they introduced new fighting techniques. Until then, archers were the main element in the armies of the Near East. The Greeks brought in the hoplite phalanx, a new tactic that proved unsurpassable for the next 200 years (Figure 38).

Unlike oriental soldiers who fought independently (1 Kgs 20:39-40), the hoplites fought in formation, shield to shield, and in several rows. Despite their heavy armament, they approached the enemy in tight formation.

Figure 37: Galleys on coins from (a) Dor the holy (ΔΩΡΑ ΙΕΡΑ) and (b) from Jerusalem, where the motif appears three centuries later than at Samaria (*NEAHL* 4: 1309), at first during the reign of Herod Archaeleus (4 BCE–6 CE) (a Meshorer 1985, #20; b Madden 1881, #116).

Showers of arrows could not keep them at bay. Tribal contingents were no match. However, the hoplite had to finance his own bronze armour and helmet and he had to train. Hence, the Greeks did not invent sport for recreation but for military training. They relied more than others on the labour of their wives and slaves to work their farms.

When Cyrus ascended the throne of Babylon, he also ruled over the "kings sitting on thrones" of Syria-Palestine and "the kings of Amurru who live in tents" (*CoS* 2.124 in *ANET* 316). Kedar was noteworthy among these tent-dwellers (Gen. 25:13; Isa. 21:16-17; 42:11; 60:7; Jer. 2:10; Ezek. 27:21). Besides his mention in Nehemiah 6, the Kedarite sheikh Gusam (biblical Geshem) is named in several inscriptions. The oasis of Dedan was ruled by the king of Lihyan and a Persian governor (Aramaic *peḥa'*, Arabic

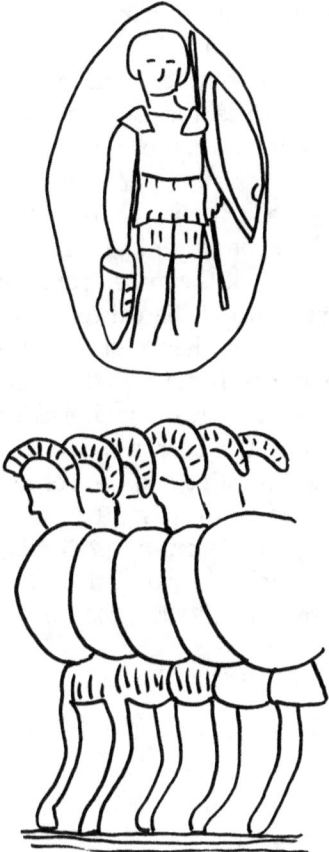

Figure 38: (a) Hoplite on a bulla from the late fourth century BCE, from Samarian documents discovered at Wadi Daliyeh and from Dor. The bag in the right hand of the hoplite points to the myth of Perseus. In that bag, Perseus put the head of the Gorgon. Jonah's boarding of a boat at Joppa (Jon. 1:3) is another echo of that myth. (b) Hoplite phalanx in tight formation on a bulla from Dor (a after Leith 1997, 32; b after *CSAPI* 2 Dor #12).

Faḥat). As indicated by an inscription from Dedan, long-distance trade was in the hands of Gusam:

> Nuran bin Khadir has registered in the days of Gusam bin Sahr and 'Abd, the governor (*faḥat*) of Dedan, under the ru[le of PN, King of Lihyan (Knauf 1989, 105).

On the eastern border of Egypt, Gusam's son left a silver bowl with an inscription (ca. 400 BCE): "What Qain bin Gusam, king of Kedar, dedicated to han-'Ilāt" (Eph'al 1982, 194). Herodotus (1.131) mentions the goddess han-'Ilāt as ΑΛΙΛΑΤ, which simply means "the goddess." The three places where Geshem/Gusam is mentioned—Yehud, Dedan, and the eastern Nile

Delta—circumscribe Kedar's sphere of influence under Persian rule. Kedar controlled the incense road from Saba to Gaza and as far north as Damascus and Tyre (Ezek. 27:31). In southern Arabia, the Sabeans were the partners of Kedar, but in the fifth century BCE, Saba's northern neighbour and rival Ma'in started to write inscriptions in its own language rather than in Sabean.

The Book of Job has Job's friends come all the way from Arabia, the exotic edge of the world as the writer knew it (Job 2:11). Yehud in the fifth century BCE was very much at the margin, and Herodotus, who sailed to Egypt (450 BCE), never heard of the existence of Samaria or Jerusalem. That changed around 400 BCE, when Yehud and the new Jerusalem found themselves on the frontier with an Egypt that had overthrown its Persian occupiers in 399 BCE. Persia's loss of Egypt had immediate repercussions for Kedar. The Persian clients, Kedar in the North and Saba' in the South (Job 1:15; 6:19), lost their prestige and control of the frankincense trade which they had dominated for the past 350 years. Now the Minaeans took over for the next 300 years (1 Chron. 4:41; 2 Chron. 26:7). They cooperated with Egypt well into the Hellenistic period. In the North, the Nabataeans supplanted the Kedarites (Knauf 1990b, 2009c).

CHAPTER 8
FROM ARTAXERXES I TO PTOLEMY I:
THE SECOND "SECOND TEMPLE" AND TORAH

The difficulties encountered by the Achaemenids in Egypt spur the construction of a Persian fortress at Jerusalem with an adjacent sanctuary (the second "Second" Temple), the destruction of Bethel, and the construction of a cultic centre at Mount Gerizim. Such renewed imperial interest in the Levant set the stage for the formation of the Torah and the rise of a common identity based on biblical Israel that was intended to be valid among the Diaspora across the Empire.

Whatever happened at Jerusalem before the reign of Artaxerxes I (464–424 BCE) remained modest and of limited significance. The main turning point in Achaemenid policy in the southern Levant and Jerusalem was the rebellion of Egypt led by Inaros at the beginning of Artaxerxes' reign. Egypt had previously rebelled when Artaxerxes' two predecessors had ascended the Persian throne, in 522 BCE (Darius) and in 486 BCE (Xerxes). These rebellions had been quickly extinguished, but this time the threat was more serious, because Inaros was in league with Athens, which provided naval support to the Egyptian rebels. The involvement of Greek forces in Egyptian affairs revealed the need for a tighter integration of Yehud into the imperial apparatus: campaigns in Egypt would require the provisioning of large numbers of troops on the Via Maris.

With this aim in mind, a Persian garrison was stationed at Jerusalem to ensure the collection of agricultural surpluses to supply the coastal overland route between Egypt and Phoenicia and to guard the route from Jericho, Ammon, and Moab to the coast. The passage of troops towards Egypt required the storage of large amounts of food and fodder. Due to the cost of overland transport, food had to be produced locally. The historical problem is that Mizpah was already administering the affairs of Yehud, and it remains unclear what motivated the decision to shift from this existing provincial capital back to the previous one. Doubts regarding the loyalty of Mizpah is a likely factor in the Achaemenid change of policy; Mizpah had been made the provincial capital by Nebuchadnezzar, and since that time the affinities of the Benjaminite elite with Babylon could have proved problematic when the Achaemenids encountered difficulties in Egypt and when Megabyzos rebelled in 448 BCE. Jerusalem's access to perennial water may have also played a role in the Persians' decision to shift the provincial seat (Edelman 2005, 344).

The wall Nehemiah is said to have restored is the city wall of Manasseh, a wall that protected a population of 15,000–25,000 in the seventh century BCE (Ussishkin 2006). With only 3,000 inhabitants in late Persian times (Nehemiah 11), most of the intramural area in Jerusalem was dedicated to the gardens of the military colony (Neh. 7:3). Gardens were always surrounded by walls in ancient cities, and they played as important a role as access to a perennial spring in case of siege.

8.1 Nehemiah and the Persian Fortress of Jerusalem

The Bible only transmits the names of three Persian governors (פחא, *peḥa*) at Jerusalem: Zerubbabel (Hag. 1:1) and Sheshbazzar (Ezra 5:14), probably in that order, and Nehemiah. Seals and bullae preserve the names of other governors active in Yehud (Avigad 1976; Figure 39).

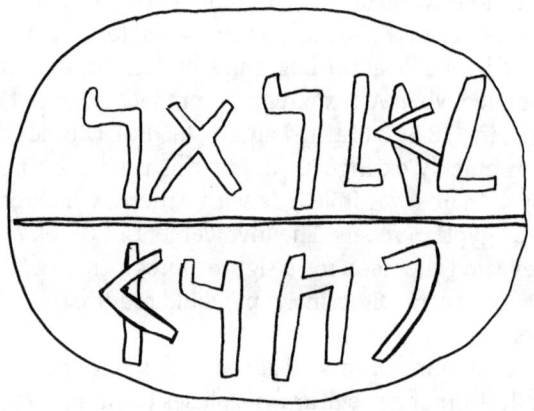

Figure 39: Aniconic seal of Elnatan Yehuda (לאלנתן יהדא), possibly mentioned in 1 Chronicles 3:19 (after Avigad 1976, #5).

Nehemiah himself mentions previous governors (Neh. 5:15), making it clear that the Books of Ezra-Nehemiah reflect but a fraction of what went on in Persian Yehud.

According to 1 Chronicles 6 and Ezra-Nehemiah, it is Haggai and Zechariah who laid the foundations of the temple. Then, Ezra proclaimed the Torah and, finally, Nehemiah rebuilt Jerusalem. The joint performances of Ezra and Nehemiah in the Book of Nehemiah (8:9; 12:26, 36) are chronologically impossible. According to Nehemiah 2:1, Nehemiah is still in Susa in year 20 of the reign of Artaxerxes I (445/444 BCE), while Ezra went from

Babylon to Jerusalem in year seven of Artaxerxes (Ezra 7:7-9). Which Artaxerxes? The seventh year of Artaxerxes I would be 458 BCE. The seventh year of Artaxerxes II would be 398 BCE. There are good reasons to ignore Artaxerxes III and to reverse the biblical sequence by placing Nehemiah before Ezra, since Ezra reads the Torah in front of the Water Gate (Neh. 8:1). As this gate was repaired in the days of Nehemiah (Neh. 3:26), it is likely the order Ezra–Nehemiah is a literary device modelled on the Moses-Joshua sequence. Ezra the law-giver corresponds to the figure of Moses. Nehemiah the governor must follow Ezra because he corresponds to Joshua, Moses' successor.

The Nehemiah memoir (Neh. 1:1–7:3, 10; 12:27–14:31), a vindication of Nehemiah's conduct in office, is one of the first biblical texts written in the first person singular. As is the case with other texts classified as Diaspora novellas (the story of Joseph in Genesis 37–47, Esther, Aramaic Daniel, and Tobit), the aim of the memoir is to show that one can be both a loyal Persian official and a pious Israelite at the same time.

The lists in Ezra–Nehemiah circumscribe the realm controlled by Jerusalem: Benjamin in the north, with Bethel and Jericho. Hebron is not mentioned, which suggests that it was under the jurisdiction of Edom/Idumea. Neighbours appear as Nehemiah's opponents (Neh. 2:10, 19; 4:3, 7; 6:1, 12, 14). The main opponent is Sanballat (*Sîn-uballiṭ* 'Sin revived him'), the governor of Samaria, whose grandson occupied the same position half a century later.[1]

In the East, the Judean family of the Tobiads was involved in the government of the province of Ammon as indicated by the title "Ammonite official". In the West, Ashdod was a gateway to the Mediterranean traders, who are depicted as fish merchants, trying to ply their trade on the Sabbath (Nehemiah 13). The territories of Ashkelon and Gaza were not in direct contact with Yehud.

The villains of Nehemiah 4:7 belong to the model of the conspiracy theories that were as common in Egyptian and Assyrian historiography as they are today. It is not clear which "villain" was the most threatened by Nehemiah's activities in Jerusalem. If the notion of a hostile Kedar is accepted, Geshem was directly affected by Nehemiah's fortification of Jerusalem. The Kedarites would have perceived it as the first stage of a programme designed to regain control of the Hebron region and the incense route in the Negev, and thus to ensure a cut in the profit seeing

---

1 Altogether there are three Samarian governors named Sanballat, all probably from the same family: the contemporary of Nehemiah (445–432 BCE), the Sanballat mentioned in the Elephantine correspondence (410–408 BCE), and the Sanballat of the Wadi Daliyeh papyri (332 BCE).

that the Kedarite sheikhs were less controllable. This is what eventually happened in the second and first centuries BCE, under Hasmonean rule, but with the support of Rome.

Since the fortification of Jerusalem was part of the Achaemenid endeavour to recover control of Egypt, it is unlikely that the Persians would have allowed Jerusalem to upset another vassal whose position towards Egypt was even more strategic than that of Jerusalem. Yehud's southern extension, half-way to Hebron (Ezra 2; Nehemiah 7), probably presupposes the demise of Kedar and the establishment of the province of Idumea in the 380s. As for Ashdod, it is equally difficult to imagine how it could have been threatened by Jerusalem. Tensions with Ammon and with Samaria are more likely.

The conflict with Tobiah was an internal affair. The Tobiad family was indigenous and its position was challenged by Nehemiah (6:17, 19; 13:4, 7-8). The issue, however, was not the fortification of Jerusalem as such. The walls were a convenient pretext for covering up the threat that Nehemiah's political and financial activities (Neh. 5:10) posed to the small elite that had secured a hold over the affairs of Yehud after Nebuchadnezzar had deported the Judean elite of the time. With the military backing of the Persians and his financial connections with the Babylonian Golah, Nehemiah was a formidable rival to local networks. Nehemiah's entourage offered interest-free loans to undercut rival lenders (Lev. 25:36-37). Repayments were postponed and taxes cancelled (Neh. 5:11-17) to gain an edge over longer-established rivals (Guillaume 2010; Miller 2010).

With Samaria, relationships would have been tense due to the abolition of the common sanctuary at Bethel and the subsequent Deuteronomistic claim that Yehud and Jerusalem were the only true Israel. The "foreign plot" depicted in the Book of Nehemiah obscures the source of the main opposition to Nehemiah's actions: the indigenous Benjaminite and Ammonite elite that had much to lose with the transfer of the provincial capital of Mizpah to Jerusalem (Neh. 3:7). Like the Canaanites and Gibeonites in the Book of Joshua, the Book of Nehemiah projects internal rivalries onto external enemies in order to preserve the illusion that the "returnees" were the only legitimate inhabitants of the province.

According to Nehemiah 2:1, Nehemiah was Artaxerxes' cup-bearer, a high court official who used his access to the great king to ask favours regarding relatives who had "returned" to Jerusalem and found themselves in a precarious situation. Exaggeration and simplification notwithstanding, the proximity of the Babylonian Diaspora to the Achaemenid court is clear. As is the case in many Middle Eastern countries today, the Diaspora plays a crucial role in the affairs of the home country. From the Persians' point of view, Nehemiah's mission may be considered a reward for the loyalty of the Jews in the Empire during the revolt of the Egyptian

Inaros in Egypt (460-454 BCE) and later, in the revolt of the Persian Megabyzos in Transeuphrates (448 BCE). There is a risk, however, of exaggerating the importance of the small Jewish minority of the Empire.

8.2 Economic Crisis in Yehud?

The events described in Nehemiah 5:1-5 have been read as evidence of a social crisis that accelerated the process of class formation and led to a landless proletariat. Exegetes imagine a similar scenario already in the eighth century BCE to explain the social critique of the "prophets" Amos and Hosea (Chaney 1993). In the face of huge reserves of uncultivated arable land, aggravated by low demography throughout the entire biblical period, landlessness is meaningless. Until the end of the nineteenth century CE, arable land was not privately owned and there was as much as anyone needed, for remainees as well as for returnees and newcomers (Guillaume 2012, 92-97). A famine explains the situation described in Nehemiah 5:1-3. The question is whether Nehemiah 5:4-5 implies destitution.

Today, failing to reimburse loans leads to foreclosure of the assets pledged as security, but for the Persian Yehud—as for the entire ancient world for that matter—arable land was not lost through foreclosure. It was not an asset, because it had no intrinsic value. What *was* valuable, because of its scarcity, unlike land, was man and animal power. Since animals were far too "volatile" to secure loans, grain traders—the only sources of credit at the time—secured the fruit of the work of their debtors. Instead of taking the land of their debtors or enslaving their means of production, creditors secured exclusive access to their debtors' future harvest. Most loans were antechretic (Wells 2011, 143-147), and merchants lent grain in the hope of collecting the same amount of grain plus a 50% yearly interest (Wunsch 2002). To modern eyes, this seems outright usury, but this is a misunderstanding. The cost covered the seasonal fluctuation of the value of grain, which rose greatly in the months preceding sowing and at harvest time when farmers borrowed, but which later fell to a low point in the months after the harvest when farmers sold their surplus. The risks and the costs involved in storage and transport need to be taken into consideration as well. All in all, the presence of grain-traders as sources of credit was beneficial to farmers, even though farmers always complain about their creditors (Hos. 12:7-8; Mic. 6:10-12). Such complaints cannot be taken as descriptions of economic facts. Famines were indeed recurrent but not for the reasons commonly advanced for the Persian period.

According to the extra-biblical story, a reform by Darius I had forced all the countries of the Empire to pay a fixed amount of tribute independently of actual yields and to pay it in silver rather than in produce (Herodotus 3.89-97). From this it is inferred that farmers were fleeced when they exchanged produce against silver to pay their taxes. The result was supposedly

> a far-reaching and long-lasting social crisis which shook post-exilic Judah to the core. The creeping decline of increasing numbers of population, which at times became acute, to a level below the minimum needs of existence, grew into an abuse which could no longer be overlooked by anyone who held a position of responsibility in the community. (Albertz 1994, 497)

In fact, sweeping views of crushing taxation, silver shortage, and general impoverishment before and after Darius' fiscal reform have long been denounced as flawed (Stolper 1985, 143–145). Food shortages followed a seasonal pattern, and for this reason there were well-established procedures to deal with them, such as the regular cancellation of debts formulated by the Mesopotamian *mišarum* edicts and the *šemiṭṭah* of Deuteronomy 15:12-13. The Persian period would have collapsed earlier had Darius' reform provoked a structural crisis.

In Yehud, the arrival of wealthy settlers from the Golah had positive effects on the overall economic situation. From the Persians' point of view, the likely aim of the resettlement of Yehud was to increase the output of the province dramatically in order to supply their troops on the way to Egypt. The new settlers were assigned fallow land so as not to displace those farmers who were already present. This is the well-attested practice from Ugarit to Ottoman times (Guillaume 2012, 75–80). Nevertheless, a crisis may have resulted from the rise of a new phenomenon; namely, the transformation of the consequences of debt slavery. Until then, debt slavery had not implied dislocation (Guillaume 2012, 142–145). Beginning in the late Persian era, however, slaves became an internationally traded commodity. Whereas the value of slaves before then seems to have been fairly stable, at 20–30 shekels of silver, at Athens they were worth 90 shekels. The cause of the inflation was the great demand for silver following the spread of monetization in the Persian Empire. Athens controlled the silver mines at Laurion, where a rich vein was discovered in 482 BCE (Treister 1996). Due to exhausting work conditions, the miners were slaves and had a short life expectancy. In the Roman period, *damnatio ad metalla*, "condemnation to the mines" was tantamount to a death sentence. In consequence, the demand for slaves followed the demand for silver. The Persians would not have allowed the wholesale export of slaves to Athens from the Levant when they were engaged in a mortal fight against Athens over the control of Egypt. Yet, the high demand for slaves generated slave trafficking behind their backs. The indications of the export of slaves in the Hebrew Bible (Amos 1:6, 9; Joel 4:3-6) reflect the beginning of this new phenomenon. The daughters mentioned in Nehemiah 5:5 and 5:8 do not belong to this category. The reproductive potential of young women was far too precious to imagine that the displaced daughters were sent to Athens' silver mines. The availability of daughters to reimburse secure loans is a tribute to the booming birth rate of Persian Yehud and a reflection of the exhortation to multiply and fructify (Gen. 1:28; 9:1, 7; 16:10; 35:11; Lev. 26:9). There is no indication that the economic situation in Persian Yehud was worse than before. On the contrary, imperial involvement must have improved the overall situation compared with the times that followed the destruction of Jerusalem (Figure 40).

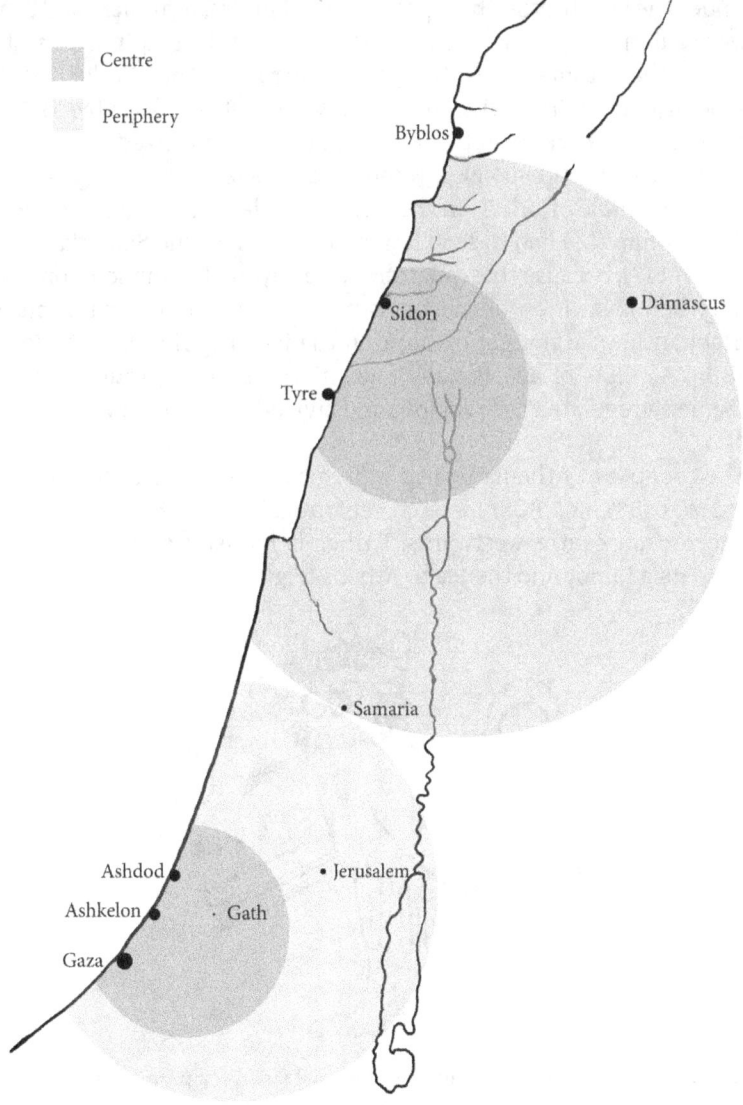

Figure 40: Centre and periphery, fifth century BCE to sixth century CE (T. Guillaume).

Despite the improvement, the majority of the Diaspora did not feel any urge to swap life in Babylonia for a precarious existence in Israel/Palestine, nor did it have the opportunity to do so. A massive return did not happen. The texts that claim otherwise are propaganda for the homecoming (Genesis 11–17; Numbers 11; 13–14; Deut. 11:10-12; Isaiah 40–48). Those who did "return" were soldiers and officers of the garrison of Jerusalem, and some priests, Levites, and scribes, all accompanied by their staff and households.

Under the new proto-ethnic policy of the Empire, Jerusalem and Samaria were put in charge of Jewish affairs throughout the Empire. In a system similar to the Ottoman *millet* that is still current in the Middle East, the state delegated affairs relative to the personal status of its subjects (marriage, divorce, inheritance) to the court of each recognized proto-ethnic group. Hence, around 400 BCE, when an authorization was necessary to restore the temple of YHWH in the fortress of Elephantine (today Aswan), the local committee had to send letters to Jerusalem and Samaria (Porten 1996, 139–147), because these matters were beyond the jurisdiction of the military administration of the garrison. The Persian officer responsible for Elephantine did not get involved in the internal affairs of the Jewish garrison. As seats of an officially recognized "ethnic" group, Jerusalem and Samaria regulated the religious and civil affairs of the Jews across the Empire.

The collapse of Athenian naval supremacy at the end of the Peloponnesian War (431–404 BCE) fostered centrifugal forces that expanded the Mediterranean centre westwards. Earlier it had shifted from Tyre and Sidon to Asia Minor and thence to Athens (Figure 41).

Figure 41: Athena owl on Tyrian coin. The owl stood for pure silver (after Elayi and Elayi 2009, #1378).

Now Carthage, and later Rome, entered the scene. In Egypt, rebellions continued to plague the Persians. In 404 BCE, Amyrtaios freed Egypt of Persian occupation and ruled for five years as the first and only pharaoh of the Twenty-Eighth Dynasty. From between then until 343 BCE, two more dynasties followed. These were the last Egyptian dynasties proper. Stability only returned with the Ptolemies, who were Macedonian pharaohs.

8.3 The Military Colony at Elephantine

The correspondence of the Judean military colony in Elephantine with Samaria and Jerusalem is crucial for understanding the evolution of Judaism from the sixth to the fourth century BCE. The military colony on the southern border of Egypt was taken over by Cambyses when he conquered Egypt in 525 BCE. The origins of this colony probably went back to 582 BCE, if not earlier, and it may have been founded by the Assyrians to guard the southern frontier of Egypt. Among others, it was manned by Judean mercenaries in the service of the Twenty-Sixth (Saite) Dynasty. In the fifth century BCE, the military colony of Elephantine was 500-men strong, with at least 2,500 dependants, women, and children —about the same number as the garrison of Jerusalem.[2] In 410 BCE, the temple of Yaho (YHWH's Aramaic name) was destroyed during an Egyptian pogrom. Vidranga, the local Persian official, sided with the Egyptians, probably as an outlet for the tensions between the local Egyptian population and the Achaemenid colonial administration. The pogrom was sparked by a squabble over a piece of land: the temple happened to block convenient access to a planned enlargement of the Khnum temple on the cramped island just downstream from the First Nile Cataract (Figure 36). The Achaemenid administration, however, could not leave the assault against its occupation force unpunished. When a new Persian military governor was named, the Judean community at Elephantine sent a request to rebuild their temple to the governor of Jerusalem. The letter remained unanswered. A second request was sent to Jerusalem *and* Samaria. This time Samaria and Jerusalem ruled that the temple could be rebuilt, but animals were omitted from the list of sacrifices that could be offered at Elephantine.

The cult of YHWH as it was celebrated in Bethel survived in fifth-century Elephantine. The courts of Samaria and Jerusalem did not specify that, besides discontinuing animal sacrifices, YHWH should divorce his wife, Anat-Bethel, and abandon his son,'Ashim-Bethel. Both are mentioned

---

2   There were three to four battalions (Aramaic *daglin*) in the Judean brigade (Aramaic ḥayla'), each consisting of at least two centuria (Knauf 2002c).

as beneficiaries at the end of an accounting record of silver donations to the temple by members of the Elephantine Jewish community: 12 karsh 6 shekels for Yaho, 12 karsh for Anat-Bethel and 7 karsh for 'Ashim-Bethel (TAD C3.15). Either Samaria and Jerusalem did not know of the presence of these divinities besides Yaho of Elephantine, or they chose to ignore them. Nor did they specify that the cult of YHWH at Elephantine should be aniconic from then on. It may have been iconic, since the silver collected for the temple was divided into three parts and clearly designated for each of the gods of the colony: the largest sum for Yaho, a smaller one for his consort, and the smallest for Ashim-Bethel. A bulk amount would have been more likely if the silver had been collected for general temple supplies. Divided in this way, it could have been used to adorn three different-sized statues.

The holdings of the temple library at Elephantine are also revealing. Two well-known textbooks were found there, textbooks with which local Jews learned to read and write Aramaic and thus manifest their loyalty to the Persian Empire: the Ahiqar novel and the Aramaic version of the Bisutun inscription of Darius I. The temple of Elephantine apparently owned no biblical texts, or at least, come down to the present, and the absence of cultic texts indicates that cultic matters were transmitted orally.

Among the other Elephantine papyri (all in Aramaic) are two private archives with certificates of purchase, loans, marriage, and divorce. In contrast to what is specified in the Hebrew Bible, daughters were entitled to inherit, and women could initiate divorce proceedings. Wages and prices featuring in the private documents give an idea of the purchasing power of a silver shekel at the time: a house was worth 20–30 shekels, and 1 shekel was a worker's monthly wage. Twenty per cent of the Jews in Elephantine owned gardens, houses, and other assets, and 95% could write their own name (Porten and Yardeni 1999; Knauf 2002a, 2002c).

8.4 Arabia and Idumea

The consequence of the rebellions in Egypt was the collapse of Persian rule in Arabia. Local elites who had cooperated with the Persians lost their position to their rivals in the Arabian tribes and tribal kingdoms. The Kedarite confederation disintegrated in east Jordan, northwest Arabia, and the Sinai. Kedarite clans became Nabateans. Around 400 BCE, the Sabeans, who had previously cooperated closely with Tema (Job 6:19), lost their hold over the frankincense trade to the Mineans. The Mineans cooperated with Egypt and established a colony at Dedan. Southern Palestine found itself in the frontier area between Egypt-friendly Arabs and the Achaemenid Empire. In retaliation for Arab support of Egypt's struggle for independence, the Kedarite territory west of the Arabah was turned into a separate sub-province around 387–385 BCE and into the province of Idumea before 363 BCE (Diodorus 15.2.4). To secure the frontier, large fiefs were granted to military personnel in Idumea, as place names such as Beth-marcaboth ("chariot-estate") and Hazar-susah ("cavalry farm") indicate (Josh. 19:5).

Judean small silver coins were struck in the fourth century BCE, when Jerusalem backed up the Idumean frontier. The coin emissions of Yehud in the fourth century correlate with the Persian campaigns against Egypt (385, 373, 360, 350, and 343 BCE). Culturally, Yehud and Idumea were close. Idumea had been southern Judah before 586 BCE, then northern Edom until 553 BCE. The more than 1,800 Edomite ostraca from Arad, Tel Beersheba, and probably from the provincial capital of Maresha attest to names formed with the name of the Edomite God Qaus in combination with Canaanite, Aramaic, and Arabic predicates. Typical Arabic and Judean names are also found. Evidence for the ancient Edomite God Qaus comes almost entirely from the Persian and Hellenistic periods. Strabo considered the Edomites to be "runaway Nabateans" because, in the first century BCE, the Arabic language prevailed among them. Near Maresha, a temple of Yahweh (בית יהו) stood next to a temple of the Arab goddess al-ʿUzza and the Babylonian God Nabû (Porten and Yardeni 2007).

The fact that Maresha was sited far to the northwest of Idumea shows that the province was turned towards the coastal economy. Phoenicia experienced increasing economic pressure from the Greeks and from Gaza, where a Minean colony traded with Egypt and bypassed Achaemenid control. The Gaza–Arab cooperation is reflected in 2 Chronicles 17:11, 21:16, and 26:7. Gaza struck coins for Arab tribal leaders, who used them as status symbols. The Greek, Phoenician, and local coins that circulated in the southern Levant were expressions of the identity of local tribes and cities and prepared the way for the rise of proper ethnicities in the Hellenistic era. The Persian Empire functioned largely on the principle of subsidiarity, i.e., everything that could be done on the local level was left for the locals to decide, while the emperor dealt with foreign policy. This is demonstrated by the so-called Lists of Hierodules (temple slaves) from Maʿîn (South Arabia):

> Hāni binʿ Abd, of the family Sʾaqīm, of the tribe Gabʾān, has made a relative and paid the bride-price for (the woman) Salambō from Gaza. (Translated from Capuzzi 1974, 115–124)

The original publication assumed that the women mentioned were gifts to a temple. In reality, these lists document marriages of Minean merchants with women abroad, probably to make them and their offspring legal in the home country (Knauf 1989, 157). Salambō (שלמבעל) is a Phoenician name, but most women originate from Gaza (29), followed by Dedan (9),

Egypt (8), Kedar (3), Qatabān (2), Greece (1), Sidon (1), Ammon (1), and Moab (1) (von Wissmann 1970, 957).

8.5 Yehud and Samaria

The Elephantine correspondence shows that in 407 BCE the governors at Jerusalem and Samaria, together with their council of notables, were the ultimate authority in Jewish religious affairs. It is difficult to imagine how Samaria and Jerusalem could fulfil this role together, but having the Torah in common is evidence for this arrangement and suggests that the split between them occurred after the Persian era, when Jerusalem insisted on having a prophetic canon besides the Torah. That each had its own temple was no grounds for divorce, but differences in Torah-observance may be detected in the iconography of coins. Except for the earliest issues that depict anthropomorphic deities, the coins of Yehud comply with the Torah's prohibition of images. By contrast, the coins of Samaria represent YHWH as a Baalshamim type god with Athena under the Canaanite traits of Asherah-Astarte-Anath (Figure 42). In Samaria, the prohibition of images was still understood in its original sense of a ban on *cultic* images in the narrowest sense, which did not exclude the representation of divine images (Figure 42b-e), while Jerusalem extended the ban to two-dimensional representations of the deity.

Samarian coins transmit the following minting authorities (governors?): Pharnabazus, a Persian name, Bodiah (Phoenician and Samarian), Delaiah (Samarian), Hayyim (non-specific), Mabbogay (north Syrian), Sanballat (Babylonian-Samarian), Mazday (Persian), Bagabat (Persian), Hananiah (Yehudite or Samarian), Jeroboam (Samarian), Shelemiah (Yehudite or Samarian), Yaddu' (non specific), Jeho'ana (Yehudite or Samarian), WNY (Persian? Arabic?), Abdiel (non-specific), Bod-jahbol/Bod-yehi-Bel (Phoenician or Aramaic), and Sahru (Arabic). These names show a great variety of origins. The Samarian hoard of 332 BCE (Meshorer and Qedar 1991) displays a similar variety, with 48% of the coins being Samarian, 34% Phoenician (Tyre, Sidon, Arwad) and 18% non-specific coins.

The provincial coinage gradually included silver coins of smaller denominations, which does not necessarily indicate a broader use of coins in trade since trade was, in peaceful times, based on credit and on precious metals that continued to be weighed. The weight of coins could never be taken at face value (Graeber 2011, 22–23). Hence, the invitation in Isaiah 55:1-3 to get food without silver presupposes and reacts against fourth-century soldiers buying food on the local market with the newly introduced smaller silver coins. In Yehud, the difference between the Jerusalemite region and Benjamin remained. Half of the population of the province and over 80% of its economic potential were concentrated in

Figure 42: Samarian coins. Samarian coinage (375–332 BCE) displays a much broader iconographic repertoire than the coinage of Yehud. (a) Drachma, the most valuable and rarest coin, here with Athena's head on one side and the Persian king fighting a lion on the other. (b) Athena head and orientalized owl (compare Figure 41). (c) Bes and doe on a quarter obole, the smallest Samarian coin. The grimacing gnome Bes was a very widespread *daemon* (secondary deity) venerated particularly as protector of pregnant women and babies. The doe was a symbol of love (Song 2:7; 3:5). (d) Obol with enthroned Persian king in front of a fire altar and the Greek inscription "Zeus" on one side and a Persian rider on the other side, with an Aramaic inscription YHW'NH, "YHWH has answered." (e) Half obol with Bes head and galley, a reminder of the original function of coinage (Figure 37) (a–e after Meshorer and Qedar 1991, #23, 40, 88, 152, 179).

Benjamin, as evidenced by the distribution of coins, seals, and agricultural installations (Carter 1999, figs 21, 24)). Jerusalem was mostly peopled by the garrison it housed and mainly fed with Benjaminite produce. For this reason, Jerusalem must have appeared parasitic to the Benjaminites. Yet, the Hebrew Bible mostly transmits Jerusalem's point of view in the form of anti-Benjaminite literary resentment (Judges 19–21).

With a population of 45,000–60,000 (Ezra 2; Neh. 7) at the end of the fourth century BCE, Yehud was by no means over-populated. Yet, it was a country of emigration. Besides Damascus (Acts 9:1-25), and later Alexandria, the main destination was Galilee (Josh. 18:1-10; Judges 17–18). In the second century BCE, Yehudites formed a sizeable segment of the Galilean population (1 Maccabees 5; 2 Maccabees 12).

8.6 Ezra and Torah

According to Ezra 7:12-26 (Aramaic), Ezra was appointed by Artaxerxes as scribe-priest of the law of the God of the Heavens. As a Persian official, he delivered to Jerusalem a large sum of money for the temple and its community. He was charged with the upkeep of the temple and the management of the affairs of Yehud and Jerusalem according to "the law of your God, which is in your hand" (Ezra 7:14). What kind of law was this and how did it come into Ezra's hand? Any assumption that it was not the final Torah (Genesis 1–Deuteronomy 34) has been hard to sustain, although it is clear that the mass of narrative material and of contradicting laws contained in the Torah could not serve as a law code, unlike as found in Roman Law. The Torah was a collection of traditional material that provided ancestral roots and legitimated the personal status of every Jew recognized as such across the Empire (Ezra 7:25). In practice, actual cases were arbitrated according to a combination of interpretations of the Torah with common law, as is still the case with interpretations of the Quran in the Islamic world, and in areas where religious and common law coexist. The purpose of the official endorsement given to the Torah by the Persian authorities was to lend legitimacy to the enforcement of the rulings of the central courts of Jerusalem and the Gerizim. The personal status of Jews was said to derive directly from Israel's past and YHWH's commands dictated to Moses.

The endorsement of the Torah by the Persian administration has given rise to the notion of "imperial authorization," which claims that the Achaemenids granted a large measure of autonomy to their subjects, allowing them to follow their traditional customs once these traditions were filed at court and declared compatible with the loyalty due to the Persian crown (Frei 1996). The theory has received much criticism (Watts 2001). Nevertheless, some sort of autonomy was granted by the Persian administration. A similar process is attested to by the redaction of Egyptian common law that Cambyses ordered after the conquest of Egypt (Blenkinsopp 1987). In Tema, a stele records the setting up of the cult of a Mesopotamian god, ṢLM, at a place called HGM, already worshipped there as ṢLM of MḤRM alongside two other gods, ŚNGL' and 'ŠYR'. ṢLM (statue, image) is the Babylonian god Salmu, closely associated with kingship

(Dalley 2010). Hence, the Persian imperial treasury contributed a fifth of the yearly cost of the upkeep of the sanctuary:

> (On the.....) in the 22nd year of .... (the king), ṢLM [of MḤRM and ŚNGL' and 'Š]YR', the gods of Tema (gave entrance into Tema) to ṢLM of [HGM. Therefore] they have appointed him this day (a place) in Tema...............which[ ]...... Therefore............... [this monument], which ṢLMŠZB, son of PṬSRY, [has set] up [in the temple of] ṢLM of HGM. Therefore the gods of Tema have dealt generously with ṢLMŠZB son of PṬSRY, and with his seed, in the temple of ṢLM of HGM. If any man harms this monument, let the gods of Tema remove him and his seed and his posterity from Tema. This is the grant which ṢLM of HGM and MḤRM and ŚNGL' and 'ŠYR', the gods of Tema, shall [give] to ṢLM of HGM, namely from the (temple) estate 16 palms and from the property of the king 5 palms, making 21 palms in all, year by year. Neither gods nor men shall eject ṢLMŠZB, son of PṬSRY, from this temple, or his seed or his posterity, priests in this temple for ever.
> ṢLMŠZB the priest. (Gibson 1975, 150)

Rather than an imperial authorization, the granting of local autonomy may be regarded as the outworking of an "Imperial Religious Police Department". As Jerusalem and Elephantine were Persian military colonies, the military administration had to know on which holy days the Jewish troops might be expected to be released from duty. In 419 BCE, the Jews of Elephantine received instructions of this nature and in 408/407 BCE, the Persian governor in Egypt had to know how the temple of YHWH in Elephantine was to be rebuilt (*CoS* 3.52).

The new Jerusalemite elite had mobilized the colonial powers in their own interests against the old Benjaminite elite. Nevertheless, it is unlikely that the squabbles between the members of the Golah in Nehemiah's time and the Benjaminites and Samaria put peace and stability at risk. The internal evidence of the Torah shows that it is a compromise document in which the relevant conflicts are erased, if not settled. The place YHWH chose for his name to reside at (Deuteronomy 12, 14, 16) is left open so that Jerusalem, Samaria, and any other sanctuary may claim it for themselves. The identification of *the* place with Jerusalem (Gen. 14:18-20; 22:1-14) or Gerizim (Deut. 11:29; 27:12) is a matter of interpretation. Monotheism and aniconism in the cult were in vogue in the fifth century BCE, the century of the religious critic Xenophanes of Colophon. The Empire-friendly Priestly Narrative provided the chronological and narrative thread of the compilation of the Torah. Upon this structure were inserted the additions dealing with the temple cult. The Deuteronomistic tradition was marginalized, as the position of Deuteronomy at the end of the Torah indicates, but it was not suppressed. While the Priestly Narrative places Ishmael on the same level as Isaac (Genesis 17; 25:12-18), the Deuteronomists want to drive him out (Genesis 21). Eventually, Isaac is with Ishmael just as Jacob was with Esau, when they buried their respective fathers in the family grave at Hebron. The Torah is also a compromise between "returnees" and the local population. Abraham is accepted (contrary to Ezek. 33:24) as the ancestor of every Judean, Benjaminite, Samarian, Arab, and Edomite, although he arrives from Babylonia, Ur, and Harran.

Rather than a law code, the Torah is a charter with a detailed preamble (Genesis 1–Exodus 19), with material relating to God, mankind, Israel, and the other nations of the world. With the final editing of the Hexateuch (Genesis to Joshua) and the enactment of the Torah (Genesis to Deuteronomy), the long pre-history of biblical Israel is completed. Eight centuries after Merenptah destroyed the first Israel, 398 BCE marks the birth date of biblical Israel made up of Yehud and Samaria, as the first people of the Bible. The category "Bible" designates an authoritative theological text that is no longer secret.

But in Ezra's time, there probably existed Torah scrolls only in the sanctuaries of Jerusalem and on Mount Gerizim. We can assume that every trained scribe also possessed his own partial copy as part of the homework he would have produced during his training. To this day, liturgical reading in synagogues is only allowed from scrolls that have not changed their physical appearance since Ezra: the Torah must be written on a leather scroll by hand, in the orthography of the Persian period without the vowel signs and accents that were developed a millennium after the consonantal text.

8.7 Torah and Identity

The reception of the Torah in Jerusalem and Samaria revolutionized the sacrificial system. Previously, except for the hide, the holocaust fed the god without any sharing of the parts of the victim with those who offered the sacrifice. The temple profited from the sale of the hides and provided labour for tanners and the manufacturers of the many leather products. Burning the animal made it rise to the heavens to appease the gods above (Gen. 8:20-22).

In the Bible, holocausts become irrelevant to YHWH, who announces he needs no food (Ps. 50:9-14). Instead, holocausts atone for human sins. As the creator of the entire world is said to reside only in Israel, the country must be regularly cleansed of its accumulated evil, because its people can never attain the ideal of righteousness YHWH expects of it (Leviticus 17–25). Hence, the accumulated evil must be compensated. To shield Bethel from Xerxes' wrath against the "demons," the Priestly Narrative had downplayed the importance of sacrifices and presented the scapegoat expelled at Yom Kippur as the basis of bloodless atonement (Guillaume 2009b: 96-101), but the final text of the Torah prescribes a host of sacrifices on that day (Leviticus 16). The notion of a priestly people as a living temple would prove crucial to the survival of Judaism after 70 CE, when the sacrificial cult in the temple at Jerusalem was discontinued. In practice, little changed. The changes in the finality of the holocaust were beyond the immediate concerns of the population. The other sacrifices continued being shared between mankind and YHWH. The main difference was in the change of the setting of the sacrifice at the temple, which modified the position of YHWH from that of guest to that of host in the sacrificial meal.

Besides sacrifices, food taboos strengthened the separate ethnic identity of Jews. Whatever the origins of the pork taboo, it combined with the blood taboo (Gen. 9:4) and the "kid in its mother's milk" taboo to underline the importance of ritual cleanliness, expressed repeatedly in the Torah as an anxious aversion to contamination (Leviticus 11–15). Besides the cooking of a kid in milk or in fat (Sasson 2002), the prohibition of Exodus 23:19 and 34:26 and of Deuteronomy 14:21 may concern the origin of rennet used to curdle heated milk into cheese (Guillaume 2002–2003, 2011, but see Knauf 1988c). Later, Judaism extended the ban to the serving of milk and meat products in the same meal, rendering table hospitality difficult, especially in the Diaspora, where Jewish ethnic identity was in danger of being lost through integration.

Food taboos were not the only way to express identity. The promulgation of the Torah froze the written Hebrew of the text into a sacred language. The distance from the languages spoken by Jews increased. In Yehud, the mostly Benjaminite population spoke a southern Israelite dialect in which the relative particle was not *ašer* (אשר) but *še-* (ש), as is found occasionally in the Gideon and Elisha stories (Judg. 6:17; 7:12; 8:26; 2 Kgs 6:11) and more systematically in later books such as Ecclesiastes and Song of Songs (Blau 1998; Hurvitz 2000; Knauf 2006; Young and Rezetko 2008). The Benjaminite dialect became the spoken language of Persian and Hellenistic Yehud. It became a literary language at the end of the second century CE, when it was used for the codification of the Mishnah, hence Middle or Mishnaic Hebrew. The population of Jerusalem originating from the Babylonian Golah proudly preserved their ancient Judean dialect that differentiated it from the populace. Hence, diglossia prevailed in Yehud, with the coexistence of two different but closely related dialects (southern Israelite and Jerusalemite) besides two written languages (Biblical Hebrew and Aramaic), as is the case today in Switzerland (Swiss-German dialects besides Schrift Deutch and Hoch Deutch) and in Arab countries (local Arabic dialects, Qur'anic Arabic, and Standard Arabic). Interference between the different dialects and languages was inevitable and gave rise to Late Biblical Hebrew, a literary language influenced by spoken Middle Hebrew. The level of education was revealed by mastery of the classical language. By contrast, anyone writing in Late Biblical Hebrew was a child of his time.

The difference between Biblical Hebrew and Late Biblical Hebrew is more syntactic than semantic, lying not so much in differences of vocabulary as in different ways of constructing phrases. The main difference is played out between what grammarians describe as aspects and tenses. Instead of clearly defined tenses to express whether the action described by a verb took place in the past, the present, or the future, as is the case with most European languages, the syntax of Biblical Hebrew is based on aspects. In Biblical Hebrew, both *qatal* and short *yiqtol* (or *wa-yiqtol* in prose) are available for the perfective aspect (completed operations or actions). Long-*yiqtol* forms express the imperfective aspect (uncompleted tasks or actions). On the other hand, Middle Hebrew and Late Biblical Hebrew use tenses with *qatal* for the past and *yiqtol* for future action. The difference between long and short *yiqtol* is lifted. As is the case in modern Ivrit, the participle of presence represents the present tense.

In the fifth and fourth centuries BCE, Aramaic was the language of officialdom and the *lingua franca* of the Persian Empire. Every scribe mastered it, including those of the Jerusalem temple. To what extent and by whom it was spoken outside Syria has to be assessed from case to case. Judeans in Galilee, Idumea and in the Babylonian, Egyptian, and Arab Diaspora also spoke various forms of Aramaic at an early date because they lived in multiethnic contexts, so that these varieties of Aramaic became their first language within a few generations. Jerusalem, however, kept Middle Hebrew alive. That someone wrote in Aramaic says nothing about his daily vernacular(s).

Compared with ancient oriental literary phenomena, the Torah marks the abolition of the monarchy. In the ancient Orient, the supreme god appointed the king, who handed down the law to his subjects, at least in theory. To his Amorite subjects, Hammurabi presented himself as a wise legislator who gives them the common law they already had. In the Torah, it is the law that tells the king what to do (Deut. 17:14-20). In short, a king in Israel is deprived of a foreign policy, an army, diplomatic marriages, and a financial policy, because he must not accumulate riches. Instead, he must listen to the Torah day and night. From now on, every human being can be considered the image of God, something formerly reserved exclusively for the king. This is a significant contribution of the history of biblical Israel to human dignity.

8.8 Literary Developments after the Torah

The completion of the Torah enabled the Jerusalemite scribes to concentrate on the other preserved texts and traditions and prepare them for a second canon that would forge a Judean memory different from that of the Samarians. Besides the Book of Joshua, which was an organic supplement to the Torah, or the first Deutero-canonical book, because it contained the logical conclusion to the Exodus, the next book the Jerusalem scribes worked on was Job, which is one of the rare non-Torah biblical books found among the Dead Sea Scrolls that was written in Palaeo-Hebrew characters (4QPaleoJob^c; Skehan *et al.* 1992). Job begins with the Chaldeans and Sabeans in Arabia, which betrays a date of production between 553 and 404 BCE, when this political configuration prevailed. By contrast, the Deuteronomistic "History of the First Temple" in 1 Samuel–2 Kings, not to be confused with the standard "Deuteronomistic History" (Deuteronomy–2 Kings), still had a long process of redaction in front of it. It was broken down into several prophetic editors and two separate books, with Kings becoming less a continuation of Samuel than the introduction to Isaiah. By the end of the fourth century BCE, what would eventually become the prophetic canon was composed of six main literary bodies in progress: Joshua, Kings–Isaiah, Samuel, Jeremiah, Judges, and the Minor Prophets, who at the time were numbered at only 10. Within the temple school, the political virulence of Deuteronomistic texts was contained. By way of compensation, proto-apocalyptic texts (Isa. 54:11–55:5; 60–62; Joel 3–4; Zeph. 1:14-18; Hag. 2:21-23; Zechariah 1–8) elaborated various utopias and dystopias (Ben Zvi 2006), but no one in Jerusalem had any inkling of what was going to occur after 333 BCE.

The authority of the temple of Bethel was recognized during the first attempts to rebuild a temple in Jerusalem (Zech. 7:2),[3] although the project was marked by the expectation of a Davidic restoration (Haggai; Zechariah 1–8). Bethel's prestige survived the completion of the temple of Jerusalem under Persian aegis. Davidic notions were abandoned. The new temple was inspired by the spirit of what is described in exegetical literature as the Priestly Narrative in the Hexateuch. This narrative starts in Genesis 1 with the neutral designation of the Creator as Elohim (God). It is only in Exodus 6:3 that Moses is told that the name of El-Shaddai, who appeared under this name to Abraham, Isaac, and Jacob, is in fact YHWH. This long period of anonymity provided a space for the recognition of YHWH's universalism and his equation with Marduk, Ahuramazda, or any other creator god, while recognizing that the differences were only a matter of names. Hence, the militancy of the Deuteronomistic YHWH was defused. The reality of the Empire was accepted. A wedge was driven between political sovereignty and proto-ethnic identity. It was possible to worship YHWH without being ruled by a descendant of David.

---

3 Bethel cannot possibly be a personal name.

As a consequence of the de-territorialization of divine rule, people belonging to different proto-ethnic groups could live side by side in any given territory. This was a crucial step towards the emergence of Judaism as a world religion. Yet, it is too early to speak of religion at this stage, because the concept of religion as a distinct sphere is a later phenomenon. This momentous shift occurred in stages; in the Bible, it is actualized in the Priestly Narrative, which presents the entrance of the children of Israel into Canaan (Josh. 5:10-12) as the climax of a long story that is rooted in Creation (Genesis 1) rather than in any military conquest (Kratz 2005).

However, the adjective "Priestly" is confusing, because the Priestly Narrative, contrary to later priestly layers in the Pentateuch, is very discreet about priestly matters. It focuses on the portable sanctuary built in the wilderness by the children of Israel. YHWH's residence in the midst of his people is delimited by curtains embroidered with cherubim that guard it (Exod. 40:17, 34). The residence (מִשְׁכָּן miškan) is *not* a temple, and it remains distinct from the intricate descriptions of the tent of meeting and of the tabernacle that were later added as prototypes of the Jerusalem temple (Guillaume 2009a: 62–68). The residence is finally put to rest in Shiloh (Josh. 18:1), and in the subsequent stories it never makes it to Jerusalem.

This hiatus between the wilderness and Jerusalem tends to be downplayed in exegetical literature, although it is at the root of the Torah and Judaism. The Priestly Narrative refers only to Bethel and Hebron/Machpelah as sacred places. The absence of Jerusalem is hardly surprising. Contrary to a widely held notion, the Torah does not identify "the place where YHWH lets his name dwell" with Jerusalem or any other place.

A likely context for the elaboration of such a priestless narrative is Xerxes' "demon-hunt," when temples in rebellious areas were destroyed (Guillaume 2009b: 177–187). Once Artataxerxes I ordered the fortification of Jerusalem and the transformation of the fortress-chapel into the central sanctuary of the province, the Deutero-Isaiah group added the descriptions of the tabernacle and of the tent of meeting (Exodus 25–30; 35–40) as the prefiguration of Solomon's temple (Hurowitz 1992). The Ezekiel group, however, waited for the "true" temple that would be built as the result of divine intervention rather than as a Persian project. That true temple could only be the result of a new creation (Ezekiel 40–48).

8.9 Bethel's Legacy

The province of Yehud was too small for two temples (Carter 1999, fig. 7). A clash was inevitable between the "returnees" in Jerusalem, where the members of the second Golah of 586 BCE increasingly set the tone, and the old-timers at Mizpah and Bethel. This was given several narrative expressions, projected back to the time of Jeroboam in 1 Kings 13 and also set in a mythical period when "there were no kings in Israel and everyone did what was right in his own eyes" (Judges 17–21). Eventually, the venerable sanctuary of Bethel was destroyed. The destruction was justified via an antecedent attributed anachronistically to Josiah (2 Kgs 23:15-18). Politically, such an outrage became thinkable under the influence of Xerxes' repeal of the Marduk cult in Babylon in 484 BCE and his programme for the destruction of temples in rebellious areas deemed consecrated to the worship of demons.

The number of returnees living in Yehud was fewer than that of the locals, but they were funded by the Babylonian Diaspora and they acted on behalf of the Persian state. In this way, the so-called "returnees" were in the same position as the deportees of the Assyrian Empire: a small elite ruling an unwilling local majority. Their loyalty to the Empire was guaranteed by their numerical inferiority and the benefits they derived from more direct access to the centres of power. The success of every empire since the Neo-Assyrians (the first with a central and provincial administration) has depended on the ability to maintain tension between ruler and ruled (Lamprichs 1995, 33–45). Whenever the elite enters into collusion with ordinary people, at the periphery or at the centre, the empire breaks up into kingdoms or tribes. The biblical notions of the empty land and mass return cover up this essential tension by ignoring the predominantly Benjaminite population of Yehud. On the practical level, however, Benjamin had to be ruled, not ignored. However much the "returnees" claimed to be more legitimate than the Benjaminites, the destruction of the temple of Bethel was soon made up for by the construction of a temple on Mount Gerizim, which the Samaritan tradition designates as Bethel, while the associated settlement is called Luzah (לוזה). Archaeologically, the foundation of the Gerizim sanctuary is now firmly dated to the first half of the fifth century (Magen 2007). The literary migration of Bethel is reflected in Judges 1:22-26. Against this, the "returnees" in Jerusalem could do nothing because, to maintain their control over the area, the Persians played on the geographical structure that made Samaria and Jerusalem rivals. Were the one tempted to side with the Egyptians, the other would automatically take the opposite stance and denounce the first as a "rebel" to the Persians, which recalls the rivalry of the Amarna Age.

The destruction of Bethel and its replacement for those living in Yehud by the temple of Jerusalem marked the revenge of the Deuteronomists after the failure of Zerubbabel. Their heroes Joshua and Josiah embodied the concept of killing, expelling from, or converting (Gibeonites, Rahab) the Canaanites of the Promised Land because they might draw Israel into idolatry (Exodus 34; Deuteronomy 7, 20; Joshua 6; 8–9; 10:28-31; 11). Ezra 9:1 reveals who the Canaanites of the fifth century BCE were:

> After these things had been done, the officials approached me and said, "The people of Israel, the priests, and the Levites have not separated themselves from the peoples of the lands with their abominations, from the Canaanites, the Hittites, the Perizzites, the Jebusites, the Ammonites, the Moabites, the Egyptians, and the Amorites [...]".

The sin of Jeroboam and the Baal of Samaria (1 Kings 16–2 Kings 10) are Deuteronomistic theological constructs elaborated against YHWH's competitors, from Sin of Harran to Baalshamim of the Phoenicians. In deference to the new sanctuary on Mount Gerizim, the idea of a single legitimate sanctuary is never clearly formulated in the Torah, but the story of the discovery of the scroll in 2 Kings 22–23 paved the way for the destruction of the Gerizim sanctuary in the second century BCE. In the meantime, the victory of the Deuteronomistic concept of Israel culminated in the founding of Jerusalem as the capital of Yehud under Nehemiah.

8.10 Alexander and the Diadochi

The audience of the Torah in 398 BCE was the elite of the Persian provinces of Yehud and Samaria at the temples of Jerusalem and the Gerizim. Relations between Yehud and Samaria grew tense in the course of Alexander's campaign, but they did not break down before the second century BCE. Within Ioudaia itself, the appearance of religious parties (Sadducees, Pharisees, Essenes, Zealots, and many others) revealed the existence of increasing internal tensions.

Alexander's legacy was the foundation of a Hellenistic world that stretched from what is today southern France, Rome, and southern Italy to Libya and Egypt, and eastwards as far as Pakistan. At the time of his death, however, the mark he left on the structures he found in the Orient was continuity. The conflict between the Greek free West and the Persian despotic East (Herodotus 1.1–5, Aeschylus, *Persians*) is an ideological construct. In Macedonian propaganda, Alexander is the new Achilles who conquered the Troy of his time.

Economically, the rise of Greece was a result of the Mediterranean economic system. Greece developed on the fringes of the ancient Near East. Ugaritic epics, Homer, and the myths of the Bible connect Greece and the Orient more than they divide them. The difference Hellenism introduced was to turn the wish of pharaohs and Mesopotamian great kings to be "kings of the four cardinal directions" into a cultural, if not political, reality.

Alexander's father, Philip II (359–336 BCE), controlled more productive silver mines than did Athens. The Macedonian kingdom was a chieftaincy: the king was responsible to the people's assembly. Philip II created a power base from knightly vassals. It was not until he came to the Orient that Alexander learned autocracy. Macedonians considered themselves

Greeks, but the Greeks despised them as barbarians. Aristotle officiated for a time as Alexander's tutor; whether this fact explains his megalomania is an open question. The battle of Chaeronea (338 BCE) subjected the Greeks to Philip, who mobilized them against the Persians around the slogan, "revenge for the destructions wrought by the Persians."

At Chaeronea, the Macedonian phalanx proved superior to the Greek hoplite phalanx. The length of the spears made some difference in combat. The Macedonian *sarissa* was 6.3 m long, compared with the 2-m Greek spears. Moreover, the Macedonian phalanx was deeper. The first six rows brought their lances to bear in both attack and defence and produced an inertia that was almost impossible to stop or to dislocate. The Macedonians were also the first to deploy cavalry in tactical formations.

The Macedonian vanguard had already crossed the Hellespont when Philip II was assassinated in 336 BCE. The following year, Alexander had to subdue his neighbours yet again. He destroyed Greek Thebes in the process. In 334 BCE, he marched with 5,600 riders (of which 600 were Greeks) and 37,000 infantrymen (7,000 of them Greeks) into Asia Minor and defeated the satraps of Asia Minor at the Granicus River (Figure 36). In Syria he defeated Darius III in person at the battle of Issus (333 BCE). Syria-Palestine fell without a fight, with the exception of Tyre and Gaza. Tyre was besieged for seven months, the time it took to pile up a causeway from the mainland to the island. In 332 BCE, the impregnable island of Tyre was stormed for the first time and razed (Zech. 9:3-4). Gaza resisted for two more months before it was also razed. At Memphis, Alexander was crowned pharaoh. In 331 BCE he founded in Egypt the most important of the 30 Alexandrias that he planted throughout the Orient. Also in Egypt, he was adopted by the god Zeus-Ammon at the oasis of Siwa, and coins thus depict Alexander with the deity's ram horns. The same year, Alexander dealt the final blow to the Persian Empire at Gaugamela River east of the Tigris, near Nineveh (Roisman 1995; Green 2007; Heckel and Tritle 2009). The visit of Alexander to Jerusalem is legendary (Josephus *Antiquities* 11.8.4-7 [Neise's edition §§321–345]).

After Gaugamela, the Persian Empire fell apart. Darius was murdered by his own troops, and Alexander had to claim the Persian provinces one by one. For lack of a better solution, Persian satraps or client kings were often left in place. In 331 BCE, Alexander had the temple of Marduk rebuilt before he left Babylon. In Susa, the equivalent of two billion modern US Dollars was plundered from the Persian treasury (40,000 talents of silver and 9,000 darics).[4] Persepolis was burned down. The Greek soldiers were dismissed at

---

4   1 daric = 8.42 g of gold x 9000 = 75.78 kg = 2673.01587 oz = \$3,458,347.94. 1 talent = 25.8 kg x 4 x 10^5 = 1,032,000 kg = 122,565,321 oz = \$2,375,315,914. New York spot silver

Ecbatana (modern Hamadan; Arrian, *Anabasis* 3.19.5–8). Alexander claimed the inheritance of Darius and incorporated Persian contingents into his army (*Ana*. 6.4–5, 7.23.3–4, 24.1). In 330–327 BCE, he conquered Iran and Afghanistan (Wood 2001, 136). To this day, Alexander and Genghis Khan are the only military leaders who ever successfully pacified Afghanistan, though in both cases few Afghans survived the pacification. Alexander founded the last of the Alexandrias: Khujand in Tajikistan, Alexandria in Aria (Herat), and Alexandria in Arachosia (Kandahar). He married Roxane, a Persian prisoner, in 327 BCE. In 327–325 BCE he continued eastwards into Pakistan. He believed he had reached the sources of the Nile when he beheld the Indus (*Ana*. 6.1.4). At this point, the Macedonians mutinied and forced a retreat (*Ana*. 6.25–27). A mass wedding celebrated Persian–Macedonian brotherhood at Susa in 325 BCE (*Ana*. 7.4). At that moment, Alexander ceased behaving like a Macedonian tribal leader on a looting spree. As the successor of the Great Kings, he decided that the capital of the world would be Babylon. From there he planned to subject Arabia, but he died of malaria or alcohol poisoning or both in 323 BCE.

At the local level, Alexander followed the Persian principle of local autonomy, illustrated by an inscription cited below that records Alexander's letter to the inhabitants of the island of Chios. Autonomy, however, was strictly defined. Contrary to the cities in Greece, for which constitutions were to remain unchanged, Alexander interfered in the internal affairs of the cities of Asia Minor:

> In the prytany of Deisitheos. From King Alexander to the people of Chios. All the exiles from Chios shall return, and the constitution in Chios shall be a democracy. Law-writers [*monographoi*] shall be elected, who shall write and correct the laws, so that nothing shall be contrary to the democracy or to the return of the exiles; what is corrected or written shall be referred to Alexander. The Chians shall provide twenty triremes at their own expense, and these shall sail as long as the rest of the Greek fleet sails with us. Of those who betrayed the city to the barbarians, those who have already left shall be exiled from all the cities sharing the peace, and shall be liable to seizure in accordance with the resolution of the Greeks; those who have been left inside shall be taken and tried by the council [*synedrion*] of the Greeks. If there is any dispute between those who have returned and those in the city, in connection with this they shall be tried before us. Until the Chians are reconciled, there shall be a garrison among them from King Alexander, as large as is sufficient; this shall be maintained by the Chians.
>
> (Rhodes and Osborne 2003, 420–421)

May 20, 2014, 11 h ZULU was quoted at 19.380 $/ounce and gold at 1293.8 $/ounce. Together $2,378,774,262, or $2–2.5 billion, which had at least twice the real purchase power as today's money (based on the buying power of silver).

After the death of Alexander, his generals, the Diadochi (from Greek "successor") vied for his legacy. Against the supporters of a central government under the leadership of Antigonus Monophthalmos, the centrifugal forces prevailed. Ptolemy secured Egypt. Seleucus established himself in Babylon (312 BCE). This date became the starting point of the first "era," a calendar system beginning from one single point, instead of starting again with each new ruler. The Seleucid "Alexander era" was used by Jews until the late Middle Ages, when they replaced it with their own "creation era" based on the biblical chronologies from Genesis 1 onwards. Against Seleucus, Ptolemy claimed Egypt's eastern glacis, southern Syria, and Israel/Palestine, as the pharaohs of the Eighteenth to Twentieth Dynasties, Twenty-Second, and Twenty-Sixth Dynasties had done before him. With a Ptolemaic Egypt and a Seleucid Mesopotamia, the geopolitical constellation of the ancient Near East, based on Egypto-Mesopotamian bipolarity, was restored after the long interruption from 716 to 331 BCE. For the next century, the Seleucids and the Ptolemies fought over control of the southern Levant (Grainger 2010).

Of the five "Syrian Wars" (274–271, 260–253, 246–241, 219–217, and 202–195 BCE), only the last two affected Ioudaia. Josephus (*Antiquities* 12.1.1 [Niese edition §§5–6) mentions an attack on a Sabbath (see Zech. 14.2); however, attacks made during the Sabbath because Jews did not fight back out of respect for the day of rest is a literary topos already refuted by the story of the seven-day siege of Jericho (Joshua 6), which necessarily included a Sabbath. Yet, rigorous Torah obedience may have already brought forward this kind of issue, which is attested in the second century BCE (1 Macc. 2:32-41; 2 Macc. 5:25-26). Psalm 79 may also refer to a Ptolemaic storming of Jerusalem. As Seleucid pressure on the southern Levant grew, it can be expected that the Ptolemies tightened their control over Jerusalem, which lost some of the autonomy it had gained during the late Persian era. The date of the coins of Hezekiah (Figure 43) and those of Yohanan the priest (Figure 44) are too uncertain to support a comparison between Ioudaia's status under the Achaemenids and under the Ptolemies.

Ezra 1–6 may nevertheless reflect an attempt to defend the privileges of the local elite, notably the temple, against the new rulers.

After the capture of Tyre in 332 BCE, the Jerusalem high priest is said to have paid homage to Alexander at Kfar Saba, Aphek/Antipatris (Babylonian Talmud Yoma 69a). As could be expected, Jerusalem's stance was the opposite to that of the Samarians, who remained loyal to Darius. The Macedonians conquered Samaria and established a Macedonian colony on the site in 331 or 296 BCE. The Samarian coins and papyri hidden in a cave at Wadi Daliyeh witness to the downfall of Achaemenid Samaria. According to Josephus (*Antiquities* 11.8.2–4), Manasseh, the brother of the Jerusalem chief priest, Jaddus, had married Nikaso, the daughter of the Samaritan

Figure 43: Yehud coin of Hezekiah the Governor (YḤZQYH HPḤ' A, ca. 330 BCE). The owl of Athena is the most frequent theme on Yehud coins (after Meshorer 2001, #3,22).

Figure 44: Yehud coin of Yohanan the priest (YWḤN[N HKWHN) featuring the owl of Athena (after Meshorer 2001, #3,20).

governor Sanballat. Having refused to divorce his wife, Manasseh escaped to his father-in-law, who promised to obtain from Darius the authorization to build for Manasseh a temple like the one at Jerusalem, on condition Manasseh did not divorce his wife. When Alexander besieged Tyre, Sanballat betrayed Darius and submitted to Alexander in return for his permission to build a temple on Mount Gerizim for Manasseh.

This fictitious story about the origin of the Gerizim temple has been used by many to date the "Samaritan schism," the alleged founding of Samaritan "Israelitism" vis-à-vis Jerusalemite Judaism and related forms practised in the Judean Diasporas, but it is contradicted by what we know of the behaviour of the elite in both provinces and by the archaeology of the Gerizim temple. The imaginary relationahip between Manasseh and Sanballat condenses events that took place in the ensuing 200 years, but the overthrow of the Persian-era elite in Yehud and Samaria was the starting point for a development that eventually turned Yehudites into Jews and Samarians into Samaritans, each claiming to be the true successors of Israel to the exclusion of the other. The final development cannot be projected back to its beginnings. Since, according to Josephus (*Antiquities* 12.1.1 [Niese edition §10]), Jews and Samaritans in Ptolemaic Alexandria argued over which temple should be the recipient of their contributions, they still formed a joint community.

Despite Alexander's stunning successes, the Hebrew Bible remembers him in rather bleak terms. His apparent overthrow of traditional order fuelled proto-apocalyptic expectations (Zech. 9:1-8). In light of developments during Hellenistic times, the fascination with the figure Alexander elicited did not erase the horror his destructions generated. Daniel 11:3 heralds the arrival of a great despot who does whatever he wants. The construction of the causeway to storm the island of Tyre was an example of Alexander's *hubris*, which paid no respect to the divinely established boundaries between the dry land and the sea (Ps. 104:9; Prov. 8:29-30). Hence, Daniel 7:7 envisions Alexander as terrifying and dreadful. The final biblical verdict on Alexander is a sober assessment of the violence of his career and of the illegitimacy of his successors:

> He fought many battles, conquered strongholds, and put to death the kings of the earth. He advanced to the ends of the earth, and plundered many nations. When the earth became quiet before him, he was exalted, and his heart was lifted up. He gathered a very strong army and ruled over countries, nations, and princes, and they became tributary to him. After this he fell sick and perceived that he was dying. So he summoned his most honored officers, who had been brought up with him from youth, and divided his kingdom among them while he was still alive. And after Alexander had reigned twelve years, he died. Then his officers began to rule, each in his own place. They all put on crowns after his death, and so did their descendants after them for many years; and they caused many evils on the earth. (1 Macc. 1:2-9)

Alexander's trail of destruction resulted in the restoration of the pervasive geographical structures: the Seleucids in the East (from Antioch to Kabul) and the Ptolemies in the South (from Tyre to Tripoli and Aswan). As successors of the Assyrians and of the pharaohs, the Diadochi fought relentlessly for the control of Syria/Palestine (Manning 2010). In the meantime, Asia Minor and Greece reverted to small- and medium-sized states that Rome would take over at an opportune time. In 300 BCE, Rome controlled only central Italy, from Rome to Naples; in the next 50 years, however, it brought the whole of Italy under its control and collided with the Carthaginians, the heirs of the Phoenician Mediterranean colonies. By 238 BCE, Carthage had lost western Sicily, Corsica, and Sardinia to Rome. After the First Punic War (264–241 BCE), Rome became the undisputed power in the western Mediterranean. After the *de facto* elimination of Carthage in the Second Punic War (218–201 BCE), Rome was ready and willing to intervene further east. The Roman Republic in the third and second centuries BCE is an example of imperialism without an emperor (Harris 1979).

India and Afghanistan soon slipped away from Seleucid control, but not before having taken over the language of the Greeks, as they had earlier taken over Aramaic from their Persian neighbours. The oldest written records of Buddhism are the Greek and Aramaic inscriptions of the Indian King Ashoka (272/269–232 BCE) found in the vicinity of Kandahar (Nikam and McKeon 1959).

In the meantime, the Ptolemies in Egypt not only continued the centralized rule of the pharaohs; they perfected it. The state held major monopolies in salt and exports, and the fiscal pressure on producers resulted in a dramatic increase in agricultural surpluses, as can be assessed by the number of shipwrecks (Figure 5). The Persian Nile-Red Sea canal was revived (Burstein 2008), which enabled the Ptolemies to compete with the Arabian caravan trade for the export of African and Arabian luxuries to the Mediterranean. Every king was called Ptolemy, although modern scholarship also numbers them, from I to XIII. The queens were mostly named Cleopatra, the most famous being the seventh (Chaveau 2000). In ancient times, the Ptolemies were distinguished by epithets: Ptolemy II was Philadelphus "Lover of siblings" (282–246 BCE), Ptolemy III was Euergetes "Benefactor" (246–221 BCE), Ptolemy IV was Philopator "Loving the father" (221–204 BCE) and Ptolemy V was Epiphanes "God manifest" (204–180 BCE).

Part III

The Disintegration of Biblical Israel

CHAPTER 9
FROM PTOLEMY II TO ANTIOCHUS III:
THE BIBLE IN GREEK

The construction of Alexandria and the translation of the Torah into Greek introduce Judaism into the thriving Hellenistic scene and foster the production of Jewish literature besides the Torah.

9.1 Alexandria

The language of the Ptolemaic administration was Greek, and Greeks and Macedonians filled the upper levels of the administration. Hellenized Egyptians filled government positions to a limited extent (Hölbl 2001). The royal family remained a closed circle. The crown prince often married his own sister, continuing an old pharaonic tradition (Buraselis 2008). Hellenism supplanted, but did not suppress, the Egyptian language and traditions, which continued to be used in rituals, temple architecture, and sacred art. The syncretism of Zeus-Ammon and Serapis (Osiris-Apis) is the result of the translation of Egyptian traditions into Greek. To establish Alexandria as the successor of Athens, the Ptolemies set up the library of Alexandria to collect the entire knowledge of the ancient world and attract the intellectual elite. The library was burned down several times, around 48 BCE as collateral damage in the Roman civil war between Julius Caesar and Pompey and again in 391 CE by a Christian mob (Pollard and Reid 2006). Egyptian Alexandria was the first major city in the world where Greeks, Jews, and barbarians lived next to one other instead of in ethnic ghettos. The Jewish community flourished in Alexandria and had a huge influence on the spread of the Hebrew Bible and of Jewish culture.

Ptolemy I and his successors recognized the religious autonomy of the Persian province of Yehud, but Macedonians and Greeks dominated the political and economic spheres and marginalized the Jerusalemite elite. The only administrative post opened to locals was that of tax farmer, as it was more expedient to put the delicate task of collecting taxes in the hands of locals than in the those of hated foreigners. Improving Darius' fiscal reform, the tribute of each district was set by the highest bid placed by a local in the auction for the position of tax collector, who delivered the sum to the treasury in advance. Hence, the costs and the risks were transferred to the local elite, who had the best knowledge of the economic situation in the province. Modern scholarship tends to reproduce the New Testament's negative view of tax farmers, considering them to be collaborators who enriched themselves on the backs of the peasants, repeating the standard interpretation of the prophetic fulminations against merchants (Hos. 12:7; Amos 2:6; 8:6; Mic. 2:2). Tax farming, however, had hidden benefits for everyone concerned, since it is likely that the local elite conferred among themselves before bidding and thus assessed jointly the most realistic sum that could be expected for each year. The "Tale of the Tobiads" (Josephus *Antiquities* 12.4.1–4 [Niese edition §§154–177]) supports the view that higher bids by outsiders were unlikely, because without an intimate knowledge of local conditions, it was very risky. Moreover, resistance was real when landlords and tenants stood together. A letter sent to Zenon, the agent of the Ptolemaic Finance Minister, on April 5, 258 BCE reports that the person sent to recover a debt was thrown out:

> [Alexan]dros to Oryas, greetings. I have received your letter, to which you added a copy of the letter written by Zenon to Jeddous saying that unless he gave the money to Straton, Zenon's man, we were to hand over his pledge to him (Straton). I happened to be unwell as a result of taking some medicine, so I sent a lad, a servant of mine, with Straton, and wrote a letter to Jeddous. When they returned they said that he had taken no notice of my letter, but had attacked them and thrown them out of the village. So I am writing to you. (Tcherikover and Fuks 1957, 129)

In Palestine, Aramaic remained the *lingua franca* in the markets, while at home people continued to speak Phoenician, Hebrew, or Arabic. In Jerusalem, knowledge of Greek would have been confined to the narrowest circles of the elite. Another letter found in the archive of Zenon illustrates the difficulties a Syrian or Sidonian camel-trader encountered to get paid by Zenon's agent (Westermann 1934, 16–21; Bagnall and Derow 1981, 193–194). One of the pretexts evoked against him is that he was a barbarian. As a non-Greek, he did not belong to the upper levels of the trade networks and was thus abused.

A few commercially strategic cities were elevated to the rank of a polis by the Ptolemies: Acco-Ptolemais and Amman-Philadelphia, for example. Other places were Hellenized by the settlement of veterans without obtaining a city charter: Philoteria (Khirbet el-Kerak on Lake Kinneret), Gadara, Gerasa, Pella, Scythopolis (Beth-She'an), and Samaria.

9.2 Hellenistic Biblical Texts

The shockwaves from Alexander's conquests left traces in Zechariah 9–11, but the change from Ptolemaic to Seleucid rule in 201–198 BCE is not discernable, although it was initially received with enthusiasm in Jerusalem. Since Daniel (final edition between 168 and 165 BCE) is not classified among the prophetic books of the Hebrew Bible, the prophetic canon must already have been formed by the time Daniel was produced, by the beginning of the second century at the latest. The prophetic canon tones down apocalyptic hopes revived in the wake of Alexander's campaign (Isaiah 24–27, the Apocalypse of Isaiah). As a whole, the canon of the Prophets is dominated by the voice of the Deuteronomists (Ben Zvi 2004). The collapse of Persian rule led to the repudiation of the aristocracy loyal to the Achaemenids, which became politically marginalized under the Ptolemies. Anti-Deuteronomic theology is nevertheless found in the prophetic corpus, especially in the Book of Jonah, in the early layers of the Book of Jeremiah, and in parts of 1 Kings 17–19 and 2 Kings 2.

Non-Deuteronomistic texts are also found in the third part of the Hebrew Bible: Ecclesiastes and Song of Songs. Both display the syntax and semantics of Late Biblical Hebrew. Song of Songs is a collection of love poems and Jerusalem's response to Plato's *Symposium* (Hagedorn 2003). The philosophical depth of the Song should not be underestimated; love is the only sensible answer to the questions of Job and Ecclesiastes about the meaninglessness of life in the face of death (Song 8:6).

Ecclesiastes/Qohelet is the first Jewish philosopher. Received wisdom is questioned critically and tested empirically. As the first biblical book written entirely in the first person, Ecclesiastes is the only "author" in the Hebrew Bible, although Qohelet is a title rather than a proper name. The systematic use of empirical falsification also makes Qohelet the first biblical scientist. His scepticism reflects a high level of education and a detachment from the centres of political decision making that were now located in Alexandria. Undoubtedly from Sadducee circles, Ecclesiastes reflects a Priestly theology of a stable creation order, but in contrast to Genesis 1, a pessimistic epistemology. Qohelet is clearly against the Deuteronomistic notion of a glorious past (Eccl. 7:10), and against apocalyptic hopes (Eccl. 1:9). Although the name Qohelet is a feminine form, the author shows no esteem for women (Eccl. 7:26-28), but his opinion on the subject is balanced by his theory of "pleasure while it lasts" (Eccl. 3:12-13; 8:15; 9:7-10) and a dispassionate view of marital love (Eccl. 9:9).

The Book of Chronicles is a compendium of the biblical narrative from Genesis 1 to 2 Kings 25, introduced by nine chapters of genealogies. The listing technique is inspired by the Priestly Narrative, as is the suppression of military conquest under Joshua. Chronicles presupposes Ezra–Nehemiah, although this does not mean that the three were written by the same person (Japhet 1991). Hellenistic traits in Chronicles are detectable: the large numbers of soldiers in Judah's armies and the ethnic division of arms according to tribes (1 Chron. 12:2), the numerous personnel at the royal court (1 Chronicles 27), and the use of the Torah and the Prophets as sources to write a history. The prophets are viewed as divinely inspired historiographers and, from then on, the Torah *of* Moses was understood as the Torah written *by* Moses, just as each prophetic book was thought to be written by the person whose name was attached to it. David became the founder of the temple music school. Like the work of the other Hellenistic Jewish historians (Artapanus, Demetrius the Chronographer) the biblical Books of Chronicles are works of Jewish self-assertion in the Hellenistic world, but written in Hebrew.

The Psalter is more than a sequence of individual Psalms. It is a programmatic theological composition. In the third century BCE, Solomon was deemed the author of Ecclesiastes and Song of Songs. A similar honour was ascribed to his father, to whom was attributed a number of laments and love songs (2 Sam. 1:17-18). Supplanted during the Persian era, Deuteronomism represented David as a suffering and persecuted figure (Psalms 3, 7, 18, and 34) which prepared the way for the formation of the first Davidic collection (Psalms 3–41) as a temple songbook.

Under Ptolemy II (282–246 BCE) the Torah was translated into Greek. The Letter of Aristeas relates circumstances for the translation that are legendary, but recent scholarship recognizes that royal interest and support for the translation is plausible (Honigman 2003). According to the legend, 70 or 72 Judean translators were involved, six from each of the 12 tribes, hence the name "Septuagint." Strictly speaking, the siglum LXX (70 in Roman numerals) designates only the Greek Torah rather than the entire Old Testament in Greek. Other books from the temple library of Jerusalem were gradually sent to Alexandria and translated for the library.

Among these were biblical books that are missing from the rabbinic canon but which belonged to ancient Jewish literature as much as the canonical books. The Hebrew text of Jeremiah, Ezekiel, and of parts of Joshua to 2 Kings, which was translated and is now preserved in the Greek Bible, preserves an older form of each literary work than the current text that has been transmitted in the Masoretic Hebrew Bible. Despite the witness of Greek translations, the reconstitution of the redactional process of the biblical text is arduous, and current exegetes have less confidence in the ability to reconstruct it than had previous generations.

Chapter 10
From Antiochus III to Salome Alexandra

The transition to Seleucid rule followed by the rise of centripetal forces fosters the emergence of the Hasmoneans and their attempt to turn biblical Israel into a political reality. The Samaritan reaction initiates the disintegration of biblical Israel.

10.1 Antiochus III and Hellenism

When Antiochus III (223–187 BCE) conquered the southern Levant between 200 and 198 BCE the Seleucid Empire was at the height of its power, in contrast to the Ptolemies, who were in decline. After taking control of Asia Minor (223–213 BCE) and restoring its previous eastern border close to India (212–204 BCE), Antiochus pushed his advantage westwards into Thrace (196–194 BCE). At this stage, the Seleucids came into conflict with Rome, which had expanded its realm eastwards after its victory over Carthage in the Second Punic War. The inevitable clash took place at Magnesia in 190/189 BCE. Antiochus lost, and instead of retreating into his vast empire to replenish his forces he signed the Peace of Apamea (188 BCE) with Rome, by which he gave up Asia Minor, his war elephants, the largest part of his fleet, and accepted paying a huge war indemnity of 12,000 talents.

The Seleucids, especially Antiochus III, continued the Persian policy of granting a large amount of local autonomy to the areas they controlled (Carlsson 2010). The king claimed to be the descendant of Alexander deified as Apollo. According to Josephus (*Antiquities* 12.3.3 [Niese edition §§141–144), after the conquest of Jerusalem Antiochus issued an edict in which he reduced the city's taxes, paid a contribution to the temple cult, and granted a tax exemption to temple personnel. Although Josephus' information should always be read with scepticism, in this case, the edict in favour of Jerusalem corresponds with the measures Antiochus took to relieve other war-damaged cities.

The Antiochus Edict implies that the Torah would be recognized not only as a religious document (as had been the case under the Ptolemies), but also as the civil law of the province of Ioudaia, as it had been under the Achaemenids. Unlike the Ptolemies, the Seleucids elevated many cities to the level of *polis,* with the right to self-government through an assembly of citizens and the power to mint coins.

Confronted with Hellenism, Jews, Samaritans, Phoenicians, and Arabs either acculturated wholeheartedly or resisted acculturation vehemently. Acculturation is generally found among the elite, who profit most from the new culture. Reactions to Hellenism were nevertheless complex. Despite the notion of an irreconcilable opposition between Judaism and Hellenism in the Books of the Maccabees, from the fourth century BCE onwards, all shades of Judaism were Hellenistic to some degree. The culture and language of the victors held promises of social advancement to provincials, while reinforcing ethnic identities. Hence, the concept and the term "ethnicity" are of Greek origin, even though the autonomy that Achaemenids granted to some of their provinces formed the precedent for the *ethnoi* that became identifiable categories in the Hellenistic kingdoms. The Greeks introduced the principle of the individual author, a category that appears in the Hebrew Bible only as a fiction under the guise of the son of David in Ecclesiastes 1:1 but eventually prevails in the canon, as each book is given a particular author: "Moses wrote his book and the Book of Job. Joshua wrote his book and the last eight verses of the Torah" (bBaba bathra 14b-15a).

Hellenism did not end in 63 BCE when Pompey went to Jerusalem; political and cultural histories do not align. Today, the influence that the English language exercises over trade and technology across the world is not due to England but to the United States of America. The acquisition of the eastern Mediterranean turned Rome into a Hellenistic state in which more than 60% of the literati wrote in Greek rather than Latin. At the height of Hellenization in the second and third centuries CE, the mastery of Greek by eastern Mediterraneans was comparable to the mastery of English in India: 5% of Indians speak and write fluent English, 30-35% have working English, and 60-65% speak only the local language (Bragg 2004, 250-264).

The deutero-canonical Books of Sirach and Tobit are good examples of the impact of Hellenism on Jews who sought to preserve their Jewish heritage. Jesus ben Sirach is the non-fictitious author of the Book of Sirach (or Ecclesiasticus), a textbook of the wisdom of the Torah (Rey and Joosten 2011). The "Praise of the Fathers" in Sirach 44-49 is the first attestation of the prophetic canon, which can be dated around 180 BCE thanks to the indications of Sirach's grandson, who went to Egypt in 135 BCE to translate the work of his grandfather into Greek (Sirach prologue).

Sirach may have left Jerusalem with the Ptolemaic governor when Antiochus took the city (McKechnie 2000). He opened a school in Egypt, and the translation of the textbook by his grandson shows there was a need to continue teaching Hebrew wisdom, but in Greek. Because Sirach wrote in his own name, his book was not accepted in the Hebrew canon of Writings, in contrast to Ecclesiastes, whose work could be ascribed to Solomon thanks to the introductory verse that attributes the book to the son of David.

The Book of Tobit, contemporaneous with Sirach, suffered the same fate, although it claims to have been written before the fall of Nineveh (Tob. 14:1-4). The problem with Tobit is that he is presented as a descendant of the tribe of Naphtali, which was deported by the Assyrians. According to the biblical scenario, Tobit belonged to the 10 "lost" tribes of Israel. Tobit shows how a member of the northern tribes could remain faithful to the Torah and exempt from the "sin of Jeroboam." Rather than proselytizing among the Samaritans, the author's intention might have been to safeguard Galilean Jews against reproaches of lax orthodoxy "far from Jerusalem." A typical Hellenistic novelette, Tobit alternates moral teachings with entertaining stories of adventure and miracles (Weeks et al. 2004).

Like Ecclesiastes and Song of Songs, Sirach and Tobit were written outside the scribal school of the temple of Jerusalem. Both know the Torah and the Prophets, which suggests their authors studied at Jerusalem. But after 180 BCE, as a result of the tensions between Antioch and Rome and the ensuing fragmentation of the Jerusalem elite, the temple lost its monopoly over the ownership and maintenance of biblical literature.

Egypt continued to be an attractive destination, and after his removal from office in Jerusalem, the high priest Onias built his own temple in Leontopolis (Josephus *Antiquities* 13.3.1-3 [Niese edition §§62-73]). Onias may have owned a private library with copies of the Torah and Prophets that he took with him to Leontopolis. The diversity of biblical and parabiblical texts found among the Dead Sea Scrolls attests to the multiplication of types and versions that disseminated the Hebrew and Greek Bible to a growing variety of Jewish sects far beyond the few known Jewish temples that existed at the time. The plurality of forms of biblical text reflects the plurality of Jewish groups, which defied the normative claims of the Jerusalem temple. After the Ptolemaic period and prior to the ascendancy of Rabbinic Judaism from the third through to the sixth centuries CE, it is difficult, if not impossible, to identify any form of "mainstream Judaism."

10.2 The Breakup of the Seleucid Empire and the Rise of the Hasmoneans (187-130 BCE)

The Books of Maccabees and Josephus describe the rise of a virulent Hellenist party in Jerusalem followed by a religious persecution under Antiochus IV. Circumcision was supposedly banned, as well as the Sabbath and the possession of Torah scrolls. A pig was supposedly sacrificed on the altar of Jerusalem to signify the end of traditional Judaism. This horror story serves as the backdrop to the heroic restoration of Judaism led by the priestly family of Mattathias. One of his sons was later nicknamed

"Hammer" (Hebrew *maqqevet*, Aramaic *maqqâbâ'*) for his terrorist actions against the Seleucids, through which the Maccabees restored "true religion" and Judean independence from foreign domination. This is the winner's point of view. The overthrow of Seleucid control over Jerusalem occurred in the wider context of the struggle of the Seleucids against Rome, in particular during the aftermath of the Sixth—and last—Syrian War (170–168 BCE).

To meet the conditions of the Peace of Apamea, Antiochus III raided temples in his realm, and he died at Susa while plundering the treasure of the temple of Bel in 187 BCE. His successor, Seleucus IV Philopator (187–175 BCE), appointed Olympiodorus as chief administrator of all the temples of the province Coele-Syria and Phoenicia (Lebanon and Palestine), with the intention of accessing their financial resources. An inscription that was probably erected in the temenos of Apollo's temple in the provincial capital of Mareshah records the event (Gera 2009; Jones 2009). According to 2 Maccabees 3:1-13, Heliodorus (Seleucus' prime minister), was present in person in Jerusalem to collect a large levy from the temple treasury but was prevented from doing so by a miraculous intervention. Nevertheless, the temple delivered 5,000 shekels to Demetrius II around 178 BCE (1 Macc. 10:40; Josephus *Antiquities* 13.2.3 [Niese edition §55]). This may have motivated the Hellenists in Jerusalem to seek to secure the status of *polis* for Jerusalem, which would have sheltered them from further impositions and granted greater self-government rights to the city and its temple.

The Maccabean revolt was primarily a Jewish civil war. It was less a conflict of traditionalists versus Hellenists and more a communal uprising against the big families. Inevitably, it spurred a military response from the Seleucid state. By 161 BCE, the revolt had failed. Despite the terms of the Peace of Apamea, the Seleucid Empire thrived to such a point that it was about to take over the Ptolemaic realm. Prior to this momentous event, Rome had used the Seleucid hostages it held in the framework of the Peace of Apamea to stage coups against the Seleucid rulers who followed Antiochus III. Rome also supported the Ptolemies against the Seleucids to maintain the balance of power in their favour.

In 168 BCE, however, indirect interference did not suffice, and a Roman emissary was in Alexandria when Antiochus IV (175–164 BCE) was about to take the city and annex Egypt. Such a revival of the Assyrian Empire would have proved fatal to Rome's ambitions. As the story goes (Livy, *Ab Urbe Condita* 45.12), Rome's emissary drew a circle around Antiochus, stating that stepping out of it would be taken by Rome as a declaration of war. As with Antiochus III after Magnesia, Antiochus IV complied with Rome's demand.

Misinterpreting Antiochus' withdrawal as a defeat, anti-Seleucid leaders took control of Jerusalem and organized a rebellion. The rebels had probably been prompted by Roman promises, but the blunder was theirs. They paid for it when, on his way back to Antioch, Antiochus quenched the revolt and set up a Seleucid garrison in Jerusalem to secure the region. Despite claims to the contrary in 1 Maccabees 1:29-40 and 2 Maccabees 5:5, 11-23, the "persecution" had nothing to do with Hellenism. Fuelled by Rome, the ongoing conflict between the Seleucids and Ptolemies translated in Jerusalem into heightened rivalry between the local elites, who chose opposing camps in the hope of securing their position against their local rivals.

The Books of Maccabees and Josephus depict the Tobiads as rural aristocrats and tax farmers, in distinction to the Jerusalemite Oniads, who, as is generally the case with urban elites, leaned more towards the Empire than their rural counterparts. The power struggle between Antioch, Alexandria, and Rome took the form of a bitter rivalry in Jerusalem over control of the position of high priest, who obviously had prerogatives unknown in previous eras. Like tax farming, the position was secured from Antioch through some sort of unofficial auction or payment of a bribe. In 172 BCE, Menelaus replaced Jason in exchange for an increase in tribute. Civil war broke out. During Antiochus' first campaign against Egypt (170 BCE), Jason attacked Menelaus in Jerusalem to recover his lost high priestly position. Antiochus quashed the unrest by turning Jerusalem into a Seleucid military colony (1 Macc. 1:34-38). The biblical presentation of the various anti-Seleucid rebellions that led to the rise of the Hasmonean dynasty as the consequence of the actions of impious Hellenist Jews and of Seleucid oppression should not be taken at face value. The Hasmoneans, whose legitimacy in occupying the high priestly office was questionable, had every interest in discrediting their competitors.

The Maccabean revolt broke out when the Jerusalemite priest Mattathias killed a Jew and a Seleucid official in Modein (compare Numbers 25; Sir. 45:23-26). Mattathias then escaped to the hills with his sons, as the ʽapiru used to do in the Bronze Age. His son Judas became a self-appointed guerrilla leader and gained the nickname Maqqabi (מקבי), "Hammer".

The Mattathias episode is missing in 2 Maccabees, which begins with the rebellion of Judas. Judas received support from the circles of the Ασιδαιοι (חסידים Hasidim) and other marginalized groups that had gone into the "desert" (1 Macc. 1:29-44). In 166-165 BCE, Judas beat some small Seleucid contingents, while Antiochus IV died on a campaign in Parthia. Judas took this opportunity to occupy Jerusalem and "purify" the temple (1 Macc. 14:12). In 163 BCE, the regent Lysias defeated Judas at Beth-Zur and almost conquered Jerusalem but, having to defend his own position in northern Syria, Lysias made a truce with Judas and officially handed over the temple to the Maccabees. Menelaus was deposed and executed. His successor Alcimus soon lost the support of the Maccabees when he executed some Hasidim extremists. Alcimus fled and returned with the Seleucid army. After one last victorious battle, Judas was killed (161 BCE). Alcimus reigned and the Hellenists confiscated the land of the rebels, marking the end of the revolt of the Maccabees.

After the death of Judas Maccabeus, his brother Jonathan kept the Maccabean legacy alive by organizing guerrilla actions. Alcimus governed as high priest until 159 BCE while the Seleucid general Bacchides built strongholds in Galilee. In 157 BCE, a truce between Bacchides and Jonathan secured a mutual release of prisoners, indicating that even from the Maccabees' point of view, the rebellion was over. Jonathan lived on as a "judge" in Michmash (157-152 BCE). In 153 or 152 BCE, however, disputes over the succession of Demetrius I broke out in Antioch and both parties courted Jonathan with a view to recruiting him to their side. In his new position as a mercenary leader courted by the high officials, Jonathan lost the allegiance of one element of the Deuteronomists of the day, the Hasidim, but gained the support of some elements among the Sadducees, while ultra-Orthodox Hasidim may have seceded as Essenes. In the eyes of some Hasidic circles, Jonathan was as bad as the Hellenists once had been (1QpHab 8:11). As military governor of Coele-Syria, Jonathan conquered Joppa, Ashdod, and Ashkelon in 148/147 BCE, officially for the Seleucids, but *de facto* as part of his own power base. In 145 BCE, Demetrius II handed over the administration of the districts of Iouda, Ephraim, Lydda, and Ramathaim to Jonathan, under the supervision of the Seleucid garrison that remained in the citadel of Jerusalem. Jonathan met his fate in another campaign conducted in the service of the Seleucids in 142 BCE. As guerrilla turned condottiero, Jonathan recalls the career of David in 1 Samuel 16-30 and that of Idrimi of Alalakh.

Whoever ruled, or hoped to rule, in Antioch could not ignore the Hasmonean power factor. The weaker the position of the pretender to the Seleucid throne, the greater the concessions he granted to local rulers. In 142 BCE, Simon succeeded his brother Jonathan as ethnarch (chief, נשיא *nasi'*), strategos (provincial governor) and high priest. Iouda became a semi-autonomous Seleucid province. Immediately after his appointment, Simon captured Gezer, where he performed the first Jewish ethnic cleansing, expunging its residents according to the programme of Deuteronomy 7 and 20 (1 Macc. 13:43-48). In 141 BCE, he expelled the Seleucid garrison from the citadel in Jerusalem. In the course of the Seleucid attempt to recapture Jerusalem and the Philistine coast, Simon was murdered (135 BCE) and his son succeeded him.

After a seemingly uneventful career in the service of the Seleucids, Simon was succeeded by his son John Hyrcanus. Since 135 BCE, Antiochus VII (138-129 BCE) had reasserted Seleucid supremacy over Jerusalem and the Philistine coast. As a vassal, Hyrcanus followed Antiochus VII to Parthia in an attempt to regain the eastern parts of the Seleucid Empire. This campaign was disastrous. Antiochus died and Hyrcanus returned to Jerusalem, where he ruled unchallenged (129 BCE). The turmoil of the years 175-129 BCE is paradigmatic. The struggle between the leading families reflected broader geopolitical issues. An "independent" state in Israel/Palestine was and remains possible only with the active or passive support of the powers of the moment.

The Maccabean crisis left some traces in the Greek Bible (de Troyer 2003). Produced between 167 and 165 BCE, the Book of Daniel reached its final form in the Latin Vulgate. Daniel transmits a number of short Diaspora stories: Daniel 2-6, Susanna (Latin Daniel 13), and Bel and the Dragon (Latin Daniel 14). These stories were updated at the beginning of the second century BCE with apocalyptic visions that culminated in the "abomination of desolation" of 167 BCE. Yet, the book ignores the feast of Hanukkah. The juxtaposition of Aramaic (Daniel 2-7) and Hebrew texts (Daniel 1 and 8-12) reflects the status of these languages in the third and second centuries BCE. Daniel is portrayed as a member of the first deportation, and the time ever since the destruction of the "First Temple" is depicted as one of exended "foreign rule," which will end only by divine intervention. Daniel seems to originate from among the Hasidim, who disapproved of the Maccabean revolt and viewed it as an illegitimate human endeavour to liberate Israel.

In the wake of Jonathan's need for legitimation following his accession to the high priesthood, the Pentateuch was slightly edited again. The begetting ages of three of the antediluvian ancestors in the Hebrew text of Genesis 5 were lengthened (Jared, Methuselah, Lamech) so that the Exodus could be dated in year 2666 after the creation of the world, two thirds of the way towards Hanukkah, the celebration of the rededication of the temple by the Maccabees occurring in year 4000. In Joshua, Hebrew text missing from the Greek version (Josh. 10:15, 43) makes Joshua a forerunner of Judas Maccabaeus. The burden of the Maccabean or Hasmonean edition was the consolidation of the link between the Torah and the Prophets, with a concluding editorial note in Malachi 3:22-23.

The Book of Judith is a historical novel that reveals the techniques of biblical historiography. In it, the contemporary Seleucids are represented in the guise of Nebuchadnezzar, anachronistically presented as the "King of Assyria"—chronology was no great concern in this kind of historiography in which all biblical heroes are more or less contemporaries. Judith belongs to the Syro-Palestinian literary tradition written in Aramaic that goes back to the seventh century BCE and the Story of Ahiqar (Conybeare et al. 1913).

10.3 From John Hyrcanus to Salome Alexandra

Following the collapse of the Seleucid Empire, John Hyrcanus (134/129/128–104 BCE) was *de facto* independent, but he did not take the royal title (Barag 1992–1993). His coins represent him as "Jonathan the high priest, head of the Congregation (חבר) of the Jews," which corresponds to the functions of high priest and ethnarch (Figure 45). Hyrcanus hired mercenaries and settled them in military colonies (Ps. 108:8-11). According to Josephus (*Antiquities* 13.11.7 [Niese edition §§299–300]; *Jewish War* 1.2.8 [Niese edition §§68–69]), Hyrcanus was also a prophet, and a David *redivivus* after the image of David in the Psalter.

Figure 45: Coin of John Hyrcanus I (135–104 BCE). Jehohanan the high priest and the guild/congregation of the Jews (יהוחנן הכהן הגדל וחבר היהודים). The other side features a double cornupia, a pomegranate, and ears of grain (after Ostermann 2005, #1).

Between 129 and 112/110 BCE, John Hyrcanus extended Iouda as far as Madaba in the east, Idumea in the south, and Shechem in the north. The Idumeans were offered the choice between death, emigration, or conversion to Judaism, described in the sources as forced circumcision, although, technically, all Abraham's progeny were already circumcised. The eventual Edomite revenge for this forced conversion was Herod the Great, an Edomite who became the most powerful ruler Jerusalem ever had.

The plateau of Medaba (Moab, north of the Arnon) was conquered from the Nabateans. This conquest requires that Perea, the southern Jordan Valley, and the slopes leading to the Ammonite plateau were already in Judean hands. Otherwise, the conquest of the region between the Jordan River and the Madaba plateau would need to have been mentioned too. In the heart of this mountainous zone, the Tobiads acquired a large estate in the Wadi es-Sir, known today as Qasr al-'Abd. It is the only Hellenistic monumental architecture in Israel/Palestine and Jordan still standing (Rosenberg 2006).

The kingdom of Hyrcanus, up until the time of Herod the Great, was as extensive as the kingdom of David as described in the Bible. It was neither the first nor the last time that a literary tradition would be given concrete political expression.

After the destruction of Samaria by one of the generals of Alexander, the Samaritans built a new capital adjoining the temple on Mount Gerizim. It is named לוזה Luzah in Samaritan literature, after the model of Genesis 28:19, 35:6, and 48:3; Joshua 16:2 and 18:13; and Judges 1:23-26. At 40 hectares, it was large (Magen *et al.* 2004). The persecution of the Samaritans under Antiochus IV (2 Macc. 5:23; 6:2) is unlikely, but the story reveals that, for the author of 2 Maccabees, the Samaritans were not schismatic, despite Josephus (*Antiquities* 12.5.5 [Niese edition §§257–264]), who claimed that the Samaritans had replaced YHWH with Zeus Hellenios, or "Zeus Xenios" (2 Macc. 6:2). This is a polemical depiction of the Samaritans, who rendered in Greek their ancestral god YHWH as a Zeus figure without implying idolatry. In 112/111 BCE, however, Hyrcanus destroyed Luzah and the temple on Mount Gerizim. From then on, the schism was unbridgeable (Mulder 2011). To this day, the Samaritans celebrate Passover on their sacred mountain, albeit denying that there ever was a temple there. The development of the Samaritan religion and theology, between the first century BCE and the fourth century CE, gives rise currently to a plethora of open questions. In 108/107 BCE, Hyrcanus destroyed the new Samaria, which Herod then built again as a *polis* under the name of Sebaste (Augusta in Greek).

The Book of 1 Maccabees goes back to a Hebrew original that was probably composed at the court of John Hyrcanus. It is inspired both theologically and stylistically by Joshua-Kings, Chronicles, and Ezra-Nehemiah. Sequences of events are condensed or distended and interpreted in speeches, hymns, and anecdotes. The military successes of the Hasmoneans make them legitimate rulers over the whole of Israel. Judas Maccabaeus is portrayed as a David *redivivus*. Second Maccabees begins with two letters sent from Jerusalem to Alexandria. It is an epitome of a five-volume work by Jason of Cyrene on Judas Maccabaeus, and besides Wisdom of Solomon, it is the only Old Testament book written by someone whose first language was Greek or who was highly educated while remaining true to Judaism.

Even if some Psalms contain old material, the final shape of the Psalter is the product of the first half of the first century BCE. Some Psalms are dated to the time of the Maccabean revolt. So, for example, Psalm 79 refers more to the "abomination of desolation" in 167–165 BCE than to the destruction of the temple in 586 BCE. Psalm 110 is an oracle that designates a non-Zadokite priest as a ruler; thus, it legitimizes the pontificates of Simon and of his son Hyrcanus (1 Macc. 14:41-44). In the Dead Sea Scrolls, Psalm 89 (the end of Book III of the Psalter) is present in a short version. After Psalm 89, the text of the Psalms in the Dead Sea Scrolls deviates significantly from the Massoretic Text, which indicates that until 150 BCE the first Psalter contained only Psalms 2–89.

Hyrcanus was succeeded by his son (Judah) Aristobulus I who, like his father and brother Alexander Yannai (Jannaeus), had both a Hebrew and a Greek name. Despite his short reign (104–103 BCE), Aristobulus was the first Hasmonean to take the title of king. He conquered Galilee from the Ituraean Arabs, who had seized it along with the Lebanese Beqa' after the breakdown of Seleucid rule in the area (Knauf 1998; Maoz 2011). In Genesis 25:15, Jetur is a son of Ishmael and grandson of Abraham. In the Greek Psalter, the Hebrew expression, "Judah my sceptre" (Pss. 60:9; 108:9) is rendered "O king Judah" (Pss. 59:7; 108:8; the NRSV's "king of Judah" is a mistranslation), which suggests that the Psalter was translated into Greek in Jerusalem at the time of Judas Aristobulus or shortly thereafter.

Alexander Jannaeus (103–76 BCE) added the title of king to that of high priest on his coins (Figure 46). Alexander conquered Acco at the beginning of his reign. Around 93 BCE, he captured Gaza and Gadara but then had to relinquish Gadara and Hyrcanus' Moabite conquests to the Nabatean King Obodas I. Now in open rebellion, the Pharisees fought Alexander with Seleucid help for six years, a repeat of the Maccabean civil wars. In 88 BCE, Alexander was defeated at Shechem by a Seleucid pretender, but the last Seleucid died in 87 BCE in a battle against the Nabateans, and the Hasmonean kingdom was saved *in extremis*. In 83–80 BCE, Alexander conquered Pella, Dium, Gerasa, and Gamala. In 76 BCE, he died in Gilead before the fortress of Ragaba.

Figure 46: Coin of Alexander. The meaning of the anchor is not clear. It might reflect integration into the Mediterranean trade system. The surrounding Greek inscription reads ΑΛΕΞΑΝΔΡΟΥ ΒΑΣΙΛΕΩΣ (King Alexander). The reverse bears the Hebrew words in Phoenician letters המלך יהונתן (the king Yehonatan) inscribed between the eight rays of the royal diadem or star, which might be one source for the star sighted by the shepherds in the Christmas story (both after Ostermann 2005, #10).

From the sixth century BCE until the death of the last Hasmonean rulers, the history of Israel/Palestine is mostly a history of Israelites and Judahites, Judeans and Samaritans, and Arabs. Jews and Nabateans were the only vassals Rome tolerated within the province of Syria for some time. The Nabateans emerged from Kedar during the Persian period (Knauf 1990a; Patrich 1990; Healey 2001). Due to their control of the caravan routes leading to Gaza and Damascus, they became major regional players: they controlled the Hauran, northwest Arabia, Moab, Edom, the Negev, and Sinai. The leading tribe numbered about 10,000 men, and their territory was populated by Aramean peasants and other Arab tribes that used Aramaic as their *lingua franca*. The Maccabees maintained good relations with the Nabateans (1 Macc. 5:25; 9:35). Their seasonal cult centre and royal necropolis was at Petra in Edom. The Hellenization of the Nabateans meant the supplementation of their tribal chieftainship with the props of a Hellenistic kingdom, beginning with Aretas III (87–62 BCE). After the collapse of Seleucid rule, Aretas III controlled Damascus for a short time to prevent a takeover by the dreaded Itureans. Aretas III was the first Nabatean king to issue his own coins, initially with a Greek legend. At the height of Nabatean rule under Aretas IV (9 BCE–40 CE, Figure 47), the Nabatean consul who headed the Nabatean colony in Damascus seems to have been influential, since Aretas is mentioned in 2 Corinthians 11:32 as having the power to arrest the Apostle Paul.

Figure 47: Coin of Aretas IV (9 BCE–40 CE), whose reign marks the apex of the Nabatean kingdom, expressed in the Hellenistic architecture of Petra. The coin features the king's portrait on one side with the legend "Ḥariṭat, king of the Nabateans, carer of his people 1 silver ma'ah." On the other side is the portrait of the queen with the legend "Ḥuldu, Queen, year xy" (after Meshorer 1985, #49).

The economic base of the Nabateans was undermined by the Roman occupation of Egypt in 30 BCE. The peaceful relations the Nabateans had entertained with the Maccabees turned to rivalry with the Hasmoneans and Herodians and several battles, although these wars did not affect the daily lives of the Jews living in Nabataea, as evidenced by the archives of

Babatha (Lewis 1989; Yadin *et al.* 2002) and the Salome Komaise papyri (Cotton and Yardeni 1997).

Alexander's successor was his widow, Salome Alexandra (שלמציון), who had a peaceful reign (76–67 BCE). She relied on the Pharisees (moderate Deuteronomists), who sympathized with her son Hyrcanus and allowed her to make him high priest because she could not exercise the office herself. Representatives of the Pharisees were included in the high council (Gerousia or Sanhedrin). The Pharisees began to take revenge on their old enemies for the persecutions they had suffered under Jannaeus. That was the beginning of the end and should, therefore, be treated in the next chapter. The history of the Hasmoneans thus closes with a woman on the throne and nine years of peace.

The Hebrew and Greek versions of the Book of Esther could have been written in Jerusalem during the reign of Queen Salome (Ilan 2006). Like Salome Alexandra, Esther is a wise Jewish queen who avoids a Jewish catastrophe. Hence, Salome Alexandra lives on as a subtext in Purim, the Jewish carnival.

The final redaction of the Psalter and its inclusion in the canon of theological reading reflects most of the theological themes of the rest of the Hebrew Bible. A doctrinal compendium of early Pharisaic theology, the Psalter was probably finalized under Salome Alexandra and her son Hyrcanus, when the Pharisees dominated the political sphere. To celebrate the wedding of Yannai and Salome Alexandra, Psalm 2 was turned into an acrostic poem, so that the combination of the first letter of each line reads 'For Yannay and his wife, by a Pharisee' (Atkinson 2008; Knauf 2009b). Apart from this reference to earthly politics, the Psalter projects political issues onto a messianic expectation where Israel is only a community of believers. For this reason, the Psalms are by far the most quoted biblical book in the New Testament.

Chapter 11
"Pax" Romana and Jewish Wars

The vagaries of Roman rule in the Levant, the replacement of the Hasmoneans by the Herodians and the chaotic misrule of ethnarchs and procurators pave the way for a series of Jewish wars that complete the disintegration of biblical Israel into Rabbinic Israel and Christianity.

"You, Roman, be sure to rule the world (be these your arts), to crown peace with justice, to spare the vanquished and to crush the proud" (Virgil, *Aeneid* 6.851–853). This motto sums up the programme of Caesar Augustus (30 BCE–14 CE), the first Roman emperor, who saw himself as the first citizen (*princeps*) of the Republic. Acquiring an empire of about 50 million subjects changed Rome into a city of marble, transformed the rest of Italy, and brought about the end of the Roman Republic (Ball 2000; Erskine 2010). Whatever one thinks of the relative value of republics and empires, Rome's domination of the Near East was a golden age overshadowed by two devastating Jewish Wars and the elimination of the temple in 70 CE. What survives of the legacy of biblical Israel was the Bible, which gave rise to the Mishnah (the Oral Torah), the Christian Bible, and the Qur'an.

Rome was a stratified society with three classes defined by one's fortune. Whoever owned more than 1 million sesterces invested in land and belonged to the patrician class. This ruling nobility was represented by the senate and its members held the highest offices: the consulate (for one year, and in pairs) and the proconsulate (the administration of a province after holding the consulate). To the middle layer, of the eques or "knights," belonged those who possessed landed estate worth at least 400,000 sesterces. The knights originally represented the Roman cavalry, but this role had been outsourced to allies and in the first century BCE; the knights were middle-rank army officers and civil servants who were often employed in the administration of the provinces.

Ordinary citizens had voting rights, and in exchange they were theoretically bound to compulsory military service. This third class was made up of small farmers, merchants, and craftsmen, and of the proletariat, the people who owned nothing besides their progeny and lived as day labourers or from grain distributions. The rights of citizenship also came to include freedmen (former slaves attached to their previous owners as clients) and the residents of the provinces.

Slaves and women constituted a major element of Roman society but were subject to the authority of the male head of the household (*pater familias*). The growth of the proletariat went hand in hand with the extension of the realm, and was the motor of the Empire. As was the case with the Neo-Assyrians, in Macedonia in the days of Philip II, and generally in most subsequent empires, social peace at home was obtained by absorbing the wealth of the new provinces, which in turn made the integration of new provinces a constant necessity.

Roman law and the Latin language only prevailed outside Italy in the colonies of Roman veterans who were settled in frontier areas to pacify and develop the fringes of the Empire. Otherwise, the language of the administration in the eastern part of the Empire was Greek. Beyond the coveted status of Roman citizen (Acts 22:25-29; 23:27), the Roman class system was opaque to the provincials. The patrician provincial governor of Syria and the knightly procurator (administrator) of Judea are both erroneously designated as governors in Luke 2:2 and 20:20.

The Roman army was originally a militia, an army of conscripted peasants who returned to their farm, like the "army" of ancient Israel. By the time Rome reached the Orient, the army had become a body of professionals. The core was the infantry of the legions, which consisted only of Roman citizens, who received a farm in a veteran colony after 25 years of service. At the head of a legion (brigade) was a Legate, of patrician origins. A legion was composed of 10 cohorts (battalions), each made up of six centuries (companies), about 80 men under arms. The basic tactical unit was the maniple, made up of two centuries. Cohorts and maniples were commanded by military tribunes from the knightly or patrician class. The Romans owed their victories to new tactics and a radically new weapon. Whereas the Macedonian phalanx was a single body of several thousand men who, once in motion, were unstoppable but hardly manoeuvrable, the Romans divided the unwieldy phalanx into tactically usable small units. The maniple, a group of two cohorts, was able to move in any direction without disbanding. The maniples of the second line stood in the gaps of the first line. In this way, the Roman legion was far more mobile and flexible than its adversaries. The Romans also abandoned the long and unwieldy lances of the hoplites. Instead, the legionaries were protected against enemy fire by large rectangular shields that guarded the maniple effectively from the front, the sides, and from above. They had two javelins and a short sword (*gladius*).

While the Assyrians preferred killing the enemy at a distance with bowshots and the Greeks did so at lance-length, the Romans killed in direct physical contact using their swords. The javelin's only function was to deprive the enemy of their shields, which became useless once a javelin was stuck in it. Striking the enemy at close range was a hitherto unheard of apogee of brutality that ensured Roman military successes. Roman society expressed the same brutality in the enjoyment of the games of the circus with animal hunts, gladiator fights, and cruel and unusual executions. In addition to the legions, auxiliary troops were recruited from among non-Roman citizens, who were organized into cohorts (infantry) and alae (squadrons, cavalry). Whereas the provinces provided the cavalry and archery for the legions, the main Roman army developed very sophisticated engineering skills. Many roads, bridges, tunnels, and aqueducts built by the Roman army are still visible in the Mediterranean world and beyond.

11.1 Pompeius (63 BCE)

In Rome, the conquest of the East was fatal to the Republic (Ball 2000). The party of the "Optimates" (like the British Tories of the eighteenth and nineteenth centuries CE) and the "Popular" party (the Whig or Liberal Democrats) were engaged in a deadly combat. Strong men formed triumvirates to subjugate the senate and the rest of the world. At the end of the Republic, the Empire grew primarily as the result of the competition between the Triumvirs, who needed a power base to assert themselves against their rivals. Hence, Gnaeus Pompeius conquered the east and Caesar conquered Gaul; the clash between them was inevitable (Welch 2010). The trigger was the conquest of the Roman possessions in Asia Minor by Mithridates VI, king of Pontus (northeast Asia Minor on the Black Sea,) for the third time, in 74 BCE (Højte 2009). In 67 BCE, Licinius Lucullus was sent to fight Mithridates and Pompey was sent to the eastern Mediterranean to suppress rampant piracy (de Souza 2002). Having solved that problem, Pompey conquered Pontus and Armenia (65 BCE) and continued into Syria, where he liquidated the last Seleucids (64 BCE). In 63 BCE, he entered Jerusalem.

Before the arrival of Pompey, Hyrcanus, the son of Salome Alexandra, was high priest and her designated successor. With the support of the Sadducees, Aristobulus, Salome's other son, secured several forts shortly before Salome's death. In the ensuing civil war, Aristobulus II (67–63 BCE) besieged Hyrcanus II at Jericho in 67 BCE. The Seleucid governor of Idumea, Antipater, himself an Idumean and the father of Herod the Great, supported Hyrcanus II, who escaped to the Nabatean king Aretas III and returned with a Nabatean army to besiege Aristobulus II in Jerusalem.

When Pompey arrived in Damascus in 63 BCE, three Jewish ambassadors went out to meet him: one from Hyrcanus II, one from Aristobulus II, and one sent by the "people," that is, the Pharisees, who no longer wanted a king. Their position may be reflected in the fact that the messiah-king is prominent in the earlier Psalter but disappears from its end, Psalms 146–150. In the autumn of 63 BCE, Pompey went to Jerusalem in a peacemaking mission to restore law and order.

The Hellenistic cities Hyrcanus I and Alexander Jannaeus had conquered were "liberated" and added to the Roman province of Syria. Their combined territories correspond to the Decapolis mentioned in Matthew 4:25 and in Mark 5:20 and 7:31. Some autonomy was granted, consisting of local government and the right to mint coins. Judea, with Idumea, Samaria, and Galilee, were placed under Hyrcanus II, who ruled only as high priest (63-40 BCE) and paid tribute to Rome, thus restoring the status of Jerusalem to that before 129 BCE when Simon, the last of the Maccabeans, rose to the rank of ethnarch. Rather than an echo of the Roman relation with the Maccabees (1 Macc. 8:17-31; 12:1-4; 14:16-19; 15:15-24), the status granted to Jerusalem reflects the basic principle of eastern and Roman politics. Rome regarded the Judeans as independent allies while they were still under Seleucid rule and as vassals inherited from the Seleucids as soon as Rome controlled this part of the Seleucid Empire. In 62 BCE, the Nabateans were made tributary and had to evacuate Philadelphia (Amman).

The brother of Hyrcanus did not give up, and the ongoing civil war led to further Roman interventions. In 57 BCE, Aulus Gabinius, proconsul of Syria, increased the powers of the high priest and placed five provincial Gerousia (councils) under his supervision: Jerusalem, Gezer, Amathous in Perea, Jericho, and Sepphoris. Idumea and Samaria were apparently left out (Figure 48).

Figure 48: Coin of Gabinius, proconsul of Syria (57-55 BCE) and founder of many Roman cities in Syria-Palestine. This coin is from Marisa (after Hendin 2001, #874a).

The next development was the civil war between Julius Caesar and Pompey (49-45 BCE), which continued after the murder of Pompey and his followers in 48 BCE. In 49 BCE, the Pompeians had murdered Aristobulus II, and Hyrcanus II replaced him as a puppet of the Edomite Antipater. In 47 BCE Julius Caesar restored the arrangements of Gabinius: Hyrcanus was ethnarch, while Antipater became a Roman citizen and procurator of

Judea. Antipater's sons, Phasaelus and Herod, were military commanders and provincial governors of Jerusalem and Galilee, respectively. Without consulting the Sanhedrin, Herod caught a rebel (or resistance fighter) named Hezekiah in Galilee and had him executed. The Sanhedrin indicted Herod, but the Romans rewarded him by extending his jurisdiction to Coele-Syria (now Lebanon) and Samaria.

In the next round of the Roman civil war, Julius Caesar was assassinated (44 BCE). In 43 BCE, Herod and Phasaelus supported the murderers of Julius Caesar as actively as they had once supported Julius Caesar at the expense of the people. The residents of four of 11 districts who could not pay their taxes were sold into slavery. In 42 BCE, the brothers swore loyalty to the new winning pair, Octavian (Augustus) and Anthony. Hyrcanus remained ethnarch; Herod and Phasaelus became tetrarchs.

11.2 Herod the Great (40/37-4 BCE)

Overextended and crippled by civil wars, Rome could not fill the eastern power vacuum created by the breakdown of Seleucid rule. A new player appeared from the east, and Rome lost Syria to the Parthians between 40 and 36 BCE. Antigonus allied with the Parthians and Hyrcanus II lost his ears and thus, the priesthood (see Lev. 21:21). Mattathias Antigonus (Figure 49) served as high priest and vassal king to the Parthians (40–37 BCE).

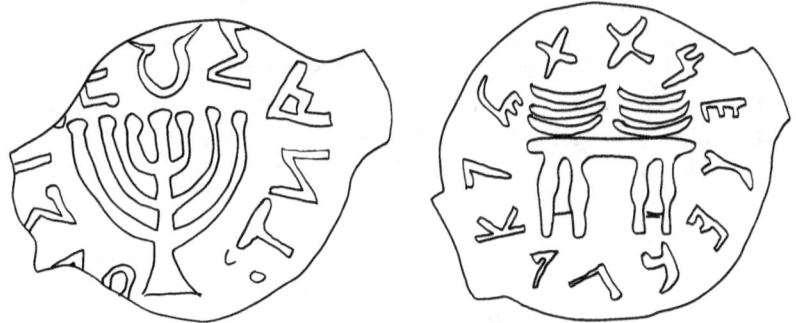

Figure 49: Coins of Mattatias Antigonus (40–37 BCE), featuring for the first time temple furniture: (a) the seven-branch Menorah (Exod. 25:31; 39:37) and (b) the showbread and its table (Exod. 25:30; 39:36). The table and bread appear again on a coin of Herod the Great (both after Ostermann 2005, #41–42).

At the same time, the Roman senate proclaimed Herod as king of Judea and sent him home to conquer his kingdom. The rural population of Judea and Galilee supported Antigonus, while the estate owners of Idumea and

Samaria sided with Herod. In 37 BCE, Herod conquered Jerusalem with Roman support. Antigonus was beheaded, ending the Hasmonean dynasty.

The Idumean Herod the Great was the greatest king who ever ruled in Jerusalem. He built the temenos wall of the Tomb of the Patriarchs in Hebron and the Abraham sanctuary at Mamre. He founded the cities of Caesarea Maritima and Sebaste (former Samaria), both named after Caesar Augustus (Latin *augustus*, Greek σεβαστος, "illustrious"). He reigned from Dan to Beersheba, and a little beyond. He was the great builder that Solomon was only in legend. He rebuilt the Jerusalem temple on a scale that exceeds its biblical descriptions. The platform of the Temple Mount (*Ḥaram aš-Šarīf*) still preserves its Herodian dimensions; the lowest courses of the Western Wall exhibit Herod's monumental ashlars. As a good Hellene, he donated generously to the Olympic Games in honour of Zeus. He continued Alexander Yannai's efforts to rid the province of guerrilla groups by building fortresses in the desert (Alexandrium, Machaerus, Masada, and Herodium).

Herod rebuilt the Hasmonean winter palaces at Jericho (Netzer 2006). He ruled with an iron fist. He tried to be a Hellene to the Hellenes and a Jew to the Jews, though not altogether successfully. The Sadducees were loyal to him, so the Pharisees and the radical circles hated him. Despite the vilification he receives in the New Testament, he was the more acceptable choice from among the bad options for Judea, given internal and external political circumstances.

In 24 BCE, the Romans added Trachonitis, Batanaea (Bashan), and the Hauran to Herod's kingdom. These fringe regions, with a predominantly Arab population, had a problem with bandits who roamed the desert from Damascus to Duma. The Romans considered Herod the best-suited to deal with them. The bandits can be identified with the Safaite Bedouin, who were divided into over a hundred tribes. The ancient Arabic inscriptions they left behind make no secret of their militancy (Ababneh 2005). Herod the Great, however, died in 4 BCE before the problem was solved.

11.3 Ethnarchs and Procurators

After the death of Herod, none of his surviving sons proved capable of taking up the legacy of their father in full. The Herodian vassal kingdom was divided into tetrarchies. The Herodian kingdom is comparable in this respect to the kingdom of David as a state based on the personal abilities of its founder that disintegrates into its previous components at his death. While the heirs were quarrelling, guerrilla chiefs who called themselves kings were stirring up Galilee, Perea, and Judea, preparing the way for the conflagration of 66 CE. The rebels were suppressed by the Syrian legate Quintilius Varus. Three of Herod's sons were eventually designated as tetrarchs, without having the resources to fulfil their task (Kokkinos 1998). In 4 BCE, Archelaus received Judea, Samaria, and Idumea, but he was exiled to southern Gaul ten years later, in 6 CE. Judea was then placed under the administration of procurators of equestrian rank as a second-class province, loosely under the province of Syria. The census of Quirinius (Lk. 2:2) was carried out in 7 CE. Between 26 and 36 CE, Pontius Pilate officiated as prefect (Bond 1998). In 41–44 CE, Judea became a kingdom again, ruled this time by King Herod Agrippa I who sympathized with the Pharisees. He was assassinated by poison, probably by the Romans, due to his attempts to show a certain degree of independence.

Judea was managed by procurators again between 44 and 66 CE. Agrippa II was granted the royal prerogative of appointing the High Priest in 48 CE, though he never ruled over Judaea. Herod Antipas (4 BCE–39 CE) ruled Galilee and Perea in the days of Jesus (Jensen 2010). He built Sepphoris and founded Tiberias in honour of the reigning emperor. But he was banished to Lugdunum (Lyons), and his tetrarchy went to Agrippa I (Figure 50).

Figure 50: Coin of Herod Agrippa I (37–43 CE) featuring the alliance with Rome symbolized with a handshake (after Madden 1881, #136).

A third son of Herod, Philip (Figure 51), was tetrarch over Batanaea, Trachonitis, Auranitis, Gaulanitis, (the former southern) Iturea, southwest Syria, and southern Lebanon (4 BCE–34 CE). He founded Caesarea Philippi (Paneas) at the eastern source of the Jordan River and Julias (Bethsaida) on Lake Kinneret (not identical with the site of that name currently excavated east of the Jordan River). Philip was the only peaceful man of the family. His tetrarchy went back and forth between the province of Syria and Philip's nephew, King Agrippa I (Acts 12:1).

Agrippa II (Marcus Julius Agrippa, see Acts 25:13-26, 32) was the son of Herod Agrippa I. When his father died, Claudius kept him in Rome and entrusted his kingdom to procurators until 48 CE, when he received the kingdom of Chalcis, the tetrarchy of Philip. In 53 CE, Agrippa II lost the

Figure 51: A Greek temple on the reverse of a coin of Herod Philip II (4 BCE–34 CE) (after Madden and Fairholt 1864, 101).

kingly title for that of governor but received a larger territory. Then, in 55 CE he also received Tiberias and Julias (in Perea) from Nero. In 66 CE, at the outbreak of war, he supported Vespasian with 2,000 men and after the destruction of Jerusalem in 70 CE, he retired to Rome.

This constant restructuring shows Rome's helplessness in dealing with a situation that was becoming explosive. Rome's domination of the east was dependent on the ability of a handful of Roman aristocrats to find a local upper class that could mediate between rulers and ruled. In Judea, however, the presence of the temple, over which various irreconcilable factions fought, made it difficult to find a reliable local partner. The theological subtleties of these sects were beyond the understanding and interest of the Romans, who were more concerned with the nearby Parthian threat.

The cities of the province of Syria were the first to be granted semi-autonomous status, thanks to the presence of a Hellenized upper class in the cities of the Decapolis, the coastal plain, and Phoenicia. From there, the pacification of the "wilderness" progressed slowly. Iturea was annexed in 20 BCE, Judea in 6 CE, 70 CE, and 136 CE, and Nabatea in 106 CE. In the case of the Nabateans and Itureans, the annexation of the kingdom—i.e., the switch from indirect to direct Roman rule—was irrevocably accepted by the population, who saw the benefits of the new situation. In the case of Judea, it took three tries and two very bloody wars to complete the pacification. Not only did the Romans and the Zealots have incompatible notions of a just world order but, after the death of Augustus (14 CE), Rome became too unstable to stabilize Judea. Tiberius (14–37 CE) was paranoid (Tacitus *Annals* 6.1.1, 15.3). None of his followers died of natural causes. Caligula (37–41 CE) was a murderer and a megalomaniac (Dio Cassius 59.8.4–7, 59.28.2; Suetonius 26.1; Josephus *Jewish War* 2.186–188); Claudius (41–54 CE), under whom Britain became part of the Roman Empire, was a shy scholar unprepared for the throne (Suetonius 3.5.6.2; Cassius Dio 60.2.4-5, 60.2.1; Tacitus *Annals* 3.2.3). He was a careful administrator but not a soldier, and he lacked charisma. In 54 CE, his wife Agrippina had him murdered (Tacitus *Annals* 12.66-69; Suetonius 44-45) and succeeded by his great-nephew Nero, who, out of narcissistic vanity, incompetence, vacillation, and sadism, made a mockery of the *imperium* througout the Roman world (Tacitus *Annals* 13.17.1, 13.25.1, 14.3-8, 14.20.1, 15.33, 48-63, 16.6; Suetonius 22.3, 26.1-2, 34.2-4).

11.4 The Jewish Wars (66-73 and 132-136 CE)

Since the middle of the second century BCE, segments of Palestinian Judaism had been in a state of apocalyptic fever, which events in Rome and at home worsened by seeming to confirm that the world had reached its end. The level of violence and injustice was felt to have reached such a level that YHWH was bound to send the messiah (Arbel 2009). As the economic *conjoncture* in Israel/Palestine continued on the favourable trend initiated during the Ptolemaic period, social inequalities grew, as they do in such contexts. Everybody got richer, but the rich did so faster, on a bigger scale, and more conspicuously, so that others felt relatively poor in spite of the general economic improvement.

Revolutions do not occur during economic downturns (except in subsistence crises). The prophets and messiahs Josephus repeatedly mentions in addition to bandits presuppose prosperity. According to the prevailing view expressed in Hasmoaean historiography people reasoned that if the small family of Mattatias and a few supporters had successfully resisted the Seleucids, what could prevent new Maccabees from succeeding against Rome and liberating Israel?

What this perspective missed was the decline of the Seleucids and the real reasons for the Hasmonean ascendency. The political incompetence of the emperors of Rome and of the procurators in Jerusalem and Caesarea Maritima was blatantly apparent and generated exasperation. The structures of Roman power, however, were not affected. The legions had lost none of their combative power, and the estate owners and merchants provided a stable economy, even if trading in the Mediterranean declined slightly (Figure 5).

The pre-revolutionary bands in the forests of Galilee and in the desert of Judea were inferior to Roman soldiers in their weaponry and tactics, but in the moral sphere, they had a deadly weapon: belief in the bodily resurrection of the righteous. In the third century BCE, the belief had arisen that the souls of the righteous, instead of going down to the underworld of Sheol, as was previously believed, went up to heaven and to fellowship with YHWH (Pss. 49:14-16; 73:23-26; Dan. 3:86; compare Eccl. 3:18-21). The evidence for the resurrection of the flesh in the Hebrew Bible is late and controversial (Isa. 26:19; Dan. 12:2; 2 Macc. 7:9-23), and it remains unclear how many contemporaries accepted it. The Sadducees rejected the idea of resurrection, but around the turn of the era they were a minority. In the rock tombs of the Iron Age, the deceased were left in the tomb until their place was needed for the next generation, at which point their bones were added to the pile of their ancestors' dry bones. The Bible describes this as being gathered to one's fathers (Gen. 25:8; 25:17; 35:29). In the first century BCE, burial customs changed (Hachlili 2005). After the decomposition process, the bones were collected in individual boxes or ossuaries. Of the approximately 2,000 ossuaries from the necropolis of Jerusalem, 25% are inscribed with the name of the occupant in Greek, Hebrew, or Aramaic. This shows that people expected the resurrection and that this Pharisaic doctrine was disseminated throughout the highest levels of society. According to Ezekiel 37:1-10, this care of the bones was not necessary for the Day of Judgment; nevertheless, it was thought to make the angels' job easier and the practice has provided archaeological evidence for a religious conviction.

With Roman occupation, a "left wing" appeared among the Pharisees (Josephus *Antiquities* 18.1.1 [Niese edition §§1–10], 18.1.6 [§§23–24]) as a religio-political opposition movement. Among these, the Zealots, modelled after Pinehas in Numbers 25 and Mattatias in 1 Maccabees 2, were the most radical avatars of the Deuteronomists. An evolution similar to that of the early stages of dynastic formation in the Iron Age took place among the Zealots and the Maccabees. In the first generation, Hezekiah was executed by Herod. In the second generation, we find Judas ben Hezekiah of Gamala (Acts 5:37). In the third generation, Simon and Jacob ben Judah ben Hezekiah were crucified by the procurator Tiberius Alexander. The fourth generation is represented by Menahem ben Judah ben Hezekiah, or Menahem ben Jair, a leader of the 66–70 CE uprising, and his brother Jair. In the fifth generation, Eleazar ben Jair was the commander of Masada 66/70–73 BCE. With Eleazar we no longer have Zealots but Sicarii ("dagger men"), a group that assassinated Romans as well as Jewish "collaborators," real or perceived.

The previous paragraphs describe the political, social, and mental context in which Jesus ben Miryam lived. Since Jesus was a Jew, he has a place in a history of biblical Israel. He was an apocalyptic preacher of his time. But sources on his life are particularly scarce, because he belonged to Aramaic-speaking Galilean Judaism. In this language, nothing concerning Jesus has reached us, since the rabbinic tradition about Jesus was produced in reaction to Christian claims. The legacy of the Jesus movement survived in Hellenistic Judaism and mainly outside Israel/Palestine.

The earliest evidence of Christian unrest in the Jewish community is found in Suetonius (5.25): in 49/50 CE, Jews were expelled from Rome because a certain "Chrestus" instigated unrest among them. The Jesus movement shared the Zealots' radical itinerant lifestyle. Himself a Galilean, Jesus roamed his home region around the northern shores of Lake Kinneret, where he could live year round with his group without a roof over their heads, thanks to the favourable climate. The city of Tiberias is the only *polis* mentioned in the New Testament (Jn 6:1, 23; 21:1).

As is the case with other charismatic leaders, Jesus came from the middle class. His father was a τεχνίτης, a skilled carpenter—a master builder rather than a cabinet-maker. Jesus' religious rigor suggests that he was influenced by Pharisaic doctrines, even if he was not a Pharisee himself. He was executed as a rebel while Pontius Pilate was in office (26–36 CE). If his triumphal entry into Jerusalem is factual, the Romans had no choice but to eliminate someone who was called Joshua and who came up from Jericho (Joshua 6–10).

The Zealots and Sicarii targeted the Roman occupants and their Sadducee collaborators, but the Romans occasionally used them to eliminate members of the Jewish elite they disliked. The Sadducees recruited bodyguards from among the Zealots, which meant that the Romans controlled nothing and that the country was in the hands of gang leaders. In short, everyone fought against everyone. The country sank into anarchy and became ungovernable. The procurators were unable to deliver the overdue taxes owed to Rome and to get their own share in the revenues of the area.

When Florus Gessius, the last procurator, seized the temple treasury, the First Jewish War broke out. It was no less a Jewish civil war than the Maccabees' insurrection had been. The Twelfth Legion marched in from Syria but was destroyed in 66 CE at Beth Horon. The Sadducee Mattityahu ben Joseph (later Flavius Josephus) became commander of Galilee. That even the Sadducees joined the rebellion reveals the condition of the Roman Empire in the later years of Nero's reign. In 67 CE, at the head of the Fifth, Tenth, and Fifteenth legions, 23 auxiliary cohorts and six alae (at least 30,000 men in all), General Vespasian conquered Galilee and captured Josephus, who, according to legend, correctly predicted that Vespasian would become emperor. In 68–69 CE, the Zealots massacred the Sadducee elite in Jerusalem and then each other. Like Beirut in the 1980s, different parts of the city were controlled by rival factions.

Meanwhile, Vespasian occupied Perea and Samaria and waited to see how the Roman civil war evolved after the death of Nero (June 68 CE). Then, he occupied the south of Judea (June 69 CE) and left for Rome when the legions in Egypt proclaimed him emperor (July 69 CE). In 70 CE, his son Titus restored the Twelfth Legion and stormed the temple on the tenth day of the month of Ab. The next four years were necessary to eliminate the last pockets of resistance in the desert fortresses (Herodium, Machaerus, and Masada). The table of showbread and the menorah looted from the temple were immortalized on the triumphal arch of Titus in Rome. Roman coins underlined the submission of Judea (Figure 52).

Figure 52: *Iudaea capta* coins were produced across the Roman Empire to celebrate Vespasian's victory over the Jews. This one shows the Emperor standing in victorious pose on one side of the palm tree. On the other side sits a wailing woman. On other *Iudaea capta* coins, the woman is replaced by a man with hands tied behind the back (after Brin 1986, #93).

In 70 CE, the Tenth Legion was stationed at Jerusalem, which was transformed into a military camp. Veterans were settled on the former royal estates confiscated from the rebels. The majority of the Jewish population had the status of *coloni* (tenant farmers), which meant no change from their previous situation, except that their taxes went directly to the Roman treasury instead of transiting via the temple. The Pharisees survived the elimination of the Sadducees by the Zealots and of the Zealots by the Romans. For the majority of Jews in 70 CE, the loss of the temple was not final. They were still convinced that God was on their side. This radical mentality is expressed in 2 Maccabees 7:32-33:

> For we are suffering because of our own sins. And if our living Lord is angry for a little while, to rebuke and discipline us, he will again be reconciled with his own servants.

A small group of former Pharisees gathered around Johanan ben Zakkai in Jamnia (Hebrew Yavne) under Roman protection. This group did not form a "Council of Jamnia," but the term serves as an abbreviation for a lengthy discussion process out of which gradually emerged the general acceptance of the Hebrew Bible as we know it today. Basically, it is the canon of the Pharisees, which was fairly identical with the theological textbooks of the temple school used since the days of Salome Alexandra. The significance of the work of the sages of Jamnia would appear later with the rise of Rabbinic Judaism to normativity from the third to the sixth centuries

CE (Cohen 2010). For the time being, most Jews still wanted to get rid of the Romans and regain their temple.

In his identification of Jerusalem and its temple as the source of the Judean problem, Titus was correct, but he failed to realize that instead of quenching the radical-apocalyptic frenzy, the destruction of the temple would spread the fever further. It infected the Jewish Diaspora in Egypt, Cyrenaica (eastern Libya), and Cyprus, and turned Judea into a bloodbath in 115–117 CE (Eusebius, *Ecclesiastical History* 4.2.1–5; Stern 1984, 29–30). In the shadow of the two legions now stationed in Judea, the province remained quiet, and P. Aelius Hadrian decided in 132 CE that the moment had come to reward the Jews with a rebuilt Jerusalem, larger and more beautiful than before: Aelia Capitolina (Speller 2003). The plan included a colony that would be granted Roman citizenship and a temple for YHWH under the guise of Jupiter Capitolinus. At the same time, however, the Roman ban on castration was extended to include circumcision. In Jewish eyes, Hadrian was turning into a second Antiochus Epiphanes. Hence, a new *nasi'* (נשיא) "prince" arose, flanked with a priest named Eleazar (cf. Num. 20:25-28; Ezekiel 40–48, and the figures of Moses/Aaron, Pinchas/Joshua, Ezra/Nehemiah). His name this time was Simon Bar Kosiba, remembered as Bar Kochba, "Son of the star," by his partisans, and Bar Koziba, "Son of the liar," by his opponents (Schäfer 2003; Cotton and Eck 2011). Under the slogan "For the freedom of Jerusalem," Bar Kochba set up a parallel administration over the countryside but was careful to leave Jerusalem and its legion alone. Bar Kochba overstruck Roman coins with his own marks, that often represent the façade of a building that may have symbolized the "Third Temple" the rebels hoped to build (Figure 53).

Had the Second Jewish War found a historian like Josephus, there would have been little he could have recorded except continuous mutual

Figure 53: Coin of Bar Kochba (132–135 CE) featuring a flat-roofed temple (compare Figure 51) with the name Jerusalem around it (YRWŠLM) and what may represent a Torah niche in the centre. On similar issues in the ensuing years, a star was added above the temple (after Madden 1881, #202).

atrocities. As in every asymmetric war, each Roman casualty was a victory for the rebels and boosted the morale of the freedom fighters/terrorists, who performed hit-and-run operations in rugged terrain. It took three years and at least four legions with their best generals and engineers to smoke out the rebels from their caves and underground passages (Stern 1980, 134–137). Losses on both sides were high (Stern 1980, 177). Hadrian virtually depopulated Judea (Cassius Dio 69.12.1–14.3, 15.1; Stern 1980, 391–393). Fanatical apocalyptic Judaism was vanquished at the cost of the extermination of the population that provided tactical support to the rebels.

The First and Second Jewish Wars were a resounding refutation of the Deuteronomistic doctrine that claims that the welfare of a Jewish state is dependant on obedience to the Torah and the right kind of worship. It is no coincidence that the third part of the Hebrew Bible is dominated by the voice of Priestly theology (Ecclesiastes, Song of Songs, Job, and Proverbs), which militates in favour of a universal concept of God and men.

The following letter was sent by Simon Bar Kosiba to some uncooperative people (Papyrus Yadin 49, 133/134 CE):

> From Shim'on, son of Kosiba' to the men of 'Ein Gedi; to Mesabbala' and to Yehonathan, son of Ba'yan: Peace! In good (circumstances) you are dwell[i]ng; eating and drinking of the property of the House of Israel, but showing no concern for your brothers in any manner. And (as regards) the boat(s) *which they have inspected* at your place – you have not done anything at all. However, be informed that your case is (under consideration) by me. And regarding the fruit that is with you – you are to handle them carefully, and you are to bale them quickly from off the boat that is with you, and (which is) at the port. You are to *provide necessities for [...]*
> (Yadin et al. 2002, 282)

11.5 From Judea to Palestine

The Roman colony of Aelia Capitolina (Aelii was the name of Hadrian's family) replaced Jerusalem. The temple of Jupiter Capitolinus (the Roman version of Olympian Zeus) stood in the Forum and became the precursor to the Holy Sepulchre. The Temple Mount was left as a heap of rubble to signify the victory of Rome.[1] It remained so until Omar, the first Muslim

---

1 The story that the Romans built the temple of Jupiter Capitolinus on the Temple Mount is a Christian misinterpretation of Cassius Dio (69.12) "instead of the temple of the god he raised a new temple of Jupiter" (Isaac and Roll 1979; Isaac 1980). Constantine's church was built on the site of a (perhaps dilapidated) temple of Aphrodite at the Forum, and probably with stone material from the (perhaps unfinished) temple of Jupiter next to or opposite Aphrodite.

conqueror of the city, erected a shrine on the site of the temple to set Islam as the true heir of Israel. Rome changed the name of the province from Judaea to Palaestina, which is based on the designation of the coast by Herodotus (1.105, 2.104, 2.106, 3.5).

Palestinian Jews survived in rural Galilee, while Christianity became the religion of Hellenistic urbanites. Although its eponymous man-of-god was himself a rural Galilean, its founder, however, was a Hellenistic Jew from Asia Minor, Paul of Tarsus. Jews and Christians lived in different worlds and from the fourth century CE onwards, Christianity suppressed its Jewish heritage as much as possible. After 136 CE, new Israels arose as non-governmental religious associations.

With the settlement of the early rabbis and the Sanhedrin of Jamnia in Tiberias, this city became the cultural centre of Palestinian Judaism. There, the codification of the Mishnah was completed, which led to discussions that were included in the Jerusalem Talmud, a misnomer for the Palestinian Talmud that, in Judaism, plays but a role secondary to that of the Babylonian Talmud. The Masoretic vocalization of the Hebrew Bible reflects the pronunciation tradition of the biblical text by the Tiberian families of Ben Asher and Ben Naphtali in the ninth century CE, who otherwise spoke Arabic and Aramaic in the streets and arbitrated their disputes according to the customary law of the province in which they lived, rather than according to the Mishnah. While Rabbinic Judaism and post-Constantinian Christianity grew out of centres away from Galilee, a late antique Greco-Aramaic-Arab culture emerged in the first half of the seventh century CE and gave rise to the Qur'an, the youngest shoot from the stump of Jesse (Isa. 11:1).

At the end of this presentation of the history of biblical Israel, we hope to have disproved the claim that if

> historical (verifiable) truth should be our only concern, the history of ancient Israel should not only be very short (written on ten pages or so), but it would be so utterly boring. (Barstad 1997, 64)

What has been presented in this story can be called into question by new archaeological or epigraphic finds and thus corrected as time goes on. It is a challenge to make the reconstruction of the history of Israel nearly as enthralling as the stories transmitted in the Bible, but the data currently available makes it impossible to do that in 10 pages. The biblical image of YHWH developed through confrontation with Assur, Sin, Marduk, and Ahuramazda. It has integrated subversive and constructive features of these gods. The disasters the different Israels experienced (734–701 BCE, 597–582 BCE, 66–136 CE) were largely self-inflicted. These battles were lost, but the defeats were intellectually processed. The legacy of this history is the Bible.

Appendix

Years of enthronement of Israelite and Judean kings, plus final regnal years for Hosea, Zedekiah, and Gedaliah, according to Jepsen (1964), Thiele (1983), Hayes and Hooker (1988) and Galil (1996, 147) and. The right-hand column indicates the highest and lowest likely dates. Dates which, according to recent researchers, are clearly erroneous are not taken into account in the composite column.

IsraelJudah	Jepsen	Thiele	Galil	Hayes-Hooker	Composite
Jeroboam	927	931/930	931/930	927	932/922
Rehoboam	926	931/930	931/930	926	932/922
Abijam	910	913	914	909	916/909
Asa	908	911/910	911	906	914/906
Nadab	907	910/909	909	905	911/901
Baascha	906	909/908	908	903	910/900
Elah	883	886/885	885	881	887/877
Zimri	882	885/884	884	880	886/876
Omri	882	885/884	884	879	886/876
Jeoshaphat	868	873/872	870	877	874/868
Ahab	871	874/873	873	868	875/868
Ahaziah	852	853	852	853	853/850
Jehoram	847	853	851	852	853/847
Jehoram	851	852	851	851	853/849
Ahaziah	845	841	843/842	840	845/840
Jehu	845	841	842/841	839	845/841
Athaliah	845	841	[842/841]	839	845/841
Jehoash	840	835	842/841	832	845/841
Jehoahaz	818	814/813	819	821	821/813
Jeohash	802	798	805	804	805/798
Amaziah	801	796	805/804	802	805/796
Jeroboam II	787	793/792	790	788	793/783
Uzziah	787	792/791	788/787	785	792/768
Zechariah	747	753	750/749	[748/747]	753/746
Schallum	747	752	749	[747/746]	752/745

Israel/Judah	Jepsen	Thiele	Galil	Hayes-Hooker	Composite
Menahem	747	752	749	746	752/745
Jotham	756	750	758/757	759	758/740
Pekahiah	737	742/741	738	736	742/736
Pekah	735	752	750?	734	741/734
Ahaz	741	735	742/741	743	743/733
Hoshea	731	732/731	732/731	730	732/729
until	723	723/722	722	722	724
Hezekiah	725	716/715	726	727	727/714
Manasseh	696	697/696	697/696	698	698/696
Amon	641	643/642	642/641	643	643/641
Josiah	639	641/640	640/639	641	641/639
Jehoahaz	609	609	609	[609/608]	609/608
Jehoiakim	608	609	609	608	609/608
Jehoiachin	598	598	598	[598/597]	598/597
Zedekiah	597	597	597	596	597/596
until	587	586	586	586	587/586
Gedaliah until	[587]	[586]	[586]	[582/581]	582

Abbreviations

ANEP. *Ancient Near Eastern in Pictures Relating to the Old Testament*, edited by J.B. Pritchard. 1954. Princeton, NJ: Princeton University Press.

ANET. *Ancient Near Eastern Texts Relating to the Old Testament*, edited by J.B. Pritchard. 1969. Princeton, NJ: Princeton University Press.

CoS. *Context of Scripture*, edited by W. Hallo. 1997–2003. Three volumes. Leiden: Brill.

CSAJ. *Corpus der Siegel-Amulette aus Jordanien*, edited by J. Eggler and O. Keel, 2006. Orbis Biblicus et Orientalis Series Archaeologica 25. Fribourg: Fribourg Academic Press and Göttingen: Vandenhoeck & Ruprecht.

CSAPI. *Corpus der Stempelsiegel Amulette aus Palästina/Israel*, edited by O. Keel, 1997–2013. Orbis Biblicus et Orientalis Series Archaeologica 13, 29, 31, 33. Fribourg: Fribourg Academic Press and Göttingen: Vandenhoeck & Ruprecht.

DDD 1. *Dictionary of Deities and Demons in the Bible*, edited by K. van der Toorn, B. Becking and P.W. van der Horst. 1995. Leiden: Brill.

DDD 2. *Dictionary of Deities and Demons in the Bible*, edited by K. van der Toorn, B. Becking and P.W. van der Horst. Second edition. 1999. Leiden: Brill.

GGG. *Gods, Goddesses and Images of God*, edited by O. Keel and C. Uehlinger. 1998. Minneapolis, MN: Fortress Press.

IPIAO. *The Iconography of Palestine/Israel and the Ancient Near East*, edited by S. Schoerer and O. Keel. 2005–2015. Four volumes. Fribourg: Fribourg Academic Press.

NEAHL. *The New Encyclopedia of Archaeological Excavations in the Holy Land*, edited by E. Stern. 1993. Jerusalem: Karta.

Bibliography

Ababneh, M.I. 2005. *Neue safaitische Inschriften und deren bildliche Darstellungen*. Semitica et semitohamitica Berolinensia 6. Aachen: Shaker.

Achenbach, R., R. Albertz and J. Wöhrle. eds. 2011. *The Foreigner and the Law*. Beihefte zur Zeitschrift für altorientalische und biblische Rechtsgeschichte 16. Wiesbaden: Harrassowitz.

Aharoni, Y. 1981. *Arad Inscriptions*. Translated from Hebrew by J. Ben-Or, edited and revised by A. Rainey. Jerusalem: Israel Exploration Society.

Aḥituv, S. 1984. *Canaanite Toponyms in Ancient Egyptian Documents*. Jerusalem: Magnes Press.

–. 2005. *HaKetav veHamiktav*. Jerusalem: Bialik.

Albarella, U., F. Manconi, J.-D. Vigne and P. Rowley-Conwy. 2007. The Ethnoarchaeology of Traditional Pig Husbandry in Sardinia and Corsica. In *Pigs and Humans: 10,000 years of Interaction*, edited by U. Albarella, K. Dobney, A. Ervynck and P. Rowley-Conwy 285–307. Oxford: Oxford University Press.

Albertz, R. 1994. *A History of Israelite Religion in the Old Testament Period*. Two volumes. Translated by J. Bowden. London: SCM Press.

Andersson, J. 2011. A Modest Addition to Early Syro-Mesopotamian Calendars. In *Akkade is King: A Collection of Papers by Friends and Colleagues Presented to Aage Westenholz on the Occasion of His 70th Birthday 15th of May 2009*, edited by G. Barjamovic, J.L. Dahl, U.S. Koch, W. Sommerfeld and J. Goodnick Westenholz, 29-36. Uitgaven van het Nederlands Historisch-Archaeologisch Instituut te Istanbul 118. Leiden: Nederlands Instituut voor het Nabije Oosten.

Arbel, Y. 2009. *Ultimate Devotion: The Historical Impact and Archaeological Expression of Intense Religious Movements*. London: Routledge.

Arie, E. 2008. Reconsidering the Iron Age II Strata at Tel Dan: Archaeological and Historical Implications. *Tel Aviv* 35(1): 6-64.

Artzy, M. 2003. Bronze Trade in the Late Bronze-Early Iron Period: Tel Masos and Tel Kinrot in Eastern Mediterranean Context. In *Saxa loquentur: Studien zur Archäologie Palästinas/Israels: Festschrift für Volkmar Fritz zum 65. Geburtstag*, edited by C.G. den Hertog, U. Hübner and S. Münger, 15-23. Münster: Ugarit-Verlag.

Athas, G. 2003. *The Tel Dan Inscription: A Reappraisal and a New Interpretation*. Journal for the Study of the Old Testament Supplements 360. London: T & T Clark.

Atkinson, K. 2008. The Salome No One Knows. *Biblical Archaeology Review* 34(4): 60-65, 72.

Avigad, N. 1976. *Bullae and Seals from a Post-exilic Judaean Archive*. Qedem 4. Jerusalem: Hebrew University Press.

Avigad, N. and B. Sass. 1997. *Corpus of West Semitic Stamp Seals*. Jerusalem: Israel Academy of Sciences and Humanities/Israel Exploration Society/Institute of Archaeology, Hebrew University of Jerusalem.

Azize, J. 2003. The Ammonite Bottle and Phoenician Flasks. *Ancient Near Eastern Studies* 40: 62-79.

Badè, W.F. 1933. The Seal of Jaazaniah. *Zeitschrift für die Alttestamentliche Wissenschaft* 51: 150-156.

Bagnall, R.S. and P. Derow. eds. 1981. *Greek Historical Documents: The Hellenistic Period*. Chico, CA: Scholars Press for the Society of Biblical Literature.

Ball, W. 2000. *Rome in the East: The Transformation of an Empire*. London: Routledge.

Barag, D. 1992-1993. New Evidence on the Foreign Policy of John Hyrcanus I. *Israel Numismatic Journal* 12: 22-26.

Barstad, H.M. 1996. *The Myth of the Empty Land: A Study in the History and Archaeology of Judah during the "Exile" Period*. Stockholm: Ascheoug.

-. 1997. History and the Hebrew Bible. In *Can a "History of Israel" Be Written?*, edited by L.L. Grabbe, 37-64. Sheffield: Sheffield Academic Press.

Beaulieu, P.A. 1989. *The Reign of Nabonidus, King of Babylon (556-539 B.C.)*. New Haven, CT: Yale University Press.

Becking, B. 1992. *The Fall of Samaria: An Historical and Archaeological Study*. Studies in the History of the Ancient Near East 2. Leiden: Brill.

Bedford, P.R. 2001. *Temple Restoration in Early Achaemenid Judah*. Journal for the Study of Judaism Supplements 65. Leiden: Brill.

Ben Zvi, E. 1996. Prelude to a Reconstruction of the Historical Manassic Judah. *Biblische Notizen* 81: 31-44.

-. 2004. The Prophets: References to Generic Prophets and their Role in the Construction of the Image of the "Prophets of Old" within the Postmonarchic Readership(s) of the Books of Kings. *Zeitschrift für die Alttestamentliche Wissenschaft* 116(4): 555-567.

–. ed. 2006. *Utopia and Dystopia in Prophetic Literature*. Publications of the Finnish Exegetical Society 92. Helsinki and Göttingen: Finnish Exegetical Society and Vandenhoeck.

Benichou-Safar, H. 2004. *Le tophet de Salammbô à Carthage: Essai de reconstitution*. Collection de l'École française de Rome 342. Rome: École française de Rome.

Berlejung, A. 2006. Erinerungen an Assyrien in Nahum 2, 4–3, 19. In *Die unwiderstehliche Wahrheit. Studien zur alttestamentlichen Prophetie*, edited by R. Lux and E.-J. Waschke, 323–356. Arbeiten zur Bibel und ihrer Geschichte 23. Leipzig: Evangelische Verlagsanstalt.

–. 2009. Twisting Traditions: Programmatic Absence-Theology for the Northern Kingdom in 1 Kgs 12:26–33 (the "Sin of Jeroboam"). *Journal of Northwest Semitic Languages* 35(2): 1–42.

Betts, A.V.G. 1992. Eastern Jordan: Economic Choices and Site Location in the Neolithic Periods. In *Studies in the History and Archaeology of Jordan 4*, edited by M. Zaghloul, K. Amr, F. Zayadin, R. Nabeel and N.R. Tawfiq, 111–114. Amman: Department of Antiquities.

Bietak, M. 1996. *Avaris, The Capital of the Hyksos: Recent Excavations at Tell el-Dabca*. The First Raymond and Beverly Sackler Foundation Distinguished Lecture in Egyptology. London: British Museum Publications.

Blau, Y. 1998. *Topics in Hebrew and Semitic Linguistics*. Jerusalem: Magnes Press.

Blenkinsopp, J. 1987. The Mission of Udjahorresnet and those of Ezra and Nehemia. *Journal of Biblical Literature* 106(3): 409–421. http://dx.doi.org/10.2307/3261065

Bond, H.K. 1998. *Pontius Pilate in History and Interpretation*. Society for New Testament Studies Monograph Series 100. Cambridge: Cambridge University Press. http://dx.doi.org/10.1017/CBO9780511585166

Bragg, M. 2004. *The Adventure of English: The Biography of a Language*. London: Sceptre.

Braudel, F. 1972. *The Mediterranean and the Mediterranean World in the Age of Philip II*. Translated by S. Reynolds. New York: Harper & Row.

Breasted, J.H. 1906. *Ancient Records of Egypt*. Five Volumes. Chicago: Chicago University Press.

Briant, P. 2000. Histoire impériale et histoire régionale. À propos de l'histoire de Juda dans l'Empire achéménide. In *Congress Volume: Oslo 1998*, edited by A. Lemaire and M. Sæbø, 235–245. Leiden: Brill. http://dx.doi.org/10.1163/9789004276055_016

Briant, P., W.F.M. Henkelman and M.W. Stolper. eds. 2008. *L'archive des fortifications de Persépolis: état des questions et perspectives de recherches: actes du colloque organisé au Collège de France par la "Chaire d'histoire et civilisation du monde achéménide et de l'empire d'Alexandre" et le "Réseau international d'études et de recherches achéménides" (GDR 2538 CNRS), 3-4 novembre 2006*. Paris: De Boccard.

Brin, H.B. 1986. *Catalogue of Judaea Capta Coinage*. Minneapolis, NM: Emmett Publishing.

Bulliet, R.W. 1977. *The Camel and the Wheel*. Cambridge, MA: Harvard University Press.

Bunimovitz, S. 1994. Socio-Political Transformations in the Central Hill Country in the Late Bronze – Iron I Transition. In *From Nomadism to Monarchy: Archaeological and Historical Aspects of Early Israel*, edited by I. Finkelstein and N. Na'aman, 179–202. Jerusalem: Yad Izhak Ben-Zvi.

–. 1995. On the Edge of Empires – Late Bronze Age (1550–1200 BCE). In *The Archaeology of Society in the Holy Land*, edited by T.E Levy, 320–331. Leicester: Leicester University Press.

Buraselis, K. 2008. The Problem of the Ptolemaic Sibling Marriage. In *Ptolemy II Philadelphus and His World*, edited by P. McKechnie and P. Guillaume, 291–302. Leiden: Brill.

Burstein, S.M. 2008. Elephants for Ptolemy II: Ptolemaic Policy in Nubia in the Third Century BC. In *Ptolemy II Philadelphus and His World*, edited by P. McKechnie and P. Guillaume, 135–148. Leiden: Brill. http://dx.doi.org/10.1163/ej.9789004170896.i-488.24

Byrne, R. 2003. Early Assyrian Contacts with Arabs and the Impact on Levantine Vassal Tribute. *Bulletin of the American Schools of Oriental Research*, 331: 11–25. http://dx.doi.org/10.2307/1357756

Cantrell, D. 2011. *The Horsemen of Israel: Horses and Chariotry in Monarchic Israel*. History, Archaeology, and Culture of the Levant 1. Winona Lake, IN: Eisenbrauns.

Capuzzi, A. ed. 1974. *Iscrizioni sudarabiche, I. Iscrizioni minee*. Publicazioni del Seminario di Semitistica 10. Naples: Seminario di Semitistica.

Carlsson, S. 2010. *Hellenistic Democracies: Freedom, Independence and Political Procedure in Some East Greek City-States*. Historia Einzelschriften 206. Stuttgart: Franz Steiner.

Carter, C.E. 1999. *The Emergence of Yehud in the Persian Period: A Social and Demographic Study*. Journal for the Study of the Old Testament 294. Sheffield: Sheffield Academic Press.

Chaney, M.L. 1993. Bitter Bounty. In *The Bible and Liberation: Political and Social Hermeneutics*, edited by N.K. Gottwald and R.A. Horsley, 250–263. Maryknoll, NY: Orbis.

Chaveau, M. 2000. *Egypt in the Age of Cleopatra: History and Society Under Ptolemies*. Ithaca, NY: Cornell University Press.

Cogan, M. 2008. *The Raging Torrent: Historical inscriptions from Assyria and Babylonia Relating to ancient Israel*. Jerusalem: Carta.

Cohen, S.J.D. 2010. *The Significance of Yavneh and Other Essays in Jewish Hellenism*. Tübingen: Mohr Siebeck.

Conybeare, F.C., J. Rendel Harris and A. Lewis Smith. 1913. *The Story of Aḥiḳar from the Aramaic, Syriac, Arabic, Armenian, Ethiopic, Old Turkish, Greek and Slavonic Versions*. Cambridge: Cambridge University Press.

Coote, R.B. and K.W. Whitelam. 1987. *The Emergence of Early Israel in Historical Perspective*. Sheffield: Phoenix Press.

Cotton, H.M. and W. Eck. 2011. The Impact of the Bar Kokhba Revolt on Rome: Another Military Diploma from AD 160 from Syria Palaestina. *Michmanim* 23: 7–22.

Cotton, H.M. and A. Yardeni. 1997. *Aramaic, Hebrew and Greek Documentary Texts from the Naḥal Ḥever and Other Sites*. The Seiyâl Collection II. Discoveries in the Judaean Desert 27. Oxford: Clarendon Press.

Crowford, J.W. and G.M. Crowford, 1938. *Samaria-Sebaste II: The Early Ivories from Samaria*. London: Palestine Exploration Fund.

Dalley, S. 2010. Ṣalmu. *Iconography of Deities and Demons in the Ancient Near East*. Zürich: Universität Zürich. Online: www.religionswissenschaft.uzh.ch/idd/prepublications/e_idd_salmu.pdf

Dalley, S. and A. Goguel 1997. The Sela' Sculpture: A Neo-Babylonian Rock Relief in Southern Jordan. *Hawliyyat Da'irat al-Atar al-Ammat* 41: 169–176.

Dalman, G. 1939. *Arbeit und Sitte in Palästina Volume 6: Zeltleben, Vie-h und Milchwirtschaft, Jagd, Fischfang*. Gütersloh: Der Rufer, Evangelischer Verlag.

Davies, P.R. 1997. Whose History? Whose Israel? Whose Bible? Biblical Histories, Ancient and Modern. In *Can a "History of Israel" Be Written?*, edited by L.L. Grabbe, 104–122. Sheffield: Sheffield Academic Press.

–. 2007. Beginning at the End. *Journal of Hebrew Scriptures* 7: 6–11.

de Souza, P. 2002. *Piracy in the Graeco-Roman World*. Cambridge: Cambridge University Press.

de Troyer, K. 2003. *Rewriting the Sacred Text: What the Old Greek Texts Tell Us about the Literary Growth of the Bible*. Atlanta, FL: Society of Biblical Literature.

Dearman, J.A. ed. 1989 *Studies in the Mesha Inscription and Moab*. Archaeology and Biblical Studies 2. Atlanta, FL: Scholars Press.

Dever, W.G. 1995a. "Will the Real Israel Please Stand Up?" Archaeology and Israelite Historiography: Part I. *Bulletin of the American Schools of Oriental Research* 297: 61-80. http://dx.doi.org/10.2307/1357390

–. 1995b. "Will the Real Israel Please Stand Up?" Part II: Archaeology and the religions of ancient Israel. *Bulletin of the American Schools of Oriental Research* 298: 37-58. http://dx.doi.org/10.2307/1357084

–. 2005. *Did God Have a Wife? Archaeology and Folk Religion in Ancient Israel*. Grand Rapids, MI: Wm. B. Eerdmans Publishing.

–. 2007. Ethnicity and the Archaeological Record: The Case of Early Israel. In *The Archaeology of Difference: Gender, Ethnicity, Class and the "Other" in Antiquity. Studies in Honor of Eric M Meyers*, edited by D.R. Edwards and C.T. McCollough, 49–66. Annual of the American Schools of Oriental Research 60/6. Boston: American Schools of Oriental Research.

Donner, H. 1984–1986. *Geschichte des Volkes Israel und seiner Nachbarn in Grundzügen*. Göttingen: Vandenhoeck & Ruprecht.

Dostal, W. 1985. *Egalität und Klassengesellschaft in Südarabien. Anthropologische Untersuchungen zur sozialen Evolution*. Vienna: Berger.

Douglas, M. 1966. *Purity and Danger: An Analysis of the Concepts of Pollution and Taboo*. London: Routledge & Kegan Paul.

Drijvers, H.J.W. 1976. *The Religion of Palmyra*. Iconography of Religions 15. Leiden: Brill.

Edelman, D.V. 1995. Solomon's Adversaries Hadad, Rezon and Jeroboam: A Trio of 'Bad Guy' Characters Illustrating the Theology of Immediate Retribution. In *The Pitcher is Broken: Memorial Essays for Gösta W. Ahlström*, edited by S.W. Holloway and L.K. Handy, 166–191. Sheffield: Sheffield Academic Press.

–. 1996. Saul ben Kish in History and Tradition. In *The Origins of the Ancient Israelite States*, edited by V. Fritz and P.R. Davies, 142–159. Journal for the Study of the Old Testament Book 228. Sheffield: Sheffield Academic Press.

–. 2005. *The Origins of the "Second" Temple: Persian imperial policy and the rebuilding of Jerusalem*. London: Equinox.

–. 2006. Seeing Double: Tobiah the Ammonite as an Encrypted Character. *Revue Biblique*, 113(4): 570–584.

–. 2013. Introduction. In *Remembering Biblical Figures in the Late Persian and Early Hellenistic Periods*, edited by D.V. Edelman and E. Ben Zvi, xi–xxiv. Oxford: Oxford University Press. http://dx.doi.org/10.1093/acprof:oso/9780199664160.001.0001

Edelman, D.V. and E. Ben Zvi. eds. 2009. *The Production of Prophecy*. London and Oakville, CT: Equinox.

Elayi, J. and A.G. Elayi. 2009. *The Coinage of the Phoenician City of Tyre in the Persian Period*. Orientalia Lovaniensia Analecta 188. Leuven: Peeters.

Eph'al, I. 1982. *The Ancient Arabs: Nomads on the Borders of the Fertile Crescent, 9th-5th Centuries B.C.* Jerusalem: Magnes Press.

Erskine, A. 2010. *Roman Imperialism: Debates and Documents in Ancient History.* Edinburgh: Edinburgh University Press.

Evans, R.J. 1997. *In Defence of History.* London: Granta.

Fales, F.M. and J.N. Postgate. 1995. *Imperial Administrative Records* Volume 2: *Provincial and Military Administration.* Helsinki: University of Helsinki Press.

Fantalkin, A. 2001. Mezad Hashavyahu: Its Material Culture and Historical Background. *Tel Aviv* 28(1): 3-165.

Finkelstein, I. 1994. The Emergence of Israel: A Phase in the Cyclic History of Canaan in the Third and Second Millenia BCE. In *From Nomadism to Monarchy: Archaeological and Historical Aspects of Early Israel*, edited by I. Finkelstein and N. Na'aman, 150-178. Jerusalem: Biblical Archaeology Society.

–. 1998. The Rise of Early Israel: Archaeology and Long-term History. In *The Origins of Early Israel - Current Debate*, edited by S. Ahituv and E. Oren, 7-39. Beersheva: Ben Gurion University Press.

–. 2000. Omride Architecture. *Zeitschrift des Deutschen Palästina-Vereins* 116: 114-138.

–. 2006. The Last Labayu: King Saul and the Expansion of the First North Israelite Territorial Entity. In *Essays on Ancient Israel in Its Near Eastern Context: A Tribute to Nadav Na'aman*, edited by Y. Amit, E. Ben Zvi, I. Finkelstein and O. Lipschits, 171-177. Winona Lake, IN: Eisenbrauns

–. 2011. Stages in the Territorial Expansion of the Northern Kingdom. *Vetus Testamentum* 61(2): 227-242. http://dx.doi.org/10.1163/156853311X571437

–. 2013. Geographical and Historical Realities behind the Earliest Layer in the David Story. *Scandinavian Journal of the Old Testament* 27(2): 131-150. http://dx.doi.org/10.1080/09018328.2013.839104

Finkelstein, B. Sass and L. Singer-Avitz. 2008. Writing in Iron IIA Philistia in the Light of the Těl Zayit/Zěta Abecedary. *Zeitschrift des Deutschen Palästina-Vereins* 124, 1-14.

Finkelstein, I., A. Fantalkin and E. Piasetzky. 2011. Iron Age Mediterranean Chronology: A Rejoinder. *Radiocarbon* 53(1): 1-20.

Finkelstein, I. and L. Singer-Avitz. 2004. "Ashdod Revisited"—Maintained. *Tel Aviv* 31(2): 122-135.

Fishman, T. 2011. *Becoming the People of the Talmud: Oral Torah as Written Tradition in Medieval Jewish Cultures.* Philadelphia: University of Pennsylvania Press.

Flanagan, J.W. 1988. *David's Social Drama: A Hologram of Israel's Early Iron Age.* Journal for the Study of the Old Testament Supplements 245. Sheffield: Sheffield Academic Press.

Fleming, D.E. 1999. A Break in the Line: Reconsidering the Bible's Diverse Festival Calendars. *Revue Biblique* 106(2): 8-34, 161-174.

Franklin, N. 2004. Metrological Investigations at 9th and 8th c. Samaria and Megiddo. *Mediterranean Archaeology and Archaeometry* 4(2): 83-92.

–. 2008. Trademarks of the Omride Builders? In *Bene Israel: Studies in the Archaeology of Israel and the Levant during the Bronze and Iron Ages in Honour of Israel Finkelstein*, edited by A. Fantalkin and A. Yasur-Landau, 45-54. Leiden: Brill.

–. 2011. From Megiddo to Tamassos and Back: Putting the "Proto-Ionic Capital" in Its Place. In *The Fire Signals of Lachish: Studies in the Archaeology and History of Israel in the Late Bronze Age, Iron Age, and Persian Period in Honor of David Ussishkin*, edited by I. Finkelstein and N. Na'aman, 129-140. Winona Lake, IN: Eisenbrauns.

Frei, P. 1996. Zentralgewalt und Lokalautonomie im Achämeniden Reich. In *Reichsidee und Reichsorganisation im Perserreich: Zweite, bearbeitete und stark erweiterte Auflage*, edited by P. Frei and K. Koch, 5-131. Orbis Biblicus et Orientalis 55. Fribourg: Fribourg Academic Press and Göttingen: Vandenhoeck & Ruprecht.

Gadd, C.J. 1958. The Harran Inscriptions of Nabonidus. *Anatolian Studies* 8: 35-92. http://dx.doi.org/10.2307/3642415

Gaddis, J.L. 2002. *The Landscape of History: How Historians Map the Past*. New York: Oxford University Press.

Galil, G. 1996. *The Chronology of the Kings of Israel and Judah*. Leiden: Brill.

Galpaz, P. 1991. The Reign of Jeroboam and the Extent of Egyptian Influence. *Biblische Notizen* 60: 13-19.

Garbini, G. 2003. *Myth and History in the Bible*. Journal for the Old Testament Supplements 362. Translated by C. Peri. Sheffield: Sheffield Academic Press.

Gardiner, A.H. 1947. *Ancient Egyptian Onomastica*. Oxford: Oxford University Press.

Gasche, H., J.A. Armstrong and V.G. Gurzadyan. 1998. *Dating the Fall of Babylon: A Reappraisal of Second-millennium Chronology*. Ghent: Peeters.

Gera, D. 2009. Olympiodoros, Heliodoros and the Temples of Koile Syria and Phoinike. *Zeitschrift für Papyrologie und Epigraphik* 169: 125-155.

Ghantous, H. 2013. *The Elisha-Hazael Paradigm and the Kingdom of Israel: The Politics of God in Ancient Syria-Palestine*. London: Acumen.

Gibson, J.C.L. 1975. *Textbook of Syrian Semitic Inscriptions* Volume 2: *Aramaic Inscriptions*. Oxford: Oxford University Press.

Gilboa, A. 2006. Fragmenting the Sea Peoples, with an Emphasis on Cyprus, Syria and Egypt: A Tel Dor Perspective. *Scripta Mediterranea* 27-28: 209-244.

Gillingham, S. 1999. The Exodus Tradition and Israelite Psalmody. *Scottish Journal of Theology* 52(1): 19-46. http://dx.doi.org/10.1017/S0036930600053473

Gitin, S., A. Mazar and E. Stern. 1998. *Mediterranean Peoples in Transition: Thirteenth to Early Tenth Centuries BCE: In Honor of Professor Trude Dothan*. Jerusalem: Israel Exploration Society.

Gitin, S., T. Dothan and J. Naveh. 1997. A Royal Dedicatory Inscription from Ekron. *Israel Exploration Journal* 47(1-2): 1-16.

Glassner, J.-J. 2004. *Mesopotamian Chronicles*. Atlanta, FL: Society of Biblical Literature.

Gottwald, N.K. 1979. *The Tribes of Yahweh: A Sociology of the Religion of Liberated Israel, 1250-1050 B.C.E.* Maryknoll, NY: Orbis.

Goren, Y., I. Finkelstein and N. Na'aman. 2004. *Inscribed in Clay: Provenance Study of the Amarna Letters and Other Ancient Near Eastern Texts*. Tel Aviv: Institute of Archaeology, Tel Aviv University.

Grabbe, L.L. 2000. Ancient Near Eastern Prophecy from an Anthropological Perspective. In *Prophecy in Its Ancient Near Eastern Context: Mesopotamian, Biblical, and Arabian Perspectives*, edited by M. Nissinen, 13-32. Atlanta, FL: Society of Biblical literature.

-. 2007a. *Ancient Israel: What Do We Know and How Do We Know It?* London: T&T Clark International.

-. 2007b. Mighty Oaks from (Genetically Manipulated?) Acorns Grow: *The Chronicle of the Kings of Judah* as a Source of the Deuteronomistic History. In *Reflection and Refraction: Studies in Biblical Historiography in Honour of A. Graeme Auld*, edited by R. Rezetko, T. Lim and W.B. Aucker, 155-173. Leiden: Brill. http://dx.doi.org/10.1163/ej.9789004145122.i-577.78

Graeber, D. 2011. *Debt: the First 5,000 Years*. New York: Melville House.
Grainger, J.D. 2010. *The Syrian Wars*. Mnemosyne Supplements 320. Leiden: Brill. http://dx.doi.org/10.1163/ej.9789004180505.i-450
Grayson, A.K. 1975. *Assyrian and Babylonian Chronicles*. Texts from Cuneiform Sources 5. Locust Valley, NY: J.J. Augustin.
–. 1991. *Royal Inscriptions of Mesopotamia, Assyrian Period* Volume 2: *Assyrian Rulers of the Early First Millennium BC, I (1114-859 BC)*. Toronto: Toronto University Press.
–. 1996. *Royal Inscriptions of Mesopotamia, Assyrian Period* Volume 3: *Assyrian Rulers of the Early First Millennium BC, II (858-745BC)*. Toronto: Toronto University Press.
Green, P. 2007. *Alexander the Great and the Hellenistic Age*. London: Arthur Baker.
Gruntfest, Y. and M. Heltzer. 2001. Nabonid King of Babylon (556-539 B.C.E.) in Arabia in Light of New Evidence. *Biblische Notizen* 110: 25-30.
Guillaume, P. 2000. Deborah and the Seven Tribes. *Biblische Notizen* 101: 18-21.
–. 2002-2003. Thou Shalt not Curdle Milk with Rennet. *Ugarit-Forschungen* 34: 213-215.
–. 2008. Jerusalem 720-705 BCE. No Flood of Israelite Refugees. *Scandinavian Journal of the Old Testament* 22(2): 195-211. http://dx.doi.org/10.1080/09018320802661184
–. 2009a. *Land and Calendar: The Priestly Document from Genesis 1 to Joshua 18*. London: Bloomsbury.
–. 2009b. Nahum 1: Prophet, Senet and Divination. In *A Palimpsest: Rhetoric, Ideology, Stylistics, and Language Relating to Persian Israel*, edited by E. Ben Zvi, D. Edelman and F. Polak, 129-160. Perspectives on Hebrew Scriptures and its Contexts 5. Piscataway, NY: Gorgias Press.
–. 2010. Nehemiah 5: No Economic Crisis. *Journal of Hebrew Scriptures* 10, Art. 8. Online: http://www.jhsonline.org/Articles/article_136.pdf.
–. 2012. *Land, Credit and Crisis: Agrarian Finance in the Hebrew Bible*. London: Routledge.
–. 2013. The Myth of the Edomite Threat. Arad Letters # 24 and 40. *Kleine Untersuchungen zur Sprache des Alten Testaments und seiner Umwelt* 15: 97-108.
Hachlili, R. 2005. *Jewish Funerary Customs: Practices, and Rites in the Second Temple Period*. Leiden: Brill.
Hadley, J.M. 2000. *The Cult of Asherah in Ancient Israel and Judah: Evidence for a Hebrew Goddess*. Cambridge: Cambridge University Press.
Hagedorn, A.C. 2003. Of Foxes and Vineyards: Greek Perspectives on the Song of Songs. *Vetus Testamentum* 53(3): 337-352. http://dx.doi.org/10.1163/156853303768266335
Halayqa, I.K.H. 2008. Natural and Cultural Factors Influenced the Toponyms of Al-Ahuyoukh Town in Hebron District. *Ugarit-Forschungen* 40: 405-419.
Halbwachs, M. 1992. *On Collective Memory*. Chicago: University of Chicago Press.
Halpern, B. 1998. Why Manasseh is Blamed for the Babylonian Exile: The Evolution of a Biblical Tradition. *Vetus Testamentum* 48(4): 473-514. http://dx.doi.org/10.1163/156853398774228417
–. 2001. *David's Secret Demons: Messiah, Murderer, Traitor, King*. Grand Rapids, MI: Wm B. Eerdmans.
Harris, M. 2001. *Cultural Materialism: The Struggle for a Science of Culture*. Walnut Creek, CA: AltaMira Press.
Harris, W. 1979 *War and Imperialism in Republican Rome 327-70 BC*. Oxford: Clarendon Press.
Hasegawa, S. 2010 Aram and Israel during the Jehuite Dynasty. MPhil thesis, Tel Aviv University.

Hawkins, J.D. 2000 *Corpus of Hieroglyphic Luwian Inscriptions 1: Inscriptions of the Iron Age*. Berlin: De Gruyter.

–. 2009 Cilicia, the Amuq, and Aleppo: New Light in a Dark Age. *Near Eastern Archaeology* 72(4): 164–173.

Hayes, J.H. and P.K. Hooker. 1988. *A New Chronology for the Kings of Israel and Judah and its Implications for Biblical History and Literature*. Atlanta, GA: John Knox Press.

Healey, J.F. 2001. *The Religion of the Nabataeans*. Leiden: Brill.

Heather, P.J. 2009. *Empires and Barbarians: The Fall of Rome and the Birth of Europe*. Oxford: Oxford University Press.

Heckel, W. and L. Tritle. eds. 2009. *Alexander the Great: A New History*. Chichester, UK: Wiley-Blackwell.

Hendin, D. 2001. *Guide to Biblical Coins*. New York: Amphora.

Herzog, Z. 1997. *Archaeology of the City: Urban Planning in Ancient Israel and Its Social Implications*. Tel Aviv: Institute of Archaeology, University of Tel Aviv.

Higginbotham, C.R. 2000. *Egyptianization and Elite Emulation in Ramesside Palestine: Governance and Accommodation on the Imperial Periphery*. Leiden: Brill.

Hobsbawm, E.J. 1994. *Age of Extremes: The Short Twentieth Century, 1914–1991*. London: Michael Joseph.

Højte, J.M. ed. 2009. *Mithridates VI and the Pontic Kingdom*. Black Sea Studies 9. Aarhus: Aarhus University Press.

Hölbl, G. 2001. *History of the Ptolemaic Empire*. Translated by T. Saavedra. London: Routledge.

Honigman, S. 2003. *The Septuagint and Homeric Scholarship in Alexandria: A Study in the Narrative of the "Letter of Aristea"*. London: Routledge.

Horden, P. and N. Purcell. 2000. *The Corrupting Sea. A Study of Mediterranean History*. Oxford: Blackwell.

Hornung, E. 1999. *History of Ancient Egypt. An Introduction*. Ithaca, NY: Cornell University Press.

Horwitz, L.K. and E. Tchernov. 1989. Subsistence Patterns in Ancient Jerusalem. In *Excavations in the South of the Temple Mount*, edited by E. Mazar and B. Mazar, 144–154. Jerusalem: Institute of Archaeology, Hebrew University of Jerusalem.

Hurowitz, V. 1992. *I Have Built You and Exalted House: Temple Building in the Bible in Light of Mesopotamian and Northwest Semitic Writings*. Sheffield: Sheffield Academic Press.

Hurvitz, A. 2000. Can Biblical Texts be Dated Linguistically? In *Congress Volume: Oslo 1998*, edited by A. Lemaire and M. Sæbø, 143–160. Leiden: Brill. http://dx.doi.org/10.1163/9789004276055_011

Hütteroth, W.-D. and K. Abdulfattah. 1977. *Historical Geography of Palestine, Transjordan and Southern Syria in the Late 16th Century*. Erlangen: Fränkische Geographische Ges.

Ilan, D. 1995. The Dawn of Internationalism: The Middle Bronze Age. In *The Archaeology of Society in the Holy Land*, edited by T.E. Levy, 297–319. Leicester: Leicester University Press.

Ilan, T. 2006. Silencing the Queen. In *The Literary Histories of Shelamzion and Other Jewish Women*, edited by T. Ilan, 35–72. Texts and Studies in Ancient Judaism 115. Tübingen: Mohr Siebeck.

Isaac, B. 1980. Roman Colonies in Judaea: The Foundation of Aelia Capitolina. *Talant* 12(13): 31–54.

–. and I. Roll 1979. Judaea in the Early Years of Hadrian's Reign. *Latomus* 38(1): 54–66.

Isserlin, B.S.J. 1956. Place Name Provinces in the Semitic-speaking Ancient Near East. *Proceedings of the Leeds Philosophical and Literary Society (Literary and Historical Section)* 7(2): 83–110.
Japhet, S. 1991. The Relationship between Chronicles and Ezra-Nehemia. In *Congress Volume: Leuven 1989*, edited by J.A. Emerton, 298-313. Leiden: Brill. http://dx.doi.org/10.1163/9789004275669_019
Jaroš, K. 1974. *Die Stellung des Elohisten zur kanaanäischen Religion*. Orbis Biblicus et Orientalis 4. Fribourg: Fribourg Academic Press and Göttingen: Vandenhoeck & Ruprecht.
Jensen, M.H. 2010. *Herod Antipas in Galilee: The Literary and Archaeological Sources on the Reign of Herod Antipas and its Socio-Economic Impact on Galilee*. Tübingen: Mohr Siebeck.
Jepsen, A. 1964. *Untersuchungen zur israelitisch-jüdischen Chronologie*. Beihefte zur Zeitschrift für die alttestamentliche Wissenschaft 88. Berlin : Töpelmann.
Jones, C.P. 2009. The Inscription from Tel Maresha for Olympiodoros. *Zeitschrift fur Papyrologie und Epigraphik* 171: 100-104.
Kahn, D. 2007. Notes on the Time-Factor in Cambyses' Deeds in Egypt as Told by Herodotus. *Transeuphratène* 34: 103-112.
–. 2008. Some Remarks on the Foreign Policy of Psammetichus II in the Levant. *Journal of Egyptian History* 1(1): 139-157. http://dx.doi.org/10.1163/187416608784118811
Karta 1985. *The Atlas of Israel: Cartography, Physical and Human Geography*. Jerusalem: Karta.
Keel, O. 2007. *Die Geschichte Jerusalems und die Entstehung des Monotheismus* Volume 1. Göttingen: Vandenhoeck & Ruprecht.
Kent, R.G. 1953. *Old Persian: Grammar–Texts–Lexicon*. American Oriental Series 33 New Haven, CT: American Oriental Society.
Khalidi, W. ed. 1992. *All That Remains: The Palestinian Villages Occupied and Depopulated by Israel in 1948*. Washington, DC: Institute for Palestine Studies.
Kitchen, K.A. 1964. Some New Light on the Asiatic Wars of Ramesses II. *Journal of Egyptian Archaeology* 50: 47-70. http://dx.doi.org/10.2307/3855742
–. 1996. *Ramesside Inscriptions, Ramesses II, Royal Inscriptions: Translated and Annotated, Notes and Comments* Volume 2. Oxford: Blackwell.
Kletter, R. 1999. Pots and Polities. *Bulletin of the American Schools of Oriental Research* 314: 19–54. http://dx.doi.org/10.2307/1357450
Knauf, E.A.1988a. *Midian: Untersuchungen zur Geschichte Paliistinas und Nordarabiens am Ende des 2 Jahrtausends v.Cr.* Wiesbaden: Harrassowitz.
–. 1988b. The West Arabian Place Name Province. *Proceedings of the Seminar for Arabian Studies* 18: 39-49.
–. 1988c. Zur Herkunft und Sozialgeschichte Israels: Das Böcklein in der Milch seiner Mutter. *Biblica*, 69, 153–169.
–. 1989. Ismael: Untersuchungen zur Geschichte Palästinas und Nordarabiens im 1. Jahrtausend v. Chr. Wiesbaden.
–. 1990a. Dushara and Shai' al-Qaum. *ARAM Periodical* 2(1–2): 175-183.
–. 1990b. The Persian Administration in Arabia. *Transeuphratène* 2: 201-217.
–. 1991. King Solomon's Copper Supply. In *Phoenicia and the Bible*, edited by E. Lipinski, 167-186. Studia Phoenicia 11. Orientalia Lovaniensia Analecta 44. Leuven: Peeters.
–. 1992. The Cultural Impact of Secondary State Formation: The Cases of the Edomites

and Moabites. In *Early Edom and Moab: The Beginning of the Iron Age in Southern Jordan*, edited by P. Bienkowski, 47–54. Sheffield: J.R. Collis.

–. 1998. The Ituraeans: Another Bedouin State. In *Baalbek: Image and Monument 1898–1998*, edited by H. Sader, T. Schaeffler and A. Neuwirth, 269–277. Stuttgart: F. Steiner.

–. 2000a. Kinneret and Naphtali. In *Congress Volume: Oslo 1998*, edited by A. Lemaire and M. Sæbø, 219–233. Leiden: Brill. http://dx.doi.org/10.1163/9789004276055_015

–. 2000b. The "Low Chronology" and How not to Deal with it. *Biblische Notizen* 101: 56–63.

–. 2001a. History, Archaeology and the Bible. *Theologische Zeitschrift* 57(2): 262–268.

–. 2001b. Saul, David and the Philistines: From Geography to History. *Biblische Notizen* 109: 15–18.

–. 2001c. Shoshenq at Megiddo. *Biblische Notizen* 107/108: 31.

–. 2001d. Solomon at Megiddo? In *The Land That I Will Show You: Essays on the History and Archaeology of the Ancient Near East in Honor of J. Maxwell Miller*, edited by J.A. Dearman and M.P. Graham, 119–134. Sheffield: Sheffield Academic Press.

–. 2002a. Elephantine und das vor-biblische Judentum. In *Religion und Religionskontakte im Zeitalter der Achämeniden*, edited by R.G. Kratz, 179–188. Gütersloh: Gütersloher Verlagshaus.

–. 2002b. The Queens' Story: Bathshebah, Maacah and Athaliah and the "Historia" of Early Kings. *Lectio Difficilior* 2/2002. Online: http://www.lectio.unibe.ch/02_2/axel.htm

–. 2002c. Towards an Archaeology of the Hexateuch. In *Abschied vom Jahwisten: Die Komposition des Hexateuch in der jüngsten Diskussion*, edited J.C. Gertz, K. Schmid and M. Witte, 275–294. Berlin: De Gruyter. http://dx.doi.org/10.1515/9783110886887.275

–. 2003. 701: Sennacherib at the Berezina. In *Like a Bird in a Cage: The Invasion of Sennacherib in 701 BCE*, edited by L.L. Grabbe, 141–149. Journal for the Study of the Old Testament Supplements 363; European Seminar in Historical Methodology 4. Sheffield: Sheffield Academic Press.

–. 2004. Prophets that Never Were. In *Gott und Mensch im Dialog: Festschrift für Otto Kaiser zum 80*, edited by M. Witte, 451–456. Beihefte zur Zeitschrift für Alttestamentliche Wissenschaft 345/1. Berlin: De Gruyter. http://dx.doi.org/10.1515/9783110910001.449

–. 2005a. Deborah's Language. In *Studia Semitica et Semitohamitica Festschrift für Rainer Voigt anläßlich seines 60*, edited by B. Burtea , J. Tropper and H. Younansardaroud, 167–182. Münster: Ugarit-Verlag.

–. 2005b. The Glorious Days of Manasseh. In *Good Kings and Bad Kings*, edited by L.L. Grabbe, 164–188. Library of Hebrew Bible / Old Testament Studies 393. London: T&T Clark.

–. 2006. Bethel: The Israelite Impact on Judean Language and Literature. In *Judah and the Judeans in the Persian Period*, edited by O. Lipschits and M. Oeming, 291–349. Winona Lake, IN: Eisenbrauns.

–. 2007. Was Omride Israel a Sovereign State? In *Ahab Agonistes: The Rise and Fall of the Omri Dynasty*, edited by L.L. Grabbe, 100–103. Library of Hebrew Bible / Old Testament Studies 421. London: T&T Clark.

–. 2008. From Archeology to History, Bronze and Iron Ages. In *Israel in Transition: From Late Bronze to Iron IIa (c. 1250-850 B.C.E.) Volume 1: The Archaeology*, edited by L.L. Grabbe. 72–85. London: T&T Clark.

–. 2009a. Arabia, Ancient. 1. In the Bible. In *Encyclopedia of the Bible and its Reception*

Volume 2, edited by H.-J. Klauck, B. McGinn, P. Mendes-Flohr, C.-L. Seow and H. Spieckermann. 578–580. Berlin: De Gruyter.
–. 2009b. Ashurites. *Encyclopedia of the Bible and Its Reception* Volume 2, edited by H.-J. Klauck, B. McGinn, P. Mendes-Flohr, C.-L. Seow and H. Spieckermann, 1004–1005. Berlin: De Gruyter.
–. 2009c Salome Alexandra and the Final Redaction of Psalms. *Lectio Difficilior* 2/2009. Online: http://www.lectio.unibe.ch/09_2/knauf_salome_alexandra.html.
–. 2010a. History in Joshua. In *Israel in Transition: From Late Bronze to Iron IIa (c. 1250-850 BCE)* Volume 2: *The Texts*, edited by L.L. Grabbe, 130–139. London: T&T Clark.
–. 2010b. History in Judges. In *Israel in Transition: From Late Bronze to Iron IIa (c. 1250-850 BCE)* Volume 2: *The Texts*, edited by L.L. Grabbe, 140–149. London: T&T Clark.
–. 2011. Against Historiography. *Inquire of the Former Age: Ancient Historiography and Writing the History of Israel*, edited by L.L. Grabbe, 49–56. London: T&T Clark.
Köhler-Rollefson, I. 1987. Ethnoarchaeological Research into the Origins of Pastoralism. *Hawliyyat Da'irat al-Atar al-Ammat* 31: 535–539.
Kokkinos, N. 1998. *The Herodian Dynasty: Origins, Role in Society and Eclipse*. Journal for the Study of the Pseudepigrapha Supplements 30. Sheffield: Sheffield Academic Press.
Krämer, G. 2002. *Geschichte Palästina: Von der osmanischen Eroberung bis zur Gründung des Staates Israel*. Munich: C.H. Beck.
Kratz, R.G. 2005. *The Composition of the Narrative Books of the Old Testament*. Translated by J. Bowden. London: T&T Clark.
Lamon, R.S. and G.M Shipton. 1939. *Megiddo I. Seasons 1925-34: Strata I–V*. Oriental Institute Publications 42. Chicago: University of Chicago Press.
Lamprichs, R. 1995. *Die Westexpansion des Neuassyrischen Reiches: Eine Strukturanalyse*. Alter Orient und Altes Testament 239. Neukirchen-Vluyn: Butzon & Bercker.
Layard, A.H. 1849. *The Monuments of Nineveh from Drawings Made on the Spot*. London: John Murray.
Lehmann, G. 2001. Phoenicians in Western Galilee. In *Studies in the Archaeology of the Iron Age in Israel and Jordan*, edited by A. Mazar, 65–112. Library of Hebrew Bible / Old Testament Studies 331. Sheffield: Sheffield Academic Press.
–. 2004. Reconstructing the Social Landscape of Early Israel: Rural Marriage Alliances in the Central Hill Country. *Tel Aviv* 31(2): 141–175.
Leith, M.J.W. 1997. *Wadi Daliyeh*. Volume 1: *The Wadi Daliyeh Seal Impressions*. Oxford: Clarendon Press.
Lemaire, A. 1977. *Inscriptions hébraïques* Volume 1: *Les ostraca*. Paris: Éditions du Cerf.
Lepsius, C.R. 1859. *Denkmäler aus Aegypten und Aethiopien*. Berlin: Neudruck der Ausgabe.
Lev-Tov, J. 2012. A Preliminary Report on the Late Bronze and Iron Age Faunal Assemblage from Tell es-Safi/Gath. In *Tell es-Safi* Volume 1: *Report on the 1996-2005 Season*, edited by A.M. Maeir, 589–612. Ägypten und Altes Testament 69. Wiesbaden: Harrassowitz.
Levin, C. 1995. The System of the Twelve Tribes of Israel. In *Congress Volume: Paris 1992*, edited by J.A. Emerton, 163–178. Leiden: Brill. http://dx.doi.org/10.1163/9789004275850_012
Levy, T.E. ed. 1995. *The Archaeology of Society in the Holy Land*. Leicester: Leicester University Press.
Lewis, N. ed. 1989. *The Documents from the Bar Kokhba Period in the Cave of Letters: Greek Papyri*. Jerusalem: Israel Exploration Society.

Lichtheim, M. 1976 *Ancient Egyptian Literature* Volume 2: *The New Kingdom*. Berkeley: University of California Press.

Lipiński, E. 1991. The Territory of Tyre and the Tribe of Asher. In *Phoenicia and the Bible: Proceedings of the Conference held at the University of Leuven on the 15th and 16th of March 1990*, edited by E. Lipiński, 153–166. Leuven: Peeters.

Lipschits, O. 1999 The History of the Benjamin Region under Babylonian Rule. *Tel Aviv* 26(2): 155–190.

–. 2003. Demographic Changes in Judah between the Seventh and the Fifth Centuries B.C.E. In *Judah and the Judeans in the Neo-Babylonian Period*, edited by O. Lipschits and J. Blenkinsopp, 323–376. Winona Lake, IN: Eisenbrauns.

–. 2005. *The Fall and Rise of Jerusalem*. Winona Lake, IN: Eisenbrauns.

–. 2006. Achaemenid Imperial Policy, Settlement Processes in Palestine, and the Status of Jerusalem in the Middle of the Fifth Century B.C.E. In *Judah and the Judaeans in the Persian Period*, edited by O. Lipschits and M. Oeming, 19–52. Winona Lake, IN: Eisenbrauns.

Lipschits, O. Sergi and I. Koch. 2011. Judahite Stamped and Incised Jar Handles: A Tool for the Study of the History of Late Monarchic Judah. *Tel Aviv* 38(1): 5–41.

Lissovsky, N. and N. Na'aman. 2003. A New Outlook on the Boundary System of the Twelve Tribes. *Ugarit-Forschungen* 35: 291–332.

Livingstone, A. 2005. Taima' and Nabonidus. In *Writing and Ancient Near East Society: Papers in Honour of Alan R. Millard*, edited by P. Bienkowski, C. Mee and E. Slater, 29–39. Library of Hebrew Bible / Old Testament Studies 426. London: T&T Clark.

Loretz, O. 1984. *Habiru-Hebräer. Eine soziolinguistische Studie über die Herkunft des Gentiliziums 'ibrî vom Appelativum habiru*. Berlin: De Gruyter.

Luckenbill, D.D. 1924. *The Annals of Sennacherib*. Oriental Institute Publications 2. Chicago: University of Chicago Press.

Machinist, P. 1997. The Fall of Assyria in Comparative Ancient Perspective. In *Assyria 1995*, edited by S. Parpola and R.M. Whiting, 179–195. Helsinki: Neo-Assyrian Text Corpus Project.

Madden, F.W. 1881. *Coins of the Jews*. London: Trubner & Co.

Madden, F.W. and F.W. Fairholt 1864. *History of Jewish Coinage and of Money in the Old and New Testament*. London: Bernard Quaritch.

Maeir, A. and J. Uziel. 2007. A Tale of Two Tells: A Comparative Perspective on Tel Miqne-Ekron and Tell es-Sâfi/Gath in Light of Recent Archaeological Research. In *"Up to the Gates of Ekron": Essays on the Archaeology and History of the Eastern Mediterranean in Honor of Seymour Gitin*, edited by S. White Crawford, A. Ben-Tor, J.P. Dessel, W.G. Dever, A. Mazar and J. Aviram, 29–42. Jerusalem: W.F. Albright Institute of Archaeological Research and the Israel Exploration Society.

Magen, Y., H. Misgav and L. Tsfania. eds. 2004. *Mount Gerizim Excavations* Volume 1: *The Aramaic, Hebrew and Samaritan Inscriptions*. Judaea and Samaria Publications 4. Jerusalem: Israel Exploration Society.

Manning, J.G. 2010. *The Last Pharaohs: Egypt under the Ptolemies 305–30 BC*. Princeton, NJ: Princeton University Press.

Maoz, Z.U. 2011. *Itur in Galilee*. Archaostyle Scientific Research Series 10. Qazrin: Archaostyle.

Marfoe, L. 1998. *Kamid el-Loz 14: Settlement History of the Biqa' up to the Iron Age*. Saarbrucker Beitràge zur Altertumskunde 53. Bonn: Habelt.

Mazar, A. 2003. Three 10th–9th Century B.C.E. Inscriptions from Tel Rehov. In *Saxa*

loquentur: Studien zur Archäologie Palästinas/Israels: Festschrift für Volkmar Fritz zum 65. Geburtstag , edited by C.G. den Hertog, U. Hübner and S. Münger, 171–184. Münster: Ugarit-Verlag.
McDermott, J.J. 1998. *What are They Saying about the Formation of Israel?* Mahmah, NJ: Paulist Press.
McKechnie, P. 2000. The Career of Joshua Ben Sira. *Journal of Theological Studies* 51(1): 3–26. http://dx.doi.org/10.1093/jts/51.1.3
Mendelsshon, H. and Y.A. Yom-Tov. 1999. Report of Birds and Mammals which have increased their Distribution and Abundance in Israel due to Human Activity. *Israel Journal of Zoology* 45(1): 35–47.
Mershen, B. and E.A. Knauf. 1988. From Gadar to Umm Qais. *Zeitschrift des Deutschen Palästina-Verein*, 104: 128–145.
Meshel, Z. 2012. *Kuntillet 'Ajrud (Ḥorvat Teman): An Iron Age II Religious Site on the Judah-Sinai Border*. Jerusalem: Israel Exploration Society.
Meshorer, Y. 1985. *City Coins of Eretz-Israel and the Decapolis in the Roman Period*. Jerusalem: Israel Museum.
–. 2001. *A Treasury of Jewish Coins: From the Persian Period to Bar Kokhba*. Jerusalem: Amphora.
Meshorer, Y. and S. Qedar. 1991. *The Coinage of Samaria in the Fourth Century BCE*. Jerusalem: Numismatic Fine Arts International.
Mildenberg, L. 1998. *Vestigia Leonis: Studien zur antiken Numismatik Israels, Palästinas und der östlichen Mittelmeerwelt*. Novum Testamentum et Orbis Antiquus 36. Fribourg: Fribourg Academic Press and Göttingen: Vandenhoeck & Ruprecht.
Miller, J.M. and J.H. Hayes. 2006 [1977]. *History of Ancient Israel and Judah*. Louisville, KY: Westminster John Knox Press.
Miller, M.L. 2010. Nehemiah 5: A Response to Philippe Guillaume. *Journal of Hebrew Scriptures* 10 Art. 13. Online: http://www.jhsonline.org/Articles/article_141.pdf
Mittmann, S. 2000. Tobia, Sanballat und die Persische Provinz Juda. *Journal of Northwest Semitic Languages* 26(2): 1–50.
Moran, W.L. 1996. *The Amarna Letters*. Baltimore: Johns Hopkins University Press.
Moore, M.B. 2006. *Philosophy and Practice in Writing a History of Ancient Israel*. London: Continuum.
Motro, H. 2011. Archaeozoological Analysis of the Faunal Remains. In *Tel Aroer: The Iron Age II Caravan Town and the Hellenistic-Early Roman Settlement*, edited by Y. Thareani 265–297. Jerusalem: Hebrew Union College.
Mulder, O. 2011. New Elements in Ben Sira's Portrait of the High Priest Simon in Sirach 50. In *Rewriting Biblical History*, edited by J. Corley and H. van Grol, 273–290. Berlin: De Gruyter. http://dx.doi.org/10.1515/9783110240948.273
Mundy, M. 1986. Qada 'Ajlun in the Late 19th Century. *Levant* 28(1): 79–97.
Musil, A. 1928. *Northern Nejd: A Topographical Itinerary*. New York: American Geographical Society.
Münger, S. 2005. Stamp-Seal Amulets and Iron Age Chronology – an Update. In *The Bible and Radiocarbon Dating: Archaeology, Text and Science*, edited by T.E. Levy and T. Higham, 381–404. London: Equinox.
Na'aman, N. 1982. The Town of Ibirta and the Relations of the 'Apiru and the Shosou. *Gottinger Miszellen* 57: 27–33.
–. 1990. The Kingdom of Ishbaal. *Biblische Notizen* 54: 33–37.

–. 1995. Rezin of Damascus and the Land of Gilead. *Zeitschrift des Deutschen Palästina-Vereins* 111(2): 105–117.
–. 1996. The Contribution of the Amarna letters to the Debate on Jerusalem's Political Position in the Tenth Century B.C.E. *Bulletin of the American Schools of Oriental Research* 304: 17–27. http://dx.doi.org/10.2307/1357438
–. 1997. Prophetic Stories as Sources for the Histories of Jehoshaphat and the Omrides. *Biblica* 78(2): 153–173.
–. 1999. No Anthropomorphic Graven Images. *Ugarit-Forschungen* 31: 391–415.
–. 2000. Three Notes on the Aramaic Inscription from Tel Dan. *Israel Exploration Journal* 50(1–2): 92–104.
–. 2001. An Assyrian Residence at Ramat Raḥel? *Tel Aviv* 28(2): 260–280.
–. 2003. Ostracon 40 from Arad Reconsidered. In *Saxa loquentur: Studien zur Archäologie Palästinas/Israel : Festschrift für Volkmar Fritz zum 65*, edited by C.G. den Hertog, U. Hübner and S. Münger, 199–204. Münster: Ugarit-Verlag.
–. 2007a. Royal Inscription versus Prophetic Story. In *Ahab Agonistes: The Rise and Fall of the Omri Dynasty*, edited by L.L. Grabbe, 145–183. Library of Hebrew Bible / Old Testament Studies 421. London: T&T Clark.
–. 2007b. When and How did Jerusalem Become a Great City? The Rise of Jerusalem as Judah's Premier City in the Eighth Century B.C.E. *Bulletin of the American Schools of Oriental Research* 347: 21–56.
–. 2008. Naboth's Vineyard and the Foundation of Jezreel. *Journal for the Study of the Old Testament* 33(2): 197–218. http://dx.doi.org/10.1177/0309089208099256
–. 2011a. Textual and Historical Notes on the Eliashib Archive from Arad. *Tel Aviv* 38(1): 83–93.
–. 2011b. The Exodus Story: Between Historical Memory and Historiographical Composition. *Journal of Ancient Near Eastern Religion* 11(1): 39–69. http://dx.doi.org/10.1163/156921211X579579
–. 2014. Dismissing the Myth of a Flood of Refugees in the Late Eighth Century B.C.E. *Zeitschrift für die alttestamentliche Wissenschaft* 126(1): 1–14.
Na'aman, N. and R. Zadok. 2000. Assyrian Deportations to the Province of Samerina in the Light of Two Cuneiform Tablets from Tel Hadid. *Tel Aviv* 27(2): 159–188.
Nelson, R. 1983. Realpolitik in Judah (687–609 B.C.E.). In *Scripture in Context* Volume 2: *More Essays on the Comparative Method*, edited by W. Hallo, J.C. Moyer and L.G. Perdue, 177–190. Winona Lake, IN: Eisenbrauns.
Netzer, E. 2006. *The Architecture of Herod, the Great Builder*. Tübingen: Mohr Siebeck.
Niehr, H. 1997. In Search of Yhwh's Cult Statue in the First Temple. In *The Image and the Book: Iconic Cults, Aniconism, and the Rise of Book Religion in Israel and the Ancient Near East*, edited by K. van der Toorn, 73–96. Leuven: Peeters.
Niemann, H.M. 1997. The Socio-political Shadow Cast by the Biblical Solomon. In *The Age of Solomon: Scholarship at the Turn of the Millennium*, edited by L.K. Handy, 252–299. Leiden: Brill.
–. 2000. Megiddo and Solomon: A Biblical Investigation in Relation to Archaeology. *Tel Aviv* 27(1): 61–74. http://dx.doi.org/10.1179/tav.2000.2000.1.61
–. 2006. Choosing Brides for the Crown-prince: Matrimonial Politics in the Davidic Dynasty. *Vetus Testamentum* 56(2): 225–238. http://dx.doi.org/10.1163/156853306776907467
–. 2008. A New Look at the Samaria Ostraca: The King-Clan Relationship. *Tel Aviv* 35: 249–266.

Nikam, N.A. and R. McKeon. 1959. *The Edicts of Aśoka*. Chicago: University of Chicago Press.

Nimchuk, C.L. 2002. The Archers of Darius: Coinage or Tokens of Royal Esteem. In *Medes and Persians: Reflections on Elusive Empires*, edited by M.C. Root, 55–79. Ars Orientalis 32. Washington, DC: Smithsonian.

Nissinen, M. 2002. Prophets and the Divine Council. In *Kein Land für sich allein: Studien zum Kulturkontakt in Kanaan, Israel/Palästina und Ebirnari für Manfred Weippert zum 65. Geburtstag*, edited by E.A. Knauf and U. Hübner, 4–19. Fribourg: Fribourg Academic Press and Göttingen: Vandenhoeck & Ruprecht.

Noth, M. 1960. *History of Israel*. London: A. & C. Black.

Olivier, J.P.J. 1983. In Search of a Capital for the Northern Kingdom. *Journal of Northwest Semitic Languages* 11: 117–132.

Oren, E.D. ed. 1997. *The Hyksos: New Historical and Archaeological Perspectives*. Philadelphia: University Museum, University of Pennsylvania.

Ostermann, S. 2005. *Die Münzen der Hasmonäer*. Novum Testamentum et Orbis Antiquus 55. Fribourg: Fribourg Academic Press and Göttingen: Vandenhoeck & Ruprecht.

Parker, A. 1992. *Ancient Shipwrecks of the Mediterranean and the Roman Provinces*. British Archaeological Reports International Series 580. Oxford: British Archaeological Reports.

Parpola, S. 1993. The Tree of Life: Tracing the Origins of Jewish Monotheism and Greek Philosophy. *Journal of Near Eastern Studies* 52(3): 161–208. http://dx.doi.org/10.1086/373622

Patrich, J. 1990. *The Formation of Nabataean Art: Prohibition of a Graven Image among the Nabateans*. Jerusalem: Magnes Press.

Pearce, L.E. 2006. New Evidence for Judeans in Babylonia. In *Judah and the Judeans in the Persian Period*, edited by O. Lipschits and Manfred Oeming, 399–411. Winona Lake, IN: Eisenbrauns.

Perlitt, L. 1977. Sinai und Horeb. In *Beiträge zur Alttestamentlichen Theologie: Festschrift für Walther Zimmerli zum 70. Geburtstag*, edited by H. Donner, R. Hanhart and R. Smend, 302–322. Göttingen: Vandenhoeck & Ruprecht.

Picard, O. 2000. Monnayages en Thrace à l'époque achéménide. In *Actes de la Table Ronde Internationale d'Istanbul, 22-23 mai 1997: Institut Français d'Etudes Anatoliennes d'Istanbul*, edited by O. Casabonne, 239–253. Varia Anatolica 12. Paris: Éditions de Boccard.

Pirenne, H. 1939. *Mohammed and Charlemagne*. Translated by B. Miall. New York: Norton.

Pollard, J. and H. Reid. 2006. *The Rise and Fall of Alexandria: Birthplace of the Modern World*. London: Penguin.

Pongratz-Leisten, B. 1997. The Interplay of Military Strategy and Cultic Practice in Assyrian Politics. In *Assyria 1995*, edited by S. Parpola and R.M. Whiting, 245–252. Helsinki: Neo-Assyrian Text Corpus Project.

Popper, K.R. 1963. *Conjectures and Refutations: The Growth of Scientific Knowledge*. London: Routledge & Kegan Paul.

–. 1979. *Objective Knowledge: An Evolutionary Approach*. Revised edition. Oxford: Oxford University Press.

Porten, B. 1981. The Identity of King Adon. *Biblical Archaeologist* 44(1): 36–52. http://dx.doi.org/10.2307/3209735

–. 1996. *The Elephantine Papyri in English*. Documenta et Monumenta Orientis Antiqui 22. Leiden: Brill.
Porten B. and A. Yardeni. 1999. *Textbook of Aramaic Documents from Ancient Egypt* Volume 4: *Literature, Sccounts, Lists*. Jerusalem: Hebrew University.
–. 2007. The House of Baalrim in the Idumean Ostraca. In *New Seals and Inscriptions: Hebrew, Idumean, and Cuneiform*, edited by M. Lubetski, 99–147. Hebrew Bible Monographs 8. Sheffield: Sheffield Phoenix Press.
Prosic, T. 2004. *The Development and Symbolism of Passover*. Library of Hebrew Bible / Old Testament 414. London: T&T Clark.
Rainey, A.F. 1996. *Canaanite in the Amarna Tablets: A Linguistic Analysis of the Mixed Dialect Used by Scribes from Canaan*. Four Volumes. Atlanta, GA: Society of Biblical Literature.
–. 2007. Whence Came the Israelites and their Language? *Israel Exploration Journal* 57(1): 41–64.
Redford, D.B. 1984. *Akhenaten: The Heretic King*. Princeton, NJ: Princeton University Press.
–. 1992. *Egypt, Canaan, and Israel in Ancient Times*. Princeton, NJ: Princeton University Press.
Redmount, C.A. 1995. The Wadi Tumilat and the Canal of the Pharaohs *Journal of Near Eastern Studies* 54(2): 127–135. http://dx.doi.org/10.1086/373742
Reich, R. 2011. The Pool of Siloam in Jerusalem of the Late Second Temple Period and its Surroundings. In *Unearthing Jerusalem: 150 Years of Archaeological Research in the Holy City*, edited by K. Galor and G. Avni, 241–255. Winona Lake, IN: Eisenbrauns
Rendsburg, G.A. and W. Schniedewind. 2010. The Siloam Tunnel Inscription: Historical and Linguistic Perspectives. *Israel Exploration Journal* 60(2): 188–203.
Rey, J.-S. and J. Joosten. eds. 2011. *The Texts and Versions of the Book of Ben Sira: Transmission and Interpretation*. Leiden: Brill.
Rhodes, P.J. and R. Osborne. 2003. *Greek Historical Inscriptions, 404–323 BC*. Oxford: Oxford University Press.
Ritner, R.K. 2009. *The Libyan Anarchy: Inscriptions from Egypt's Third Intermediate Period*. Atlanta, GA: Society of Biblical Literature.
Roisman, J. ed. 1995. *Alexander the Great: Ancient and Modern Perspectives* Lexington, MA: D.C. Heath & Co.
Rosen, B. 1988. Early Israelite Cultic Centres in the Hill Country. *Vetus Testamentum* 38(1): 114–117. http://dx.doi.org/10.1163/156853388X00535
Rosenberg, S.G. 2006. *Airaq al-Amir: The Architecture of the Tobiads*. British Archaeological Reports International Series 1544. Oxford: John and Erica Hedges.
Rosenfeld, H. 1965. The Social Composition of the Military in the Process of State Formation in the Arabian Desert. *Journal of the Royal Anthropological Institute* 95: 73–86, 174–194.
Rothenberg, B. 1972. *Were These King Solomon's Mines?: Excavations in the Timna Valley* London: Stein and Day.
Rowton, M.B. 1973. Urban Autonomy in a Nomadic Environment. *Journal of Near Eastern Studies* 32(1–2): 201–215. http://dx.doi.org/10.1086/372237
–. 1977. Dimorphic Structure and the Parasocial Element. *Journal of Near Eastern Studies* 36(3): 181–198. http://dx.doi.org/10.1086/372560
Sagona, C. 2004. The Phoenicians in Spain from a Central Mediterranean Perspec-

tive. *Ancient Near Eastern Studies* 41: 240–266. http://dx.doi.org/10.2143/ANES.41.0.562930

Sancisi-Weerdenburg, H. 1988. Was There Ever a Median Empire? In *Achaemenid History* Volume 3: *Method and Theory. Proceedings of the London 1985 Achaemenid History Workshop*, edited by H. Sancisi-Weerdenburg and A. Kuhrt, 197–212. Leiden: Nederlands Instituut voor het Nabije Oosten.

Sapir-Hen, L., G. Bar-Oz and I. Finkelstein. 2013. Pig Husbandry in Iron Age Israel and Judah: New Insights Regarding the Origin of the "Taboo". *Zeitschrift des Deutschen Palästina-Vereins* 129(1): 1–20.

Sass, B. 2010. Four Notes on Taita King of Palistin with an Excursus on King Solomon's Empire. *Tel Aviv* 37(2): 169–174.

Sasson, A. 2007. Corpus of 694 Astragali from Stratum II at Tel Beersheba. *Tel Aviv* 34(2): 171–181.

Sasson, J.M. 2002. Ritual Wisdom? On "Seething a Kid in its Mother's Milk". In *Kein Land für sich allein. Studien zum Kulturkontakt in Kanaan, Israel/Palästina und Ebirnari für Manfred Weippert zum 65. Geburtstag*, edited by U. Hübner and E.A. Knauf, 294–308. Fribourg: Fribourg Academic Press and Göttingen: Vandenhoeck & Ruprecht.

Schäfer, P. ed. 2003. *The Bar Kokhba War Reconsidered: New Perspectives on the Second Jewish Revolt against Rome*. Texts and Studies in Ancient Judaism 100. Tübingen: Mohr Siebeck.

Schaudig, H. 2008. A Tanit-sign from Babylon and the Conquest of Tyre by Nebuchadrezzar II. *Ugarit-Forschungen* 40: 533–545.

Schipper, B.U. 2005. *Die Erzählung des Wenamun: Ein Literaturwerk im Spannungsfeld von Politik, Geschichte und Religion*. Orbis Biblicus et Orientalis 209. Fribourg: Fribourg Academic Press and Göttingen: Vandenhoeck & Ruprecht.

Schmid, K. 2010. *Genesis and the Moses Story: Israel's Dual Origins in the Hebrew Bible*. Siphrut: Literature and Theology of the Hebrew Scriptures 3. Translated by J.D. Nogalski. Winona Lake, IN: Eisenbrauns.

Schorn, U. 1997. *Ruben und das System der zwblf Stdmme Israels. Redaktionsgeschichtliche Untersuchungen znr Bedeutung des Erstgeborenen Jakobs*. Beihefte zur Zeitschrift für die Alttestamentliche Wissenschaft 248. Berlin: De Gruyter.

Schroer, S. 1987a. Die Zweiggöttin in Palästina/Israel. Von der Mittelbronze II B-Zeit bis zu Jesus Sirach. In *Jerusalem. Texte-Bilder- Steine. Festschrift Hildi Keel-Leu und Othmar Keel*, edited by M. Küchler and C. Uehlinger, 201–225. Novum Testamentum et Orbis Antiquus 6. Fribourg: Fribourg Academic Press and Göttingen: Vandenhoeck & Ruprecht.

–. 1987b. *In Israel gab es Bilder: Nachrichten von darstellender Kunst im Alten Testament*. Orbis Biblicus et Orientalis 74. Fribourg: Fribourg Academic Press and Göttingen: Vandenhoeck & Ruprecht.

Schulman, A.R. 1976. The Royal Butler Ramessesemperre. *Journal of the American Research Center in Egypt* 13: 117–130. http://dx.doi.org/10.2307/40001124

Skehan, P.W., E. Ulrich and J.E. Sanderson. 1992. *Qumran Cave 4* Volume 4: *Palaeo-Hebrew and Greek Biblical Manuscripts*. Discoveries in the Judaean Desert 9. Oxford: Clarendon Press.

Sinopoli, C.M. 1994. The Archaeology of Empires. *Annual Review of Anthropology* 23(1): 159–180. http://dx.doi.org/10.1146/annurev.an.23.100194.001111

Smith, A.T. 2003. *The Political Landscape*. Berkeley: University of California Press.

Smith, S. 1924. *Babylonian Historical Texts relating to the Capture and Downfall of Babylon*. London: Methuen.
Sokal, A.J. and J. Bricmont. 1999. *Fashionable Nonsense: Postmodern Intellectuals' Abuse of Science* New York: Picador.
Spalinger, A.J. 2005. *War in Ancient Egypt: The New Kingdom, Ancient World at War*. Oxford: Blackwell.
Speller, E. 2003. *Following Hadrian: A Second-century Journey Through the Roman Empire*. Oxford: Oxford University Press.
Staubli, T. 2007. Sammlung Liebefeld. In *Bilder als Quellen / Images as Sources: Studies on Ancient Near Eastern Artefacts and the Bible Inspired by the work of Othmar Keel*, edited by S. Bickel, R. Schurte and C. Uehlinger, 45-80. Orbis Biblicus et Orientalis, Special Volume. Fribourg: Fribourg Academic Press and Göttingen: Vandenhoeck & Ruprecht.
–. 2008. Hühneropfer im Alten Israel: Zum Verstandnis von Lev 1,14 im Kontext der antiken Kulturgeschichte. In *The Books of Leviticus and Numbers*, edited by T. Römer, 355-370. Bibliotheca Ephemeridum Theologicarum Lovaniensium 215. Leuven: Peeters.
Stavrakopoulou, F. 2004. *King Manasseh and Child Sacrifice: Biblical Distortions of Historical Realities*. Berlin: De Gruyter. http://dx.doi.org/10.1515/9783110899641
–. 2005. The Blackballing of Manasseh. In *Good Kings and Bad Kings*, edited by L.L. Grabbe, 248-263. Library of Hebrew Bible / Old Testament Studies 393. London: T&T Clark.
Steinberg, N. 2009. Exodus 12 in Light of Ancestral Cult Practices. In *The Family in Life and in Death: The Family in Ancient Israel: Sociological and Archaeological Perspectives*, edited by P. Dutcher-Walls, 89-105. London: T&T Clark.
Stern, E. 2001. *Archaeology of the Land of the Bible Volume 2: The Assyrian, Babylonian, and Persian Periods (732-332 B.C.E.)*. New Haven, CT: Yale University Press.
Stern, M. 1980. *Greek and Latin Authors on Jews and Judaism Volume 2*. Jerusalem: Israel Academy of Sciences and Humanities.
–. 1984. *Greek and Latin Authors on Jews and Judaism Volume 3*. Jerusalem: Israel Academy of Sciences and Humanities.
Stolper, M.W. 1985. *Entrepreneurs and Empire: The Mura su Archive, the Mura su Firm and Persian Rule in Babylonia*. Leiden: Nederlands Instituut voor het Nabije Oosten.
Stronach, D. 1997. Notes on the Fall of Niniveh. In *Assyria 1995*, edited by S. Parpola and R.M. Whiting, 307-324. Helsinki: Neo-Assyrian Text Corpus Project.
Sugerman, M. 2009. Trade and Power in Late Bronze Age Canaan. In *Exploring the Longue Durée: Essays in Honor of Lawrence E. Stager*, edited by J.D. Schloen, 439-448. Winona Lake, IN: Eisenbrauns.
Sussnitzki, A.J. 1966. The Ethnic Division of Labor. In *The Economic History of the Middle East 1800-1914*, edited by C. Issawi, 114-125. Chicago: Chicago University Press.
Swain, H. ed. 2006. *Big Questions in History*. London: Vintage.
Tadmor, H. 1994. *The Inscriptions of Tiglath-Pileser III King of Assyria*. Jerusalem: Israel Academy of Sciences and Humanities.
Tadmor, H. and S. Yamada. 2011. *The Royal Inscriptions of Tiglath-Pileser III (744-727 BC) and Shalmaneser V (726-722 BC), Kings of Assyria*. Winona Lake, IN: Eisenbrauns.
Tcherikover, V.A. and A. Fuks. 1957. *Corpus Papyrorum Judaicarum Volume 1*. Jerusalem: Magnes Press.
Tebes, J.M. 2007. A Land whose Stones are Iron, and Out of Whose Hills You Can Dig Copper. *DavarLogos* 6(1): 69-91.

Thareani-Sussely, Y. 2008. Desert Outsiders: Extramural Neighborhoods in the Iron Age Negev. In *Bene Israel: Studies in the Archaeology of Israel and the Levant during the Bronze and Iron Ages in Honour of Israel Finkelstein*, edited by A. Fantalkin and A. Yasur-Landau, 197–212. Leiden: Brill. http://dx.doi.org/10.1163/ej.9789004152823.i-308.100

Thiele, E. 1983. *The Mysterious Numbers of the Hebrew Kings*. Revised edition. Grand Rapids, MI: Zondervan.

Treister, M. 1996. *The Role of Metals in Ancient Greek History*. Leiden: Brill.

Tuplin, C. 1987. The Administration of the Achaemenid Empire. In *Coinage and Administration in the Athenian and Persian Empires: The Ninth Oxford Symposium on Coinage and Monetary History*, edited by I. Carradice, 109–166. British Archaeological Reports International Series 343. Oxford: British Archaeological Reports.

Uehlinger, C. 1990. *Weltreich und "eine Rede". Eine neue Deutung der sogenannten Turmbauerzählung (Gen 11,1–9)*. Orbis Biblicus et Orientalis 101. Fribourg: Fribourg Academic Press and Göttingen: Vandenhoeck & Ruprecht.

–. 1994. Die Frau im Efa. *Bible und Kirche* 49(2): 93–103.

–. 1997. Anthropomorphic Cult Statuary in Iron Age Palestine and the Search for Yahweh's Cult Images. In *The Image and the Book*, edited by K. van der Toorn, 97–155. Leuven: Peeters.

–. 2002. Hanun von Gaza und seine Gottheiten. In *Kein Land für sich allein. Studien zum Kulturkontakt in Kanaan, Israel/Palästina und Ebirnari für Manfred Weippert zum 65. Geburtstag*. edited by U. Hübner and E.A. Knauf, 97–127. Fribourg: Fribourg Academic Press and Göttingen: Vandenhoeck & Ruprecht.

Ussishkin, D. 1982. *The Conquest of Lachish by Sennacherib*. Tel Aviv: Tel Aviv University.

–. 1990. Notes on Megiddo, Gezer, Ashdod, and Tel Batash in the Tenth to Ninth Centuries B.C. *Bulletin of the American Schools of Oriental Research* 277/278: 71–91. http://dx.doi.org/10.2307/1357374

–. 1995. The Water Systems of Jerusalem during Hezekiah's Reign. In *Meilenstein: Festgabe für Herbert Donner zum 16. Februar 1995*, edited by A. Fantalkin and A. Yasur-Landau, 289–307. Ägypten und altes Testament 30. Wiesbaden: Harrassowitz.

–. 2006. The Borders and de facto Size of Jerusalem in the Persian Period. In *Judah and the Judeans in the Persian Period*, edited by O. Lipschits and M. Oeming, 147–166. Winona Lake, IN: Eisenbrauns.

–. 2008. The Date of the Philistine Settlement in the Coastal Plain: The View from Megiddo and Lachish. In *Israel in Transition: From Late Bronze to Iron IIa (c. 1250–850 B.C.E.)* Volume 1: *The Archaeology*, edited by L.L. Grabbe, 203–216. London: T&T Clark.

Vargyas, P. 2000. Kaspu ginnu and the Monetary Reform of Darius I. *Zeitschrift für Assyriologie und Vorderasiatische Archäologie* 89(2): 247–268.

Veijola, T. 1979. Salomo – der erstgeborene Bathsebas? In *Studies in the Historical Books of the Old Testament*, edited by J.A. Emerton, 230–250. Vetus Testamentum Supplements 30. Leiden: Brill. http://dx.doi.org/10.1163/9789004275539_015

Volney, M.C.-F. 1787. *Travels through Syria and Egypt in the Years 1783, 1784, and 1785*. London: G.G.J. and J. Robinson.

von Wissmann, H. 1970. Ophir und Ḥawila. *Real-Encyclopädie der classischen Altertumswissenschaft: Supplement 12*, edited by A. Pauly, G. Wissowa, W. Kroll, K. Witte, K. Mittelhaus and K. Ziegler, 925–967. Stuttgart: J.B. Metzler.

Wagstaff, J.M. 1985. *The Evolution of Middle Eastern Landscapes: An Outline to A.D. 1840*. Totowa, NJ: Barnes and Noble.

Wallerstein, I.M. 1984. *The Politics of the World-economy: The States, the Movements and the Civilizations*. Cambridge: Cambridge University Press.

Wallinga, H.T. 1984. The Ionian Revolt. *Mnemosyne* 37(3): 401–437. http://dx.doi.org/10.1163/156852584X00619

—. 1987. The Ancient Persian Navy and its Predecessors. In *Achaemenid History Volume 1: Sources, Structures and Synthesis*, edited by H. Sancisi-Weerdenburg, 47–77. Leiden: Nederlands Instituut voor het Nabije Oosten.

Watts, J.W. ed. 2001. *Persia and Torah: The Theory of Imperial Authorization of the Pentateuch*. Atlanta, GA: Society of Biblical Literature.

Weeks, S., S. Gathercole and L. Stuckenbruck. eds. 2004. *The Book of Tobit*: Texts from the Principal Ancient and Medieval Traditions with Synopsis, Concordances and Annotated Texts in Aramaic, Hebrew, Greek, Latin and Syriac. Berlin: De Gruyter. http://dx.doi.org/10.1515/9783110897029

Welch, K. 2010. *Magnus Pius: Sextus Pompeius and the Transformation of the Roman Republic*. Swansea: Classical Press of Wales.

Weiser, W. 1989. Die Eulen von Kyros dem Jüngeren: zu den ersten Münzporträts lebender Menschen. *Zeitschrift für Papyrologie und Epigraphik* 76: 267–296.

Wellhausen, J. 1885. *Prolegomena to the History of Israel*. Translated by J. Sutherland Black and A. Menzies. Edinburgh: A. & C. Black.

Wells, B. 2011. The Quasi-alien in Leviticus 25. In *The Foreigner and the Law: Perspectives from the Hebrew Bible and the Ancient Near East*, edited by R. Achenbach, R. Albertz and J. Wohrle, 135–155. Beihefte Zur Zeitschrift Fur Altorientalische Und Biblische Rechtsgeschichte 16. Wiesbaden: Harrassowitz.

Westermann, W.L. 1934. *Zenon Papyri: Business Papers of the Third Century before Christ dealing with Palestine and Egypt*. New York: Columbia University Press.

Wilson, K.A. 2005. *The Campaign of Pharaoh Sheshenq I into Palestine*. Forschungen zum Alten Testament 9. Tübingen: Mohr Siebeck.

Whitcher Kansa, S. 2013. The Animal Bones. In *The Nabataean Temple at Khirbet et-Tannur, Jordan Volume 2: Cultic Offerings, Vessels, and other Specialist Reports*, edited by J. McKenzie, C.S. Alexander, J. Greene, D.G. Barrett and A.T. Reyes, 73–115. Boston: American Schools of Oriental Research.

Wittgenstein, L. 1922. *Tractatus Logico-Philosophicus*. Translated by C.K. Ogden. London: Kegan Paul, Trench, Trubner & Co.

Wood, M. 2001. *In the Footsteps of Alexander the Great*. Berkeley: University of California Press.

Wunsch, C. 2002. Debt, Interest, Pledge and Forfeiture in the Neo-Babylonian and Early Achaemenid Period. In *Debt and Economic Renewal in the Ancient Near East*, edited by M. Hudson and M. Van De Mieroop, 221–255. International Scholars Conference on Ancient Near Eastern Economies 3. Bethesda, MD: CDL Press.

Yadin, Y., J.C. Greenfield, A. Yardeni and B. Levine. eds. 2002. *The Documents from the Bar-Kokhba Period in the Cave of Letters: Hebrew, Aramaic and Nabatean-Aramaic Papyri*. Jerusalem: Israel Exploration Society.

Young, I. and R. Rezetko. 2008. *Linguistic Dating of Biblical Texts: An Introduction to Approaches and Problems*. London: Equinox.

Zadok, R. 1985. Notes on Modern Palestinian Toponymy. *Zeitschrift des Deutschen Palästina-Vereins* 101(2): 156–161.

Zerubavel, E. 2003. *Time Maps: Collective Memory and the Social Shape of the Past.* Chicago: University of Chicago Press.

Zevit, Z. 2003. *The Religions of Ancient Israel: A Synthesis of Parallactic Approaches.* Chicago: University of Chicago Press.

Index of Biblical and other Ancient References

Genesis		25:8	224	21:18-32	49
1–2 Kgs	53, 201	25:9	153	23:19	185
1–Deut. 34	182, 184	25:12-18	116–118,	25–30	188
1–Exod. 19	184		133, 166,	25:30-31	219
1	187–188,		183, 212, 224	28:30	97
	201	26–35	132	32	100
1:1-8	148	26:8	61	34	155, 189
1:28	175	28:11-22	78, 133, 153	34:26	185
2–4	19	28:19	211	35–40	188
2:1-3	58	31–33	84	39:36-37	219
5	209	33:20	35	40:17-34	188
8:20-22	184	35:6	211		
9	155	35:11	175	Leviticus	
9:1-7	175, 185	35:23-29	47, 224	1:14	61
9:13	129	36	133	11–15	185
10	133	36:32	116	16	184
10	161	37–47	171	16:8	97
10:6	30	46	41	17–25	184
10:22	124	48:3	211	19:18	50
11–17	176	48:5	47	21:21	219
12–13	141	49	45, 47	25:36-37	172
12:10-20	41	49:5-7	45	25:45-49	50
13:3	155	49:13	47	26:9	175
13:14-17	141	49:21	45, 47		
14:18-20	183			Numbers	
15:18	109	Exodus		1:4-16	47
16	141	1:1-8	30	1:46	50
16:10	175	1:15	34	11	176
16:12	153	2–Josh. 10	34	13–14	176
17	153, 155,	2:15-16	32	18:19-24	51
	183	6	155	20:17-28	16, 116, 227
17:1	56	6:3	187	21:14-22	56, 116
17:12-13	51	12–23	57	25	207, 224
18–21	141	14	58, 102	26:29	47
18	61	15:21	56	26:51	50
18:7	61	15:26	124	27:1	47
18:10	58	16:23	8	32:39-40	47
21	141, 183	18:1	36	33:45-46	92
22:2	153	20:24	123	34:13	97
22:1-14	183	21–23	57, 152	36	50
24:29-30	50	21:2-6	51	36:1	47

Index of Biblical and other Ancient References

Deuteronomy		15:9	30	1 Samuel	
3:4	88	15:13	48	2:8	68
3:19	50	15:21-62	127	3:20	99
5-28	123, 126,	16:2	211	8-12	67
	155, 183,	16:10	83	8:12	90
	189, 208	17:2	48	9-2 Kgs 10	140, 187
5:14	51	17:5	91	9-10	68
6:4	153	17:11	90	10-31	63
7:15	124	17:14-18	47, 91	11-15	50
10:9	51	18:1	188	11	67
11:10-12	176	18:1-10	182	11:1-13	68
11:29	183	18:5	47	13:1-2	67
12:11	123,	18:13	211	14:41	97
	126-127	18:15	30	16-30	208
12:12-18	51	18:21-28	127	16-18	79
14:21	185	19	99, 118	17	43
14:27-29	51	19:1-9	48, 179	17:6	2
15:12-13	174	19:24-31	47	18:7-8	67
17:14-20	186	19:44	56	21-27	65
18:1	51			21-22	50
18:21-22	140	Judges		21:12	67
22:25	19	1	118	25-30	72
27:12	183	1:22-26	189, 211	27-30	78, 118
28:60	124	1:27-29	83, 91	27:8-12	48, 72
29:11	50	3-12	102, 132	28:6	97
32:8-9	30, 79, 121	3:31	56	29:5	67
32:10-14	30	4-11	102	30	68
33	45	5	10, 32, 42,		
			45-47, 54,	2 Samuel	
Joshua			56, 68, 71,	1:17-18	98, 202
1-12	46		84, 90, 98,	2-4	70
5:10-12	188		107	2	68, 73
5:11	51	6:1-5	151, 159	2:1-4	72, 73
6-12	126, 133,	6:11	111	2:4-7	72
	189, 225	6:17	185	2:9-12	70
6	193	7:12	185	3:1-6	62, 70, 71,
6:1-10	127	8:10	89		72, 76
8:18	2	8:26	185	3:10	99
10	64	9	63, 67	3:12-21:36	72
10:12-13	65, 84, 98,	10:4	20	4:3	73
	209	11:3-5	88	5:1-3	71, 73
10:28-39	127	12:6	48	5:6-10	73
10:40-43	133, 209	12:14	20	5:18-25	72, 75
13	47	17-21	181-182,	6:2	56
13:2	97		189	8	75
14	127	20:1	99	8:5-6	87
14:7-10	46	20:9-10	97	8:14	73
14:15	48			8:16-18	77

2 Samuel (cont.)		12:25-30	36, 81–83, 93, 99	13:3-25	83, 95–96, 98
9–10	68	12:32	12	14:18	155
10–12	75, 77	13	189	14:23-29	98-9
11–12	84	14	78	15:11-26	101, 108, 155
12:20	78	14:21-26	80, 82–83		
12:24	76	14:30	76, 83	16:5-10	109, 121
13–20	84	15	79	17	109, 110–111
15–18	73	15:1-13	76, 83, 120		
15:7-12	75	15:16-32	77, 83, 86	18:1-7	120, 132
15:18	75	15:18-20	86–87	18:13-25	112–115, 121
17:1	99	15:25-32	86–87		
20	68, 73	16–2 Kgs 10	54, 190	19:9	113
20:19	73	16:8-18	86-7	19:37	122
20:23-26	77	16:21-24	48, 87–88	20	12, 112
21	73	16:27-34	83, 88, 92, 120	20:1	115
23:8-39	73			21:1-18	119–120, 123
24:2-15	99	17–2 Kgs 8	88		
		17–19	201	21:16-29	120, 123, 125–126
1 Kings		17:7	77		
1–11	62, 76, 133	18:43-45	58	21:19–22:1	125
1	77, 78, 84	19:15-17	95	22–23	126, 190
3	75	20–22	87, 98	22:	122
3:4-15	78	20:1	87	22:2-3	120, 125
3:16-28	76	20:23	132	23:5-12	132
4	76	20:34	96, 98	23:8-30	82, 115, 120, 123, 126–127, 189
4:2-19	77, 78, 90–91	20:39-40	165		
		22:20-45	86, 89, 98, 126		
4:25	99			23:31-35	135
5:1	95			24:1-2	134-5
5:9-14	76, 79	2 Kings		24:7-18	79, 125, 135-6, 139
6–7	98	1	90		
6	78	1:17	88	25	137, 138
8:12	79	2	73, 201	25:1-5	123, 127
8:12-13	78–79, 84, 123	2:24	43	25:7-21	137–138
		3:4-5	92	25:11-12	139, 141, 155
9	8	3:6-27	98		
9:15-21	56, 78, 81, 90, 99	6	136	25:22-26	122, 125, 137–139, 150
		6:8-7:20	98		
10:1-13	76	6:11	185		
10:28-29	99	8:6	62	25:27-30	135, 140, 146, 154
11:5	115	8:7-15	87, 95		
11	79, 118	8:26-9	86–89, 93		
11:14-22	79, 115	9–10	86, 88, 93	Isaiah	
11:23-25	75, 79, 87	9:30-33	93	1–66	97, 107
11:29-40	79	10:32	95	1–39	36
11:30-32	46, 90, 115	11	96	1:5-8	115, 118
11:40-41	80, 133	11:1-20	62	6–9	133
12	73, 79, 84	12:18-19	96		
12:20	82				

Index of Biblical and other Ancient References 257

6	102	36:10-12	125	4–11	132
7:4–8:4	108	36:25	125	7:11	110
7:3	112	37:4-11	137	8:4	101
8:23	16	39–41	137	8:13–13:4	36, 110
9:1-7	126	39:3-14	138, 146	9:10	30
10:9	109	49:8	148	10:3	132
11:1	229	40–42	141, 150	11:1	30
14:4-20	112	40:5-14	138, 139,	12	140
19:2-15	122		141	12:7-8	173, 200
20:1	112	41:1-15	138, 139	12:12-13	133
21:11-17	148, 153,	42–44	139		
	166	46:25	122	Joel	
22:9	141	49:7-22	147	3–4	187
24–27	201	49:28-33	135	4:3-6	174
26:19	224	52	137, 139,		
29:22	141		155	Amos	
36–39	113, 122	52:7	123	1–9	133, 141,
36:2	112	52:12	134		173
40–48	141, 154,	52:28-30	136, 137,	1:1	99, 102
	176, 188		139, 151	1:6-9	174
41:8	141	52:31-34	154	2:6-8	101, 200
42:11	166			3:10–5:12	101
44–45	149	Ezekiel		5:3	111
44:24–45:13	141	8:5	128	7:10-17	99
45:1	149	11:1-21	140	8:6	200
51:1-2	141	16:3	73, 30	8:14	10
54:11–55:5	187	18:2	140	9:1	102
55:1-3	180	20:5-9	30, 140		
60–62	187	21:25	136	Obadiah	
60:7	166	24:1-2	137	1-21	136, 147
63:16	141	25:12-14	148		
		26–28	140, 146	Jonah	
Jeremiah		27:21	166	1–4	201
1:1	138	27:31	168	1:3	167
2:10	166	28:25	140	1:7	97
6:23	2	30:14-16	122		
7	132, 141	33:23-29	140, 150,	Micah	
7:12-14	68		152, 154,	1–7	141
26	141		184	1–3	36
26:6-9	68	37:1-10	224	1:3-7	133
26:24-26	125	37:25	140	2:2	200
27:6-8	141	40–48	140, 188,	2:12	118
28:1	127		227	6:10-12	173
29:1-10	125, 141,				
	154, 159	Hosea		Nahum	
30:18-22	138	1–14	97, 141, 173	1–3	97, 132, 141
31:29-30	140	1:1	132	1	97
34:1-7	137	2:15-17	36	3:8	122
35	50				

Habakkuk
1–3	141
3:7	32
3:17	118

Zephaniah
1:14-18	187
1–3	131, 162

Haggai
1–2	3, 150, 159, 170, 187
1:1-6	162, 170
2:1-9	162
2:15-20	150
2:20-23	162, 187

Zechariah
1–8	159, 187
1–14	150, 162, 170
1:7-17	162
3:1-2	160
4	130
4:5-10	162
6:1-9	160
6:9-15	159
7:1-2	159, 187
8:20-23	150
9–11	200
9:1-8	191, 195
14:2	193

Malachi
3:22-23	209

Psalms
2–89	212
2	214
3–41	202
3	202
7	202
15	127
18	302
24	127
34	202
45	98
47	127
48	119
49:14-16	223
50:9-14	184
59:7	212
60	135
60:9	212
68	127
72	152
73:23-26	223
78:60	68
79	193, 211
82	126
89	211
104	57
104:9	195
108:8-11	210, 212
110	212
120	139
146–150	217

Proverbs
1–31	228
8:29-30	195
22–23	57
25–29	133

Job
1–41	187, 204
1	148
1:6–2:7	160, 168
2:11	168
6:19	168, 178
38–41	55
39:23	2

Song of Songs
1–8	19, 185, 201, 202, 205, 228
2:7-3:5	181
8:6	201

Ruth
	50

Qohelet (Ecclesiastes)
1–12	185, 201, 202, 205, 228
1:1	204

3:18-21	223

Esther
	3, 10, 171, 214

Daniel
1–12	3, 171, 200, 209
2–9	134
2–6	209
3:86	223
4–5	148
5:28	149
6:8-15	149
7:7	195
11:2-3	162, 195
12:2	224
14	146

Ezra
1–Neh. 10	13, 139, 170, 171, 201, 211
1–6	150, 162, 193
1:2-4	149
1:5-11	159
2	172, 182
2:69	160
4	163
5:2	162
5:14	170
5:16	159
6	159
6:3-5	149
6:15-22	162, 163
7:7-9	171
7:11–8:35	159, 182
8:1	171
9:1	189

Nehemiah
1–7	171
2–6	150
2:1	170, 172
2:8	159
2:10-19	171
3:7	150, 172

3:26	171	Judith		Mark	
4:3-7	171		10, 209	5:20	218
5:1-8	173–174			7:31	218
5:7	152	Tobit			
5:10-17	172		10, 171, 204,	Luke	
5:15	170		205	2:2	216, 221
6	166, 171, 172	Wisdom of Solomon		20:20	216
7	172, 182		211	Acts	
7:2-3	159, 170			5:37	224
7:70-72	160	Sirach		9	182
8:1	171	44–49	204	12:1	221
8:9	170	45:23-26	207	22:25–23:27	216
11	170	48:17	113	25:13-32	221
12:1-8	159				
12:27–14:31	171	Susanna		2 Corinthians	
12:26-36	170		209	11:32	213
13	171				
13:4-8	172	1 Maccabees		Babylonian Talmud	
13:16	164	1:2-9	195	Baba bathra	
		1:29-44	207	14b–15a	204
1 Chronicles		2	224		
3:17-24	140, 162, 170	2:32-41	193	Dio Cassius	
		5	182	59	222
4:41	168	5:25	213		
6	170	8–15	218	Jewish War (Josephus)	
7:24	83	9:35	213	1.2	210
8:33	70	10:40	206	2.186–188	222
9:39	70	13:43-48	208		
12:2	201	14:12	207	Antiquities (Josephus)	
27	201	14:41-44	211	11.8	191, 193
29:1-19	159, 160			12.1.1	193, 195
		2 Maccabees		12.3	203, 205
2 Chronicles		3:1-13	206	12.4	200
8:6	56	5:5-23	211, 227	12.5	211
17:11–26:7	179	5:25-26	193	13:2	206
26:7	168	6:2	211	13:11	210
33:10-14	119–121	7:9-23	224	18.1.1-6	224
33:25	125	7:32-33	226		
35:20-24	126	12	182	Suetonius	
36:20-23	137, 139, 159	Matthew		26.1	222
		4:25	218		

Index of Modern Authors

Ababneh, M.I. 220
Abdulfattah, K. 14
Achenbach, R. 49
Aharoni, Y. 135–136
Aḥituv, S. 21, 115
Albarella, U. 59
Albertz, R. 49, 174
Andersson, J. 107
Arbel, Y. 223
Arie, E. 83
Armstrong, J.A. 11
Artzy, M. 64
Athas, G. 95
Atkinson, K. 214
Avigad, N. 119, 138, 170
Azize, J. 124

Badè, W.F. 60
Bagnall, R.S. 200
Ball, W. 215
Bar-Oz, G. 59
Barag, D. 210
Barstad, H.M. 137, 229
Beaulieu, P.A. 147
Becking, B. 110–111
Bedford, P.R. 157
Ben Zvi, E. 97, 119, 187, 201
Benichou-Safar, H. 120
Berlejung, A. 83, 97
Betts, A.V.G. 18
Bietak, M. 30
Blau, Y. 185
Blenkinsopp, J. 182
Bond, H.K. 221
Bragg, M. 204
Braudel, F. 4
Breasted, J.H. 37, 41
Briant, P. 157
Bricmont, J. 5
Brin, H.B. 226
Bulliet, R.W. 18

Bunimovitz, S. 31, 42
Buraselis, K. 199
Burstein, S.M. 157, 196
Byrne, R. 157

Cantrell, D. 99
Capuzzi, A. 179
Carlsson, S. 203
Carter, C.E. 151, 181, 188
Chaney, M.L. 101, 173
Chaveau, M. 196
Cogan, M. 103, 107, 108, 112
Cohen, S.J.D. 227
Conybeare, F.C. 209
Coote, R.B. 23
Cotton, H.M. 214, 227
Crowford, J.W. and G.M. 100

Dalley, S. 157, 183
Dalman, G. 57
Davies, P.R. 3, 98
de Souza, P. 217
de Troyer, K. 209
Dearman, J.A. 92
Dever, W.G. 42, 101, 129
Donner, H. 8
Dostal, W. 48
Dothan, T. 118
Douglas, M. 61
Drijvers, H.J.W. 18

Eck, W. 227
Edelman, D.V. 22, 65, 79, 97, 150, 159, 160, 162, 170
Elayi, J. and A.G. 176
Eph'al, I. 150, 167
Erskine, A. 215
Evans, R.J. 5

Fairholt, F.W. 222
Fales, F.M. 110

Index of Modern Authors

Fantalkin, A. 135
Finkelstein, I. 12, 30, 31, 42, 56, 59, 65, 68, 73, 75, 78, 86, 98
Fishman, T. 98
Flanagan, J.W. 76
Fleming, D.E. 59
Franklin, N. 56, 82
Frei, P. 182
Fuks, A. 8, 200

Gadd, C.J. 148
Gaddis, J.L. 4
Galil, G. 12, 239
Galpaz, P. 82
Garbini, G. 132
Gardiner, A.H. 40
Gasche, H. 11
Gathercole, S. 205
Gera, D. 206
Ghantous, H. 95
Gibson, J.C.L. 183
Gilboa, A. 52
Gillingham, S. 36
Gitin, S. 52, 118
Glassner, J.-J. 10
Goguel, A. 157
Goren, Y. 30
Gottwald, N.K. 46, 101
Gurzadyan, V.G. 11
Grabbe, L.L. 9, 10, 66, 97
Graeber, D. 180
Grainger, J.D. 193
Grayson, A.K. 10, 134, 135, 147
Green, P. 191
Greenfield, J.C. 214, 228
Gruntfest, Y. 147
Guillaume, P. 43, 51, 71, 98, 110, 136, 140, 172–174, 184–185, 188

Hachlili, R. 224
Hadley, J.M. 99
Hagedorn, A.C. 201
Halayqa, I.K.H. 21
Halbwachs, M. 5
Halpern, B. 10, 72, 83, 119
Harris, M. 7
Harris, W. 196
Hasegawa, S. 95
Hawkins, J.D. 38, 107

Hayes, J.H. 9, 12, 230
Healey, J.F. 213
Heather, P.J. 38
Heckel, W. 191
Heltzer, M. 147
Hendin, D. 218
Herzog, Z. 17, 31, 103
Higginbotham, C.R. 34
Hobsbawm, E.J. 23
Højte, J.M. 217
Hölbl, G. 199
Honigman, S. 202
Hooker, P.K. 230
Horden, P. 25
Hornung, E. 11
Horwitz, L.K. 61
Hurowitz, V. 188
Hurvitz, A. 185
Hütteroth, W.-D. 14

Ilan, D. 30
Ilan, T. 214
Isaac, B. 1980 228
Isserlin, B.S.J. 21

Japhet, S. 201
Jaroš, K. 29
Jensen, M.H. 221
Jepsen, A. 230
Jones, C.P. 206
Joosten, J. 204

Kahn, D. 135, 137, 156
Karta 14
Keel, O. 77, 100, 125, 128, 130
Kent, R.G. 10, 161, 163, 164
Khalidi, W. 14
Kitchen, K.A. 35, 38
Kletter, R. 127
Knauf, E.A. 4, 5, 12, 21, 25, 34, 44, 47, 65, 71, 78, 79, 82, 84, 85, 88, 92, 97, 98, 113, 115, 119, 127, 133, 151, 167, 168, 177, 178, 179, 185, 212, 213, 214
Koch, I. 119
Köhler-Rollefson, I. 19
Kokkinos, N. 221
Krämer, G. 14
Kratz, R.G. 10, 188

Lamon, R.S. 81
Lamprichs, R. 189
Layard, A.H. 94, 121
Lehmann, G. 52, 61
Leith, M.J.W. 167
Lemaire, A. 48
Lev-Tov, J. 59
Levin, C. 46
Levine, B. 214, 228
Levy, T.E. 7, 18
Lewis, N. 214
Lichtheim, M. 34, 52
Lipiński, E. 47
Lipschits, O. 119, 149, 151, 157
Lissovsky, N. 16
Livingstone, A. 148
Loretz, O. 31
Luckenbill, D.D. 10

Machinist, P. 124
Madden, F.W. 166, 221, 222, 227
Maeir, A. 65
Magen, Y. 221
Manning, J.G. 195
Maoz, Z.U. 212
Marfoe, L. 31
Mazar, A. 52, 93, 118
McDermott, J.J. 45
McKechnie, P. 204
McKeon, R. 196
Mendelssohn, H. 60
Mershen, B. 44
Meshel, Z. 55
Meshorer, Y. 166, 180, 181, 194, 213
Mildenberg, L. 1
Miller, J.M. 9, 12
Miller, M.L. 172
Misgav, H. 221
Mittmann, S. 138
Moran, W.L. 30
Moore, M.B. 11
Motro, H. 60
Mulder, O. 211
Mundy, M. 16
Musil, A. 76
Münger, S. 12

Na'aman, N. 16, 30, 31, 32, 36, 70, 89, 92, 95, 101, 108, 110, 111, 119, 136, 152

Nelson, R. 122
Netzer, E. 220
Niehr, H. 101, 129
Niemann, H.M. 76, 78, 87, 90, 91
Nikam, N.A. 196
Nimchuk, C.L. 161, 165
Nissinen, M. 97
Noth, M. 8

Olivier, J.P.J. 83
Oren, E.D. 30
Osborne, R. 192
Ostermann, S. 210, 212, 219

Parker, A. 25
Parpola, S. 132
Patrich, J. 213
Pearce, L.E. 153
Perlitt, L. 132
Piasetzky, E.
Picard, O. 165
Pirenne, H. 24
Pollard, J. 199
Pongratz-Leisten, B. 121
Popper, K.R. 5
Porten, B. 134, 154, 176, 179
Postgate, J.N. 110
Prosic, T. 58
Purcell, N. 25

Qedar, S. 180, 181

Rainey, A.F. 30, 31
Redford, D.B. 29, 32
Redmount, C.A. 157
Reich, R. 113
Reid, H. 199
Rendsburg, G.A. 110
Rey, J.-S. 204
Rezetko, R. 185
Rhodes, P.J. 192
Ritner, R.K. 81
Roisman, J. 191
Roll, I. 228
Rosen, B. 21, 54
Rosenberg, S.G. 210
Rosenfeld, H. 86
Rothenberg, B. 33
Rowton, M.B. 17

Index of Modern Authors

Sagona, C. 85
Sanderson, J.E. 187
Sancisi-Weerdenburg, H. 134
Sapir-Hen, L. 59
Sass, B. 38, 119, 138
Sasson, A. 97
Sasson J.M. 185
Schäfer, P. 227
Schaudig, H. 146
Schipper, B.U. 40, 52
Schmid, K. 36, 152, 154
Schniedewind, W. 110
Schorn, U. 47
Schroer, S. 61, 131
Schulman, A.R. 37, 40
Sergi, O. 119
Shipton, G.M. 81
Singer-Avitz, L.
Skehan, P.W. 187
Sinopoli, C.M. 106
Smith, A.T. 17
Smith, S. 146, 147
Sokal, A.J. 5
Spalinger, A.J. 107
Speller, E. 227
Staubli, T. 61, 82
Stavrakopoulou, F. 120
Steinberg, N. 58
Stern, E. 52, 118, 150
Stern, M. 228
Stolper, M.W. 174
Stronach, D. 124
Stuckenbruck, L. 205
Sugerman, M. 19
Sussnitzki, A.J. 17, 20
Swain, H. 4

Tadmor, H. 10, 116
Tcherikover, V.A. 8, 200
Tchernov, E. 61
Tebes, J.M. 64
Thareani-Sussely, Y. 136
Thiele, E. 12, 230

Treister, M. 174
Tritle, L. 191
Tsfania, 221
Tuplin, C. 150

Ulrich, E. 187
Uehlinger, C. 101, 113, 129, 131, 132, 161
Ussishkin, D. 38, 82, 114, 123, 170
Uziel, J. 65

Vargyas, P. 161, 165
Veijola, T. 77
Volney, M.C.-F. 76
von Wissmann, H. 180

Wagstaff, J.M. 7, 19
Wallerstein, I.M. 7
Wallinga, H.T. 164
Watts, J.W. 182
Weeks, S. 205
Welch, K. 217
Weiser, W. 165
Wellhausen, J. 7, 8, 126
Wells, B. 173
Westermann, W.L. 200
Whitcher Kansa, S. 61
Whitelam, K.W. 23
Wilson, K.A. 80
Wittgenstein, L. 6
Wood, M. 192
Wunsch, C. 173

Yadin, Y. 214, 228
Yamada, S. 10
Yardeni, 154, 178, 179, 214, 228
Yom-Tov, Y.A. 60
Young, I. 185

Zadok, R. 21, 110, 111
Zerubavel, E. 22
Zevit, Z. 55

Index of Subjects

Ahuramazda 149, 155–156, 161–163, 187, 229
Akkadian language 30–31, 106, 124
Amarna 30–31, 40, 75, 189
Amman 21, 115–116, 124, 200, 218
Ammon 109, 113–118, 121, 123, 138, 147, 169, 171–172, 180, 190–191, 210
Amon (god) 2, 32, 40, 53, 78, 122, 199
Amon (king) 122–125, 231
anachronisms 46, 91, 97, 126, 162–163, 189, 209
'Anat (goddess) 54–56, 71, 129, 132, 177–178, 180
'Apiru, Habiru 31–32, 36, 45–46, 51, 72, 79, 207
Arabia 3, 13–15, 18, 23, 32, 44, 76, 89, 103, 111–113, 116–119, 139, 147–148, 151–153, 157, 161–162, 168, 178–179, 187, 192, 196, 213
Arabic 14, 21, 42, 117–118, 167, 179–180, 185, 200, 220, 229
Arad 30, 123, 135–138, 159, 179
Aram, Arameans, 21, 37–38, 59, 73, 75, 86–89, 92–98, 108–109, 121, 129, 132–135, 147, 213
Aramaic (language) 6, 21, 24, 32, 38, 47–48, 106, 111, 117–118, 148–150, 154–156, 160, 166, 171, 177–182, 185–186, 196, 200, 206, 209, 213, 224, 229
Arnon 14, 47, 210
Ashdod 14, 38–40, 52, 59, 65, 112–115, 131, 136, 171–172, 208
Asherah (goddess) 55–56, 102, 120, 127–132, 180
Ashkelon 1, 14, 35, 38–39, 52, 54, 59, 65, 112–113, 134, 171, 208

Baal (god) 53–54, 70, 73, 77–78, 86, 101–102, 180, 190

Bay/Beya (vizir) 36
Beersheba 13, 91, 99, 102, 123, 179, 200
blood 19, 49, 50, 120, 184–185, 222
bones 7, 19, 59–61, 97, 224

calendar 11–12, 58, 84, 193
camels 18–19, 40, 89, 115, 118, 200
cavalry *see* horses
children 19, 50–51, 61, 67, 100, 109, 120, 125–126, 139, 151, 177
chronology 6, 10–13, 22, 29, 67, 92, 126, 170, 183, 193, 209
circumcision 51, 205, 210
clans 17, 32, 42, 48–50, 61–62, 67, 93, 153, 178
conjoncture 4, 7, 17, 22–25, 44, 85, 116, 152
copper 1, 15, 20, 32, 37, 40, 44, 52, 64, 70, 75, 79, 96, 116, 151
corvée *see* labour
credit (finance) 19, 51–52, 62, 98, 161, 172–173, 175, 178, 180
crises 32, 37, 52, 173–176, 209, 223

Damascus 15–16, 75, 79–80, 86–89, 92–99, 105–109, 116–118, 124, 147, 157, 168, 182, 213, 217, 220
demography 17–19, 31, 43–44, 52, 67, 75, 85, 90, 101, 110–112, 115–116, 124, 137–141, 148–149, 151–152, 170–175, 177, 180–184, 220, 226, 228
deportations 31, 106, 110, 120, 135, 140, 145–146, 151, 154–155, 161, 209
deserts 13–14, 19, 46, 56, 111, 127, 135, 157, 207, 220, 223, 225
Deuteronomistic History 10, 187
donkeys 17–20, 40, 115

Edom 14, 36, 41, 50, 59–60, 64, 73, 75, 79, 85, 96, 109, 112–118, 130,

Index of Subjects 265

135–136, 139, 147–151, 153, 171, 179, 184, 210, 213, 218
egalitarianism 20, 46, 48
Ekron 38–39, 52, 59, 63, 65, 67, 72, 75, 87, 103, 111–115, 118, 131, 134, 136
El (god) 35, 53, 55–56, 78–79, 101
Elephantine 151, 154–156, 159, 171, 176–179, 183
Elijah/Elisha 88, 92, 98, 102, 185

food 7, 37, 43, 51–52, 59–63, 85–86, 90, 169, 174, 180, 184–185

Gath 38–39, 52, 63, 65, 72–73, 75, 78, 96, 118
Gaza 13–16, 38–40, 52, 59, 65, 103, 108–116, 136, 151, 157, 162, 168, 171, 179, 191, 212–213
Gibeon 16, 21, 64–65, 68, 70, 73, 75, 78, 80–81, 127, 172, 189
Gilead 14, 21, 47–48, 68, 70–71, 78, 87–88, 91, 93, 98, 108, 212
Golan 14, 16, 30

Hazael 72, 75, 87–89, 93, 95–99, 103–105, 109
Hebrew (language) 21, 34–35, 47, 64, 70, 84, 117, 154–155, 185–187, 200–202, 224
Hittites 7, 34, 37, 190
horses 18, 21, 76, 89–91, 94–95, 99, 107, 115, 163, 179, 191, 215, 217

incense 15, 117–118, 123, 147

Jacob (patriarch) 45–48, 68, 79, 84, 123, 132–133, 138, 140–141, 152–154, 183
Judah (etymology) 43

Kedar 118, 150–153, 159, 166–168, 171–172, 178–180, 213

Lab'ayu (king) 31, 68, 75
labour 17, 20, 34, 47, 51–52, 86, 90–91, 111, 166, 173
Lachish 39, 41, 103, 113–114, 119, 125, 127–128, 137

law 10, 50, 57, 127, 152, 161, 171, 182–186, 192, 203, 216, 229
Lebanon 13, 17, 30, 34, 38, 52, 57, 83, 85, 87, 117, 122, 135, 206, 212, 219, 221

migration 14, 37–38, 45, 111, 182, 189
monotheism 24, 32, 34, 53, 72, 84, 127, 129, 132, 148, 153, 155, 163, 183
Moses 8–9, 24, 34, 36–37, 45, 50, 56, 72, 84, 132–133, 140, 171, 182, 187, 202, 204, 227

Nabatea 16, 153, 168, 178–179, 210, 212–213, 217–218, 222
Negev 13–14, 48, 60, 64, 75, 78, 81, 99, 113, 117–119, 136, 139, 150, 153, 171, 213
Nile 7, 15, 30–40, 58, 109, 112, 146, 157–160, 167, 177, 192, 196
nomads 7, 17–21, 31, 41, 43, 45, 58, 117

Ottoman Empire 7, 16, 19

Palastin (kingdom) 38, 40, 124, 152, 174, 176
pigs 18, 59–61, 205
postmodernism 5
Priestly narrative/document 129, 141, 184, 187–188, 201

Sea People 37–39, 52
shasu 29, 31–38, 40–45
Shephelah 13, 57, 81, 84, 91, 113, 115, 119, 127, 136
silver 96, 101, 115, 161, 165–167, 173–180, 190–192, 213
Sinai 16, 40, 99, 117, 132, 178, 213
slaves 15, 24, 31–32, 40–41, 49, 86, 101, 138, 166, 174, 179, 215–216, 219
sun 2, 19, 32, 34, 41, 55, 65, 76, 79, 101, 128–131, 163
surplus 19–20, 37, 43–52, 63, 90–91, 107, 116, 150, 169, 173, 196
Syria 7, 11, 16–17, 30–31, 34, 38–40, 44, 54, 58, 80, 82, 86–87, 95–97, 100, 107–109, 118, 125, 135, 140, 147, 151–152, 162, 166, 180, 186, 191, 193, 200, 206–208, 213, 216–222, 225

taboo 59–61, 185
taxation 19–20, 49, 52, 61–62, 86, 90, 92, 101, 111, 119, 135, 149, 172, 174, 199, 200, 203, 207, 219, 225–226
trade 7, 19, 23, 25, 37, 40–44, 52, 64, 67, 70, 75–79, 83–86, 90, 96, 99, 103, 105, 108, 112, 116–119, 147–148, 151, 153, 160–168, 171–174, 178–180, 196, 200, 204, 212
Tyre, Tyrians 47, 85, 89, 93, 95–96, 103, 107, 113, 140, 145–146, 168, 176, 180, 191–195

Ugarit 37, 39, 52, 54, 56, 174, 190
utopia/dystopia 140, 187

wives 39, 45, 50, 82–83, 87, 101–102, 133, 166, 177, 194, 214, 223
women 19, 50–51, 61, 67, 109, 127, 174, 177–179, 181, 201, 214, 216, 226
writing 20, 22, 34, 71, 84, 89, 97–98, 106, 122, 185

Zeus-Ammon 191, 199
Zoroastrianism 156, 163

www.ingramcontent.com/pod-product-compliance
Lightning Source LLC
Chambersburg PA
CBHW052105230426
43671CB00011B/1940